Prevailing and Emerging Dilemmas in INTERNATIONAL TAXATION

Prevailing and Emerging Dilemmas in INTERNATIONAL TAXATION

2022

Edited by
Parthasarathi Shome

Foreword by
Vito Tanzi

ITRAF
INTERNATIONAL TAX RESEARCH AND ANALYSIS FOUNDATION

OakBridge

Published by
OakBridge Publishing Pvt. Ltd.
M 35, 1st Floor, Old DLF, Gurugram, 122001, Haryana, India
Tel.: +91 124 4305970, E-mail: info@oakbridge.in
www.oakbridge.in

ISBN: 978-93-91032-45-6

Printed and bound at Sai Printo Pack Pvt Ltd

Foreword

When my long-time friend Dr. Partho Shome sent me the manuscript of his new book and asked me to write a foreword, I thought this was going to be an easy task. I headed the Tax Policy Division of the IMF for seven years and had been the Director of the IMF Fiscal Affairs Department for 20 years. During those 20 years, I attended, as an observer, the bi-yearly meetings in Paris of the OECD Fiscal Affairs Committee. In 1987, I had written one of the very first articles which worried about the way the World Tax Systems were developing[1]. In 1985 I contributed to the Brookings project on globalization by writing, perhaps, the first book that expressed worries about the ongoing tax competition that was developing among countries[2].

By that time, I was convinced that the world might need to create a specialized World Tax Organization[3], or World Tax Authority, one with more power, more leverage, and more resources, and one that would be less identified with specific groups of countries such as the OECD, with more leverage than the United Nations. Such an organization would aim at promoting rules and principles and be seen as fair and objective by all or most countries, and not just by some of them. I repeated this call in an article published in 2016[4].

I learned from the articles in Partho's interesting and informative new book that my early worries were indeed correct, and that the world of taxation has changed to an extent that I did not fully realize until I read this book. Reading Partho's edited book turned out not to be a pleasant and easy walk in a known park, but it was very demanding and informative. Reading the book, I found myself in the "selva oscura", ("dark jungle") that Dante had described in his *Devine Comedy*, a jungle where it is difficult for one to find the "right path".

I learned that the tax principles that had guided tax work several decades ago, have become almost irrelevant in the new highly globalized, and a digitized world that exists today. Furthermore, and unfortunately, the erstwhile broadly accepted principles have not been replaced by new ones. To some extent, chaos has reigned, and tax lawyers have to a large extent replaced tax economists in many of the relevant debates. Complexity has replaced the simplicity of past principles. Economists do less well than lawyers when issues become too messy.

---

1. Tanzi, Vito. 1987. "Forces that Shape Tax Policy," in *Tax Policy in the Twenty First Century*, edited by Herbert Stein New York: John Wiley and Sons.
2. --------------. 1995. *Taxation in an Integrating World*, Washington: The Brookings Institution.
3. --------------. 1999. "Does the World Need a World Tax Organization?" in The Economics of Globalization, edited by Assaf Razin and Efraim Sadka, Cambridge University Press.
4. ---------------. 2016. "Lakes, Oceans and Taxes: Why the World Needs a World Tax Authority", edited by Thomas Pogge and Kishen Mehta, Oxford University Press.

For a long time, the main tax principles established by the League of Nations a century ago, were in practice. At that time income taxes were still in their infancy, the rates were low, the tax revenue needs of countries were limited, many economic activities were domestic, and most of the limited intercountry activities were connected with investments by enterprises that had their residence in colonial countries while the investments were often in developing countries where the natural resources were located (iron ore, aluminium, petroleum, etc.) and that in several cases were still, or had been colonies. The investments were in products that had real, physical content and the countries of residence of the enterprises could easily be determined.

To a significant extent that was still the world encountered by the OECD at the time of its creation. It represented mostly advanced countries, and its Fiscal Affairs Committee naturally came to be chaired by experts from rich colonial countries, especially from the UK and France. Those who participated in its bi-yearly meetings were mostly civil servants from the member countries. They brought to the meetings the knowledge and the biases of their daily work. That knowledge and those biases inevitably influenced their thinking, their decisions, and the tax principles that they tried to promote. Those principles might have been seen as favouring advanced countries.

By that time there was another world organization, the United Nations, where all the countries of the world were members and naturally the developing countries had more of a say. The UN tried to promote tax rules that were more favourable to developing countries. However, it had fewer resources and continued to have less influence than the OECD. This conflict is illustrated well in several of the chapters in Shome's book.

Starting sometime around the decade of 1970s the world that had existed in the past started to change at a rapid pace. Globalization was one factor. Deregulation of many activities was another. And the transformation that started to take place from the production of real or concrete goods to that of bodyless transactions, that were no longer conditioned by the concept of scarcity, became important. The Digital Economy and the Gig Economy became important, making both domestic and international taxation more difficult as some chapters show. The main tax problem in part changed from that aimed at avoiding double taxation to that aimed at avoiding no taxation. Both the OECD and the UN have been trying to find their ways in the new and even darker "selva oscura". Several interesting chapters in the book discuss these attempts and some focus on the new rules that the OECD has recently been trying to promote.

Other issues such as the challenges that are coming from financial innovations are discussed. I found especially informative the discussion of Special Purpose Acquisition Companies that some decades ago had made it possible for some companies, such as General Electric, to inflate their annual profits and to become more valuable.[5] The specific experiences of some countries, such as India, will also be of great interest to some readers.

The bottom line and the final question that this valuable book raises is: will the countries' tax administrators be able to cope with the growing complexity that the new world is creating? On this issue, the author of this note remains pessimistic, as long as the fragmentation of jurisdictions continues while "public goods" and "public bad" become increasingly global.

Vito Tanzi

Washington D.C.

5. David Gelles. 2022. *The Man Who Broke Capitalism,* New York: Simon and Schuster.

Preface

This is the sixth annual volume of ITRAF on the deliberations of its sixth annual conference held in December 2021. The various chapters—eleven in all—contain a wide array of issues. The first six chapters, comprising Part A, pertain to the major debates and dilemmas currently prevailing in the international taxation arena. The subsequent five chapters, comprising Part B, discuss several challenges in the Indian international taxation scene. Together, they provide a rich mix of concerns, analyzes, and policy recommendations for the interested professional, policymaker, and administrator.

Each year, we bring together a variety of international and domestic tax experts for debates and discussions, and subsequently, write their views in the form of a scholarly analytical paper for an associated volume. This year too, we have experts from Argentina, Denmark, Netherlands, South Africa, the United Kingdom and of course from India, representing both academia and the professions. Some authors are contributing for the first time to ITRAF, while others have contributed to earlier volumes as well. Several authors have written rejoinders to the subject matter of a primary chapter, thus raising discussion issues on the chapter itself. A total of twenty one authors have contributed to the present volume lending a high tone to the nature of the discussions.

Part A begins with the discussion of the prevailing lack of a stable core in international taxation by pointing to the flux and non-resolution of various contended matters that have lingered on the table of multilateral organizations for some years. Two authors have addressed this matter and supported each other regarding the views taken. Other chapters discuss the OECD model versus the UN model tax conventions and the recent international discussions and controversies on a minimum corporate income tax. The four authors who examined this topic have taken comparable views on related issues. This is followed by a chapter on the deleterious role of a tax incentive in Scandinavia, a topic that is usually discussed in the context of emerging economies. The two authors here have, effectively, critiqued tax incentives as an appropriate fiscal instrument. Part A ends by examining the taxation of a universally emerging sector, the gig economy. Again, the two authors here hold similar views on the matter. In sum, Part A explores a wide variety of international tax issues pertaining to the wider global economic community.

Part B, focussed mainly on India, begins by examining the challenges associated with the taxation of an emerging financial instrument, namely, 'special purpose acquisition of companies (SPACs), and the challenges thereof. Part B continues with the international arbitration award of the Government of India versus Cairn, which is available publicly and is, therefore, amenable to study and analysis. Note that in earlier ITRAF volumes, the comparable case of the Government of India versus Vodafone had been analyzed thus rendering a continuum in topics in successive volumes. All four authors concluded that retroactive taxation goes against the principle of 'fair and equitable treatment' (FET), and by injecting unanticipated uncertainty in business decisions and activity, an 'impossibility to perform' situation is invoked for the businesses so taxed. This is followed by a critical examination of the 'faceless assessment' of taxpayers, a recently introduced aspect of the Indian tax administration whose application and implementation are drawing criticism from practising experts. The final chapter addresses the problematic aspects of India's Goods and Services Tax (GST) that persist though practical solutions to the problems exist and are proposed. I deeply appreciate the nuanced and thought provoking articulations of senior international professors Philip Baker, Johann Hattingh, Leandro Passarella and Vito Tanzi, among the other brilliant contributions.

This being the sixth annual ITRAF volume, it adds to the consolidated collection of any international tax expert and imparts a sharp yet interesting analysis of emerging and challenging issues in international taxation over time. I appreciate the authors who have presented their analyzes at the conference and followed up with very analytical papers. Needless to say, the individual authors are solely responsible for the contents and views expressed in their chapters and rejoinders. The editor of this volume, or ITRAF as an organization, or the publisher of the volume bear no responsibility for the contents provided by individual authors. I appreciate Rohit Roy's timely assistance in checking the typeset files with me in the final phase. I also thank Shreesh Chandra, the publisher, and his copy-editing team led by Priyanka Srivastava that provided meticulous work and designed the cover. I also thank Mary Hilna Paul and Hema Muralidhar for the logistics of the conference, tracking the timetable for the volume, and assisting along the way.

It is hoped that the reader of ITRAF volumes will find this volume interesting and useful, and add it to their collection of ITRAF volumes on the shelf.

London
Summer 2022

Parthasarathi Shome
Editor and
Chairman, ITRAF
Bangalore

About the Contributors

(in order of Chapters)

Vito Tanzi was Director, Fiscal Affairs Department, and Chief, Tax Policy Division, at the International Monetary Fund (IMF) from 1975-2000. In that role, he advised the governments of many countries on fiscal issues and on tax reforms while supervising several highly trained fiscal economists from various countries. After the IMF, he served in the Italian Government as Undersecretary for Economy and Finance at the ministerial level. Subsequently, he spent some years as a visiting scholar at the Inter-American Development Bank in Washington DC. From 1990-94 he was the president of the International Institute of Public Finance (IIPF) He is now the honorary president of IPPF. He was awarded several honorary degrees from universities in Italy, Argentina, and Portugal.

During 1967-75, he was Professor of Economics (Department Chair, 1970-73), American University, Washington DC, and taught Public Finance and Income Theory at the graduate level. He visited the universities of Munich, Bocconi, Torino, Rome, and others. During 1959-1961 he worked for the Joint Economic Committee of the US Congress. From 1965-67 he was a senior economist in the Joint Tax Program of the Organization of American States (OAS) in Washington. He has been a consultant to the UN, European Commission, European Central Bank, World Bank, Organization of American States, and Inter-American Development Bank. He continues to participate and lecture at many international conferences.

In recent years, he has dedicated himself to the economic role of government in market economies, and the role that complexity plays in government's activities. He is also a prolific author, published by Cambridge University Press (2022, 2018, 2011), Elgar (2018), Oxford University Press (2020), and others.

He has contributed to the economics of corruption, tax evasion, money laundering, the underground economy, and the impact of inflation on tax systems. American Economic Review, Journal of Political Economy, and Economic Journal, and several other refereed journals have published his research papers. The "Tanzi effect"—the impact of inflation on the real value of government revenue—was named after him.

He is an MA (1963) and a Ph.D. (1967) from Harvard University and a BA with special honours (1959) from George Washington University where he has also done his first MA in 1961.

Dr. Parthasarathi Shome is Chairman, International Tax Research and Analysis Foundation (ITRAF), Bengaluru, India, and Visiting Senior Fellow, London School of Economics. He received Brazil's highest civilian honour, Commander of the Order of the Southern Cross, for his contributions to Brazilian fiscal reform. He was Adviser (Minister of State) to the Indian Finance Minister and chaired the Tax Administration Reform Commission (TARC). Earlier, he was Chief Economist, UK Revenue and Customs; Chief of Tax Policy, IMF; and Professor, American University, Washington DC. He chaired India's Ninth and Tenth Five Year Plan Task Forces on tax policy and administration. He was Director of the National Institute of Public Finance and Policy (NIPFP) and the International Council for Research on International Economic Relations (ICRIER), New Delhi, India. His publications in peer-reviewed journals include *IMF Staff Papers, National Tax Journal* (US), *Bulletin for International Taxation* (Netherlands), *Oxford Economic Papers* (UK), *Oxford Review of Economic Policy* (UK), *Public Finance* (Europe), *Public Finance Quarterly* (US), and several other international and national journals. He has edited and published many books with renowned publishers such as Business Standard Publishers, Cambridge University Press, CenTax, International Monetary Fund, Lexis Nexis, OakBridge, Orient Blackswan, Oxford University Press, Routledge, Springer, and Wolters Kluwer. His latest book, *Taxation History, Theory, Law, and Administration* is from Springer, Cham: Switzerland, 2021. He received the Jeanne S. Mattersdorf Award of the National Tax Association of America as "an outstanding student in the field of taxation and public finance" for his Ph.D. thesis on the incidence of the corporation income tax. He regularly participates in international debates and discussions on international taxation and is invited to speak across the globe.

Johann Hattingh is a professor in the law faculty of the University of Cape Town, South Africa. He is an advocate of the High Court of South Africa and formerly practised with PwC. Prof Hattingh got his academic degrees at Cambridge, Leiden, Cape Town, and Stellenbosch universities. He is the chief editor of IBFD's Bulletin for International Taxation and part of the management of the IBFD Centre for Studies in African Taxation. Outside of academia, he has acted as a senior international consultant for the UN Economic Commission for Africa, the IMF, and for NEPAD on behalf of the African Union. He serves as rapporteur for Africa in the International Law Association's Study Group on International Taxation and is an executive board member of the International Fiscal Association-South Africa.

K. R. Girish is a founder member and director on the Board of ITRAF. Previously he was a senior tax partner, and the national head of Tax Litigation and Disputes Resolution Practice in KPMG. After 20 years, he became an entrepreneur and set up his own practice under K. R. Girish & Associates, specialising in direct tax and regulatory issues. He was the president of the Bangalore Chamber of Industry and Commerce (2009-10) and continues to be the chairperson of the Finance Committee of the Chamber. He is a Fellow Member of ICAI and an Associate Member of the Australian Taxation Institute. He is a regular faculty member of the ICAI's diploma programme in international tax. He has a law degree from the Karnataka State Law University.

Rahul Chowdhury is a senior associate at K.R. Girish & Associates. An Associate Member of the ICAI, he is a young professional, enthusiastically working in the field of direct taxes. Earlier, he worked with EY's Transfer Pricing Practice for around four years. He is also a qualified Company Secretary (ICSI)and a commerce graduate from the University of Calcutta.

Mukesh Butani is the managing partner of BMR Legal and a founder member of ITRAF. A Chartered Accountant and an LLB, He practices as an advocate in various tribunals, high courts, and the Supreme Court of India. He is the president of the International Fiscal Association (IFA), India; earlier, he was a member of the Permanent Scientific Committee of IFA,. He is presently the vice chairman of the Taxation Commission of the International Chamber of Commerce (ICC), Paris. He is on the MoF Standing Committee on TDS and Foreign Tax Credit. He served as a member of the Expert Task Force on International Tax and Transfer Pricing, MoF, in July 2012. He was a member of the Focus Group on Administrative Practices on Tax Disputes at the Tax Administration Reform Commission (TARC), set up in August 2013 by the MoF. He was a member of the Tax Bureau of OECD – BIAC. and

Dr. Rohit Roy is an assistant professor of law at Christ University, Bangalore. He has a Ph. D. in International Trade Law and Policy and International Environmental Law, and a master's in International Commercial Law, both from Cardiff University, UK. His current research interests lie in various aspects of international taxation as well as climate change law. His areas of teaching comprise international tax law and policy, environmental law, and food security policy. Before teaching, he was a tax research consultant at ITRAF, Bengaluru.

Ananya Raghavendra is an associate with the Indirect Tax (Advisory) Team at Lakshmikumaran and Sridharan, Bengaluru. Her current research interests lie in various aspects of indirect tax laws and international taxation.

Indraneel Roy Chaudhury is a founder member and director on the Board of ITRAF. He is a tax partner in PW & Co LLP, Bangalore. He is also a former Leader of South India Tax, and PW & Co LLP's Tax Leadership Team. He currently chairs the Tax Policy Panel of PW & Co LLP. He specialises in international tax, and transfer pricing. He has nearly 30 years of experience in advising domestic and multinational clients on tax, legal and regulatory issues, inbound/outbound transactions, tax structuring, mergers & acquisitions, transfer pricing planning and compliance issues, MAPs, and APAs. He has been associated with several professional and trade bodies and delivered lectures at various forums, including PwC's Leadership Development programs at Genesis Park. He is a Fellow Member of the Institute of Chartered Accountants of India (ICAI).

Dr. Leandro M. Passarella is a founder partner and the tax practice leader of Passarella Abogados, a boutique Argentine tax law firm, advising on inbound and outbound investments. He is also a professor of Personal Income Taxation in the Tax Law master's programme at Universidad Torcuato Di Tella (Buenos Aires, Argentina). At Universidad Torcuato Di Tella, he also coordinates UTDT Global Tax Talks, a platform fostering an interdisciplinary dialogue among faculty members, global tax policymakers, and practitioners on hard tax topics of international taxation. He holds a JD degree (with honors) from Universidad de Buenos Aires, and an LLM degree from Harvard Law School, jointly obtained with the Harvard International Tax Program certificate. He has contributed chapters for several books, the latest being the Argentine chapter for "Taxation of Crypto Assets" (Wolters Kluwer, 2020).

Hitesh D. Gajaria is a senior partner in the tax practice at KPMG India with more than three decades of tax, transfer pricing, and regulatory consulting experience. He is also a member of the Board of ITRAF. Prior to his role as the senior partner in KPMG, Hitesh led the Industrial and Consumer Manufacturing Sector Corporate Tax Practice and has also co-led KPMG's transfer pricing practice in India. He has co-authored several BCAS' publications - 'Taxation of Non-Residents, FERA / FEMA' and 'Transfer Pricing Manual' and was Country Reporter for India at IFA international conference. He is also a mentor at KPMG India's, Enactus initiative, guiding college students in developing socially sustainable community projects. He is a Fellow Member of ICAI.

Yvette Lind is currently an assistant professor of tax law at Copenhagen Business School, Denmark. Swedish jur.dr. specialising in international taxation with an emphasis on challenges arising from globalization, increased taxpayer movement, and the fragmentation of law. She was awarded Swedish TOR/Skattenytt post-doc between 2017-2019 in connection with defending her doctoral thesis. She is a regular guest researcher and teacher at the Faculty of Law, Lund University, and the Max Planck Institute for tax law and public finance in Munich.

Karnik Gulati is a Chartered Accountant from India. He also holds Baccalaureate in Law (LL.B.) and Advanced Diploma in International Taxation from the Chartered Institute of Taxation (CIOT), London. The areas of his expertise include advising clients on international taxation, corporate taxation, transfer pricing, foreign exchange regulations matters, and start-up consulting.

He is currently associated with Coinmen Consultants LLP in New Delhi, India. In the past, he has also worked with consulting firms of international repute, including KPMG (New Delhi), Deloitte (New Delhi), and T.P. Ostwal & Associates (Mumbai).

He has authored numerous articles, research papers, and case studies on international taxation, and transfer pricing. He is also a core committee member of the International Taxation Committee of the Bombay Chartered Accountants' Society, Mumbai.

He has been awarded twice with the 'Certificate of Fellowship' by Professor Roy Rohatgi and Adv. Mukesh Butani, on behalf of Foundation for International Taxation, Mumbai, for the years 2015 and 2019, respectively.

He has a personal website (https://www.karnikgulati.com), where he shares papers and articles, both technical and non-technical technical that he has authored.

Krupa Venkatesh is an indirect tax professional with 30 years of experience. She is a Cost Accountant and Company Secretary by qualification. She has worked for 10 years with the Government of India, 14 years with Deloitte, and three years at Amazon India. She frequently speaks on the topic of indirect tax. She has been recognized by the International Tax Review as one of India's leading indirect tax professionals successively during her stint at Deloitte. She has been on various committees of trade associations, notably, she is a special invitee to the FICCI Indirect Tax Committee on GST. She is currently a partner with Consark, a boutique financial advisory services firm.

Suranjali Tandon is an assistant professor at the National Institute of Public Finance and Policy (NIPFP). She is a Chevening Financial Services Fellow 2019 at King's College London. She leads NIPFP's work on international and corporate tax and has published several papers on the subject. She is a special invitee to the sub-group on Finance and Regulation, Task Force for Sustainable Finance, Ministry of Finance, Government of India. She completed her Ph.D. at Jawaharlal University, New Delhi.

K. R. Sekar is a founder member and director on the Board of ITRAF. He is a tax partner with Deloitte and leads Deloitte Private for Deloitte India. Sekar has served as the president of the Bangalore Chamber of Industry & Commerce (BCIC), is a member of the India Board of International Fiscal Association, and works closely with other chambers, including NASSCOM. He has more than 30 years of experience in the field of direct taxes, mergers and acquisitions, international taxation, and transfer pricing. His client portfolio includes leading companies in technology, media, telecommunications, manufacturing, and engineering. Sekar's key areas of expertise include inbound structuring, litigation support, and advising on cross-border tax issues. He advises inbound global companies coming into India on entry strategy, and inbound structuring and assists them in mitigating tax risks. He is also associated with landmark litigation cases for global companies. He was recognized as one of the leading tax controversy leaders by *International Tax Review*, UK.

Aditya Vora is an advocate with the Chambers of Porus Kaka. He studied law at Jindal Global Law School before obtaining an LLM from the LSE. His professional and academic engagements are focused on international taxation. Professionally, he has advised and represented various multinationals on tax treaty issues. Academically, his interests lie in dispute resolution, particularly international tax arbitration, on which he has spoken at conferences and written in reputed journals.

Hans Mooij is an independent tax counsel specialising in international tax compliance and controversy. He assists corporate clients as well governments. As a tax treaty consultant, he has worked for various international organizations, including OECD, United Nations, and IMF. He is a visiting professor at the International Tax Centre (ITC) Leiden, and at the University of Amsterdam School of Law. He served the Netherlands Government as a tax treaty negotiator, as a competent authority in tax treaty matters, and as the prime litigator in tax treaty and EU law cases before the Dutch Supreme Court and the Court of Justice of the European Union. He was also a delegate to the OECD Working Party No 1 on the Model Tax Convention and a member of its Steering Group. He chairs the TRIBUTE organization, an independent, global initiative of leading experts in international taxation, which seeks to spread awareness of tax arbitration and tax mediation among the global tax community and avails experts for appointment as arbitrators, mediators, or technical advisors in disputes on tax treaty or cross-border tax issues.

Dr. Philip Baker is Queen's Counsel, Field Court Tax Chambers, Gray's Inn, London, and a visiting professor at the Law Faculty, University of Oxford. He has a Ph.D. from London University. He specialises in international tax issues, particularly in double tax conventions, EU tax law, and taxation and human rights (especially the European Convention on Human Rights). He has appeared in a significant number of cases before courts and tribunals at the highest level, including the European Court of Justice.

S. Krishnan is an international tax professional with significant on-ground experience in globalizing a company's operations. He is a founder member of ITRAF. He is an Associate Member of ICAI and the Institute of Cost Accountants of India. His book, *Investing in Indian & Foreign Start-up Companies,* provides an overview of income tax consequences and forex requirements for start-ups. He advises companies on international tax structuring and performs the role of a virtual international tax manager, providing 'tax health check-up' and compliance oversight of international tax, employee mobility, and transaction taxes. He provides advisory services to US citizens and green card holders on tax compliance, reporting obligations, and estate planning. Earlier, he was Vice President and Group Head – International Taxation at Infosys Limited, Bengaluru.

P.V.S.S. Prasad is a practising Chartered Accountant and partner in Prasad & Prasad, Chartered Accountants, Hyderabad. He is the past chairman of the Hyderabad Branch of ICAI and past president of The A.P. Tax Bar Association. He was the chairman of the All India Federation of Tax Practitioners (AIFTP), South Zone, for the term 2010-2011. He is an eminent speaker; he was invited to speak at IFA Asia / Africa Conference held in Mauritius in May 2012, May 2014, and May 2016, and IFA Asia-Pacific Regional Tax Conference 2016 held in Seoul, South Korea, in May 2016. He was the elected vice chairman of the IFA India for the term2018-20. He has co-authored the book "International Taxation - A Basic Study".

Brief Contents

PART B

CONTINUING CHALLENGES IN TAX STRUCTURE AND ADMINISTRATION IN INDIA

Detailed Contents

PART A

DEVELOPING COUNTRY CHALLENGES WITH OECD AND UN MODELS, AND INTERNATIONAL TAX EXPERIENCES

PART B

CONTINUING CHALLENGES IN TAX STRUCTURE AND ADMINISTRATION IN INDIA

PART A

DEVELOPING COUNTRY CHALLENGES WITH OECD AND UN MODELS, AND INTERNATIONAL TAX EXPERIENCES

CHAPTER 1

The Absence of a Stable Core in the International Taxation Regime[1]

Parthasarathi Shome

I. Introduction

Despite sincere attempts over the last decade by the international tax expert community and the increasing participation of emerging economies in the deliberations, finding a stable core for the international taxation regime has proved challenging. This article notes and analyzes selected issues relating to this topic. These issues pertain to a continuing flux in the acceptance of the source principle of taxation over the residence principle despite the OECD's increasing recognition of the former; the OECD's relative ineffectualness in challenging tax havens; various lingering issues in the adequacy of taxing the rapidly evolving global digital economy, including the OECD's Pillar One[2] and Pillar Two[3] proposals, the UN's proposals and unilateral actions in the form and variants of a levy to equalise its taxation with that of other productive sectors; and the OECD's reticence in taking measures against the retroactive enactment of tax law. In light of these shortcomings, the chapter considers some of the alternatives proposed by international experts for locating the international taxation regime in the UN or even creating an independent global tax authority. In the process, the author has expressed their views on the problems arising from the lack of a stable core in the current international tax regime, together with ways in which this issue could be resolved.

---

1. © IBFD. Originally published in 75 Bull. Intl. Taxn. 11/12, Journal Articles & Opinion Pieces IBFD. For more information, visit www.ibfd.org. Reproduced with permission.
2. OECD, *Secretariat Proposal for a "Unified Approach" Under Pillar One. Public Consultation Document*, 9 Oct.-12 Nov. 2019 (OECD 2019), available at https://www.oecd.org/tax/beps/public-consultationdocument-secretariat-proposal-unified-approach-pillar-one.pdf (accessed 8 June 2021).
3. OECD, *Statement by the OECD/G20 Inclusive Framework on BEPS on the Two-Pillar Approach to Address the Tax Challenges Arising from the Digitalisation of the Economy* – January 2020, OECD/G20 Inclusive Framework on BEPS (OECD 2020), available at https://www.oecd.org/tax/beps/statement-by-the-oecd-g20-inclusive-framework-on-beps-january-2020.pdf (accessed 8 June 2021).

II. Permanent Establishments and Source versus Residence

The changes that have occurred in recent years with the advance and acceleration of digital access during the COVID-19 pandemic and beyond include remote business operations with no local presence while maintaining management functions in more than one jurisdiction. The spread of "home office" work has been significant. Many employees seem to prefer this situation. Some multinational enterprises (MNEs) have cut back on local presence. Given this development, the concept of a permanent establishment (PE) may need to be revisited and redefined. The question is whether such changes should apply only to certain industries or become the general rule. In turn, this could be perceived as the virtual - rather than the physical - presence of a business in determining the source for taxation purposes.

The OECD has essentially endorsed a move from residence taxation to source taxation by way of the OECD/G20 Base Erosion and Profit Shifting (BEPS) Project.[4] This action is commendable and it must be pushed to the fore, as it attempts to reassign tax revenue allocation among trading countries in the right direction. In the 1990s, the United States changed its rules and permitted related foreign companies to be "de-linked" from their US parent by way of the "tick the box" rules - a set of loose criteria - resulting in a lack of relationship for tax purposes. That is, if they did not remit profits to the United States, there was no tax to be paid. In other words, the tax was "deferred". This change destabilised the parent-PE relationship and contributed to the OECD/G20 BEPS Project.[5]

India and several emerging economies had steadfastly argued well before the OECD/G20 BEPS Project that, justly, tax revenue must accrue in the source jurisdictions where the value-added was created in the international supply chain in respect of a commodity or service. By and large, advanced economies had ignored this stance, their position being that revenue should accrue where the risk-taking and management decisions were made, and where the capital resided. However, with the collapse of revenue in advanced economies due to the 2008 global economic and financial crisis,[6] these economies began to realise the potential revenue benefits of applying the source principle, given the limits of international capital movement.

---

4. *See*, for example, at the outset OECD, *Addressing Base Erosion and Profit Shifting* (OECD 2013), Primary Sources IBFD.
5. *See Base Erosion and Profit Shifting (BEPS): The Global Taxation Agenda* (P. Shome ed., ITRAF/Wolters Kluwer 2016), for several research papers by scholars who considered the initial challenges of the OECD/G20 BEPS Project.
6. *See The G20 Macroeconomic Agenda: India and the Emerging Economies* (P. Shome ed., Cambridge U. Press 2014), for a comprehensive treatment of the macro-economic challenges that prevailed during that period.

Accordingly, it has been argued increasingly that the source principle should assume permanence in the international taxation regime. Such a move would be rational. Both emerging and advanced economies, other than the United States, have been progressing towards accepting the ramifications of this principle.[7] Nevertheless, the debate over the OECD's Pillar One and Pillar Two proposals, in the context of the taxation of the digital economy, indicates that the United States continues to be reluctant when it comes to the taxation of its MNEs in source jurisdictions. It continues to insist that tax revenue should accrue, by and large, to the United States where digital companies are headquartered.[8] In sum, as Baker (2016) commented, "The MNE tax avoidance problem could be linked primarily to those MNEs with headquarters in the US".[9]

Should the concept of a PE, therefore, be redefined? The OECD's 2014 proposal of a permanent virtual establishment (PVE) was not poor.[10] Once an MNE's sales reach a certain level in a jurisdiction, it would be deemed to have a PE in that jurisdiction. In that case, the source jurisdiction would tax the profits of the MNE that were attributable to the virtual PE.

In effect, providing a healthy customer base should suffice to entitle a source state with the right to tax profits arising in, or from, that state. Such a concept would apply based on the continuous and commercially significant business activity of a non-resident enterprise in the source country. This idea matches the fundamentals behind source-based taxation. In practice, however, whether a sufficiently high sales revenue creates a legal right for a country to claim the ability to tax an enterprise, other than VAT or a goods and services tax (GST), of course, is not accepted by all, as evidenced by the ongoing international deliberations.[11]

In fact, the OECD's PVE discussion draft states that the varieties of a "virtual" presence PE are included "only for the sake of completeness".[12] Perhaps "for the sake of completeness" means that the OECD is not proposing to move forward with these suggestions at least at this time. In other words, this situation reflects a

7. *See* H.P. Khincha, N. Khincha & P. Kothari, *Source and Nexus of Income*, in *Reimagining International Taxation* ch. 8 (P. Shome ed., ITRAF/OakBridge 2021).
8. *See* H.D. Gajaria, J. Golani & R. Karadkar, *OECD's Pillar One and Pillar Two – An Overview*, in Shome ed., *supra* n. 7, at ch. 7.
9. P. Baker, *BEPS: Emergence of International Tax Law and Future Direction*, in Shome ed., *supra* n. 5, at ch. 3.
10. OECD, *BEPS Action 1: Address the tax Challenges of the Digital Economy, Public Discussion Draft*, 24 Mar.-14 Apr. 2014 (OECD 2014), available at https://www.oecd.org/ctp/tax-challenges-digital-economy-discussion-draft-march-2014.pdf (accessed 8 June 2021).
11. *See India in a Global Pandemic—Macro-economic and Tax Considerations*, in Shome ed., *supra* n. 7, at ch. 1.
12. OECD, *supra* n. 10, at sec. 3.3.

lack of enthusiasm for these alternatives as noted by experts, such as Girish[13] and others.

To sum up, countries have expressed an increasing keenness that the international taxation regime should attribute revenue among tax jurisdictions fairly. As a backdrop, it must be recalled that the international taxation regime has not been fair over past century. This situation arose as the value-added was not recognized as an appropriate criterion but capital ownership was. That is, tax revenue did not accrue to those countries where the capital was exported and the value-added was created but, rather, to those countries from where the capital was exported.

That convention and practice reflected the pattern of the global colonial past, although, unfortunately, it continued well after the colonies had vanished. It reflected the predominance of the OECD, an advanced economy grouping, which remained powerful in consolidating its interests. But the OECD/G20 BEPS Project challenged that pattern due to the broader inclusion of countries in the G20. Ironically, today the United States appears to be the sole visible adherent of the superiority of the residence principle.

III. Use of the Inclusive Framework to Eradicate Tax Havens

A crucial issue is the continuance of tax havens, which are an instrument for tax avoidance essentially installed and run under the auspices of various advanced economies. If the OECD in itself has a limited number of regular member countries, can it meaningfully use its Inclusive Framework, comprising 135 countries, which it formed to take forward its work on the OECD/G20 BEPS Project, to initiate reform leading to the eradication of tax havens?

It must be noted that the European Union has issued lists of tax havens of its Member States. Accordingly, should this work not be taken further by a group comprising the majority of nations, such as the Inclusive Framework? Some multilateral action is also being taken on tax havens. The European Union took up the issue of tax havens directly in the period 2016-2019 by issuing a code of conduct, and drawing up a blacklist[14] and a grey list of offenders. Yet,

13. *See* K.R. Girish, *A Comprehensive Overview of Shifts in International Taxation*, in *International Taxation in the Digital Era* ch. 11 (P. Shome ed., ITRAF/OakBridge 2020).

14. In 2019, Oxfam named 23 jurisdictions that were expected to be included in a blacklist by the European Union. These jurisdictions were: American Samoa, Bahrain, Cabo Verde, the Cook Islands, Dominica, Fiji, Grenada, Guam, the Marshall Islands, Morocco, Nauru, New Caledonia, Niue, Oman, Palau, Saint Kitts and Nevis, Samoa, Trinidad and Tobago, Turkey, the Turks and Caicos Islands, the United Arab Emirates, the US Virgin Islands and Vanuatu. *See* Oxfam, *Assessing Jurisdictions Against EU Listing Criteria,* (Oxfam Mar. 2019), available at

(Footnote No. 14 contd.)

unsurprisingly, Oxfam, a non-governmental organization (NGO) that monitors MNE misbehaviour, has provided its view on this topic, raising issues with the European Union as to why some countries were on the latter list and not the former, and why some had not been included in either list. "Nevertheless, it has to be recognized that the European Union is at least addressing the issue".[15] Enhanced action against tax havens would require the global economic community to bring the entire tax haven matter into the open, such that the role of selected OECD member countries appears in full view of the emerging economies. Otherwise, such advanced economies can continue to hide behind initiatives like the OECD/G20 BEPS Project, while effectively enabling pervasive international tax avoidance. In such a scenario, there is not enough bite in calling for action against tax avoidance through limited efforts like the OECD/G20 BEPS Project.

IV. Taxation of the Digital Economy

IV.1. Introductory remark

Another lacuna that has loomed large on the OECD's unfinished agenda is the taxation of the digital economy.

IV.2. OECD's Pillar One and Pillar Two proposals[16]

The OECD's Pillar One and Pillar Two proposals regarding digital economy taxation have been deconstructed by several tax experts.[17] To recount, the backdrop was the G20's direction suggesting cross-country taxing rights to enable the taxation of the digital economy. Pillar One and Two are the vehicles that emerged from the OECD's efforts.

(Footnote No. 14 contd.)

https://oxfamilibrary.openrepository.com/bitstream/handle/10546/620625/tb-off-the-hook-tax-havens-methodology-070319-en.pdf (accessed 9 June 2021). In a 2020 update, Oxfam commented that many tax havens that facilitated tax avoidance through zero-tax rates, such as Bahamas, Bermuda, British Virgin Islands, Guernsey, Isle of Man and Jersey, were also excluded from the blacklist. The reason was that the European Union did not consider zero-tax rates, or minimal tax rates, a criterion to identify tax havens; such rates were merely a "risk indicator" for the EU blacklist assessment. It is obvious that there is reason to support an argument that they should be included in a blacklist. *See* Oxfam, *EU tax haven blacklist review* (Oxfam Feb. 2020), available at https://oi-files-d8-prod.s3.eu-west-2.amazonaws.com/s3fs-public/2020-02/2020-02-17%20Oxfam%20background%20briefing%20-%20EU%20tax%20haven%20list.pdf (accessed 8 June 2021).

15. *See* P. Shome, Rejoinder to P. Baker, *The Need for A New International Tax Architecture*, in Shome ed., *supra* n. 7, at p. 67.
16. *Id.*, at ch. 31.
17. *See*, for example, H.D. Gajaria, J. Golani & R. Karadkar, *supra* n. 7, at ch. 7.

Pillar One (i) focuses on the allocation of taxing rights among countries, and (ii) seeks to undertake a coherent and concurrent review of the profit allocation and nexus rules.[18] Pillar Two recommends the introduction of a minimum tax on the digital economy by all jurisdictions.[19] There is more agreement on Pillar Two than on Pillar One, reflecting the fact that the United States is more at ease with Pillar Two's minimum tax recommendation, which it itself employs.

In January 2020, the OECD's Inclusive Framework, comprising 135 countries, reiterated its commitment to the two-Pillar approach. It developed a note called, "Outline of the Architecture of a Unified Approach on Pillar One".[20] An updated Programme of Work identified 11 building blocks for further work towards a solution.[21] A progress note on Pillar Two was also agreed.[22] An Inclusive Framework meeting in October 2020 moved towards the agreement of a package. Yet, subsequently, a statement was issued that the work was being set aside.[23] This clearly indicates the underlying lack of consensus on the issue. The crux of the final position rested on the United States essentially disagreeing with the view that its MNEs should be taxed in source jurisdictions and insisting that tax revenue should accrue to the United States where the digital companies have their headquarters.

However, the reality is that the recent business models of the digital economy and/or cyberspace and their reliance on outsourcing allow non-residents to have a significant presence in countries without a taxable PE being there.[24] In essence, the United States does not want such non-residents to be subject to any tax on digital economy activities if the taxable nexus is based on the site of the server. Accordingly, a tax based on the source of such income generated within its jurisdiction, which is often the emerging economy, is unacceptable to the United States.

In the absence of a multilateral consensus, countries have begun to take unilateral measures that are designed to generate revenue on a source basis to tax the digital economy. India's equalization levy could be perceived as an aspect of source-based taxation, i.e., where the turnover is generated. Accordingly, perhaps the source

18. OECD, *supra* n. 2, at section 2.1.
19. OECD, *Global Anti-base Erosion Proposal ("GloBE")-Pillar Two*, Public consultation document, 8 Nov.-2 Dec. 2019 (OECD 2019), available at https://www.oecd.org/tax/beps/public-consultation-document-global-anti-base-erosion-proposal-pillar-two.pdf.pdf (accessed 8 June 2021).
20. OECD, *supra* n. 2, at Annex 1.
21. OECD, *supra* n. 2, at Annex A.
22. OECD, *supra* n. 2, at Annex 2.
23. OECD, *Cover Statement by the Inclusive Framework on the reports on the Blueprints of Pillar One and Pillar Two* (OECD 2020), available at https://www.oecd.org/tax/beps/cover-statement-by-the-oecd-g20-inclusive-framework-on-beps-on-the-reports-on-the-blueprints-of-pillar-one-and-pillar-two-october-2020.pdf (accessed 8 June 2021).
24. *See* P. Shome, Rejoinder to H.D. Gajaria, J. Golani & R. Karadkar, *OECD's Pillar One and Pillar Two – An Overview*, in Shome ed., *supra* n. 7, at ch. 7.

principle should assume permanence in international tax rules. Being the rational choice, both emerging and advanced economies, other than the United States, have been progressing towards accepting the ramifications of the source principle.

There has been criticism as to how much revenue source countries should obtain if the source principle were to be followed.[25] This situation reflects the calculation of revenue accruals based on tranches that would ensure that residence jurisdictions would continue to receive a significant portion of the revenue. Essentially, under the OECD's proposals, (i) the first allowable Amount (A) is too small, while (ii) the subsequent Amount (B) is truncated by prevailing limits and arbitration that are likely to favour residence countries.[26] Gajaria, Golani, and Karadkar (2021) have explained the calculations in some detail.[27] Tax experts have expressed views that, given the various checks and balances of thresholds and the mandatory acceptance of any arbitration that may result, the likely revenue outcomes would not be great.[28]

Pillar Two was based on the US Tax Cuts and Jobs Act (TCJA) of 2017[29] and implemented as a modified version of the US Global Intangible Low-taxed Income (GILTI) and the Base Erosion and Anti-abuse Tax (BEAT), which are minimum taxes on both outbound investment and inbound investment. Under Pillar Two, there should be a minimum residence tax if the source country does not tax such as in GILTI, and a minimum source tax if the residence country does not tax, which is a modified version of the BEAT. The minimum tax rates under Pillar Two would be low and subject to limits. So, the revenue raised would not be significant.

A final question remains. As electronic commerce (e-commerce) is mobile, where do "mind and management" – the principle behind residence-based taxation – really reside? It remains difficult to pin this principle down, particularly in the context of the digital economy.

---

25. *See*, for example, H.P. Khincha, N. Khincha & P. Kothari, *supra* n. 6, at ch 8.
26. The original Pillar One of 9 October 2019 set up three taxing rights for the market economies: amounts A, B, and C. The Blueprint for Pillar One dropped Amount C. As a result, now there are now only Amounts A and B. *See* G. DeSouza, *Blueprint on Pillar One – What's New and Important* (3 November 2020), Bloomberg Tax (3 Nov. 2020), available at https://news.bloombergtax.com/transfer-pricing/blueprint-on-pillar-one-whats-new-and-important (accessed 15 Apr. 2021).
27. Gajaria, Golani & Karadkar, *supra* n. 8, at secs. 3 and 4.
28. *See*, for example, R.S. Avi-Yonah, *UTDT Global Tax Talks*, Universidad Torcuato Di Tella (UTDT) (26 Aug. 2020), available at www.youtube.com/watch?v=FmNqrFXoT5U&list=PLmZkgXYrGwgjLtF0z62Thp1_My9OZyqU9&index= (accessed 15 Apr. 2021).
29. US: Tax Cuts and Jobs Act (TCJA) of 2017, 131 Stat. 2054.

IV.3. UN recommendations on the taxation of the digital economy

The OECD was not the only player in relation to the taxation of the digital economy. The UN has made its own proposals. In August 2020, the UN proposed to add an optional provision to the UN Model (2017),[30] granting additional taxing rights to countries where an automated digital services provider's customers are located.[31] The tax base would include payments for services provided on the Internet or an e-network requiring minimal human involvement from the service provider. Consequently, the tax base would include the sale, and other alienation, of user data.

The activities covered would include online advertising services, online intermediation platform services, social media services, digital content services, cloud computing services, and standardized online teaching services. Drawn up by an ad hoc drafting group, the UN proposal differs from the OECD's Inclusive Framework in the unified approach to Pillar One, though both the OECD and the UN proposals have as their objective the granting of greater taxing rights to source countries. The UN proposal cites the following two routes for source countries to tax cross-border payments for automated digital services: (i) a "gross-based tax" at a rate agreed upon by the two treaty parties; and (ii) a net income-based tax using an apportionment formula. However, the UN also highlights problems with route (i).

The UN net income formula would apportion 30% of net income from automated digital services to the countries where the sales revenues arise. This position is broader than that of the OECD, as it does not have the size, profitability, or local revenue thresholds as in the OECD's Pillar One. It is also more straightforward in determining taxable income in the source country without any thresholds.

IV.4. Equalization levies: Cross-country experience

Under Action 1 of the OECD/G20 BEPS,[32] which laid the foundation for the taxation of the digital economy, a Task Force for the Digital Economy (TFDE) identified an alternative to taxing the digital economy. It was an equalization levy, a unilateral interim measure that a country could take to tax the digital economy. In this context, the levy could be limited to those businesses that engaged in transactions on a digital platform.

---

30. *UN Model Double Taxation Convention between Developed and Developing Countries* (21 Nov. 2017), Treaties & Models IBFD.
31. *See* J. Martin, *UN committee proposes new model treaty provision altering taxation of automated digital services*, MNE Tax (6 Aug. 2020), available at https://mnetax.com/un-committee-proposes-new-model-treaty-provision-altering-taxation-of-automated-digital-services-39609 (accessed 15 Apr. 2021).
32. *See*, for example, OECD, *Action 1 Final Report 2015 – Addressing the Tax Challenges of the Digital Economy* (OECD 2015), Primary Sources IBFD.

In 2018, the European Union proposed a 3% digital services tax (DST) on gross revenue from activities where users played a major role in creating value. It was to be levied on a list of selected digital activities. Several countries started implementing the measure unilaterally. Italy introduced a new web tax and unilaterally amended the definition of PE to tax the digital economy, i.e., to have a PVE. The United Kingdom introduced the concept of diverted profits tax (DPT) to tax diverted profits that arose to an entity during an accounting period. France, India, and Turkey have also done so. France's tax base is narrow while India's is potentially wider.

IV.5. India's equalization levy

IV.5.1. The structure

A government-appointed committee constituted in 1999 submitted a report in 2001. The committee examined e-commerce transactions under existing taxation laws. It also considered the issue of characterising the income arising from digital transactions and advocated a broader interpretation of "royalty" and "fee for technical services".

Another government committee was constituted in 2016 to examine the taxation of the digital economy. The committee analyzed alternatives proposed by the OECD. It concluded that the option of introducing the concept of significant economic presence (SEP) or levying withholding tax would require amending tax treaties. Accordingly, India introduced a 6% equalization levy by way of its annual budget law – The Finance Act (FA)[33] – in 2016, on the turnover of non-resident taxpayers with no PE in India supplying specified digital services so as to equalize the tax burden with domestic suppliers.[34] The equalization levy was reduced to 2% by the FA 2020,[35] and its scope was extended to e-commerce companies' services intended for consumption by Indian residents and persons availing of such services using an Indian Internet Protocol (IP) address.

The equalization levy effectively includes hotel bookings and software purchases in respect of the purchase of components from overseas. It could also have an effect on the business models of e-commerce giants, such as the Walmart-owned Flipkart and Amazon and Club Factory.[36]

33. IN: Finance Act (FA) 2016.
34. *See* V. Agarwal & A.P. Kumar, *Challenges in the Design of Digital Taxation in India*, in Shome ed., *supra* n. 13, at ch. 3.
35. IN: FA 2020.
36. *See* D.P. Behera & H. Kumar, *Equalization Levy on Non-Resident E-commerce Players: India's Ace in the Hole or a Stumbling Block for Foreign Players?*, International Centre for Tax and Development (ICTD) (4 Aug. 2020), available at www.ictd.ac/blog/equalization-levy-non-resident-ecommerce-india-block-foreign-players/ (accessed 15 Apr. 2021).

IV.5.2. A lingering lack of clarity

Analysts have noted several unclear elements with regard to the equalization levy. The coverage of the equalization levy could extend to a transaction with no relation whatsoever to India. For instance, a person in India ordering goods from Amazon to be delivered to and paid for by a relative residing in the United States would be covered by its all-embracing scope. This position is contrary to the concept of equalization levies as suggested by the OECD in 2015, which limited its application to non-residents with a SEP in the country.

Secondly, many internet users resort to a Virtual Private Network (VPN) for a secure connection or to avoid geographic restrictions on websites. This situation is a challenge that must be dealt with. A literal interpretation of the provision might mean that a foreign internet user using an Indian IP address on a VPN would fall within its scope. Accordingly, applying the equalization levy based on the use of an Indian IP would compel e-commerce operators to go to great lengths to ensure that they have sufficient means and infrastructure to identify and distinguish IP addresses.

The term "consideration received or receivable" used in the FA has given rise to a dubious situation for e-commerce operators. There does not appear to be much clarity on whether the equalization levy should be levied on the gross amount received by the operator from the customer or on the fee charged by the operator for its facilitation services. The difference is significant in revenue terms and the generation of market distortions. This depends on how the payment mechanism works. Some operators retain the commission from the gross amount received from the customer before sending the balance to the seller. Under the other model, the gross amount is paid to the seller, and the operator receives the commission thereafter. These two mechanisms would have significantly different implications on the tax base. If the former base were to apply, the seller would be subject to the equalization levy in the hands of e-commerce operators on the gross amount received, as the wording of the law regarding the equalization levy could be misinterpreted to infer that the entire amount paid by the customer, and initially received by the e-commerce operator, would be subject to equalization, and not just the commission that the e-commerce operator earns from such transaction.[37]

A critique of the unilateral measures adopted by countries to tax the digital economy has been that it results in double taxation. The equalization levy imposed in India is no different. First, it leads to double taxation according to the domestic laws due to its coverage in the GST base, though the equalization levy may be regarded as an income tax. Second, the equalization levy may result in international double taxation if the state of residence does not provide any credit for the levy paid in the source country under its domestic laws.

37. *Id.*

Currently, no provisions are there under any of the tax treaties entered into by India that bind the state of residence to provide for any relief in respect of any equalization levy paid. Of course, there is no expressed or implied bar to imposing a tax that results in double taxation. Tax statutes cannot be invalidated merely on the basis of the argument that the levy results in double taxation. However, though legally there is no bar on taxing the same subject twice such a situation is undesirable if economic growth is not to be jeopardized by double taxation.[38]

Even though the equalization levy has been imposed with a sound objective, in its current form, it may be burdened with too many questions of compatibility with international taxation. Other emerging economies may emulate India and endeavour to include a digital tax within their own taxation frameworks, though it may not be the best idea to introduce an equalization levy in its prevailing form. In this regard, several tax experts in India are currently analysing the problem to be able to recommend possible ways to tax the digital economy better.[39]

IV.5.3. US reaction to the equalization levy

The United States views the equalization levy and other prevailing digital economy taxes as ring-fencing the digital economy. In 2019, the Office of the US Trade Representative (USTR) initiated an investigation into the 3% DST adopted by France on revenue generated from certain digital services provided to, or targeted at, persons in France. On completion, the USTR concluded that the French DST was unreasonable, unfair, and discriminatory towards US commerce. The French DST was applied to revenue rather than to income and, therefore, was inconsistent with accepted principles of international tax policy. Further, it was retroactive and extraterritorial in its application. It was held to discriminate against US companies. Accordingly, the United States set a deadline of 6 January 2021 to impose a 25% tariff on French cosmetics, handbags, and other imports valued at approximately USD 1.3 billion, although, at the time of writing this article, actual collection was not reported to have begun.

As events unfolded, it was reported on 7 January 2021[40] that the USTR had also found India, Italy, and Turkey had discriminated against US tech firms, such as Amazon, Apple, Facebook, and Google. The USTR elaborated that the taxes were "unreasonable" because they were:

38. *See* Agarwal & Kumar, *supra* n. 34.

39. *See* V. Agarwal et al., *Removing Roadblocks in Taxing Business Income in the Digital Era: Building Global Consensus for an Equitable Solution* (June 2020), Vidhi Ctr. Leg. Policy and BMR Leg. Advocates, available at https://vidhilegalpolicy.in/wp-content/uploads/2020/06/20200620_-Digital-Economy-report-VIDHI-and-BMR.pdf (accessed 15 Apr. 2021).

40. *See* D. Lawder, *USTR slams India, Italy, Turkey on digital taxes but holds off on tariffs*, Reuters (7 Jan. 2021), available at www.reuters.com/article/usa-trade-digital-tax/update-1-ustr-slams-india-italy-turkey-on-digital-taxes-but-holds-off-on-tariffs-idUSL1N2JH34Z (accessed 15 Apr. 2021).

inconsistent with principles of international taxation, including due to its application to revenue rather than income, extraterritorial application, and failure to provide tax certainty.

To conclude on this point, the rapidly emerging developments in the unilateral actions on the digital economy taxation and widely targeted US reaction against them could be the harbinger for retaliatory tariffs, though such tariffs were not immediately specified. Nevertheless, these countries must reflect on the need for tax revenue given the adverse effects of the COVID-19 pandemic. Can they readily abandon a revenue base simply because the international taxation community is slow in finding a solution for its appropriate taxation? They need to weigh their revenue requirements against the increased post-tariff product prices at market entry and the associated reduction in the international competitiveness of domestic firms on which the burden of US tariffs would fall.

To sum up, any equilibrium in the form of multilaterally agreed taxation of the digital economy is yet to be achieved. Instead, an increasingly fractured structure of digital taxes and commodity counter-tariffs seems to be here to stay for the foreseeable future.

V. Retroactive Taxation[41]

Another challenging issue in designing taxes that the OECD should ideally take up is how adversely retroactive taxation could affect business decisions and, therefore, a country's GDP. A concern that has emerged is that the legal constructs around retroactive taxation contradict "common sense" in the framing of tax law. And retroactive taxation can affect business decision-making adversely and severely. Let me explain.

Say a business decides to invest in year t, taking into account its risk preferences. If, for example, in year t+5, five years after its investment decision and during full-fledged operation, the government declares that the tax law has now been changed and that it will be applied from five years prior to the present, that is from year t. In these circumstances, the basis of the original investment crumbles. Effectively, the government informs the business investor today, in year t+5, that the law five years back in time, at year t, was actually different from what it had been back in time in year t.

Such retroactivity in taxation makes a business decision to invest, taken in the past, untenable. If unanticipated taxes have to be paid in significant amounts at a time in the future, the earlier cost, income, and profit calculations are made baseless.

41. P. Shome, *Tax Base Erosion and Profit Shifting (BEPS)*, in *Taxation History, Theory, Law and Administration. Springer Texts in Business and Economics*, ch. 28 (Springer 2021), Online Books Springer, available at https://doi.org/10.1007/978-3-030-68214-9_30 (accessed 20 Apr. 2021).

This situation leads to what the author terms an "impossibility to perform".[42] The effect goes beyond any risk planned or accounted for by the investor. Though the investor can assess risk based on the "attitude towards risk", a retroactive tax takes the investor into a realm of "uncertainty", about which the investor possesses little ability to assess. Accordingly, the investor is robbed of a planned approach to business decision-making and management.

Yet certain tax jurisdictions have tended to adopt this approach in redefining the legal interpretation of the law to capture revenue already apparently lost. This policy fundamentally opposes taxpayer rights that should be protected in taxpayer charters. On the other hand, if taxpayers, particularly MNEs, indulge in sustained tax avoidance by taking advantage of loopholes available in different tax statutes worldwide, global authorities can intervene and install detailed reporting requirements and mechanisms for the exchange of information amongst themselves.

MNEs have complained that retroactive legislation results in the scaling back or withdrawal of investments in such jurisdictions. And such withdrawals can be effected quickly, thereby reflecting the effective mobility of international capital. What is often missed is that lower investment leads to lower economic growth and, therefore, to lower tax revenue collection. And the deleterious effects on growth can be near-permanent, rather than merely transitory.

The effect on economic growth should be a compulsory aspect of the training of tax officers, setting aside the usual practice of keeping it outside their area of concern. It is ironic that policymakers express concern about, and attempt to measure, GDP growth rates constantly. Yet, their tax officials remain oblivious to how the positions they sometimes adopt on certain matters regarding tax legislation and their implementation could directly contradict economic growth. International taxation does not comprise the daily concern of policymakers, who, on being elected, may suddenly find themselves having to deal with the intricacies of international taxation. They may not possess the wherewithal of pushing strongly, when needed, against the explanations of actions of their tax officials.

Consequently, if tax law is not designed to protect against significant setbacks in economic growth, for example, if retroactive taxation is introduced to suit an administration's will, taxpayers are bound to express dissatisfaction eventually. And, if the judiciary is unbiased, the courts are likely to interpret the law in favour of taxpayers. Usually, however, tax laws are prospective and provide protection from both retroactivity, i.e., business transactions or activities completed, and retrospectivity, i.e., business transactions or activities in progress, for taxpayers.

42. *See* IN: Expert Committee Report on Retrospective Amendments Relating to Indirect Transfers, Ministry of Finance, Government of India (2012), which this author chaired.

These issues have assumed significance, in particular, in the context of India's recent declining GDP,[43] to rectify which increasing investment, including foreign direct investment (FDI) is crucial. To expect investment — both domestic and foreign — to increase on a large scale while a regime of retroactivity application of tax law is prevalent is folly. Unless this policy is reined in through changes in the law and prospective application of tax changes is assured, tax will continue to determine GDP, rather than tax being the outcome of GDP and GDP growth.

Several authors have made efforts to bring the issue of retroactive taxation to the attention of policymakers over the last decade.[44] Their work has been cited in ongoing academic work, court judgments, and international arbitral awards, including in the recently published arbitral award of the Permanent Court of Arbitration (PCA) in *Cairn* (2020),[45] which cited Baker and Shome's work extensively.[46] That work will continue until the issue of retroactive taxation giving rise to the impossibility for businesses to perform is resolved.

VI. New International Tax Architecture

VI.1. Locating the international taxation regime at the UN

Reflecting on the flux in the outcomes that the OECD has been able to achieve despite the appropriate direction it adopted in the OECD/G20 BEPS Project, some experts have been critical regarding this issue. For instance, Baker (2021)[47] has expressed concern about the dispersion of the prevailing international taxation architecture, which is currently spread across the OECD, the UN, the International Monetary Fund (IMF), and the World Bank. His view is that the OECD's emergence as the flag holder over the UN in this field was almost an accident. He is critical of the OECD's "consensus approach", which limits the possibilities of arriving at meaningful solutions to any issue, even while, as an organization, it possesses little democratic legitimacy. His most crucial conclusion is that, even in the G20-initiated OECD's BEPS Project, the project has been found to be focused

43. *See* P. Shome, Rejoinder to N. Nigam, *Retrospective Taxation and the Vodafone Case supra* n. 7, at ch. 4.
44. *See*, for example, H. Salve, *Retrospective Taxation – The Indian Experience*, (Bingham Centre Working Paper 2014/06), Bingham Centre for the Rule of Law, BIICL (Sept. 2014), available at https://www.biicl.org/documents/315_tax_booklet_-_final.pdf (accessed 9 June 2021).
45. UK: PCA, 21 Dec. 2020, *Cairn Energy PLC and Cairn UK Holdings Limited v. The Republic of India*, PCA Case No. 2016-07. N. Nigam, *Retrospective Taxation and the Vodafone Case,* in Shome ed., *supra* n. 7, at ch. 4, references to Baker and Shome are grouped together in Appendix 1.
46. Baker, *supra* n. 44 was referred to exhaustively in *Cairn* (2020), *supra* n. 45, at pp. 280, 281, 468, 497, 502, 503 and 504. Similarly, Shome was referred to for his previous work and roles, either directly or through committee or commission chairmanships, in *Cairn* (2020), *supra* n. 45, at pp. xi, 40, 213, 214, 220, 252, 255, 281, 289, 294, 295, 296, 297, 303, 490 and 500.
47. P. Baker, *The Need for a New International Tax Architecture*, in Shome ed., *supra* n. 7, at ch. 3.

on, and biased in favour of, advanced economies. In the final analysis, the OECD/G20 BEPS Project is found to be led by a single country, thereby jeopardizing the international taxation architecture.

Baker's view is that the correct location for the international taxation architecture should be the UN, where the interests of all countries may be appropriately represented. However, Baker himself comments that there should be fundamental reforms within the UN structure itself for taking over the functioning of the international taxation architecture meaningfully.

Further, the question must also be asked as to whether, at this time, there is any critical mass in agreeing or financing for moving the location of the international taxation architecture to the UN. In this regard, there is little evidence currently of any branch within the UN that is analysing and moving this issue forward successfully.

VI.2. A global tax authority as an ultimate goal

Against this backdrop, while awaiting cross-country agreement regarding the location of the international taxation architecture at the UN, could a global fiscal and/or tax organization be designed, and could the Inclusive Framework take the formulation of such an organization forward? Such a concept has been discussed since the 1980s, one of the initiators being Tanzi (1988).[48] Subsequently, Shome (1996) elaborated on the concept of an international tax organization.[49]

Tanzi mooted the idea of a Global Tax Authority (GTA) some time ago. Accordingly, this is not altogether a new idea. However, at that time, the required commitment from nation-states would have been enormous, as it would have implied an intrinsic change in the ways in which governments of different political persuasions functioned, i.e., some sacrifice of individual national sovereignty for the sake of the global good.

Prevailing conditions have changed in the face of repeated global economic, financial, and fiscal crises. A GTA is essential now because of the proliferation of tax evasion and the need to consolidate the exchange of information among tax authorities. An important advantage of such a consolidated approach would be that of the designated vehicle in the form of a GTA, rather than dependence exclusively on bilateral tax treaties or individual countries bearing the responsibility of attaining this global objective.

---

48. *See* V. Tanzi, *Forces that Shape Tax Policy*, in *Tax Policy in the Twenty-First Century* (H. Stein ed., John Wiley and Sons 1988).
49. *See* P. Shome, *A 21st Century Global Carbon Tax*, 50 Bull. Intl. Taxn. 11/12 (1996), Journals IBFD.

Evasion has continued to take various forms. These forms include (i) failure to file information, reports, or returns; (ii) "daisy chain" schemes involving the use of dummy companies that could claim to have paid the tax through a chain of complex paper transactions; (iii) failure to pay taxes that have been already assessed or agreed on by, say, setting up dummy corporations showing little assets; (iv) filing false returns by claiming excessive inputs; and (v) evasion associated with fuel excise taxes.[50] A GTA would be more able to address these forms of evasion on the basis of being able to access more comprehensive information.

As a result, a GTA would have to employ several methods, in relation to both direct and indirect taxation. To cite just a few, these methods would encompass (i) improving regulations for the screening, licensing, and bonding of taxpaying entities; (ii) introducing innovative measures, such as exclusive fuel colouration in the case of fuel exports and imports; (iii) enforcing cross-border invoice requirements more thoroughly than at present; (iv) developing a mechanism for carrying out selective cross-country audits; (v) continuously monitoring and practising modes of inter-administration cooperation; and (vi) enforcing criminal penalties where appropriate. Though Action 13 of the OECD/G20 BEPS Project[51] deals with issue (v), consolidating such action under a GTA would provide a much more effective instrument for achieving this end.

While it would have obvious pecuniary and opportunity costs, higher expenditure of global monies, and would be yet another international bureaucracy, its benefits should compensate for the costs. Existing multilateral institutions whose mandates mainly comprise international monetary stabilization should not be burdened with additional tasks, given the phenomenal increase in the complexities in world financial markets. A new, autonomous, and streamlined GTA, therefore, deserves serious consideration.

Tanzi (2016) has continued to write on the matter, indicating that the time may have arrived for establishing a GTA that would monitor tax developments that have global implications.[52] He elaborates on the role that such an institution could play. He also notes the obstacles to creating such an institution and the shape it might take realistically under the prevailing global environment.

50. *See* A.T. Reno, *Measures to Curtail State Fuel Tax Evasion*, Natl. Coop. HwY. Research Program Paper No. 164, Transp. Research Bd., Natl. Research Council (Oct. 1990).
51. *See*, for example, OECD, *Action 13 Final Report 2015 – Transfer Pricing Documentation and Country-by-Country Reporting* (OECD 2015), Primary Sources IBFD.
52. *See* V. Tanzi, *Lakes, Oceans, and Taxes: Why the World Needs a World Tax Authority*, in *Global Tax Fairness* (T. Pogge & K. Mehta eds., Oxford U. Press 2016), Oxford Scholarship Online, available at https://oxford.universitypressscholarship.com (accessed 11 May 2021).

Tanzi clarified that:

> [...] a GTA would not collect taxes, although a time might come for such a role to finance global "public goods", but that would help bring order in the tax policies of countries, especially in those that have cross-countries' implications. In the absence of such an institution, some of the problems connected with unfair tax competition, with international tax avoidance, and with the "poaching" of other countries' tax bases are likely to intensify, contributing to progressively more serious macro-economic difficulties for some countries and to the reduction of some governments' ability to deal with domestic social problems.[53]

To sum up, it is needless to say that immense multilateral efforts and agreements would be needed to successfully establish a GTA, but, under the prevailing global, COVID-19 pandemic-driven fiscal crisis, there could be no better moment for all of the concerned countries to move in this direction. The outcome would be the reform of the international taxation architecture through a multilateral tax organization, thereby reducing international tax avoidance, enabling the rationalization of tax structures, and promoting more efficient and streamlined national tax administrations. In turn, the reformed international taxation architecture would likely result in improved global revenue generation that is needed to move towards closing the significant fiscal gaps prevalent in most countries.

Nevertheless, it appears that the time for both the idea of shifting the international taxation regime to the UN and that of establishing an independent international taxation architecture remains uncertain. In this environment, the potential role of the Inclusive Framework must be highlighted through which major challenges that continue to haunt the adequacy of taxation can be confronted meaningfully and resolved in terms of fair revenue collection and its cross-country allocation.

VII. Conclusions

In fiscal terms, there is no way out of the COVID-19 pandemic except through a carefully designed increase in taxes. The solution lies in introducing a wealth tax and a super-rich income tax, while, at the same time, reducing incentives in respect of corporate income tax complemented by tax administrative reform and, in the area of international taxation, pushing for fairness in revenue sharing among tax jurisdictions. Poorer countries can also approach multilateral institutions for loans on easy terms that are designed, in particular, to address crisis conditions. Ironically, it would not be entirely surprising, even for advanced economies, to approach the IMF for loans to help ease their economic distress.

53. *Id.*, at ch. 11, p. 264.

Humankind has faced enormous challenges through the course of its history and has, so far, survived them. On a philosophical note, Tanzi (2021)[54] has recently stated that:

> [...] the ongoing pandemic has exposed some major weaknesses that may exist in the competitive, democratic system that we as economists have admired and have promoted, over the years. It is not easy to think of satisfactory alternatives to that system. However, it is easier to argue that, in a world in which major disasters and pandemics exist, and may become more frequent, because of climate change and other developments, we will need some new thinking, that might suggest some desirable ways to change the modus operandi that we have admired up to now. That thinking should suggest ways to still promote efficiency, an objective that cannot be abandoned, and democracy. But the new ways should do a better job in dealing with major shocks, including pandemics, and with equity consideration of economic policies that often receive little attention in mainstream economics. As Rita Levi Montalcini[55] wrote four decades ago, let us hope that some good may come from the difficult moment that we are experiencing.[56]

Tanzi goes on to quote Montalcini:[57]

> It is imperfections — not perfection — that is the end result of the programme written into the formidable complex engine that is the human brain, and of the influences exerted upon us by the environment and whoever takes care of us during long years of our physical, psychological and intellectual development ... don't fear difficult moments, [because] the best comes from them.[58]22

It is to be hoped that the COVID-19 pandemic is drawing together invaluable lessons from which humankind can take strong and meaningful action. Internationally, a global carbon tax to arrest climate change could be employed if a campaign could be instituted to introduce such a tax instrument. Easing international trade rather than putting barriers on it, with powerful countries standing back from hegemonic positions and obstacles, would also be a step forward. Domestically, all countries should enhance equity in their taxation systems for the pandemic has resulted in a rapidly worsening income distribution. Emerging economies, in particular, should improve tax administration to remove barriers to

---

54. *See* V. Tanzi, *Perfect Markets, Perfect Democracies and Pandemics*, Transformation, Integration & Global., Econ. Research Working Paper Series No. 142 (2021).
55. R.L. Montalcini, an Italian biologist, won the Nobel Prize in medicine in 1996.
56. Tanzi, *supra* n. 54, at p. 4.
57. *See* R.L. Montalcini, *In Praise of Imperfections: My Life and Work* (Basic Books 1988).
58. Tanzi, *supra* n. 54, at p. 1.

investment and enable recovery in economic growth by making the tax responsibility easier to comply with. A new era cannot emerge without such fundamental steps that have always been easy to perceive though difficult to achieve. The human race is at this doorway. A forward step must be taken globally, together, and as a whole. And it must be complemented with resolute action by individual nations to buttress the global socio-economic condition.

REJOINDER

Johann Hattingh[59]

1. Introduction

Professor Shome's perceptive analysis of why there is no stable core in the international taxation regime is based on a dynamic complex of six factors. These are: (1) a continuous flux in degrees with which the source principle of taxation prevails over the residence principle; (2) the OECD's ineffectualness in challenging tax havens; (3) lingering issues in the adequacy of proposals to tax the rapidly emerging global digital economy; (4) unilateral tax actions by states; (5) the difficulty to perform business in face of retrospective taxes in light of reticence by the OECD to address the matter; and (6) the lack of a truly central and democratised institutional architecture for the governance of the international tax regime. He has recently repeated earlier calls for the establishment of a global tax authority that would be an intermediary step to the goal of having the United Nations host the premier institutional architecture so that "the interests of all countries may be appropriately represented".[60]

In this rejoinder, I first offer a few historical notes as a way of commenting on some of the dynamic features sketched by Shome, particularly the OECD's Two Pillar proposal for reforming income taxation of the rapidly emerging digital economy. Second, against the historical trend, I reflect on the prospect of a more stable international tax regime in decades to come, if these current global tax reform proposals were to be implemented. Third, I will explain why the dilemma of retrospective taxation raises nuanced legal policy questions that are inevitably tied up to the level of commitment to liberal democratic ideals, about which there are huge differences between countries, but these are all too often papered over by institutional actors. Finally, I offer thoughts on the prospects of an international tax agency and point to some of the *realpolitik* of the day that impacts this eminently laudable ideal.

2. Can we learn from tax history? The normalcy of ascending unilateral tax measures

As seen through the history of tax, true consensus-based solutions between nations to resolve double taxation of cross-border business income have, at least since the mid-19th century, been preceded and precipitated by an escalation of various

59. Professor in the Department of Commercial Law of the Faculty of Law, University of Cape Town, South Africa. Chief Editor: *Bulletin for International Taxation*, IBFD Amsterdam.

60. P. Shome, The Absence of a Stable Core in the International Taxation Regime, 75 *Bulletin for International Taxation* 11/12 (2021), at p. 568.

unilateral tax measures. Often, these 'global' solutions were in their design prefigured in unilateral domestic efforts.

A good example is offered by the multilateral federal law agreed to in 1870 by the federal states of the erstwhile German Empire, which had the effect to limit various types of dissimilar federal taxes unilaterally imposed since the 1830s on property, trades, and putative income.[61] This federal law, styled the Imperial Double Taxation Law,[62] was to decrease the burden of multiple layers of unharmonized taxes on citizens who, in 1867 on the formation of the North-German confederation were constitutionally enjoined to move freely within the German-speaking territories.[63]

At the start of the 20th century, a similar process started to unfold in the British Empire. The well-known *De Beers*[64] case of 1906 in which the House of Lords found a South African mining company to have been liable in the United Kingdom for income tax on its global profits arising from diamonds won in the Cape colony, was to usher in a period of double taxation within the British Empire. This was because soon thereafter colonial courts were confirming that companies such as *De Beers* were also liable for income taxes in their territories.[65] The courts were of course simply declaring what the unilateral income tax legislation enacted in the United Kingdom and in the colonies respectively meant. Thus by 1916, after numerous complaints and appeals by colonial governments privately and publicly at Imperial Conferences, the United Kingdom enacted unilateral relief to partly resolve the colonial problem of double taxation.[66]

The United States of America by 1918 decided to also enact unilateral relief to lessen the burden of double income tax on US multinationals.[67] The heavy cost of

---

61. J. Hattingh, On the Origins of Model Tax Conventions: Nineteenth-Century German Tax Treaties and Laws Concerned with the Avoidance of Double Tax, in J. Tiley, Ed., *Studies in the History of Tax Law*, vol. 6, (Oxford 2013), at pp. 42, 45.
62. (No. 475) Act for the Elimination of Double Taxation of 13 May 1870, Federal Law Gazette of the North German Confederation. No 14. Issued at Berlin on the 19th of May 1870. (Government Gazette Edition).
63. Hattingh, n. 61, at pp. 33-34.
64. *De Beers Consolidated Mines Ltd v Howe* [1906] AC 455.
65. *Colonial Government v De Beers Consolidated Mines, Ltd.* (1905) 22 SC 452 and *see* J. Avery Jones and J. Hattingh, De Beers Consolidated Mines Ltd v Howe (1906) - Corporate residence: an early attempt at European harmonisation, in D. de Cogan and J. Snape, Eds., *Landmark Cases in Revenue Law* (Oxford, 2019), at pp. 74-75.
66. United Kingdom, Finance Act 1916, sec. 43, and *see* C.J. Taylor, 'Send a strong man to England - capacity to put up a fight more important than intimate knowledge of income tax acts and practice': Australia and the development of the dominion income tax relief system of 1920, (2014) 12 eJournal of Tax Research, 1, at pp. 34-36.
67. United States of America, Revenue Act of 1918, ch. 18. §§ 222(a)(1), 238(a), 240(c), and *see* M.J. Graetz & M.M. O'Hear, The "Original Intent" of U.S. International Taxation, (1997) 46 Duke Law Journal 1021, at pp. 1043-1054.

the First World War had the effect of a dramatic escalation in the level of income taxes around most of the western world. Many countries took the unilateral decision to introduce a broad-based income tax around this time (for example, South Africa in 1914, Australia in 1915, Canada in 1917, and significant re-enactment by India in 1918), the rate of which shot up significantly to fund the cost of the war effort. The USA introduced, in 1918, a foreign tax credit to support the competitive position of US taxpayers because "selling in foreign markets was essential to the restoration of prosperity in the United States".[68] It took the USA a further 12 years, and the United Kingdom another 30 years before they concluded comprehensive bilateral income tax treaties to address the problem of international double tax.

The point that these short historical examples are driving at is this: uncoordinated unilateral actions by sovereign fiscal states provided the *leitmotif*, in various unrelated scenarios, to set in motion processes that led to concrete and lasting (though imperfect) bi- or multilateral solutions to address then emerging global tax challenges. It is hard to identify historical precedent for the reverse situation, namely a pre-figured globally agreed mechanism that anticipates future unilateral taxes and prospectively resolves how countries ought to limit their sovereign capacity to tax when faced with an emerging tax policy dilemma.

Based on this briefest historical sketch, it is amusing to consider that the Two Pillar proposal that is being developed by the OECD and the members of the Inclusive Framework, is dismissive of unilateral taxes that have recently emerged as tools to address the challenges posed to direct taxes by economic activity that is rapidly digitized. To condemn such unilateral national attempts to address a legitimate tax policy concern appears to ignore the forces at play in an age-old historical process, namely that sovereign states have differing national goals and agendas that inform their own choices of how to deal with common emerging fiscal problems. This can most clearly be seen in the reasons developing countries, that have not signed up to the Two Pillar proposal by October 2021, have articulated for their choice to pursue unilateral digital tax measures to address digitised economic activity. For example, Kenya has estimated that adopting the OECD's Pillar One proposal will have a negative fiscal budgetary impact, given the number and profile of mainly non-resident taxpayers that contribute to its digital service tax.[69] The residence country of technological companies may have different policy goals, for example, to remove tax barriers that impede the competitiveness of their national

68. Mitchell B. Carroll, The Development of International Tax Law: Franco-American Treaty on Double Taxation-Draft Convention on Allocation of Business Income (1935) 29 American Journal of International Law 586, at p. 588, and *see* also Graetz & O'Hear, n. 67, at pp. 1049-1054.
69. C. Mureithi, Why Kenya and Nigeria haven't agreed to a historic global corporate tax deal, https://qz.com/africa/2082754/why-kenya-and-nigeria-havent-agreed-to-global-corporate-tax-deal/ (accessed 5 February 2022).

multinational champions, which may not feature on the policy horizon of a country such as Kenya. The public discouragement by the OECD of Inclusive Framework members like Kenya who chose to pursue unilateral tax measures is not only ignorant of history but shines a spotlight on the shortcomings of the governance structures and institutional culture under which these global proposals are being developed. In contrast to the OECD, the African Tax Administrators Forum (ATAF) put forward a model digital service tax,[70] in recognition of the needs of its members for an efficient and fair mechanism to address their domestic fiscal policy objectives. Critical differences in the actions of global member-based institutions are now clear for everyone to see: should these institutions be responsive to the needs of all members, on a broad base, or are they in fact acting like a proxy to protect what is in the best interest of powerful member/s? The call by Shome and others for an overhaul of the institutional framework within which the international tax regime is to be reformed is therefore of acute interest.

3. The undoing of cornerstones of the international tax regime

The OECD's Two Pillar proposal, at its core, has the potential to finally undo three cornerstones of the existing international tax regime, given that some have been crumbling, or have been showing cracks for quite some time.

The first cornerstone of the existing international tax regime that has been crumbling for some time is the permanent establishment threshold for source taxation of international business income. The Pillar One proposal will complete the process of dematerialising the permanent establishment threshold. One can perhaps rightly remark that this process had commenced already with the inclusion of a services clause in Article 5(3) of the United Nations Model Double Tax Convention in the 1990s, which was later accepted as an alternate clause in the OECD Model. Further, the OECD's very own work on the so-called virtual permanent establishment that started in the 2000s pointed to the inevitability of eventually jettisoning the physicality of the threshold test. It remains to be seen what the content will be of a dematerialised threshold test, or series of tests, for meaningful source taxation of international business income. It seems that first principles, such as the doctrine of the sufficient link in public international law, economic efficiency theory, and the ever-increasing importance of taxpayer rights will all have to be integrated into the design of, hopefully, a principle-based new framework for source taxation of international business income.

The second cornerstone of the existing international tax regime that will be partly neutralised under the OECD's Two Pillar proposal, is the arm's length principle.

70. ATAF, Suggested Approach to Drafting Digital Service Tax Legislation, September 2020, https://events.ataftax.org/index.php?page=documents&func=view&document_id=79 (accessed 5 February 2022).

Again, it was obvious for some time that this was a sick patient in need of some incisive surgery. Regrettably, the treatment meted out through the BEPS Action Plans 8 to 10 for so-called hard-to-value intangibles, meant as an experiment for the betterment of the OECD's transfer pricing guidelines overall, had no curing effect, but rather introduced intolerable complexity, especially for countries with lower levels of capacity to administer already complex sets of transfer pricing guidelines. It is therefore ironic that the Pillar One proposal will partly jettison the arm's length principle for an industry reliant on intangible assets, and at which BEPS Actions 8 to 10 were initially aimed. The adoption of formula-based notions like a sales-based factor in place of the arm's length principle to allocate profits to a source jurisdiction (i.e. the "market" country) is of course well-known in the context of US federal state taxes.[71] Exportation of the associated problems (and avoidance strategies) of sales-based factoring in US federal state taxes is a likely prospect for countries that will sign up to Pillar One.

The third cornerstone of the existing international tax regime that will be fundamentally eroded by the Two Pillar proposal is the de-recognition of separate corporate personality as a starting point to identify a national tax base. Instead, financial group accounts are proposed as the measure of a supranational tax base, which will need to be allocated to countries based on a factor approach. This feature of the OECD's Two Pillar proposal will cause a momentous unravelling of the separate accounts approach, which has been a stable principle for international business taxation since the 1930s when it was agreed by the members of the erstwhile League of Nations.[72] A resort to supranational financial group accounts via a multilateral treaty commitment will raise many hard tax and legal policy questions. It appears to signal a decoupling of national constitutional control over the institutional framework within which financial accounting guidelines will be developed as the measure of a national tax base for business income.

The crumbling of the above cornerstones of the existing international tax regime following implementation of the OECD's Two Pillar proposal may, cumulatively, usher in a new long period of uncertainty to be sure, and new elements of instability may also be unleashed. Most immediately the details of the above-mentioned drastic new elements of the Two Pillar proposal are being softened in the current (2022) machinations of the Inclusive Framework. Yet, in the medium to long term, a wholly new direction for the international tax regime will emerge if the notions of dematerialised source tax, factor-based allocation of business income, and

71. R.S. Avi-Yonah, The International Tax Regime at 100: Reflections on the OECD's BEPS Project, 75 *Bulletin for International Taxation* 11/12 (2021), at p. 524.

72. League of Nations, *Taxation of Foreign and National Enterprises*, Volumes 1-5 (Geneva, 1932-33); and *see* the draft Convention on the Allocation of Business Income, in Report of the Fiscal Committee of the League of Nations to the Council on the Fourth Session of the Committee, 26 June 1933, (Geneva, 1933), document C.399.M.204.1933.II.A.[F./Fiscal.76], at Annex.

supranational tax base regulation are adopted. Whether stability will be enhanced will in part depend on whether governments and policymakers heed the call to rethink governance structures over such a dramatic reformation of the international tax regime for business income.

4. Retrospective taxation

The dilemma with retrospective taxation (to say nothing of the eviller twin – retroactive taxation) appears to be twofold: When may such a measure be used, as a last resort and legitimately in the eyes of *bona fide* taxpayers, to address proven tax abuse on a scale that cannot be otherwise addressed, for example through case-by-case application of a statutory general anti-avoidance rule? And if justification may be found for the use of a retrospective tax measure, how does the legislature craft a legal mechanism that does not overreach by affecting *bona fide* business, and scare away prospective investors? It seems an incredibly fine line needs to be walked by tax policymakers who wish to resort to perhaps the most drastic of measures in the arsenal of the state to address tax avoidance.

The way in which retrospective tax measures tend to emerge tells the story of why this measure causes such unease. Tax administrators can have difficulty, due to information asymmetry, distinguishing perceived tax abuse or avoidance from actual tax abusive behaviour. To be sure, retrospective tax legislation can be justified to stop blatant abusive taxpayer behaviour.[73] However, unproven tax abuse or alleged tax avoidance is unfortunately too often used by policymakers as the *only* justification to pursue retrospective tax measures to 'correct' the alleged abusive behaviour or avoidance.[74] But on closer inspection, it might be revealed that the perceived abuse was unfounded, for example, because of tax policy miscarriage (namely when the legislation is defective, and taxpayers simply rely on the law as it is found with no abusive intent). Or the retrospective measure overreaches in its effect when transactions already concluded with no tax-avoiding or abusive intent are impinged. Tax administrators and policymakers develop blind spots for defective tax legislation, and so the corrective to stop overreach and overuse of retrospective

73. For an example, *Padmore v IRC (No 2) Chancery Division,* (2001) 3 ITLR 315 concerned retrospective legislation enacted by the United Kingdom (sec. 64(4) of Finance (No 2) Act 1987). The measure was targeted at marketed tax avoidance structures involving Jersey partnerships solely set up to claim tax exemption under the 1952 income tax treaty concluded with the UK.

74. For example, in South Africa, some Ministers of Finance have used media statements to warn perceived tax avoiders that retrospective legislation may be employed, as from the date of the media statement, to address broadly identified schemes, and then went on to so act without exhausting legal avenues to establish whether actual tax avoidance occurred in transactions affected by the retrospective tax legislation. *See* A. Titus, Pienaar Bros (Pty) Ltd v CSARS, Retroactive Fiscal Legislation and the Rule of Law: Has South Africa Just Taken a Step Back in its Constitutional Democracy? (2019) 136 South African Law Journal, 3, at pp. 418, 419.

taxation is, at the end of the day, an independent judiciary with a well-developed constitutional jurisprudence that values the rule of law in its true and highest sense. A strong judiciary is needed to unmask sophistry when retrospective legislation is misused. What may also prove to stem a tide of unwarranted retrospective tax measures is clear legal ordering rules, requiring tax administrators to first exhaust available avenues to address tax abuse and avoidance, such as through a statutory general anti-avoidance rule.

It is perhaps not out of place to remark that international actors such as the OECD and other inter-governmental tax agencies have given scant attention to retrospective tax measures, which is symptomatic of the failure to work towards a balanced regulatory framework for cross-border business investment and trade. It is, therefore, no surprise that the effect of retrospective tax measures on investors has become a concern in the field of international investment protection law.[75] The global system of international economic law is fragmented, and much work remains to synthesise taxation into allied regulatory frameworks, and vice versa.

5. The prospects for a Global Tax Authority

To bring broad-based stability to the international tax regime, Professor Shome has asked "could a global fiscal and/or tax organization be designed, and could the Inclusive Framework take the formulation of such an organization forward?"[76] He postulated this question because in his analysis there is no critical mass yet to agree to, or finance moving the location of the international taxation architecture to the United Nations. Thus, a mid-way between the OECD and the United Nations is envisaged, for which the establishment of a Global Tax Authority along the contours of the Inclusive Framework is mooted. The benefit associated with such a multilateral tax organization is envisaged to be:

> "reducing international tax avoidance, enabling the rationalization of tax structures and promoting more efficient and streamlined national tax administrations. In turn, the reformed international taxation architecture would likely result in improved global revenue generation that is needed to move towards closing the significant fiscal gaps prevalent in most countries"[77]

75. For example, *see* the arbitral award in *Cairn Energy PLC and Cairn UK Holdings Limited v The Republic of India*, PCA Case No. 2016-07; N. Jalan & A. Rao, The Cairn Arbitration Award: Retrospective Taxation of Indirect Share Transfers in India Breaches Bilateral Investment Treaty, (2021) 75 *Bulletin for International Taxation* 5, and R.J. Danon & S. Wuschka, International Investment Agreements and the International Tax System: The Potential of Complementarity and Harmonious Interpretation, (2021) 75 *Bulletin for International Taxation* 11/12, at p. 698.
76. Shome, n. 60, at p. 568.
77. Shome, n. 60, at p. 569.

Whilst advocating for these benefits, he is sceptic about prospects for their realisation:

> "Nevertheless, it appears that the time for both the idea of shifting the international taxation regime to the UN and that of establishing an independent international taxation architecture remains uncertain. In this environment, the potential role of the Inclusive Framework must be highlighted through which major challenges that continue to haunt the adequacy of taxation can be confronted meaningfully and resolved in terms of fair revenue collection and its cross-country allocation."[78]

Whilst I am in broad agreement with his prognosis, I should like to point out that forces are at play that may well bring the international tax community closer to the point where meaningful reform of the OECD's dominant institutional architecture may become possible in the next decade.

The broad legitimacy of the OECD as the premier international tax standard setter has been called into question in various quarters, especially after the global financial crisis of 2008 that was founded on disorderly financial markets of the USA. In effect, the acceptability, and hence, the dominance of American economic hegemony is suffering a slow decline. Whilst I mean no disrespect to other OECD members, the influence and sway by the USA over the OECD should not be papered over. In the arena of international taxation, there are several examples whereby solutions first developed as matters of domestic US tax policy eventually find their way into global OECD tax standards. While decay in US economic hegemony inevitably translates into a legitimacy crisis of the OECD in the eyes of non-members, the BRICS and allied countries are ascending. In particular, the People's Republic of China has asserted itself broadly in most spheres of foreign and economic policy, which has meant that non-OECD members for the first time since the Second World War have begun to see possible alternates to the institutions conceived under the Marshall Plan for the restoration of Europe, in which the OECD was birthed. What this all means, is that fiscal proposals emanating from the OECD tend to suffer from an inevitable lack of credibility, despite widely used platitudes by the OECD Secretariat that non-members participate "on an equal footing" in the work on international taxation. But crises of legitimacy or credibility do not necessarily correlate with declining power and influence. The OECD is set to continue its dominance for as long as the USA believes that there is merit in pursuing multilateral solutions to questions of international fiscal regulation through the OECD's infrastructure. Furthermore, it is noteworthy that Brazil is in enhanced discussion to attain OECD membership. Brazil has been one of the most vocal adherents of alternate orthodoxy to OECD transfer pricing regulations but appears to be willing to let go of its long-standing position on alternate transfer pricing

78. *Ibid.*

methodologies in exchange for OECD membership.[79] The OECD's image among large emerging economies may receive a boost should Brazil take up membership, and the appropriateness of its tax policies for this cohort of countries may receive a measure of legitimisation by such a move.

Yet not much is known about the People's Republic of China's position on OECD membership. As the only real potential economic counterbalance to the USA's dominance over the OECD, China occupies the game-changing spot at this point of the 21st century. China is one of the key partner countries of the OECD along with India, Brazil, Indonesia, and South Africa, but there is no public record of any ambition to achieve full OECD membership. Nor does China appear to be willing to abandon any of its unique domestic international tax policies (for example around transfer pricing) in favour of OECD orthodoxy. Yet, there is also little sign of Chinese opposition to emerging OECD tax work such as the Two Pillar proposal.[80] What is clear though, is that most recently in 2017[81] and in 2018,[82]

---

79. *See* OECD, Transfer Pricing in Brazil: Towards Convergence with the OECD Standard, 18 December 2019, https://www.oecd.org/tax/transfer-pricing/transfer-pricing-in-brazil-towards-convergence-with-the-oecd-standard.htm (accessed 5 February 2022); and C. Ayub, Brazil: Advancing towards global transfer pricing convergence, International Tax Review, 23 July 2020, https://www.internationaltaxreview.com/article/b1mm864qdjxlyl/brazil-advancing-towards-global-transfer-pricing-convergence (accessed 5 February 2022).
80. *See* J. Li, China's Rising (and the United States' Declining) Influence in Global Tax Governance? Some Observations, (2021) 75 *Bulletin for International Taxation* 11/12, at pp. 736-737.
81. *See* Ministerial Declaration, forty-first annual meeting of the Group of 77 and China, New York 22 September 2017, https://www.g77.org/doc/Declaration2017.htm (Accessed 5 February 2022), at point 49 where it was declared: "The Ministers highlighted that there is still no single global inclusive forum for international tax cooperation at the intergovernmental level. While it may be indicated that a certain level of dialogue and initiative actions are taking place at the international level regarding cooperation on tax matters, they underscored that the United Nations is the only universal forum where these issues can be discussed in an open, transparent, and inclusive manner, considering that other processes might be outlined from a perspective that safeguards the interests of constituents from developed countries. In that regard, the Ministers reiterated the need to fully upgrade the Committee of Experts on International Cooperation in Tax Matters to an intergovernmental body, provide adequate resources to the Committee to fulfil its mandate and increase the participation of experts from developing countries at its meetings. Doing so would be critical to transforming the current Committee from experts acting in their own capacity to an intergovernmental subsidiary body of the Economic and Social Council, with experts representing their respective Governments."
82. *See* Statement on behalf of the Group of 77 and China by Mr. Sameh Elkhisin, First Secretary of the Permanent Mission of Egypt to the United Nations, at the ECOSOC Special Meeting on International Cooperation in Tax Matters (New York, 18 May 2018), https://www.g77.org/statement/getstatement.php?id=180518b (accessed 5 February 2022), in which it was stated that: "While the establishment of the inter-Agency Platform for Collaboration on Tax (PCT) reflects an urge to strengthen coherence, coordination and consensus building in international tax matters, we need to bear in mind that such an effort must be conducted though intergovernmental cooperation and negotiations. Again, the establishment of a universal, intergovernmental UN tax body would be the appropriate way forward on these issues."

China joined with the G77 countries in a call for the establishment of a UN-headed international tax agency to replace the OECD-dominated system. Joining forces with the G77 countries is in line with China's general international tax policy position of acting as a "responsible major developing country".[83]

How the relationship between China and the USA will develop in the next decade is likely to have material consequences for the ongoing reforms of the international tax system, including the prospects for any real shift in the institutional framework. An assessment of the convergence or divergence of the fiscal interests of China and the USA will be an important element, despite all their known disagreements and opposing world views.

83. United Nations Practical Manual on Transfer Pricing for Developing Countries, Part D, Country Practices (UN 2021), at sec. 2.1.2; and *see* Li, n. 80, at p. 738.

CHAPTER 2

USA Advocation of a Global Minimum Corporate Tax and its Impact on Developing Economies

K.R. Girish with Rahul Chowdhury

I. Introduction

The Organisation for Economic Co-operation and Development ('OECD') through its Base Erosion and Profit Shifting ('BEPS') action plan has made consistent efforts through the years to address international tax challenges. The objective of BEPS has been to counter structures adopted by Multinational Enterprises (MNEs) to avoid or reduce their global tax burden, which is termed 'tax efficiency' by them. Assets—capital and people are the factors that determine the country in which corporate tax is to be levied, collected, and revenue retained. It is a practice for MNEs to shift their profits from one country to another to minimise tax outgo. These structures technically may not strictly breach laws but take benefit from prevailing, often outdated, tax laws.

Rapid changes in business models led by digital transformation have preoccupied several countries. This led to the need for regenerating responsibility on framing policies for rightly taxing income without any tax leakage and its administration. Countries across the globe realized that old taxation rules are not capable of addressing the latest business strategies. Some of the fundamentals for determining taxation were based on profit allocation strategy using physical presence, which may not suffice for taxation where recent business models are being used. In these models where intangibles are the major drivers of a business, the physical proximity of the business is not a requirement, and existing profit allocation and taxing rules may not be effective. As per the OECD, some of the elements of digitization that contribute to this dilemma are scale without mass, reliance on intangible assets, and the centrality of data in the headquarters. It has been challenging for governments to segregate the digital economy and give boundaries around its businesses for taxing income earned from it in a jurisdiction. The speed at which these changes have occurred has multiplied the consequential tax challenges.

Many countries have adopted 'makeshift' unilateral actions to address these issues that were initiated pre-and post- BEPS guidance. However, coordinated efforts across the globe like the Multilateral Instrument (MLI) arising from BEPS actions projects are expected to provide a more predictable and efficient tax system for economic growth. It should give an opportunity to governments to address the issue and figure out a solution that can be easily administered and, at the same time, ensure that the growth of the business sector is not affected. In this light, OECD and G20 members have been focused for the past few years on arriving at a consensus-based solution to resolve the challenges arising from digitization.

II. Developments in Resolving Tax Challenges from Digitization

Diagram 1. Developments in the Emergence of the Pillars

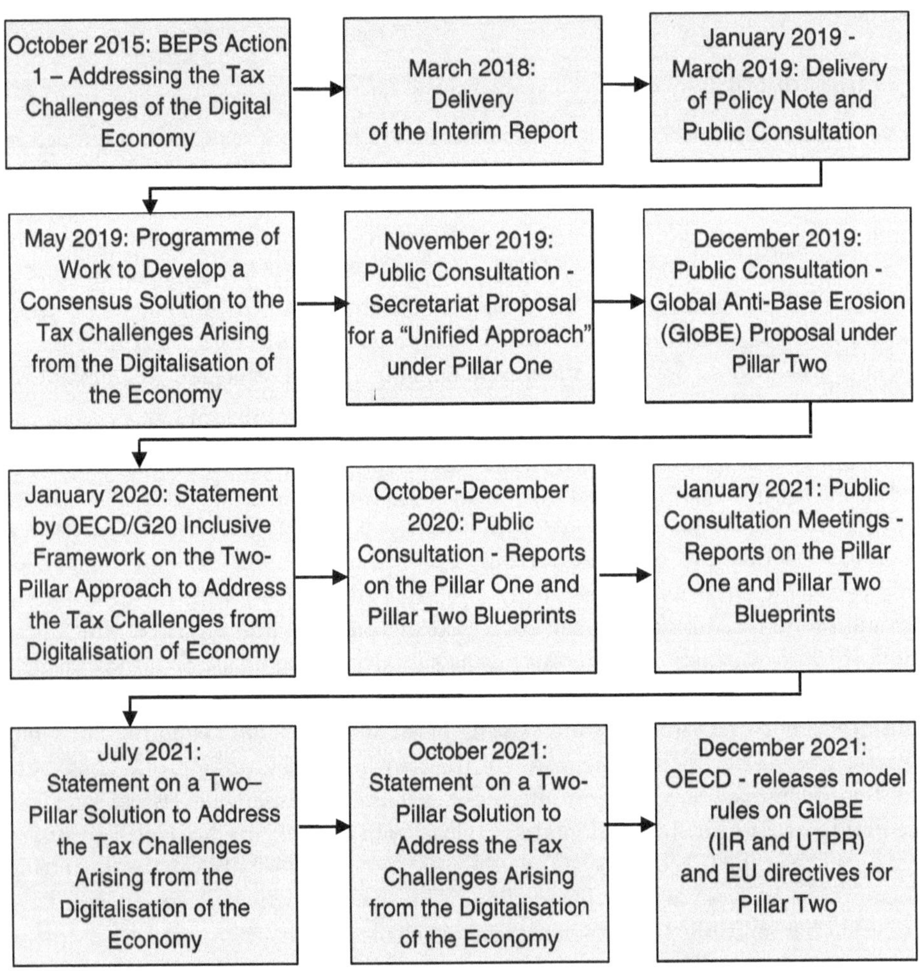

Source: Depiction of OECD Developments on BEPS Action Plans

In early 2019, BEPS 2.0 came up to reaching a global consensus through a two-Pillar approach as a solution to address these tax challenges. While Pillar One focuses on the location where large MNEs pay tax, Pillar Two focuses on levying a minimum tax to avoid location/ jurisdiction benefits. Both the Pillars require consensus for implementation.

II.1. Pillar One

To deal with businesses that generate income from market jurisdictions, Pillar One reallocates income based on users' jurisdictions. It will re-allocate some taxing rights over MNEs from their home countries to the market jurisdiction where they undertake business activities and earn profits. This re-allocation will be immaterial of their physical presence.

II.2. Pillar Two

Pillar Two aims to address tax challenges that are not addressed in Pillar One. The BEPS action plan aimed at arresting the shifting of profits to avoid/ reduce tax. Certain countries have set low/no tax rules to attract investment, and MNEs utilize this route to shift their investments to favourable jurisdictions. The intention of Pillar Two is to restrain countries from reducing tax rates or providing tax incentives to attract investment. Effectively, Pillar Two rules are set to ensure that large MNEs pay a minimum tax irrespective of their country of headquarters or country of operations. The intention of having a universal minimum tax rate is to restrict competition between governments and encourage MNEs to repatriate capital to their headquarters with the effect of eventually boosting their economies.

It was surprising that the outcome was a very low bar for the minimum corporate tax, being only 15%. However, in view of the prevailing global tax rates in tax havens such as Ireland, Cayman Islands, and Switzerland, to take a few examples, a 15% tax is not a small number. Below we take up Pillar Two with its Global Anti-Base Erosion ('GloBE') Rules, and its specifications for developing countries. Implementing GloBE must be a globally integrated effort. It is imperative that developing countries should not just be aware of GloBE Rules by its terms but also of its impact on their economies while ensuring a balance with international tax standards.

Table 1. Timeframe for Implementation of the Pillars[1]

Timeline	Pillar One	Pillar Two
Early 2022	Text of the Multilateral Convention to implement Pillar One and Explanatory Statement to implement Amount A to be agreed	Model GloBE Rules to be agreed

1. OECD Secretary-General Tax report to G20 Finance ministers And Central Bank Governors, February 2022.

Timeline	Pillar One	Pillar Two
Mid 2022	Model Rules for domestic implementation of Pillar One to be agreed	Model treaty provision to give effect to the Subject to Tax Rule (STTR)
	High-level signing ceremony for the MLC	A multilateral instrument for the implementation of the STTR in bilateral treaties
End 2022	Finalisation of work on Amount B	Implementation framework to facilitate coordinated implementtation of the GloBE Rules
2023 – Implementation of the Two-Pillar solution		

Source: OECD Secretary-General Tax Report to G20 Finance Ministers and Central Bank Governors, February 2022

In simple terms, the OECD's Global Minimum Tax ('GMT') proposal involves paying a 'top-up tax' at the level of the parent company if income made further down the ownership chain has been taxed below the GMT rate. The blueprint is targeted at profit shifting involving intangibles, rather than substance-based incentives. Pillar Two proposals are not 'minimum standards', like some BEPS 1.0 proposals. GloBE Rules under Pillar Two will have a 'common approach'. To explain, BEPS Inclusive Framework ('IF') members are not mandatorily required to adopt GloBE Rules, but if they choose to adopt them, they must implement and administer them in a way provided under Pillar Two. Further, IF members should also accept the application of GloBE Rules by other members including an agreement to rule order and application of any safe harbour rules. One could say that GMT proposed under Pillar Two is an easy fix, at the same time rendering it harder for corporates to avoid tax.

In sum, the IF's intention of negotiation on GloBE Rules was to have minimum taxation introduced so that no income escapes taxation and also minimise the difference in taxing cross-border income.

Some of the main points considered by OECD while drafting Pillar Two rules were:

- Payment of minimum tax, at the same time avoiding double taxation or taxation where there is no economic profit
- Transparency
- Level playing field
- Minimising administrative procedures and compliance costs
- Coping with tax systems in different jurisdictions, and
- Coping with varied business operating models.

II.2.1. Global Intangible low-taxed Income

The blueprint of rules structured under Pillar Two also discusses the co-existence of the GILTI ('Global Intangible low-taxed Income') regime in the US. A few years earlier, the US adopted GILTI, a new way of taxing foreign income, to charge minimum tax on foreign earnings of US companies. GILTI has inspired many countries. Rather than having similar rules in each interested country, it was thought that a global rule would be preferable.

Although GloBE is inspired by GILTI, there are many differences between the two right from the tax rate to the structure of the tax base. The US expressed its willingness to adopt a modified GILTI. The world was waiting for the US to take the first step of Pillar Two implementation. However, the Republican members of the Committee of Finance of the US Senate had written to the US Treasury Secretary that the developments in Pillar Two would harm jobs and businesses in the US.

III. Interlocking Rules and Detailed Structure under Pillar Two

Pillar Two consists of three rules, the Income Inclusion Rule, the Undertaxed Payments Rule, and the Subject to Tax Rule.

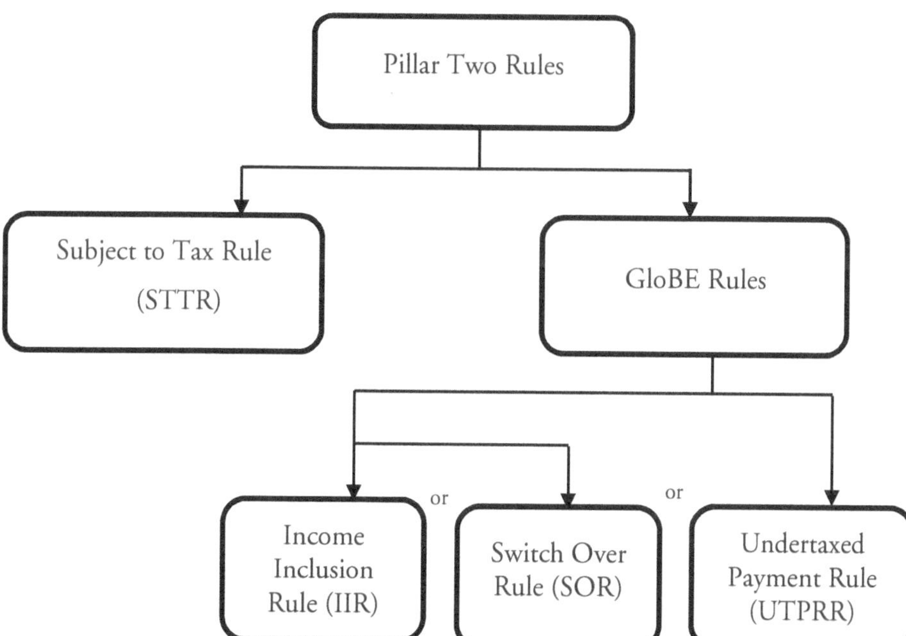

Source: OECD Report 2021 on Pillar Two Approach

On the adoption of Pillar Two, countries can choose their tax regulations; however, they must bear in mind that a corresponding jurisdiction has the right to impose tax based on the internationally agreed Pillar Two regulations, where an income is taxed below the minimum rate.

While the Pillar Two objective of a minimum global corporate tax appears to be simple, its design is quite complex with the objective to ensure that the total calculated tax is in effect collected on a global basis. In addition, Pillar Two also focuses on the rights that a jurisdiction has for collecting revenue on a taxable event in view of what is being, or not being, collected on it in a related jurisdiction.

III.1. Subject to Tax Rule

STTR is the primary rule that applies under Pillar Two. It targets BEPS structures that involve intra-group payments taking the treaty protection in the source country and remaining untaxed or taxed at a lower than the minimum rate in the resident country.

Specific payments included and excluded under STTR are:

Inclusions	Exclusions
• Interest and royalties • Insurance premium • Franchise fee • Guarantee, brokerage, and financing fee • Use of movable property • Intermediary services	• Payment to individuals • Dividend • Low-return payments • Payment to entities excluded under GloBE Rules • Payments that are not covered

STTR protects the source country's taxing right; at the same time, it does not restrict the resident country from taxing a transaction. STTR prescribes a gross basis for withholding in respect of intra-group payments, and it is unlikely to impact payments made to unrelated parties. It targets a minimum level of taxation referred to as the 'trigger rate' set at a rate lower than the minimum tax rate for GloBE Rules, i.e., at 9 percent. Where interest, royalties, and certain other payments are taxed below STTR rates, the bilateral treaties should be amended to set the minimum rate, even if not obliged to do so.

STTR is proposed to be implemented under any of the following mechanisms:

- Tax in the hands of the recipient at the end of the year
- Withholding tax provisions to be applied by the payer or

- A combination whereby a lower withholding tax is imposed and the remaining tax is collected from the recipient at the end of the year. Given the STTR mechanism, there are some aspects that need further consideration.

As STTR may require withholding, it will be implemented through changes in tax treaties and suitable amendments in domestic tax laws. Selected aspects may need further elaboration:

- IIR and UTPR (discussed next) are the principal mechanisms under Pillar Two. However, STTR is to be applied first.
- STTR is applied on a gross basis, more like TDS where consequent expenditure is not considered. This could result in lower or higher taxation.

III.2. GloBE Rules

Primarily, the GloBE Rules concern the taxation of foreign companies. Secondly, if domestic tax laws, levy tax at less than the GMT rate, then an additional charge of top-up tax could arise, if domestic tax laws are not amended to ensure taxation of profits at a minimum rate. There were 140 countries participating in Pillar Two negotiations and among them, 137 countries have signed the proposal[2].

Some of the key parameters of Pillar Two are:

- Similar to the CbCR threshold, the MNE group's consolidated revenue as per Consolidated Financial Statements of the Ultimate Parent Entity should be more than EUR 750 million in two of the four fiscal years immediately preceding the tested Fiscal Year.
- GloBE Rules apply to MNE groups that have a presence in 2 or more jurisdictions, i.e., each entity having a different tax residence or PE in another jurisdiction.
- Minimum Tax Rate for GloBE Rules are agreed at a rate of 15 percent.
- Exclusion: for jurisdictions where MNCs' global revenue is below EUR 10 million and profit is below EUR 10 million
- Carve-out: 8% carrying value of tangible assets and 10% of payroll costs phasing down to 5% over 10 years
- Implementation of GloBE Rules is optional, but once adopted by a jurisdiction, it has to be consistent. Also, GloBE Rules adopted by other IF members should be accepted.

---

2. https://www.oecd.org/tax/beps/oecd-g20-inclusive-framework-members-joining-statement-on-two-pillar-solution-to-address-tax-challenges-arising-from-digitalisation-october-2021.pdf.

III.3. Mechanism of GloBE Rules

There are five broad steps that an MNE will have to go through to determine tax liability under Pillar Two Model Rules:

Step 1: Identify Multinational Groups within the scope of Pillar Two and the location of each constituent entity within the group.

Step 2: Determine the GloBE income of each constituent entity.

Step 3: Determine the covered taxes attributable to the income of the constituent entity.

Step 4: Calculate the effective tax rate of all constituent entities located in the same jurisdiction

Jurisdictional ETR is compared with MTR:

$$\text{ETR} = \frac{\text{Aggregate adjusted covered taxes of all constituent entities in the jurisdiction} * 100}{\text{Aggregate adjusted GloBE tax base of all constituent entities in the jurisdiction}}$$

Step 5: Determine the consequent top-up tax. Top-up tax is to be determined when jurisdictional ETR is lesser than MTR. Top-up tax is the difference between MTR and ETR.

Step 6: Impose top-up tax under IIR or UTPR in accordance with the agreed rule

III.3.1. Rule 1: IIR

When the income of a controlled foreign entity is taxed below the minimum effective level, i.e., below the effective tax rate of 15%, then IIR triggers inclusion at the shareholder level.

Basically, the IIR would impose top-up tax in the parent jurisdiction on the income of a foreign-controlled entity / foreign branch if that income is taxed at less than the agreed minimum rate.

Also, countries are free to apply IIR to MNEs headquartered in their countries even if their consolidated income does not exceed the threshold.

III.3.2. Rule 2: UTPR

Top-up tax under UTPR applies to implemented countries when a constituent entity is not already subject to IIR. It acts as a backstop to the IIR rule. This rule order is supposed to mostly respond to compliance and minimal considerations.

Constituent entities are not allowed any deduction under UTPR rules, therefore UTPR top-up tax allocated to a jurisdiction could be an additional tax expense.

III.3.3. Rule 3: SOR

SOR is contemplated to remove treaty obstacles. It applies to foreign branch income.

IIR and UTPR will be implemented by changes in domestic tax laws and supported by MLIs and switch-over rules that ensure the application of the former when jurisdictions have adopted the exemption methods.

III.4. GloBE Rules - Chapters

GloBE Rules have been prescribed to provide a common approach to tax income that is either not taxed, or undertaxed. It consists of 10 Chapters:

Chapter 1: Defines scope

Key operative Rules:

Chapter 2: IIR and UTPR charging provisions

Chapter 3: Computation of GloBE income

Chapter 4: Computation of adjusted covered tax;

Chapter 5: Computation of ETR and Top-up tax;

Chapter 6: Corporate restructuring and Holding Structures;

Chapter 7: Treatment of tax neutrality and distribution regimes;

Chapter 8: Administration – provides an international coordinated approach

Chapter 9: Transition Rules

Chapter 10: Definitions

III.4.1. Chapter 1: Defines scope

Chapter 1 provides the definition of certain important terms like Group, MNE Group, Constituent Entity, Excluded entity, Ultimate Parent Entity, etc. It also provides the scope of the rules.

III.4.2. Chapter 2: Charging provisions

Chapter 2 addresses questions like:

- Who is liable to pay top-up tax?
- What is the proportion of top-up tax that is charged?
- Which entity in the ownership chain is liable for top-up tax?
- Whether IIR would apply or UTPR?

IIR is intended to be applicable to ensure that MNEs are subject to minimum taxation in every jurisdiction they operate. Further, UTPR acts as a support to IIR. Some specific scenarios of applicability of GloBE Rules that are provided in this Chapter are:

- If the ultimate parent entity is located in a jurisdiction that has not implemented IIR, then the highest parent entity located in that jurisdiction that has implemented IIR should pay the top-up tax.
- In the case of companies owned by two entities, the ultimate parent entity that applies IIR will have to reduce the share of allocable top-up tax, by an amount equal to the top-up tax imposed on the partially owned parent entity.
- UTPR does not apply to constituent entities that are investment entities.

III.4.3. Chapter 3: Computation of GloBE income or loss

In chapter 3 GloBE income or loss is determined for the constituent entity considering the Financial Accounting net income, to which adjustments are made as per prescribed rules. This exercise may require the maintenance of an additional set of data.

These are the broad steps of computation of global income or loss under this chapter:

Step 1: Consolidating Financial Statements prepared in accordance with the financial accounting standard of the Ultimate Parent Entity or other acceptable financial accounting standards

Step 2: Adjustment of certain expenses/ income like dividends, taxes, gains or losses from disposition of assets, equity gains or losses, foreign currency gains or loss, prior period errors and changes in accounting principles, and many other considerations.

Step 3: Exclusion of international shipping income.

Step 4: Allocation of net income attributable to the Permanent Establishment as the same is not included in GloBE income or loss

Step 5: income/ loss so determined is allocated to the Constituent entities in accordance with the Ownership interest

III.4.4. Chapter 4: Computation of Adjusted Covered Tax

Chapter 4 defines the computation of adjusted covered taxes (based on current tax expense) used in ETR calculation and provides:

- rules for allocation of adjusted covered taxes.
- mechanism to address timing differences – this requires complicated adjustments and recalculation

III.4.5. Chapter 5: Computation of ETR and Top-up tax

Chapter 5 provides a mechanism for determining the Effective Tax Rate for a jurisdiction and Top-up tax for constituent entities located in low-tax jurisdictions. It also provides for de minimis exclusion and a method for calculating additional top-up tax and ETR for minority-owned parent entities.

De minimis exclusion – No top-up tax shall be determined/ applicable for constituent entities located in a jurisdiction, where the:

- average GloBE revenue in such jurisdiction is less than EUR 10 Mn and
- average GloBE Income/ loss is less than EUR 1 Mn

Further, for minority-owned constituent entities, GloBE Rules apply on a stand-alone basis, as if they were a separate MNE group.

The broad steps for determining ETR and Top-up tax are:

Step 1: Aggregating GloBE income of each constituent entity in a jurisdiction.

Step 2: Aggregating adjusted covered taxes of each constituent entity in the same jurisdiction.

Step 3: Divide aggregate GloBE income by aggregate adjusted covered taxes to determine ETR for the jurisdiction.

Step 4: Identifying jurisdictions having ETR less than the minimum rate.

Step 5: Computing top-up tax for low-taxed jurisdictions

Step 6: Computation of substance-based income exclusion

Step 7: Determining excess profits in the jurisdiction

Step 8: Determining top-up tax.

Step 9: Allocating top-up tax in low-tax jurisdictions

III.4.6. Chapter 6: Corporate restructuring and holding structures

Chapter 6 provides means in GloBE Rules in the following cases:

- For determining consolidated revenue threshold in case of merger and demerger that took place four prior years
- To bring certain joint ventures within GloBE scope
- Rules to deal with the transfer of assets and liabilities
- Rules that apply to multi-parented MNE groups
- Rules to deal with entry and exit of constituent entities from MNE groups

III.4.7. Chapter 7: Treatment of tax neutrality and distribution regimes

Chapter 7 provides GloBE Rules applicable in specific cases:

- When UPE is subject to a tax neutrality regime.
- When an entity is taxed on earnings that are distributed.
- For controlled investment entities

III.4.8. Chapter 8: Administration – provides an internationally co-ordinated approach

Chapter 8 provides guidance on administration and compliance matters like:

- Filing GloBE information return – significant information, that may be different from the requirements so far, will have to be maintained
- Optional safe harbour rules
- Implementation framework – to be released in 2022 giving a tight timeline for giving effect to it in 2023

III.4.9. Chapter 9: Transition rules

Chapter 9 provides the timing, condition, and transition of GloBE Rules that apply to an MNE group along with regular rules in a jurisdiction for the first time.

The transition period will be 10 years with substance-based income exclusion during the period:

- starting from 8% and scaling down to 5% of the carrying value of tangible assets by end of the period
- starting from 10% and scaling down to 5% of the carrying value of payroll by end of the period

III.4.10. Chapter 10: Definitions

Definitions of some of the major terms like Permanent Establishment, Flow-through Entity, Hybrid Entity, Excluded Dividend, Excluded Equity Gain or Loss, etc. are provided in this Chapter

III.5. Proposed timeline for implementation of Pillar Two

The proposed timeline for implementation of Pillar Two is provided below[3]:

Period	Implementation Strategy
Year 2022	GloBE implementation framework covering administration and co-ordination to be released and Pillar Two to be brought into law

3. Refer Action 1 - OECD BEPS.

Period	Implementation Strategy
Year 2023	IIR to come into effect
Year 2024	UTPR to come into effect

Countries representing more than 90% of the Global GDP have agreed for the implementation of Pillar Two. This unanimous approach should give an advantage to multinational players as they can expect a stable and certain international tax system.

III.6. Rules may need further clarification

Interlocking rules adopted by many jurisdictions comprise more stringent provisions, which should curb the incentive for MNEs to shift their profits to low-tax jurisdictions as the Rules will still apply and enhance consistent and coordinated implementation of GloBE Rules. In turn, this should lead to a minimum tax on MNEs in each jurisdiction. Further, a carve-out applicable to a wide range of industries should help in continuing tax incentives for enhancing regular investments that are not made merely with the objective of global tax avoidance.

Given the set of rules and guidance, some aspects that MNEs should be mindful of while applying GloBE Rules are listed as follows:

- Even if there are exclusion rules for certain entities, their revenue should still be considered in determining the overall threshold provided of EUR 750 million.
- How the exchange rate should be applied for arriving/ determining the applicable amounts.
- There is an effort to include entities that are not subject to country-by-country reporting, by giving options to jurisdictions to apply IIR to MNEs headquartered in their jurisdiction even if they don't meet the threshold condition.
- The purpose of IIR tax is to negate treaty benefits and ensure that minimum tax is paid by MNCs. One important aspect is that the proposed GloBE Rules should be read in line with the treaty negotiations and their intentions.
- Inclusions in covered tax need further deliberation. Unilateral measures adopted by various countries (like the equalization levy introduced in India) could result in additional taxation if not considered as part of the covered tax.
- Outbound investments made by MNCs in low tax jurisdictions, may be taxed in HQ country under IIR.

- If IIR is unable to levy top-up tax and UTPR comes into play, then there could be many complexities like - in what capacity should the payer pay tax? What if the payee is a non-resident? Will the levy be extraterritorial, etc.?
- Whether STTR supersedes the MFN clause is something that needs more clarity.

IV. Impact of Pillar Two Rules on Developing Countries

It may be concluded from the previous analysis that the BEPS Action Plan represents a significant change in the international tax system. This was implemented through changes in domestic tax laws and tax treaties. Further, MLI's entry into force in 2018 accelerated the implementation of treaty-related measures. Additionally, to address the tax challenges arising from the digital economy, the priority of OECD and the G20 members since 2015 was to establish a stable international tax framework and prevent 'makeshift' unilateral actions.

IV.1. Benefits for the economy

In addition to the various tax benefits of Pillar Two, additional positive ramifications for the economy that developing economies may expect are the following:

- Jurisdictions with an effective tax rate higher than GMT may attract more investment based on other attractive investment criteria
- Tax may not be one of the primary factors influencing business strategy. Non-tax factors like location, infrastructure, and labour may play a vital role so that countries will realise the benefits of improving non-tax factors and take measures accordingly.
- Increased collection of taxes should help governments to rebuild the public finances, reduce government debt that shot up during the Covid 19 pandemic, and enhance public social expenditures crucially needed in the post-pandemic scenario.
- Capital and technology importing countries could anticipate benefits from STTR as these rules provide taxing rights on payments made to foreign associated enterprises.

IV.2. OECD's promise to developing countries

The OECD has noted that developing countries are members of the IF on an equal footing, and they have played an active role in the negotiations. Hence, the Two-Pillar Solution includes several features that address the concerns of low-capacity countries. The OECD is, therefore, expected to monitor and ensure that the rules can be effectively and efficiently administered, and also offer comprehensive capacity-building support to countries that need it. This work is going to be carried out in partnership with regional organizations and development banks, as well as through extensive technical assistance programmes.[4]

It is to be noted, however, that the OECD is not a legislative body and can only make recommendations. Nevertheless, time has proven the analytical emphasis and ability of the OECD, and an increasing number of developing countries, by signing on to the MLI, and subsequently, the two Pillars, have expressed confidence and trust in the OECD's recommendations. In the final analysis, recommendations of the OECD may be implemented only when countries sign on to a multilateral agreement.

V. An Assessment of Any Real Tax Benefit from the Pillars

V.1. Transfer of revenues across jurisdictions

As per the OECD, Pillar One will reallocate more than USD 125 billion to 150 billion of additional global tax revenues annually, which will accrue from the top 100 profitable MNEs with the implementation of Pillar One. The impact may not, however, be similar across countries or even among developing countries. This would depend on the number, size, and profitability of the MNEs functioning in a particular country. Given that developing countries are likely to have smaller MNEs (i.e., MNEs having consolidated revenue less than EURO 750 million), Pillar rules may not bring significant revenue to the developing countries. Approximately,, 85% – 90% of MNEs may be outside the scope of GloBE, which indicates that only a small or no additional share of tax revenue may accrue to the developing economies.

Further, not too many MNEs have headquarters in developing countries. MNE headquarters are concentrated in the United States, Japan, the United Kingdom, and other advanced economies. For this reason, it is reasonable to speculate that the proposed IIR would only be minimally applied among developing countries. On the other hand, advanced economies have also expressed some concern that MNEs may end up paying more tax in the countries where they operate (and have their customers) and less tax in the countries with MNE headquarters, that is, the advanced economies. Of course, the objective of the exercise if for emerging economies to correct some of the revenue injustices of the past; nevertheless, the changes are unlikely to generate a significant transfer of resources and there seems to be little reason for such a concern or fear. The bulk of the transfer, whatever its size, is likely to occur among the advanced economies themselves.

4. Action 1 - OECD BEPS.

V.2. Role of compliance

Another intended benefit of the application of GloBE Rules is reduced compliance costs. This is not always agreed upon by MNEs considering the additional data to be maintained, compliances to be made, checks to be instituted by jurisdictions, and so on which may not factually support the intent.

V.3. Schemes to attract investment

The downside of the implementation of GloBE Rules is that governments will be restrained in offering conditional lower taxes or exemptions or deductions as they would become more costly to offer particularly if corporate tax rates decline across the globe due to a lower GMT. This could impact the developing countries since benefits provided to attract investment must be curtailed, for example, tax incentives for the promotion of research & development, innovation, or regional development in their jurisdictions.

On the other hand, the GMT will have a significant dampening impact on the inbound structures of jurisdictions with very low tax rates such as in tax havens whose prevailing rates may be lower than the GMT.

V.4. Impact on MNEs

Over the past decade, many jurisdictions have considerably reduced the average corporate tax rate. However, MNEs have made little effort to enhance their global tax payment because their objective has been to singularly improve their 'tax efficiency' globally.

With the introduction of Pillar Two, the MNEs would probably re-examine existing business structures. However, because of the relatively low GMT of 15%, many MNEs may not feel the pressure and remain neutral to the introduction of Pillar Two, without making significant efforts to relocate from tax havens if, in most other location options, tax rates continue to linger above 15%.

V.5. Limitation of sovereign right

With the implementation of Pillar Two, countries will be obliged to charge a minimum tax of 15%. Otherwise, as per the IIR, additional tax will be payable in the home jurisdiction.

On agreeing to a GMT rate, the participating governments will have to limit their corporate tax rates and the power or ability to alter them. Thus, on the one hand, the sovereign state curtails its taxing powers (or reductions) in solidarity with the rest of the world. On the other hand, this represents a significant step forward in limiting global tax avoidance and the depletion in collecting legitimate tax revenue. It also improves the distribution of revenue in more equitable proportions across the globe. It sets a minimum standard for countries to implement a GMT and prevent the export of tax revenue.

V.6. Tax competition

As governments face accelerating financial strain, many of them, in particular, developing countries would want their share of taxes, which is not restricted only to income earned from the digital economy. Many of them provide investment-linked incentives, such as India, through sections 80-IA, 10AA, in its direct tax law. The benefit of such incentives may be nullified as these scenarios could fall under the ETR radar. Developing countries may find some tax incentives crucial for promoting investment and economic growth. At some point in the future, this matter could raise its head in multilateral discussions on tax preferences and concessions.

While these rules are in place to ensure minimum taxation for an MNE group, many jurisdictions, including some emerging economies may streamline their domestic tax laws to prevent any revenue leakage.

This way, the Model Rules may lead to another form of tax competition. Especially developing countries will try and further reduce corporate tax rates and provide exemptions/tax subsidies to attract more investments and remain internationally competitive. In such a case, the motto of 'race to the bottom' may not survive and may lay a floor for tax competition.

V.7. Timeline

There will be a push to amend the domestic tax laws as many aspects of the GloBE rules must be aligned by countries with their domestic tax provisions. In a way, model rules are templates that guide jurisdictions to incorporate them into their domestic laws. Although the expectation is that the Model Rules would assist the jurisdictions in seamless and coordinated implementation of proposed changes, given the ambitious timeline, at the current point in time, it appears to be quite challenging.

It is fair to say that India will adopt GloBE Rules. However, one must wait and watch the timeline it pursues. It is salient that it should hurry the process of amending domestic laws, but wait and watch how the Rules unfold in the multilateral community.

In the final analysis, each economy will have its own reasons and priorities in relation to the actual implementation of the Two Pillar approach. A few countries consider it as a package broadly necessary to resolve tax issues in the global digital economy, though others consider Pillar Two to be a critical anchor for global tax resilience. Certain countries also consider Pillar One as a single bargain—with Pillar Two--for the same reason.

VI. Conclusion

The tax structures of developed countries stand apart from those of developing countries in many aspects. Adopting a unanimous global corporate tax rate such as GMT could reduce the corporate tax base. The tax base of developing countries is often not broad, and they tend to depend on the share of corporate income tax more than the individual income tax, while in developed economies, it is not so.

This is corroborated by the OECD Tax Administration 2021 report which points out that developing countries are more at risk of loss of corporate tax revenues[5] reflecting the BEPS Actions. The contribution of corporate income tax to the total tax revenue of developing countries is significantly higher than in OECD countries. For example, corporate income tax share as a percentage of total tax revenue is 58% in India, 66% in Malaysia, and 52% in Indonesia as compared to 9% in France and the United Kingdom. Therefore, developing countries' higher reliance on corporate income tax implies that the tax base would significantly change if GMT were adopted and this would hinder sustainable development.

Additionally, developing countries may not have the administrative capacity to implement complicated regulations as required under BEPS. While many developing countries (like India) have agreed to implement GloBE Rules, they should have more carefully evaluated its impact and played a more active role in its design.

The GMT rules will bring substantial changes in the international tax architecture. GloBE Rules do not require a substantive activity test in the parent´s jurisdiction for applying the IIR. As a result, source jurisdictions' tax sovereignty may be affected. Pillar Two to an extent proposes what was already intended through BEPS Action Plan 3 - to strengthen controlled foreign companies (CFCs) and address weaknesses in harmful tax practices. The Pillar rules artificially segregate taxable income from the activities that generate it. The rules should aim to address not just profit shifting but also activity shifting without which the purpose for which it has been proposed will not be fulfilled.

Finally, the two most controversial questions relating to Pillar Two are the extent to which it will allow countries to engage in tax competition, and which countries will collect the tax revenues it generates. The Model Rules[6] published by the

5. https://www.oecd.org/coronavirus/en/data-insights/developing-countries-more-at-risk-of-lost-tax-revenues.
6. OECD (2021), Tax Challenges Arising from the Digitalisation of the Economy – Global Anti-Base Erosion Model Rules (Pillar Two): Inclusive Framework on BEPS, OECD, Paris. See also the Draft Directive released by the EU Commission on 23 December 2021: Proposals for a Council Directive on ensuring a global minimum level of taxation for multinational groups in the Union COM (2021) 823, and the Consultation Document released by UK authorities on 11 January 2022: HMT and HMRC, OECD Pillar 2: Consultation on Implementation.

OECD/G20 Inclusive Framework on 20 December 2021 provide somewhat unexpected answers to both questions. If Pillar One is a backstop to Pillar Two, then it would have been implemented without any pressure from G20 countries. It appears that these rules, while attempting to achieve a fairer profit allocation and taxing rights, nevertheless reveal a bias in favour of advanced economies. Implementation of Pillar Two could be a replication (to an extent) of certain laws of advanced economies hoping to solve their structural tax challenges. One could say that it may be an attempt made by the US Government to drive the tax structure for the rest of the world. A time must come when multilateral tax matters will be driven convincingly by the global community.

REJOINDER

Mukesh Butani

Problems in the Existing Tax Framework

In July 2013, due to the growing global concern about tax planning by multinational companies (MNCs) exploiting the gaps in the tax systems of a country to reduce taxable profits or artificially shift profits to low-tax jurisdictions by performing a minuscule economic activity, the OECD identified BEPS Actions Plans.

With the immense proliferation of digital means of doing business and incoherence of the existing tax systems to deal with digitisation, taxation of the digital economy has been a critical policy issue of the BEPS framework, the first plan identified was AP 1 – Taxing of Digital Economy. These digital companies heavily relied on intangibles, user participation, and the value of data, which could scale up the digital business without mass, unlike the traditional business that led to Pillar One. However, when the APs were developed, there was no separate plan identified to tax the income at a minimum level, Pillar 2.

Whilst the OECD was in the process of finalising what needed to be done on the BEPS Action Plans, countries started to take unilateral measures to address the gaps in the global tax architecture. For instance, Austria, France, India, Italy, Spain, and the UK introduced the Digital Services Tax or other unilateral measures to tax digital companies.

India introduced Equalization Levy in 2016 with a limited scope wherein a levy of 6% was imposed on digital advertising. India also legislated a Significant Economic Presence law in 2018 to tax digital companies under domestic tax laws. However, the law was kept in abeyance pending the negotiation of Two-Pillar. Considering the Trump Government backed out of the Two-Pillar solution, India widened the ambit of the Equalization Levy to cover e-commerce goods and services in 2020. As of February 2021, the government reported that the INR 1,492 crore Equalization Levy was collected in 10 months.[7]

This move of countries adopting unilateral measures led the U.S. Trade Representative to initiate an investigation of India's 2020 Equalization Levy (the DST) under section 301 of the Trade Act of 1974 in June 2020. In November 2021, the US released a report on India's Equalization Levy to state its discriminatory nature since it aims at non-resident e-commerce operators only and

7. https://economictimes.indiatimes.com/news/economy/finance/govt-collects-rs-1492-crore-equalisation-levy-between-apr-2020-jan-2021/articleshow/80879675.cms.

restricts US commerce. In November 2021, India and the US agreed on the termination of action in section 301 for Indian DST Investigation and also decided on a transitional approach on Equalization Levy with Amount A (Pillar One) The terms of such policy are yet to be finalized, however, the period applicable is from April 1, 2022, onward till the implementation of Two-Pillar Solution.

1. US domestic law legislators are the drivers[8]

The design of the income-inclusive rule draws some inspiration from the U.S. international tax rules on Global Intangible Low Tax Income (GILTI). relevant

GILTI was designed to subject foreign income of U.S. companies to a minimum tax rate. However, because GILTI was layered on top of existing U.S. international tax rules, it has created various policy challenges regarding its tax base, including the question of which high-taxed foreign incomes should be excluded from the policy. This is relevant not only for the U.S. domestic policy debate but also the designs being considered by the Inclusive Framework of the OECD: the level of blending that policymakers choose has implications for how a minimum tax will affect business decision-making. Specifically, the more granular the level of blending, the higher the associated compliance costs and the impact on expanding overseas business operations.

If the Inclusive Framework desires to minimise the impact of the income-inclusion rule on business location decisions, then a broader approach to blending will be necessary.

2. India stands to benefit or lose?[9]

In the words of Suranjali Tandon, Assistant Professor, NIPFP, "Looking at the proposal's design, one might ask if revenue gains are worth the administrative costs. It is likely that India could lose revenue from other not-so-digitized companies in the top 100 accounting for such eventualities, making the gains very tentative."

Under the new international tax regime, India gets to tax only companies with an annual turnover exceeding 20 billion euros and profitability above 10%; this comes to 100 companies.

India was arguing for a threshold of 1 billion euros, which could have covered 1000 companies. Also, the quantum of profits it gets to tax is about 25 percent of the profits in excess of 10%

8. https://taxfoundation.org/response-global-anti-base-erosion-pillar-two-proposal/.
9. https://cfo.economictimes.indiatimes.com/news/global-tax-deal-does-india-gain-or-lose/86928292.

However, in the words of Navneet Singal, Head of Taxation at Syngene International, and Mukesh Butani, Managing Partner at BMR Legal, in the long run, India will benefit under the pillar one approach. All countries seeing the bigger picture have compromised a bit. Hence, the so-called first step to a consensus has features of a deal.

3. How will IIR work for businesses which are taxed lower than 15%?[10]

While India's corporate tax rate exceeds 15%, in 2019, India offered a 15% rate to new manufacturing units. Besides, it provides tax incentives for exports and other select activities. Exemptions or preferential rates are offered to investors through treaty withholding rates or the Income Tax Act. The result of a global minimum tax may be that someone else gets the tax differential. Resultantly, what happens to investment inflows into countries offering such incentives remains to be seen.

India's current taxation policy is to phase out exemptions and lower the tax rates. Further, it has provided specific tax incentives for the growth of exports and starting up the ecosystem. It is still unclear whether such incentives will be carved out to determine 'subject to tax' so that the taxes foregone by India do not get collected by the jurisdiction of the parent of those Indian companies. Further, the fact that STTR route shall be by way of a multilateral instrument or bilateral negotiation which may also be time-consuming.

The Indian tax authorities have expressed in their personal capacity that the Pillar Two proposal of IIR and UTPR shall not be relevant since the low or no tax jurisdictions have or are introducing a corporate tax rate of 15%. For example, UAE has introduced a corporate tax rate of 15%.

4. Ambitious timelines for domestic law implementation

The timeline of implementing Pillar Two in FY 2023-24 is ambitious and will face its own set of challenges. It is yet to be decided if India should wait and watch for other countries to implement the framework to understand better the intricacies and challenges faced in the implementation of Pillar Two.

It is also pertinent to note that the earlier Multilateral Instrument was implemented in 2017; however, practically, the effect of such an instrument is yet to kick in for countries. Further, the fact that many countries have a stringent and long-drawn process for legislating tax laws also implies that the present timeline is too ambitious. For example, China deposited a provisional MLI instrument in 2017, however, it is yet to submit the final instrument.

10. https://www.bloombergquint.com/law-and-policy/india-signs-up-for-global-tax-reform-7-tax-experts-discuss-implications.

5. Should India be legislating CFC in a rush or wait?[11]

India does not have CFC provisions in its domestic income-tax legislation. However, India has implemented Country-by-Country reporting and master file requirements, wherein group taxation is collected. This will give India space and flexibility to enact CFC rules in alignment with the GLoBE framework.

6. US law vis-à-vis GloBE Rules

The similarities between the GLoBE Rules and the GILTI rules are not coincidental. However, finding a way for both ideas to co-exist is the next challenge. Representatives of many MNEs have their own views on what this interaction should look like. Some of them are:

"P&G maintains the viewpoint that the IIR should take priority over the subject to tax rule and the undertaxed payment rule in order to ensure that taxing rights under pillar two remain with the ultimate parent jurisdiction of the MNE group." Says senior vice president of finance and accounting at Procter & Gamble.

7. Sovereignty curtailed

Agreeing to a global minimum tax rate implies that governments must limit their tax rates, thus curtailing their sovereign power. However, in our opinion, multilateralism and global contribution is the way forward.

8. Bias in favour of advanced economy

On the contrary, it could be argued that residence-based rule acted as a bias favouring advanced economy/developed nations as most MNEs have their residence in such developed countries.

9. OECD assistance to developing countries

Although the OECD has promised assistance to developing countries by way of extensive technical assistance, India is not a part of any technical assistance programmes nor is it a low-capacity country. Therefore, what assistance India needs and how India exercises caution in implementing the framework only time can tell.

---

11. https://www.financialexpress.com/opinion/globe-rules-making-a-start/2400251/.

CHAPTER 3

UN Model Tax Convention: Effects on Developing Country Interests and Digital Economy Concerns

Rohit Roy and Ananya Raghavendra

I. Introduction

Taxation is the key to generating the fiscal resources necessary for poverty alleviation within a population. It is contributory to alleviating poverty and, therefore, a major enhancement in the enjoyment of economic, social, and cultural rights[1]. As a result, the idea of tax sovereignty is entrenched within the idea of State sovereignty. Tax administrations in developing countries are particularly vehement in protecting tax rights under the international tax regime.

Section II of this chapter looks at the deep-rooted relationship between the State's ability to provide social goods and services with the ability and prowess to collect tax revenue.

Section III looks at the imposition of the modern reality of globalization on such notions of insulating tax sovereignty. Global trade structures have often led to the shifting of profits and the erosion of tax bases, particularly in developing countries (which are more often source countries). However, the current global tax structure is spearheaded by the OECD which may (as argued in the chapter) as a result favour residence country interests (predominantly developed countries). The global tax structure also has a competing parallel system proposed by the United Nations (UN) which attempts to put forward developing country interests. Section III thus explores the reasons behind this dual tax leadership and its consequences on national tax interests.

1. 'Shadow Report And Recommendations Concerning The United Kingdom Of Great Britain And Northern Ireland' (Centre for Economic and Social Rights Global Justice Clinic, New York University School of Law Tax Justice Network 2016) 2 <https://chrgj.org/wp-content/uploads/2016/12/SUBMISSION-to-CESCR-UK-Responsibility-for-the-Impacts-of-Crossborder-Tax-Abuse-on-Economic-Social-and-Cultural-Rights.pdf> accessed on 12 March 2022.

Section IV analyzes the concept of permanent establishment (PE) as a limitation on source country taxation. The analysis serves to highlight the difference in approach between the UN and OECD systems. The differences highlighted are intensified under the digital economy as introduced by Section V. The section especially ponders the redundancy of the PE concept in its transition from the brick-and-mortar economy to the digital economy.

Sections VI and VII introduce the OECD and UN approaches and purported solutions to tax issues surrounding the digital economy, respectively. While the OECD favours a multilateral solution in the form of a two-Pillar approach, the UN favours a bilateral solution in the form of a negotiated treaty amendment provision. In that regard, Section VII looks at Article 12B as a suggested amending provision to the UN Model Tax Convention (MTC).

Sections VIII, IX, and X seek to provide a nuanced analysis of the advantages and disadvantages of both sets of proposals while asserting the greater developing country interests included within the UN approach. To that end, Section VIII explores the differences in the scope of taxation of the two systems, Section IX looks at the extent of accommodation of unilateral national measures by the two systems, and Section X explores the structural issues embedded in the two proposals. Section XI concludes.

II. Tax and Sovereignty

Taxes are required for raising revenue to provide public goods, infrastructure, and other public services to promote general welfare and economic progress[2]. The supply of such goods cannot take place through private market provision[3], nor can the exchange of such goods be left to an unregulated market[4]. This is because such goods and services are often the means of establishing economic rights and providing welfare.

Concurrently, taxes may also be used to influence and alter social and economic order.[5] Fiscal policy can be a powerful tool to enhance the rate of growth and,

---

2. Parthasarathi Shome, *Taxation, History, Theory, Law and Administration* (Springer, Chams: Switzerland 2021) 4; See also: Kenneth L. Sokoloff & Eric M. Zolt, 'Inequality and Taxation: Evidence from the Americas on How Inequality May Influence Tax Institutions' (2006) 59 Tax L. Rev. 167, 167-68.
3. *Ibid* 4.
4. Kyle Logue and Ronen Avraham, 'Redistributing Optimally: Of Tax Rules, Legal Rules, and Insurance', 56 Tax L. Rev. (2003) 157, 170.
5. Diane Ring, 'What's At Stake In The Sovereignty Debate? International Tax And The Nation-State' (2008) 49 Virginia Journal of International Law, 11 <https://lawdigitalcommons.bc.edu/cgi/viewcontent.cgi?article=1221&context=lsfp> accessed 12 March 2022;
   James R. Schlesinger, 'Emerging Attitudes Towards Fiscal Policy' (1962) 77 Pol. Sci. Q. 1, 1-4 and 10-13.

perhaps more importantly, the direction in which an economy is growing, not least through its impact on the nature of economic demand, employment, and price stability.[6]

As a result, the determination and effective implementation of fiscal policy is central to the social contract between the government and the people. The provision of such social goods may be thus considered a key ingredient to the "common belief that government is responsible to a given people, accountable to that people, and obliged to serve the best interests of that people"[7].[8] As an extension, therefore, such supply (and the means to supply them i.e., taxes) are also contributory to the "sense of legitimacy" required by political systems for the exercise of authority and the submission to such authority[9]. Thus, the very notion of State sovereignty is entwined with the concept of tax sovereignty.

This increasing emphasis on a State's obligation towards its citizens, within the notion of sovereignty, is reflected in various international tax arguments in favour of sovereignty. Sovereignty is often used as a defence by States against various international tax proposals[10], owing to an inevitable nexus between the taxing powers of the State and its ability to fulfil its responsibilities to its citizens. Therefore, taxation, as a concept, is entrenched in the idea of State sovereignty since the development goals of each country vary as per their resource needs and tax administration.

However, the international tax network is a stark reminder of the reality of globalization. Tax problems cross borders and their solutions must necessarily do so as well. Thus, inevitably, the international tax structure has brought about a dilution of tax sovereignty – as it has for other aspects of international law and policy as well[11]. The very preservation of sovereignty may depend on notions of international comity and cooperation[12]. Historically, conceptions of State sovereignty acknowledge and accept disparity among States in terms of both resources and

6. Ring (n 5).
7. Michael Greven, Louis W. Pauly, W. Pauly Louis, *Democracy Beyond The State? The European Dilemma And The Emerging Global Order* (Rowman and Littlefield Publishers, Inc 2000). See also David Beetham and Christopher Lord, *Political Theory And The European Union: Legitimacy and the European Union* (1st edn, Routledge 1998) 16-17.
8. Greven *et al* (n 7): "*[T]he legitimacy of a liberal democratic system depends on three criteria: an agreed definition of the people or 'political nation' as defining the rightful bounds of the polity; the appointment of public officials according to accepted criteria of popular authorization, representativeness and accountability; and the maintenance by government of defensible standards of rights protection, or its routine removal in the event of 'failure.*"
9. Greven *et al* (n 7).
10. Greven *et al* (n 7).
11. Anél Ferreira-Snyman, 'Sovereignty And The Changing Nature Of Public International Law: Towards A World Law?' (2007) 40 The Comparative and International Law Journal of Southern Africa 395, 396 <https://www.jstor.org/stable/23252645> accessed 12 March 2022.
12. Ring (n 5).

power. Resultant outcomes from asymmetric power dynamics have always been a part of international diplomacy and negotiations.[13]

Participating in, or accepting, 'less than favourable treaties' is not incompatible with the idea of State sovereignty[14]. The inevitable dilution of some tax powers should not be seen as the undermining of a State's ultimate position of sovereignty. Rather, it is a result of the competent execution of functions derived from the State's sovereign status.[15]

III. International Tax Structure and Developing Country Interests

Inasmuch as socio-economic development is intrinsically linked to welfare schemes of the State,[16] that objective is therefore dependent on increased revenue[17]. This is attainable through the direct increase in a country's tax base or through indirect measures and incentives provided to make its environment conducive for investments[18]. Inadequacies and unfulfillment in such measures are likely to lead to strains in the public budget and non-achievement of desired public expenditure.

Hybrid multinational enterprise (MNE) structures that have tailored their tax practices to cause base erosion and profit shifting (BEPS), or harmful tax regimes providing disproportionate and unjustifiable tax benefits, lead to cross-border transactions which have the potential to undermine the objective of generating much needed revenue.[19] Moreover, financial secrecy laws and liberal corporate tax policies exacerbate the ability to mobilise the maximum available resources to

13. Ring (n 5).
14. Ring (n 5).
15. This recognition of sovereignty through mutual benefit rather than an adversarial dilution of sovereignty is in consonance with the Kantian idea of 'Cosmopolitan Law' or Delbrück's concept of 'World Law' (*Weltinnenrecht*); For further reading on Cosmopolitan Law see I. Kant, '*To Perpetual Peace: A Philosophical Project*', (1795) pg. 112 in Bird G, *A Companion to Kant*, (Blackwell, 2006); For further reading on 'World Law' see Jost Delbriick 'Prospects for a "world (inter law?": legal developments in a changing international system' 2002 Indiana Journal of Legal Studies.
16. For the purpose of this chapter, it is assumed that most capital exporting countries i.e. residence countries are 'developed countries' while most capital importing countries i.e. source countries are 'developing countries'.
17. Reuven S Avi-Yonah and Yoram Margolioth, 'Taxation in Developing Countries: Some Recent Support and Challenges to the Conventional View' (2007) 1 Va. Tax Rev. 4 <https://repository.law.umich.edu/cgi/viewcontent.cgi?article=2472&context=articles> accessed 12 March 2022.
18. Yoram Margolioth, 'Tax Competition, Foreign Direct Investments & Growth: Using the Tax System to Promote Developing Country Growth', (2003) 23 Va Tax Rev. 161
19. The Tax Justice Network, *Fiscal Policy And Human Rights In The Americas: Mobilizing Resources To Secure Rights* (Thematic Report, Tax Justice Network 2015) <https://www.taxjustice.net/wp-content/uploads/2015/10/cidh_ddhh_fiscalidad_exec_summary_eng.pdf> accessed 12 March 2022

facilitate development goals.[20] Developing countries tend to depend more on corporate taxation than on individual income taxation for revenue, which creates a greater challenge for developing countries than for advanced economies.[21]

The current international tax structure, spearheaded by the OECD, may arguably be skewed in favour of developed countries (being primarily designed by the OECD and under the aegis and influence of its member countries), to the extent that it may be counterproductive to the interests of the Global South[22]. While developing countries recognize the need to reform their tax structures in accordance with OECD proposals such as under BEPS, implementation of such proposals may add to their already burdened tax administrations, which lack the capabilities to include and implement such complex reform initiatives.[23]

The UN tax model has traditionally given greater emphasis to the taxing rights of the source country as compared to the OECD model.[24] The United Nations Committee of Experts in International Cooperation in Tax Matters (UN Tax Committee) enjoys greater participation (if not greater legitimacy), as it represents all UN member States. Therefore, the Committee of Experts has the opportunity to "[ensure] the active participation of developing countries, especially the least developed ones, in relevant activities".[25] Indeed, there has been a growing need to bring about reforms in the global tax system to ensure it is inclusive and equitable as the inequity about international taxation appears to rise globally. An answer may lie

20. Alliance Sud *et al*, 'Swiss Responsibility For The Extraterritorial Impacts Of Tax Abuse On Women's Rights' (Report, Alliance Sud, Center for Economic and Social Rights, Global Justice Clinic: New York University School of Law Public Eye and Tax Justice Network, 2016) <https://www.cesr.org/sites/default/files/switzerland_cedaw_submission_2nov2016.pdf> accessed 12 March 2022.
21. UN: Economic and Social Council, 'Corporate Tax Reform Must Focus On Developing Countries: Needs, Combating Inequality, Speakers Tell Special Meeting Of Economic And Social Council' *United Nations Economic and Social Council* (2019). <https://www.un.org/press/en/2019/ecosoc6978.doc.htm> accessed on 12 March 2022.; see also Avi Yonah and Margolioth (n 17) 2.
22. Sakshi Rai, 'Tax Reforms And Global Redistribution: Situating The Global South' (2021) 33 LVI Economic and Political Weekly 16 <https://www.cesr.org/sites/default/files/2021/Tax_Reforms_and_Global_Redistribution.pdf> accessed 12 March 2022.
23. Peter Mullins, 'International Taxation and Developing Countries.' (Centre for Global Development, Policy Paper 166, Washington, DC: Centre for Global Development, 2020) 15 <https://www.cgdev.org/sites/default/files/Gupta-Mullins-International-Taxation.pdf> accessed 12 March 2022.
24. Nana Ama Sarfo, 'The Quiet Strengthening Of The U.N. Tax Model', *Forbes* (2021a) <https://www.forbes.com/sites/taxnotes/2021/05/17/the-quiet-strengthening-of-the-un-tax-model/?sh=3bfb9db3707c> accessed 12 March 2022.
25. UN: Department of Economic and Social Affairs, 'Strengthening UN Role In International Tax Cooperation', *United Nations Department of Economic and Social Affairs* (*UN Webpage*) <https://www.un.org/esa/ffd/tax-committee/tc-ta-tax-cooperation.html> accessed 12 March 2022.

in relocating more tax policymaking to the UN. Developing countries may see such a move as a shift towards a more neutral policymaking home[26].

To fully comprehend and assess the existing asymmetry in the international tax structure, it is imperative to understand the historical anomalies that continue to influence its framework and functioning to this day.

After the First World War, the League of Nations was asked to address the growing problem of 'double taxation', resulting in the differentiation and specific assignment of tax rights between residence and source countries[27]. By 1929, the League had a permanent Fiscal Committee which led to a League of Nations Model Tax Convention (MTC) with further drafts being drafted in 1943 (the Mexico draft) and 1946 (the London Draft)[28]. Considering that the entire premise of the tax structure is dependent on source countries relinquishing their tax rights – afforded to them by the 'first bite to the apple rule' (discussed below) – the two versions of the MTC mirrored the demography represented in each convention. Thus, in the Mexico convention in 1943, with most of the developed world involved in the Second World War, the Mexico draft favoured fewer compromises by source countries. Contrastingly, the post-war London draft with greater representation of developed nations resulted in a larger yielding of source country rights[29].

The League of Nations MTC was based on the work of four economists representing developed nations. With the dissolution of the League of Nations in 1946, the UN Fiscal Committee invited the UNECOSOC to review the work done thus far, in its capacity as a more varied forum, representing the different economic interests of the UN members[30]. The UN MTC, with greater emphasis on source country rights, is closer in principle to the Mexico draft of the League MTC, while the later OECD MTC with a greater transfer of rights to residence countries, has greater proximity to the London MTC[31].

---

26. Philip Baker, 'The Need for a New International Tax Architecture', in Parthasarathi Shome (ed.), *Reimagining International Taxation: Navigating through the Crises of the Pandemic, Lack of Consensus and Retrospective Taxation* (Oakbridge,2021).
27. Sebastien Leduc and Geerten Michielse, 'Chapter 8: Are Tax Treaties Worth It For Developing Economies?', in Ruud A. de Mooij, Alexander D Klemm and Victoria J Perry (eds.) *Corporate Income Taxes under Pressure* (International Monetary Fund 2021) 124.
28. League of Nations Doc. C.88M.88 1946.IIA, London and Mexico Model Tax Conventions, Commentary and Text.
29. Michael Lennard, 'The Purpose and Current Status of the United Nations Tax Work' (2008) Asia-Pacific Tax Bulletin <https://www.taxjustice.net/cms/upload/pdf/Lennard_0802_Status_of_UN_Tax_Work.pdf> accessed 22 August 2021.
30. Anna Binder and Viktoria Wöhrer, *Special Features of the UN Model Convention* (Linde Verlag 2019).
31. Michael Lennard, 'The Purpose and Current Status of the United Nations Tax Work' (2008) Asia-Pacific Tax Bulletin.

The OECD acquired its de facto leadership role in international taxation with the collapse of the UN tax efforts in the 1950s. Since then, the OECD (initially through its predecessor, the OEEC) has had an unrivalled role in formulating and updating its MTC, on which most modern Double Taxation Avoidance Agreements (DTAAs) are based. The OECD MTC has been updated regularly since 1977, progressively yielding more rights to residence countries, and consequently proving more detrimental to developing country interests[32]. Essentially, 36 developed countries took over the reins of the international tax structure.[33]

The OECD Draft Double Taxation Convention was created in 1963 giving primary importance to the interests of the OECD members, by allocating significant taxing rights to residence countries[34]. As a result, several developing nations desired an MTC which would be more sympathetic toward developing country interests, due to which the UN restarted its work on international taxation.

The UN Economic and Social Council (ECOSOC) adopted a resolution[35] requesting the Secretary-General to set up an *ad hoc* working group consisting of experts and tax administrators nominated by governments "*with the task of exploring, in consultation with interested international agencies, ways and means for facilitating the conclusion of tax treaties between developed and developing countries, including the formulation, as appropriate, of possible guidelines and techniques for use in such tax treaties which would be acceptable to both groups of countries and would fully safeguard their respective revenue interests*"[36]. Through this resolution, the UN recognizes its responsibility, as a better represented forum than the OECD, to balance the need for encouraging investments with the need for revenue collection, through taxation rights, in developing economies.

While the UN designed a new model convention that granted greater taxing rights to source countries—comprising mainly capital importing developing countries—it was nevertheless based on the 1977 OECD Model.[37]. However, the OECD continued to possess and exercise the leading role in the international tax system.

---

32. OECD Model Convention for the Avoidance of Double Taxation with Respect to Taxes on Income and Capital (1977).
33. Sarfo (n 24).
34. Luduc and Michielse (n 27).
35. UNECOSOC Resolution 1273 (XLIII).
36. UNECOSOC, 'United Nations Model Double Taxation Convention between Developed and Developing Countries 2017 Update' (UN 2017) See Introduction Section to the document.
37. Marina Castro Bosque, Hugo López López and Esther Marcos Rodríguez, 'Commentaries On Article 26 Of The OECD Model Tax Convention: Exchange Of Information' (Working Paper 2020-01, 2020) 26 <https://e-archivo.uc3m.es/bitstream/handle/10016/29846/Wp-oiti-2020-01.pdf?sequence=3&isAllowed=y> accessed 12 March 2022.

Thus, the dichotomy existent today with a dual set of MTCs – the UN and the OECD – is a direct result of this historical account. If one analyzes the ethos of either MTCs and the underlying principles that govern them, one might notice (as mentioned above) that the London Model finds its way through the OECD MTC, granting more taxing rights to residence countries, while the Mexico Model shows similarities in its content to the UN Model.[38] This difference in outlook is visible at the very outset of the UN MTC. The UN MTC preamble declares that "there is a need for international and regional organisations to provide guidelines to facilitate conclusion of tax treaties with a view to promote trade liberalisation and expansion as well as socio-economic growth"[39].

A notable difference between the two MTCs is that, while the OECD Model primarily seeks to eradicate double taxation, the UN Model, while seeking to do this, also recognizes the need for tax revenues to developing countries in furthering their socio-economic goals[40]. This is recognized in the UN MTC by either lowering the tax threshold or not defining withholding taxes for passive income and other means[41]. Thus, the UN system allows the source country to keep a greater residual amount once the equivalent of the residence country tax is returned[42]. As a result, it may be said that developing countries, in general, continue to prefer the UN model.[43]

IV. Limitation on Source-Country Taxation through PE

The OECD[44] and the UN[45] agree that corporate taxes are a "key source of revenue" for developing countries. Developing countries, which are often source countries, seek to meet their social goals and fiscal needs using tax revenue[46] or MNE

38. Sarfo (n 24).
39. United Nations Model Double Taxation Convention between Developed and Developing Countries: Preamble (UN MTC), (UN 2017).
40. UN MTC Preamble.
41. See for example Articles 11, 12, 12A and the below discussed Article 12B (Section VII below) where no income threshold is provided for these measures to be applicable.
42. UN MTC Article 5.
43. Wim Wijnen and Marco Magenta, 'The UN Model in Practice', (1997) 51(12) Bull. Intl. Fiscal Docn. 574.
44. OECD 'Corporate Tax Remains A Key Revenue Source, Despite Falling Rates Worldwide' (*OECD*, 2019) <https://www.oecd.org/tax/corporate-tax-remains-a-key-revenue-source-despite-falling-rates-worldwide.htm> accessed 12 March 2022.
45. UN Economic and Social Council (n 21).
46. OECD 'Countries Must Strengthen Tax Systems To Meet Sustainable Development Goals' (*OECD*, 2018) <https://www.oecd.org/ctp/countries-must-strengthen-tax-systems-to-meet-sustainable-development-goals.htm> accessed 12 March 2022; See also Jan Walliser, 'Making Taxes Work For The SDGs' (World Bank Blogs, 2018). <https://blogs.worldbank.org/governance/making-taxes-work-sdgs> accessed 12 March 2022; See also Chris Morgan, 'The Impact Of Tax On Delivering The Sustainable Development Goals' (*KPMG*, 2017) <https://responsibletax.kpmg.com/article/the-impact-of-tax-on-delivering-the-sustainable-development-goals> accessed 12 March 2022.

investments[47]. Such corporate tax at the source is usually levied on the taxable presence of MNEs based on a defined threshold of 'permanent establishment' (PE)[48].

The PE threshold essentially acts as a limitation on source countries to tax MNE income at source. As Article 7 (Business Profits) of the OECD MTC states, "the profits of the enterprise may be taxed in the other State *but only so much* of them as is attributable to that permanent establishment. [*emphasis added*]"[49]. Under the OECD Model, the qualification for a PE is set high, in order to reduce source-based taxation of capital-exporting enterprises. Thus, under the model, the interests of developed countries are well represented.

This contrasts distinctly with the UN approach to the concept of PE, which tends to favour source country rights. The various instances of PE employed by the UN MTC make it easier for source countries to establish a sufficient economic linkage to trigger a PE designation[50]. Examples within the UN MTC include more stringent duration tests for building and construction PEs[51], defining PE for service activities not covered by the OECD Model[52], and establishing PE for collecting premiums or insuring risks[53]. The UN MTC also extends source country rights to tax business income by including the force-of-attraction rule[54] in its PE provisions[55].

As mentioned above, PE, under the OECD model, limits the rights of source countries to tax MNE income at the source. The development of this constraint is connected to the historical evolution of the international tax structure which was discussed in Section III.

---

47. OECD 'The Contribution Of International Business Investment To The Sustainable Development Goals: Key Actors And Recent Trends' (*OECD*, 2019) <https://www.oecd.org/investment/investment-policy/The-contribution-of-international-business-investment-to-the-sustainable-development-goals.pdf> accessed 12 March 2022.
48. UN MTC Article 5 and Article 7.
49. OECD MTC Article 7.
50. UN MTC Article 5(2) and (3).
51. Michael Lennard, 'The UN Model Tax Convention As Compared With The OECD Model Tax Convention – Current Points Of Difference And Recent Developments' (2009) Asia Pacific Tax Bulletin, IBDF 4 <https://www.taxjustice.net/cms/upload/pdf/Lennard_0902_UN_Vs_OECD.pdf> accessed 12 March 2022.
52. UN MTC Article 12A; See also Lennard (n 51) 5.
53. UN MTC Article 5(6).
54. "Force of Attraction Rule: Concept under which a permanent establishment is taxed by the country in which it is located not only on the income and property, but also on all income derived by its foreign head office from source in, and all property owned by the foreign head office situated in, the country where the permanent establishment is located. *The OECD model treaty does not allow application of it.* [*emphasis added*]" The OECD Glossary of Tax Terms < https://www.oecd.org/ctp/glossaryoftaxterms.htm> accessed on 28 April 2022.
55. Lennard (n 51) 7.

The very first report on double taxation published under the League of Nations[56], recognized the "first bite to the apple rule" (hereinafter the first bite rule) – a representation of the natural order of taxation rights. This rule recognizes that the way income is placed, source countries would always get the opportunity to tax first[57] – hence the proverbial "first bite to the apple".

If residence countries were only concerned about eliminating double taxation, a unilateral effort would suffice. Due to the first bite rule, the onus lies solely on residence countries to prevent it. The international tax structure, often advertised as a means to eliminate double taxation, would therefore be rendered redundant.

However, the international tax structure also serves to increase and protect the tax base of residence countries against the natural bias of the 'first bite rule'. It does so through the 'Benefits principle' and PE.

The Benefits principle was also recognized and instituted in the international tax structure through the abovementioned League of Nations report on Double taxation[58]. The principle serves to artificially shift taxing rights on passive income – naturally within the grasp of source countries through the 'first bite rule' – to residence countries[59]. Once international tax rights have been thus allocated, PE serves to preserve the tax rights of residence countries by limiting the taxing rights available to source countries. Thus, any form of tax adventurism by source countries to increase their tax base, is nipped in the bud by criteria that determine a PE.

While the international tax structure can be inculpated to the negotiated will of sovereign States, the problem runs deeper in the modern globalised economy. Hybrid MNE structures, mentioned in Section II, are found to circumvent PE criteria, thereby shifting much-needed revenue from source countries (the BEPS problem). This issue is further exacerbated by the advent of the digital economy. The following Section V highlights these issues.

V. PE and the Digital Economy

The digital economy has created two key complexities for the international tax regime. These are (1) the elimination of physical presence to do business and, (2) the monetization of consumer data without remuneration to the source. Enterprises

56. League of Nations, 'Report on Double Taxation submitted to the Financial Committee' (Document E.F.S.73. F.19; 5 April 1923).
57. Reuven S. Avi-Yonah, 'The New International Tax Framework: Evolution Or Revolution?' (2021) 25(11) American Society of International Law. <https://www.asil.org/insights/volume/25/issue/11> accessed 12 March 2022.
58. League of Nations Report (n 56).
59. Avi-Yonah 2021 (n 57).

within the digital economy tend to rely heavily on intangibles, which allows them to move revenues across borders and thereby minimising their tax liability[60].

Furthermore, the dependence on digital assets and technology has provided enterprises with another source of income – user data. Enterprises monetise user data mined in the source country, without paying any tax in these countries, owing to the lack of 'tangible presence'.[61] For example, the Fair Tax Foundation reported the 'silicon six'[62] to have accrued combined profits up to USD 1.36 trillion between 2011 and 2020, and yet had a tax liability of a mere 3.6% on revenue and 16.1% on booked profit.[63] In the process, such MNEs have displaced valuable revenue from source countries.

It may be argued that the concept of a PE serves to limit source countries from unfettered taxation of business income through attributes such as "fixed place of business" or "physical presence". However, under the digital economy, where corporations structure business models lacking attributes required for a PE, income which cannot be attributed to a PE can be shifted outside the jurisdiction of the source country. Thus, the very attributes developed to create a PE can now serve to shift legitimate tax away from source countries.[64]

The problem is furthered where e-commerce is defined to include 'delivery that does not have to be conducted online' (such as the OECD definition) [65]. As a result, the delivery of tangible goods, which would otherwise require a physical presence, may now not meet the physical presence criteria along with the delivery of intangible goods.

Newer business models, catering to the digital economy, eventually deprive source countries, mostly developing countries, of their much-needed tax revenue.[66]

60. Avi-Yonah and Margolioth (n 17).
61. Shikha Mehra and Rohit Roy, 'What Comprises the Digital Economy? Global Challenges Going Forward' in Parthasarathi Shome (ed), *International Taxation In The Digital Era* (Oakbridge Publishing 2020).
62. Facebook, Apple, Amazon, Netflix, Google and Microsoft.
63. Freny Patel, 'No Place To Hide' (2021) Indian Business Law Journal <https://law.asia/no-place-hide/> accessed 12 March 2022.
64. Eli Hadzhieva, 'Impact Of Digitalisation On International Tax Matters: Challenges And Remedies' (Report, Policy Department for Economic, Scientific and Quality of Life Policies, European Parliament 2019) <https://www.europarl.europa.eu/cmsdata/161104/ST%20Impact%20of%20Digitalisation %20publication.pdf> accessed 12 March 2022; See also OECD, 'Action 1 Tax Challenges Arising From Digitalisation' (*OECD,* 2021) <https://www.oecd.org/tax/beps/beps-actions/action1/> accessed 12 March 2022.
65. The OECD Glossary Of Statistical Terms: Electronic Commerce <https://stats.oecd.org/glossary/detail.asp?ID=4721> accessed 12 March 2022.
66. Avi-Yonah and Margolioth (n 17).

According to the OECD, tax jurisdictions may lose anywhere between USD 100 to 240 million annually, due to corporate tax avoidance by MNEs.[67]

As a result of this increasingly recognized and burgeoning problem, both the OECD and the UN have taken seminal steps to bring the existing international tax structure in line with the digital economy and the hybrid tax structures adopted by companies. Attempts by both tax systems aim at a reduced dependency on PE. Simultaneously, States have taken unilateral measures to counter tax issues within the digital economy. The following sections (Sections VI – IX) deliberate how the OECD and UN systems, and unilateral sovereign State measures look to tackle some of these issues occasioned by the digital economy. The remaining sections of the chapter discuss the advantages and disadvantages of each system, and how they interact with each other.

VI. The OECD Response to the Digital Economy

The OECD, through its Inclusive Framework on BEPS, has sought to depart from a dependency on PE, by suggesting a "Two-Pillar solution" [68] i.e., Pillar One and Pillar Two.[69] Pillar One primarily intends to tax MNEs with a global revenue of more than 20 billion euros and a profitability rate greater than 10%, at the rate of 20-30% of the profit[70].

For this, a new special-purpose nexus rule is intended, allowing income to be allocated to a source country if the MNE in question gets at least EUR 1 million in revenue from that source country.[71] The nexus will be set at EUR 250,000 for smaller jurisdictions with GDPs less than 40 billion euros, with 25% of residual

67. OECD, 'International Collaboration to End Tax Avoidance: Understanding Tax Avoidance, (*OECD*) <https://www.oecd.org/tax/beps/> accessed 12 March 2022.

68. The latest version of which was released in October 2021.

69. OECD 'Statement On A Two-Pillar Solution To Address The Tax Challenges Arising From The Digitalisation Of The Economy' (*OECD/G20 Statement*, 2021). <https://www.oecd.org/tax/beps/statement-on-a-two-pillar-solution-to-address-the-tax-challenges-arising-from-the-digitalisation-of-the-economy-october-2021.pdf> accessed 12 March 2022.

70. Radhakishan Rawal and Madhu Agarwal, 'Pillar One And Pillar Two' (*Deloitte*, 2021) <https://www2.deloitte.com/content/dam/Deloitte/in/Documents/tax/in-tax-pillar-one-and-pillar-two-noexp.pdf> accessed 12 March 2022.; See also OECD, 'International Community Strikes A Ground-Breaking Tax Deal For The Digital Age' (*OECD*, 2021). <https://www.oecd.org/tax/international-community-strikes-a-ground-breaking-tax-deal-for-the-digital-age.htm> accessed 12 March 2022; See also OECD Statement 2021 (n 69).

71. European Commission, 'Global Agreement On Corporate Taxation: Frequently Asked Questions', (*European Commission*, 2021) <https://ec.europa.eu/commission/presscorner/detail/cs/qanda_21_3564> accessed 12 March 2022.

revenues transferred to source countries[72]. By using nexus, the OECD has effectively circumvented the PE rules for the targeted income level.

While this is certainly a step towards reversing a dated system of tax allocation, developing countries argue that the use of residual profits may be inadequate. Forums such as the G24 and the African Tax Administration Forum (ATAF) have regularly called for the reallocation of an MNE's total profits, rather than the residual profit alone. Firstly, such an approach would be simpler and have a reduced administrative burden. Secondly, the proposed range of 20-30% of the residual profits is seen as inadequate, with groups like the ATAF hinting at only ranges above 35% being meaningful.[73]

Importantly, a reversal of allocation of total profits is a call for the reversal of the Benefits principle. It is perhaps indicative of the burden the allocation of tax rights imposes on developing countries. The OECD Inclusive Framework has however failed to heed such suggestions thus far.[74]

Pillar One also contains a promise to create simpler, streamlined ways to apply transfer pricing regulations to specific arrangements, with a particular emphasis on the needs of low-capacity nations – frequently the subject of tax disputes[75]. This is done by creating a mandatory and binding dispute prevention and resolution mechanism to prevent double taxation for Amount A.[76]

Lastly, Pillar One mandates that all unilateral measures adopted or intended to be imposed by governments, be repealed.[77] This last characteristic of the Pillar One proposal highlights differences in the OECD and UN approaches. The interaction of the UN and OECD systems with unilateral measures has been discussed further in Section IX below.

Pillar Two tackles outstanding BEPS issues and is intended to guarantee that major multinational operating firms with more than EUR 750 million are subject to at least 15% taxation, independent of their place of headquarters or the jurisdictions

72. Rawal and Agarwal (n 70).
73. South Centre, 'Statement By The South Centre On The Two Pillar Solution To Address The Tax Challenges Arising From The Digitalisation Of The Economy' (*South Centre*, 2021) <https://www.southcentre.int/wp-content/uploads/2021/07/SC-Statement-on-IF-Two-Pillar-Solution-FINAL.pdf> accessed 12 March 2022.
74. *Ibid.*
75. Alison Lobb and Howard Osawa, 'How Will The G20/OECD'S Pillar One And Pillar Two Project Affect Disputes?' (*International Tax Review*, 2021) <https://www.internationaltaxreview.com/article/b1srp7qzw9dhrd/how-will-the-g20oecds-pillar-one-and-pillar-two-project-affect-disputes> accessed 12 March 2022.
76. OECD Statement 2021 (n 69).
77. See Section IX below.

in which they operate[78]. If such MNEs pay an effective tax rate of less than 15% in a jurisdiction, Pillar Two steps in to collect the difference as "top-up tax" from that MNE in the residence country[79].

Pillar One and Two adjustments are transnational in scope and, although simpler than the previous suggestion continue to remain technically challenging, particularly for developing countries[80]. Detailed source rules for certain types of transactions are yet to be defined, and the approach will have to consider the facts and conditions of a single MNE[81].

The ongoing work, as well as the need to further define and clarify the specifics of the Pillar One and Pillar Two regimes, adds another degree of complexity to enterprises' attempts to prepare for their implementation.[82] It is currently expected that the rules will be finalized in 2022 and will be effective beginning from 2023.[83] Furthermore, a date of mid-2022 is set for the signature of the proposed international agreement on the Amount A system, with the new regulations going into force globally in 2023[84].

As with previous aspects of the OECD BEPS initiative, the implementation phase will require considerable modifications to treaties and domestic legislation, as well as related processes and instructions to tax authorities and taxpayers. Therefore, the

78. OECD Statement 2021 (n 69); See also Leigh Thomas, '130 Countries Back Global Minimum Corporate Tax Of 15%' (*Reuters*, 2021) <https://www.reuters.com/business/countries-backs-global-minimum-corporate-tax-least-15-2021-07-01/> accessed 12 March 2022.
79. Naveen Aggarwal, 'Implications Of The Pillar 2 Global Anti-Base Erosion (GLoBE) Rules On Businesses' (*KPMG,* 2022) <https://home.kpmg/in/en/blogs/home/posts/2022/03/global-minimum-tax-mantra-pillar-2.html> accessed on 12 March 2022. See also OECD, 'OECD Releases Pillar Two Model Rules For Domestic Implementation Of 15% Global Minimum Tax' (*OECD*, 2021) <https://www.oecd.org/tax/beps/oecd-releases-pillar-two-model-rules-for-domestic-implementation-of-15-percent-global-minimum-tax.htm> accessed 12 March 2022; See also European Commission 2021 (n 71).
80. Jeroen Lammers, 'Can Developing Countries Do Better Than The Unified Approach?' (ICTD, 2020) <https://www.ictd.ac/blog/developing-countries-unified-approach-digital-economy-tax/> accessed 12 March 2022.
81. OECD Statement 2021 (n 69); See also Vikas Vasal, David Sites, Matt Stringer, Peter Vale and Pierre Bourgeois, 'OECD/G20 Issues Statement On International Tax Changes' (*Grant Thornton*, 2021) <https://www.grantthornton.global/en/insights/articles/OECD-G20-issues-statement-on-international-tax-changes/> accessed 12 March 2022.
82. *Lobb and Osawa* (n 75)
83. KPMG 'BEPS 2.0: Pillar One And Pillar Two' (*KPMG*, 2021) <https://home.kpmg/xx/en/home/insights/2020/10/beps-2-0-pillar-one-and-pillar-two.html> accessed 12 March 2022.
84. OECD Statement 2021 (n 69).

implementation process might still take years to complete, and it will most likely extend in scope slowly over time[85].

VII. The UN Approach – Article 12B

An alternative approach to the OECD two-Pillar solution is the introduction of Article 12B within the UN MTC.[86] While Article 12B is limited to automated digital services (ADS), it is suggestive of the UN's inclinations regarding the solution to the tax issues plaguing the digital economy. Unlike the OECD multilateral approach, Article 12B will be applicable as a bilateral proposal between two States upon negotiation, re-negotiation, or amendment of tax treaties between both parties[87].

Article 12B offers the source State new taxation rights on incomes earned from automated digital services[88]. The income from automated digital services is defined as income from a service provider with 'little to no human participation', such as online advertising services, digital content services, social networking services, and standardised online instructional services.[89] This does not, however, include revenue from 'fees for technical services' (payments for administrative, technical, or consulting services for which Article 12A would apply in theory) or customised digital services[90].

Article 12B(1) allocates taxing rights to the residence state and *prima facie* looks similar to the OECD thought process[91]. The key difference lies in the fact that Article 12B does not provide exclusivity of taxing rights to the residence country[92]. Through Article 12B(2) the UN reverses the allocation of tax by allowing source countries to tax the ADS income on gross profits, in accordance with source country domestic laws, based on a bilaterally negotiated tax rate[93].

---

85. OECD Statement 2021 (n 69).
86. Committee of Experts on International Cooperation in Tax Matters, 'Report On The Twenty-Second Session (Virtual Session, 19–28 April 2021)' (Report, United Nations 2021) <https://www.un.org/development/desa/financing/sites/www.un.org.development.desa.financing/files/2021-06/2107033E.pdf> accessed 12 March 2022; See also UN MTC Article 12B Commentary Tax Treatment of Payments for Digital Services' (UN, 2021). <https://www.un.org/development/desa/financing/sites/www.un.org.development.desa.financing/files/2020-08/TAX%20TREATY%20PROVISION%20ON%20PAYMENTS%20FOR%20DIGITAL%20SERVICES.pdf> accessed 12 March 2022.
87. Kazim Rizvi and Ayush Tripathi, 'The UN Digital Tax Solution And The Problems With This Proposal' (*The Print*, 2021) <https://theprint.in/theprint-valuead-initiative/the-un-digital-tax-solution-and-the-problems-with-this-proposal/670961/> accessed 12 March 2022.
88. Committee of Experts on International Cooperation in Tax Matters Report (n 86).
89. Committee of Experts on International Cooperation in Tax Matters Report (n 86).
90. Committee of Experts on International Cooperation in Tax Matters Report (n 86).
91. UN MTC Article 12B (1): Income from automated digital services arising in a Contracting State, underlying payments for which are made to a resident of the other Contracting State, may be taxed in that other State.
92. UN MTC Article 12B(2).
93. Committee of Experts on International Cooperation in Tax Matters Report (n 86).

The UN also allows source countries to apply a withholding tax on the gross payments at a rate mutually negotiated and agreed by both States[94]. The UN commentary on Article 12B suggests that the contracting States negotiate a modest tax rate of 3 or 4%[95]. In both cases, potential double taxation due to source-based withholding tax should be relieved by the residence State[96]. Here again, the onus is reversed to accommodate the 'first bite rule'.

Furthermore, for an assessed income from ADS, the option of being taxed on qualified profits on a net basis rather than withholding tax on gross payments also exists[97].

The most pertinent characteristic of Article 12B is the lack of requirement of a PE, fixed base, or a minimum period of presence, for the source country to be able to tax the MNE[98]. In case a beneficial owner of such businesses does carry on its business through a fixed base or a PE, Article 7 of the UN Model Convention will automatically apply instead[99].

VIII. Scope of Taxation under the UN and OECD Approach

As previously mentioned, the rights of source countries are more prominently emphasized under the UN MTC.[100] Not only does the UN approach increase the scope of taxation to include the opportunity to tax large companies within the digital economy[101], but also provides a simple and efficient method of taxation for countries with a limited or inferior tax infrastructure[102]. As the UN Committee of Experts on International Cooperation in Tax Matters (the UN Committee)

---

94. Committee of Experts on International Cooperation in Tax Matters Report (n 86).
95. Committee of Experts on International Cooperation in Tax Matters Report (n 86).
96. Committee of Experts on International Cooperation in Tax Matters Report (n 86).
97. Committee of Experts on International Cooperation in Tax Matters Report (n 86).
98. Committee of Experts on International Cooperation in Tax Matters Report (n 86).
99. Kimberly van Sande, 'An Active UN Adopts New UN Model Treaty Provision Regarding Income From Automated Digital Services' (*Tiberghien Law Blog*, 2021) <https://www.tiberghien.com/en/about-tiberghien> accessed 12 March 2022.
100. Nana Ama Sarfo, 'The U.N. Tax Committee And Developing Countries' (*Forbes*, 2021b). <https://www.forbes.com/sites/taxnotes/2021/04/13/the-un-tax-committee-and-developing-countries/?sh=721edad57fe8> accessed 12 March 2022.
101. Hamza Ali, 'Developing Countries Get UN Model For Taxing Tech Companies' (*Bloomberg Tax*, 2021) <https://news.bloombergtax.com/daily-tax-report-international/developing-countries-get-un-model-for-taxing-tech-companies> accessed 12 March 2022.
102. IBDF, 'International - Developing Countries And The Proposed Article 12B Of The UN Model: Some Known Unknowns (*IBDF*, 2021) <https://www.ibfd.org/shop/international-developing-countries-and-proposed-article-12b-un-model-some-known-unknowns> accessed 12 March 2022.

outlines, "Many developing countries have limited administrative capacity and need a simple, reliable, and efficient method to enforce tax imposed on income from services derived by non-residents."[103]

The OECD on the other hand, not only continues to confer greater taxing rights to the residence State but also places reliance on the nexus rule under Pillar one, in order for an MNE to be taxed[104]. While the nexus rule is more accommodating of source country interests than the use of PE, the risk of MNEs circumventing source country taxation continues to be a threat as newer business models develop.

However, the UN MTC Article 12B is limited to only 'automated digital services', specifying a list of what is inclusive and exclusive[105]. ADS under the UN system are defined thus:

> "The term 'income from automated digital services' as used in this Article means any payment in consideration for any service provided on the internet or an electronic network requiring minimal human involvement from the service provider. The term 'income from automated digital services' does not, however, include payments qualifying as 'royalties' or 'fees for technical services' under Article 12 or Article 12A as the case may be."[106]

Moreover, the commentaries to Article 12B do limit the list of services and activities, that are considered ADS, to *"Online advertising services, Sale or other alienation of user data, Online search engines, Online intermediation platform services,*

---

103. UN Committee of Experts on International Cooperation in Tax Matters, 'Twentieth session: Update on work on taxation issues related to the digitalization of the economy' (UN, E/C.18/2020/CRP41, October 2020) available at https://www.un.org/development/desa/financing/sites/www.un.org.development.desa.financing/files/2020-10/CITCM%2021%20CRP.41_Digitalization%2010102020%20Final%20A.pdf; See also Henrik Kleven, Claus Thustrup Kreiner and Emmanuel Saez, 'Understanding Fiscal Capacity In Developing Economies: Firms As Third-Party Tax Enforcers' (Project Report, International Growth Centre, 2012). <https://www.theigc.org/project/understanding-fiscal-capacity-in-developing-economies-firms-as-third-party-tax-enforcers/> accessed 12 March 2022.
104. KPMG, 'Pillar One: Profit Allocation And Nexus' (*KPMG*, 2021) <https://assets.kpmg/content/dam/kpmg/xx/pdf/2021/11/beps-pillar-one-web.pdf> accessed 12 March 2022.
105. Committee of Experts on International Cooperation in Tax Matters Report (n 86); See also PwC, 'UN Tax Committee Adopts Article 12B For Model Treaty Rules On Digital Services' (*PwC*, 2021) <https://www.pwc.com/gx/en/tax/newsletters/tax-policy-bulletin/assets/pwc-un-tax-committee-adopts-article-12b.pdf> accessed 12 March 2022.
106. Committee of Experts on International Cooperation in Tax Matters Report (n 86).

Social media platforms, Digital content services, Online gaming, Cloud computing services; Standardized online teaching services."[107]

Just like the OECD's dependency on 'nexus', the UN limiting income categories also has the potential for many business models to escape taxation under the provision. Consumer-facing Businesses (CFBs) is an example of income escaping taxation under the UN MTC Article 12B. On the other hand, CFBs are included by Pillar One under the OECD system[108].

The UN Committee, however, seems disinclined to explain why the scope of Article 12B is limited. When asked why the CFBs are not part of the gamut of incomes included the committee responded with unusual dismissiveness that it has no obligation to justify in the Article or its Commentary why CFBs are out of the scope of the UN proposal[109].

Apart from differences in the scope, the OECD and UN proposals also differ on income thresholds for attracting the respective measures. As discussed in Section VI, there is a minimum threshold under the OECD proposal for companies to be subject to its provisions[110]. Article 12B of the UN MTC, on the other hand, does not have any such prescribed minimum threshold[111].

The lack of specific thresholds in Article 12B allows countries to bring various companies under its ambit irrespective of their revenue and profitability, while the OECD targets only the big MNCs. This is in congruence with the UN tax agenda generally, as other provisions in the UN MTC (such as Articles 11, 12, and 12A) do not prescribe a threshold either[112].

The lack of a prescribed threshold also provides a certain amount of flexibility to developing nations in their choice of revenue collection. As already discussed above[113], developing countries may choose to fund public goods and services directly

---

107. Vikram Chand and Camille Villaseca, 'The UN Proposal On Automated Digital Services: Is It In The Interest Of Developing Countries?' (Kluwer International Tax Blog, 2021) < http://kluwertaxblog.com/2021/03/05/the-un-proposal-on-automated-digital-services-is-it-in-the-interest-of-developing-countries/> accessed 12 March 2022.

108. UN Tax Committee Update (n 103); See also KPMG, 'The OECD Pillar 1 And 2 Blueprints' (*KPMG*) <https://home.kpmg/uk/en/home/insights/2020/10/the-oecd-pillar-1-and-2-blueprints-on-a-page.html> accessed 12 March 2022.

109. UN Tax Committee Update (n 103).

110. UN Tax Committee Update (n 103).

111. Committee of Experts on International Cooperation in Tax Matters Report (n 86).

112. Committee of Experts on International Cooperation in Tax Matters, 'Tax Consequences Of The Digitized Economy- Issues Of Relevance For Developing Countries' (United Nations 2020) <https://www.un.org/development/desa/financing/sites/www.un.org.development.desa.financing/files/2020-10/CITCM%2021%20CRP.41_Digitalization%2010102020%20Final%20A.pdf> accessed 12 March 2022.

113. See Section III above.

through tax revenue or through indirect measures and incentives aimed at inviting greater investments. Therefore, some countries might seek to impose low withholding taxes to encourage investment and technology transfer.

With a significant number of transnational transactions being found within the digital economy[114], the UN MTC Article 12B approach seems in congruence with source country interests. By adopting low withholding taxes, jurisdictions can lower the cost of capital to stimulate investment and encourage the transfer of technologies. Conversely, countries wishing to increase tax revenue may impose higher rates. Hence, Article 12B permits developing countries, which are mostly capital importing countries, to exercise their tax sovereignty as per their development goals and needs.[115]

The simpler UN provision also has the added benefit of more efficient adoption and implementation – a feature welcomed by jurisdictions with lesser developed domestic tax structures and less sophisticated tax administrations. Conversely, developing countries have generally found it difficult to determine the implications of complex OECD tax proposals on their jurisdiction, let alone implement them. This is perhaps because OECD provisions (excepting those recently worked at by the Inclusive Framework) are usually drafted by and for developed countries.[116] Ironically, the OECD Ottawa Framework, 1998, recommends similar principles of efficiency, simplicity as well as flexibility for the digital economy.[117]

In that regard, a system placing importance on withholding of tax (such as Article 12B UN MTC), facilitates the easier implementation and ensures better procedural certainty for tax authorities and taxpayers[118]. As a simpler way to impose taxes on non-residents, withholding taxes also provide tax certainty, particularly in developing countries with inferior tax administrations.[119] Furthermore, withholding

---

114. OECD, 'Digital Trade – The Impact Of Digitalisation On Trade' (*OECD*) <https://www.oecd.org/trade/topics/digital-trade/> accessed on 12 March 2022.; See also World Trade Organisation, 'How Digital Technologies Are Transforming Global Commerce' (World Trade Organisation 2018) <https://www.wto.org/english/res_e/publications_e/wtr18_e.htm> accessed on 12 March 2022.
115. Luduc and Michielse (n 27).
116. Mullins (n 23).
117. OECD, 'Comments Received On Public Discussion Draft- BEPS Action 1: Address The Tax Challenges Of The Digital Economy' (*OECD*, 2014) 47 <https://www.oecd.org/ctp/comments-action-1-tax-challenges-digital-economy.pdf> accessed 12 March 2022; See also Business at OECD (BIAC), 'Business Principles For Addressing The Tax Challenges Of The Digitalizing Economy' (Position Paper, BIAC 2019) <https://biac.org/wp-content/uploads/2019/02/FINAL-2019-01-31-Business-at-OECD-Digital-Principles-Position-Paper2.pdf> accessed 12 March 2022.
118. William Byrnes, 'Recommendations For The Pillar One And Pillar Two Blueprints' (Kluwer International Tax Blog, 2020) <http://kluwertaxblog.com/2020/12/18/recommendations-for-the-pillar-one-and-pillar-two-blueprints/> accessed 12 March 2022.
119. *Ibid.*

tax systems also protect corporate tax bases in developing countries from aggressive transfer pricing, by reducing their incentive.[120]

Additionally, while the OECD proposal levies taxes on a net profit basis, the UN proposal implements gross profit-based taxation[121]. The use of gross profits by the UN (as opposed to the extremely complex proposal under Pillar one) is not only beneficial to small businesses, but it is also easier for developing countries with limited capabilities to implement. This is affirmed by the UN Committee which declares that "[s]uch a method of taxation may also simplify compliance for enterprises providing services in another State since they would not be required to compute their net profits or file tax returns unless they themselves opt for net income basis taxation."[122]

However, one of the concerns with gross-based taxation is that the cost to enterprises may be passed onto the end consumer, through a consequential increase in prices in the source country[123]. Such actions by corporations have been observed in various cases. For example, on the implementation of a digital service tax in France, Amazon stated that they would pass on the cost to the marketplace sellers.[124] Similarly, on the introduction of an equalization levy in India, Apple passed on the cost to its Indian consumers.[125]

However, not all companies chose to do so, adding credence to the argument that the passing of costs to the consumer is a matter of choice rather than a necessity for enterprises. Netflix India, as an example, decided not to pass on the cost post-implementation of equalization levy to its customers.[126] As the UN Committee had declared, "There is no reason to assume that the tax will be passed on to the consumer in all situations. In any case, such situation for ADS taxation is no

120. Luduc and Michielse (n 27).
121. UN Tax Committee Update (n 103).
122. UN Tax Committee Update (n 103).
123. Chand and Villaseca (n 107).
124. Mark Sweney, 'Amazon To Escape UK Digital Services Tax That Will Hit Smaller Traders' (*The Guardian*, 2020) <https://www.theguardian.com/technology/2020/oct/14/amazon-to-escape-uk-digital-services-tax-that-will-hit-smaller-traders> accessed 12 March 2022.
125. Sachin Dave, 'Apple Passes On 2 Per Cent Equalisation Levy To Indian Consumers' (*The Economic Times*, 2020) <https://economictimes.indiatimes.com/industry/cons-products/electronics/apple-passes-on-2-per-cent-equalisation-levy-to-indian-consumers/articleshow/78962608.cms?from=mdr> accessed 12 March 2022.
126. Sachin Dave and Gaurav Laghate, 'Netflix To Absorb Equalisation Levy: Not Passing The Charge On Consumers' (*The Economic Times*, 2020) <https://economictimes.indiatimes.com/industry/media/entertainment/netflix-to-absorb-equalisation-levy-not-passing-the-charge-on-consumers/articleshow/79011418.cms> accessed on 12 March 2022.

different from similar scheme of taxation for royalties and FTS".[127] Moreover, if gross profits are truly a disadvantage it is pertinent to note that Article 12B also provides an alternative option to implement the net basis taxation instead of gross basis taxation.[128]

IX. Unilateral Digital Taxes

While the OECD was developing proposals to tackle tax issues with the digital economy, several countries have implemented or proposed temporary bilateral measures. The most common of these measures is a digital services tax (DST) on selected gross revenue streams of large digital companies[129]. Several OECD countries in the European Union (EU) have either proposed or already implemented digital service taxes.[130] The EU has also sought to implement its own digital levy before January 2023.[131]

DSTs have also been adopted by several developing countries. Their popularity may be representative of the concerns developing countries have with a complex multilateral tax system spearheaded by the OECD. Such concerns are often combined with apprehension that the international system may provide source States with little or no opportunity to increase tax revenues.[132] In such circumstances, unilaterally developed DST better serves the developing country's interests, administrative capabilities, and economic needs.[133]

However, with the advent of Pillar One, the OECD expects unilateral national measures to be repealed by the end of 2023. According to the OECD, DSTs are a 'second best-approach' which become redundant with the implementation of Pillar One recommendations.[134]

Several OECD and EU countries have agreed to withdraw DSTs and not consider similar unilateral measures in the future in congruence with the Pillar One

127. Chand and Villaseca (n 107).

128. UN MTC Commentary para 26 page 16; See also UN Tax Committee Update (n 103).

129. Elke Asen and Daniel Bunn, 'What European OECD Countries Are Doing About Digital Services Taxes' (Tax Foundation Bog, 2021) <https://taxfoundation.org/digital-tax-europe-2020/> accessed 12 March 2022.

130. *Ibid.*

131. European Council, 'Special Meeting Of The European Council (17, 18, 19, 20 and 21 July 2020): Conclusions' (*European Council*, 2020) <http://210720-euco-final-conclusions-en.pdf (europa.eu)> accessed 12 March 2022.

132. UN, 'World Bank Group Staff Comments On Article 12B' (*United Nations*, 2020) <https://www.un.org/development/desa/financing/sites/www.un.org.development.desa.financing/files/2021-02/2020_1_19_WB%20staff%20comments%20on%20UN%20Article%2012B_FINAL.pdf> accessed 12 March 2022.

133. *Ibid.*

134. OECD/G20 Statement (n 69).

proposal.[135] However, for several countries with inferior tax infrastructure, where DSTs are already in place, retracting such measures may not be administratively feasible or beneficial. The UN Committee pointed out in 2020 that "elements of the significant economic presence proposal" had not been reflected in the OECD approach, inhibiting developing countries from being able to introduce national measures in case a business fell out of the scope.[136]

Moreover, past experiences (such as the BEPS MLI) hint at the possibility that all countries may not sign and ratify the OECD Pillar One recommendations. This will have ramifications on the Pillar One effort and the ability of countries to collect revenue using the process. Thus, the OECD may find it equitable to not suggest the removal of DSTs till such time Pillar One is effectively functional.[137]

Contrary to the approach of the OECD, the UN acknowledges DSTs, signalling to the developing countries to continue implementing such unilateral measures.[138] If the developing countries do indeed pay heed to the UN argument for DSTs, there is every possibility of increased use of DSTs by the States[139].

The UN's International Financial Accountability, Transparency and Integrity for Achieving the 2030 Agenda (FACTI) panel report, 2021[140] recognizes the fact that countries have already implemented unilateral DSTs.[141] While the OECD expects the participating States to remove all unilateral provisions, the FACTI report sees this, rather, as an opportunity to strengthen multilateralism by adopting within the UN Tax Convention, "additional proposals to allow taxation of automated digital

135. U.S. Department of the Treasury, 'Joint Statement From The United States, Austria, France, Italy, Spain, And The United Kingdom, Regarding A Compromise On A Transitional Approach To Existing Unilateral Measures During The Interim Period Before Pillar 1 Is In Effect' (US Department of the Treasury 2021) <https://home.treasury.gov/news/press-releases/jy0419> accessed on 12 March 2022.

136. UN Economic and Social Council, 'Tax Consequences of the Digitalized Economy – Issues of Relevance for Developing Countries' (Report, UN Committee of Experts on International Tax Matters, Department of Economic and Social Affairs, 2021). <https://www.un.org/development/desa/financing/sites/www.un.org.development.desa.financing/files/2021-06/2107033E.pdf> accessed 12 March 2022.

137. South Centre Statement (n 73).

138. Jefferson VanderWolk, 'Sideshow: The UN Committee Of Experts And Digital Services Taxes' (*Bloomberg Tax Blog*, 2021) <https://news.bloombergtax.com/daily-tax-report/sideshow-the-un-committee-of-experts-and-digital-services-taxes> accessed 12 March 2022.

139. *Ibid.*

140. UN Panel on International Financial Accountability, Transparency and Integrity for Achieving the 2030 Agenda, 'Financial Integrity for Sustainable Development' (Panel Report, UN:FACTI 2021) <https://uploads-ssl.webflow.com/5e0bd9edab846816e263d633/602e91032a209d0601ed4a2c_FACTI_Panel_Report.pdf> accessed 13 March 2022.

141. *Ibid.*

services".[142] The report admits that "Countries are already moving ahead with digital services taxes. Therefore, incorporating provisions to address this in the UN Tax Convention will create a multilateral framework based on international agreement and enable additional countries to start taxing the digital economy with realistic prospects of obtaining substantial revenue."[143].

While the UN system seeks to create a multilateral network of unilateral DSTs through the UN Tax Convention, which will play an integrating role, its approach so far has been that of a bilateral negotiated solution. Section X, therefore, deliberates the prudence of the UN's bilateral approach to an obviously multilateral issue. The section also highlights how the OECD approach compares in this aspect.

X. Article 12B: A Bilateral Solution to a Multilateral Problem

Article 12B and the Two-Pillar approach of the UN and OECD proposals respectively, are designed to be implemented in very dissimilar ways. The OECD approach is to make changes through a Multilateral Instrument (MLI) which then operates to modify treaties based on a country-by-country listing and approval.[144] Eventually, the amendment of a bilateral tax treaty will be dependent on both parties to the treaty applying the MLI amendment. The UN proposal, on the other hand, functions in the same way as an amending protocol to a single existing treaty. Both approaches seem to have their own merits and demerits.

For instance, tax jurisdictions favouring bright-line rules in their domestic tax systems would find treaty provisions such as the UN Article 12B more congruent to their domestic agenda. Moreover, a formulated treaty provision also comes with an agreed international framework, which the States can then use to expand and further their national tax agendas – the more tax jurisdictions that come within the framework, the more consistency and harmonization achieved between national tax systems. This results in a consistent and clear treatment of international tax issues such as double taxation[145]. Even before the provision is implemented, the prevalence of an international framework would be catalytic to its acceptance[146]. Being a part of the UN tax framework, the UN proposal has persuasive value for countries to adopt.[147]

142. UN FACTI Report (n 140) Recommendation 4A.

143. Kuldeep Sharma, 'UN Versus OECD – It's Time For The UN To Get Going' (*MNE Tax Blog*, 2021) <https://mnetax.com/un-versus-oecd-its-time-for-the-un-to-get-going-43782> accessed on 12 March 2022.

144. Nathalie Bravo and Marianna Dozsa, 'A Multilateral Convention to implement Amount A of Pillar One' (Kluwer International Tax Blog, 2021) <http://kluwertaxblog.com/2021/12/03/a-multilateral-convention-to-implement-amount-a-of-pillar-one/> accessed 1 May 2022.

145. UN: WB Staff Comments (n 132).

146. UN: WB Staff Comments (n 132).

147. Ernst & Young India, 'OECD's Pillar One And Pillar Two- Impact And Way Forward' (*EY*, 2021) <https://www.ey.com/en_in/tax/india-tax-insights/oecd-pillar-one-and-pillar-two-impact-and-way-forward> accessed 12 March 2022.

However, it is pertinent to note that the solution provided by the UN, in the form of Article 12B, is a bilateral solution to what is, undeniably, a complex multilateral issue. While developing countries may be enthusiastic about adopting the approach[148], the applicability of the provision would be limited to those developed countries with whom they have bilateral treaties, and who are willing to accept a reversal of taxing rights (Article 12B(2))[149]. Moreover, a lack of widespread adaptation of Article 12B will stem from the fact that the UN MTC is not as widely adopted as the OECD MTC is.[150]

Additionally, tax treaties concluded between developing countries and high-income countries would certainly be subject to asymmetric power dynamics[151]. As most bilateral tax treaties concluded by developing countries are with developed countries[152], it would be very difficult to expect Article 12B to be accepted and adopted through a fresh set of negotiations across thousands of treaties, where the dynamics of negotiating power are skewed against the beneficiaries *a priori*[153].

On the other hand, the OECD proposal is a consensus-based multilateral approach, and therefore, is more likely to be adopted by member countries[154]. The attractiveness of the OECD BEPS MLI approach may lie in its rapid implementation through country-by-country MLI positions which exist alongside and efficiently modify bilateral treaties[155].

The UN's International Financial Accountability, Transparency and Integrity for Achieving the 2030 Agenda (FACTI) panel report, 2021[156] had several recommendations for the implementation of UN Article 12B. Some recommendations mirror the more appreciated aspects of the OECD system. For example, Recommendation 2,

148. After all, the central agenda of the UN MTC is agreement between developed and developing countries.
149. Ayush Tripathi, Nishant Shah, Shefali Mehta, Stella Joseph, 'Taxation Of Digitalised Economy: Analysing The United Nations Article 12B Solution' (*Economic Laws Practice*, 2021) <https://elplaw.in/wp-content/uploads/2021/06/The-Dialogue-Economic-Laws-Practice-Taxation-of-Digitalized-Economy.pdf> accessed 12 March 2022.
150. VanderWalk (n 138).
151. Evert-jan Quak and Hannah Timmis, 'Double Taxation Agreements And Developing Countries' (Institute of Development Studies 2018) <https://assets.publishing.service.gov.uk/media/5b3b610040f0b645fd592202/Double-Taxation-Treaties_and_Developing_Countries.pdf> accessed on 12 March 2022.
152. Luduc and Michielse (n 27).
153. Quak and Timmis (n 151).
154. OECD, 'Tax Challenges Arising From Digitalisation- Report On The Pillar One Blueprint: Inclusive Framework On BEPS' (*OECD* 2020) <https://www.oecd.org/tax/beps/tax-challenges-arising-from-digitalisation-report-on-pillar-one-blueprint.pdf> accessed 12 March 2022.
155. See OECD: 'Signatories And Parties To The Multilateral Convention To Implement Tax Treaty Related Measures To Prevent Base Erosion And Profit Shifting' (*OECD*, 2022) <https://www.oecd.org/tax/treaties/beps-mli-signatories-and-parties.pdf> accessed 12 March 2022.
156. UN FACTI Report (n 140).

suggests that "to hasten implementation, the UN Tax Convention should contain provisions holding that its terms will be automatically incorporated into signatories' tax treaties, so that they would not need to renegotiate individual bilateral treaties."[157] The OECD MLI implementation process achieves just that.

Another concern highlighted to the UN Tax Committee was that a bilateral treaty may lead to excessive taxation as compared to a multilateral implementation of OECD Pillar One[158]. The UN Committee's retort to this argument was that "a multilateral approach also raises concerns, complexity, for instance, being one and less than a fair share of allocation of revenue being other, besides complex multilateral dispute settlement mechanism as well as complex process for the elimination of double taxation. [A] bilateral solution will work in the same way as it has worked for existing physical presence rules." [159] The Committee thereafter reiterated that "the multilateral approach is complex and difficult to implement and does not result in fair or reasonable share for developing countries." [160]

However, the committee perhaps fails to appreciate that the problem under discussion is complex and multilateral as well. A bilateral approach may be an issue for companies in source countries due to a lack of uniformity in the tax structure[161]. With a multilateral approach, such as the one adopted by the OECD, tax structures across jurisdictions acquire uniformity and thus bring consistency to the tax expectations for enterprises[162].

Another issue that may haunt the UN proposal is that the greater legitimacy the UN system enjoys over the OECD does not transition to its tax proposals. The OECD proposals have been deliberated by an experienced group of 139 government officials. The UN proposal, on the other hand, was the work of 25 revenue officials acting in their individual capacities[163]. The mandate of the Group of Experts is specified in the ECOSOC resolution 1273 (XLIII)[164], which "requests the Secretary-General to set up an ad hoc working group consisting of experts and tax administrators nominated by the Government, *but acting in their personal capacity*, both from developed and developing countries and adequately representing different regions and tax systems, with the task of exploring, in consultation with interested

157. UN FACTI Report (n 140).
158. Chand and Villaseca (n 107).
159. UN Tax Committee Update (n 103).
160. UN Tax Committee Update (n 103).
161. Tripathi *et al* (n 149).
162. Rizvi and Tripathi (n 87).
163. UN Department of Economic and Social Affairs, 'Committee Of Experts On International Cooperation In Tax Matters: Terms of Reference' (*United Nations Webpage*) <https://www.un.org/esa/ffd/tax-committee/about-committee-tax-experts.html> accessed 12 March 2022.
164. *Ibid.*

international agencies, ways, and means of facilitating the conclusion of tax treaties between developed and developing countries. [*emphasis added*]"[165]

The fact that the UN committee members do not really represent the views of their government, complicates the UN solution.[166] It may also undermine the credibility of the UN proposal, as the officials who participated in their individual capacity may not represent the opinion of their countries.[167] In contrast, the international mandate of the OECD is much higher for the simple reason that there is more participation by developed countries.

The UN approach does manage to recover some legitimacy through its penchant for equity. As the above-mentioned FACTI report observes, "Fair taxation of digitalised economic activity requires equitable treatment of digital businesses and business models with traditional business." [168] As a result, the UN proposal is developed as a formulaic approach[169].

XI. Conclusion

The ability to collect tax is entrenched within the idea of State sovereignty. This is particularly true for developing countries as taxes are essential to the supply of social goods and services which only the State can provide. Consequently, the furthering of economic, social, and cultural goals of the State, implemented through the provision of such goods and services, are dependent on tax revenue for effective implementation. This creates a strong impulse on States to protect tax sovereignty from external transborder influence.

However, as the chapter discusses, the modern notion of tax sovereignty is perhaps not subject to such bright-line demarcations and is influenced by comity and cooperation. Thus, taxation has evolved into a more conjunctive sovereign right than an insular one. As a result, participating in or accepting 'less than favourable treaties' is not incompatible with the idea of State sovereignty[170].

The modern international tax ecosystem has evolved around this fact. With the advent of globalization, Double Taxation Avoidance Agreements (DTAAs) have proliferated, binding jurisdictions into a network of agreements aimed at preventing double taxation in transborder investment and trade. More recently, this tax structure also concerns itself with the problem of double non-taxation and tax avoidance. The international tax structure has the OECD as its *de facto* head.

---

165. *Ibid.*
166. Rizvi and Tripathi (n 87).
167. Tripathi *et al* (n 149).
168. UN FACTI Report (n 140) Recommendation 4A.
169. UN FACTI Report (n 140) Recommendation 4A.
170. Ring (n 5).

However other stakeholder multilateral organizations (such as the UN, the IMF, The World Bank, etc.) are also involved.

As deliberated above, a tax system with the OECD as its head creates certain issues. The OECD is a conglomerate of developed economies, perpetuating the interest of developed economies. Even when the OECD extends its working to other nations through its Inclusive Framework, the agenda remains limited (e.g. the BEPS Project).

The UN tax ecosystem, however, has traditionally given greater emphasis on the taxing rights of the source country as compared to the OECD model.[171] The work of the UN Tax Committee represents the interests of a wider and varying set of economies[172]. The current UN tax system runs parallel to the OECD system and attempts to remedy the strong influence of developed country interests within the OECD structure.

A pertinent example of this difference in the outlook of the two systems is the concept of a PE under the brick-and-mortar economy. Corporate tax at the source country is usually levied based on the existence of a PE. In that sense, the concept is used to limit source country taxation, to preserve the tax base of residence countries, while preventing double taxation. Under the OECD system, the threshold of establishing a PE is higher while the scope of a PE is narrower (thereby favouring developed country interests) than the equivalent provisions under the UN system.

This problem is further exacerbated by the advent of the digital economy. The reliance of the developing countries on corporate taxes as a source of revenue is significant[173] and the shift to a digital economy has drastically jeopardised this income. Taxing rights of source countries can be circumvented in the digital economy leading to double non-taxation. The attribution of a PE (as a requirement of source country taxation) is avoided by MNEs in the digital economy, as they do not require a physical presence to continue trade. This results in source States (very often developing countries) forgoing valuable tax revenue. Newer business models will lead to further shifting of profit by MNEs and the continuing erosion of the tax base of source countries.

The digital economy has served to highlight the differences in approach of the OECD and UN tax systems. Both the OECD and the UN have taken steps to address the problem of BEPS in the digital economy and otherwise (and are continuing to do so). Under the digital economy, the OECD has proposed its Two-pillar solution, under a multilateral system. The UN has, on the other hand, chosen to propose targeted and specific provision-based solutions as amending protocols to

171. Sarfo (2021a) (n 24).
172. UN: Department of Economic and Social Affairs (n 25).
173. UN: Economic and Social Council (n 21).

existing bilateral treaties. Article 12B of the UN proposal is an example, which has been specifically discussed in this chapter.

The OECD's Pillar One approach is a three-step process involving the identification of MNEs for tax purposes, based on their global tax revenues; the attribution of tax income through a nexus rule; and the reallocation of residual profits to source countries, once the nexus has been established[174]. Pillar two tackles outstanding BEPS issues through a 'top-up tax' on MNEs deemed as paying inadequate tax in a particular jurisdiction.

The UN approach has thus far sought to target individual issues through amending protocols to bilateral treaties. Therefore, in Article 12B, the attempt is to define the income under 'automated digital services' (ADS). The process then reverses tax allocation to a limited degree by allowing source countries to tax such income under domestic law at a bilaterally negotiated tax rate[175]. Both the OECD and UN approaches have their own advantages and disadvantages.

The primary advantage of the UN approach is its emphasis on source country rights. By defining a new form of income, the UN increases the scope of taxing the income of technology/digital-based companies. The UN system also rolls out a far simpler method of taxation which would be easier to understand and implement for countries with inferior resources and lesser developed tax administrations.

Under the OECD system, the method of identifying MNEs, establishing nexus, and attributing tax to a source jurisdiction is complex. A complicated policy design such as the two-Pillar approach will be difficult to implement and administer, especially for low-income countries with smaller-sized tax administrations.[176]

Moreover, the OECD continues to depend on a nexus approach to identify the scope of taxation. With the advent of the digital economy and the development of new forms of income, the definition of 'nexus' has become redundant to a certain extent. International tax law and policy found itself to be reactive to a changing world of globalization and trade. To depend on the nexus as a basis of taxation is to continue down a similar path of reactive measures.

As newer forms of income manifest in the digital economy, the potential to circumvent this nexus rule increases. The UN approach, however, is not bereft of a similar problem. By targeting a specific kind of income through a list of inclusions

174. See Section VI.
175. See Section VII.
176. South Centre, 'Assessment of the Two-Pillar Approach to Address the Tax Challenges Arising from the Digitalisation of the Economy' (South Centre Tax Initiative, 2021) <https://www.southcentre.int/wp-content/uploads/2020/12/Assessment-ofthe-Two-Pillar-Approach-to-Address-the-TaxChallenges-Arising-from-the-Digitalization-ofthe-Economy-reduced.pdf.> accessed 12 March 2022.

and exclusions, the UN system leaves out other forms of income and business models[177].

Further evidence of the UN system accommodating the needs of developing countries, is the visible lack of an income threshold to impose corporate tax. Unlike the OECD Pillar One proposals, thresholds of revenue and profitability are not suggested as factors to identify MNEs for tax purposes. This allows developing countries the flexibility of chasing various revenue streams. A developing country may impose a fairly low threshold in order to increase its tax base or have a high threshold to tax, thereby creating a market more inviting to non-tax revenue[178]. While such flexibility may bring about uncertainty and a higher tax burden to certain enterprises, it undeniably includes the social and economic interests of developing countries in the tax process to a much larger degree.

The UN ecosystem is also more accommodating of the unilateral attempts of individual tax jurisdictions, specifically those tax jurisdictions which have implemented a form of DST prior to the OECD two-Pillar solution. However, with the advent of Pillar One, the OECD expectation is the systematic phasing out of the unilateral provisions.

The UN outlook is markedly different. The UN recognizes the need for individual tax jurisdictions to implement national measures to include businesses that fall out of the scope of the multilateral approach. Thus, the UN ecosystem acknowledges the need and presence of unilateral national measures and has signalled the need for coexistence[179].

The UN approach does suffer certain structural problems based on the fact that it insists on a bilateral approach based on amending existent treaties through individual negotiations. The UN approach also has a legitimacy problem as it is designed by a small group of tax experts in their individual capacity, while the OECD approach has a larger representation in its formulation[180]. However, this is countered by the fact that the UN approach is backed by the entire UN system, which cannot be disregarded in terms of global representation. The UN MTC even enjoys the recognition of other global institutions. The World Bank Group, for example, has stated that "[they] believe [they] will welcome the insertion of the proposed new Article 12B to the UN Model Tax Convention concerning the taxation of the digital economy".[181]

177. See Section VIII.
178. See Section VIII.
179. See Section IX.
180. See Section X.
181. UN: WB Staff Comments (n 132).

Practically, however, the UN approach through Article 12B will achieve true relevance when accepted by developed countries (especially the US). It was the US that had insisted on the inclusion of consumer-facing businesses within the OECD unified approach. There is reason to be optimistic that this might be the case with businesses within the digital economy (such as ADS).

However, even if the UN approach does not achieve such universality, as discussed above, it serves the purpose of signalling to the global south that their interests *viz-a-viz* the digital economy will have consideration. This may be through the incorporation of bilateral treaty amendments in the form of provisions such as Article 12B or through the acknowledgment of coexistence with unilateral national measures. At the very least, it serves as a benchmark and guidance to the developing countries on what a possible solution to tax issues within the digital economy may look like[182].

182. EY (n 139).

REJOINDER

Indraneel Roy Chaudhury

The optimal allocation of profits between residence and source jurisdiction has been a subject matter of continuous debate among revenue authorities in the developed and developing jurisdictions over the years. This debate has since intensified with the advent of the digital economy, which has engulfed the world very fast. The conventional international tax regime built for the "Brick and Mortar economy" eventually failed to adapt itself to the commercial practices of the digital economy and this has intensified the need for changes in international tax and corresponding domestic tax rules. The fact that the digital economy is a growing tax base and ripe for taxation has significantly added to the narrative[183].

In their chapter, "UN Model Tax Convention - Effect On Developing Country Interests and Digital Economy Concerns", Dr. Rohit Roy and Ms. Ananya Raghavendra make interesting observations on the aspect of "Tax and Sovereignty", providing insights into the history of Model Tax Conventions (MTC) - how they came into being after the world wars to address the growing problems of Double Taxation, thus generating a greater sense of tax sovereignty. The authors have also brought out the differences between the Mexico and the London drafts and their eventual merging into the UN MTC and the OECD MTC, respectively. As the authors have pointed out, while the OECD model sought to eradicate Double Taxation, the UN model, while also seeking to do this, recognized the need for tax revenues of developing countries in furthering their socio-economic goals[184].

Both OECD and the UN had commenced their agenda for re-evaluating the interface of tax regimes with the digital economy around 1997 / 98, then under the nomenclature of Electronic Commerce. The broad taxation principles of electronic commerce set out in the Ottawa Conference of the OECD were – neutrality, efficiency, certainty and simplicity, effectiveness, fairness, and flexibility. In its first report on Digital Taxation, the OECD concluded that "such international taxation principles should maintain the fiscal sovereignty of the country to achieve fair sharing of tax space and should avoid double taxation as well as unintentional non-taxation[185]". Closely following the same, in the 10th meeting of the Ad Hoc Group of Experts on International Co-operation in tax matters, the UN addressed the issue of eCommerce transactions for the first time. It had observed that the direct taxation of electronic commerce is fundamentally more problematic than the indirect

183. Taxation of Digital Economy in India – The Way Forward, Vidhi Centre for Legal policy – Report March 2019.

184. UN MTC Preamble.

185. OECD Electronic Commerce : Taxation Framework Condition – Report of Committee of Fiscal Affairs – October 1998.

taxation of commerce. This was for two reasons – the absence of international consensus on what would constitute a permanent establishment (PE) in the digital economy and disagreements on the characterization of the transactions[186].

For any tax system to be effective, four fundamental requirements must exist – jurisdiction, identification of the taxpayer, transaction information, and a collection mechanism[187]. Jurisdiction is defined as the common authority and control in a territory where taxation authority is exercised. Accurate identification of the taxpayer responsible for remitting tax revenue is a fundamental element of any tax system. Transaction information is essential for tax administrators to effectively assess and collect taxes. Mechanism to collect taxes effectively is an integral part of any tax system – if taxes cannot be collected or the cost of collection is unacceptably high, the tax system becomes ineffective. Any new tax, while dealing with technological advancements and new business models, must keep these fundamental issues in mind.

The new economy business models have raised doubts concerning the fundamental tax principle of allocation of profits to the source country based on functions physically performed in the host country. Any new rules under source rule taxation and or the attribution of profits to PE should have an international consensus and result in equitable sharing of revenue between residence and source country, which can only happen with joint efforts of developed and developing nations. The rules should not only be neutral, efficient, and effective but should also keep pace with the digital economy. It is important that the concerns of developing countries are effectively addressed failing which they would be forced to adapt novel measures for the protection of their tax space.

A Peruvian report presented to International Fiscal Association states, "The principle of territoriality either has to adapt to this new way of doing business through digital means and bits, or simply new criteria will have to be devised that will very clearly and with all due respects apply to the various tax principles such as Neutrality, Efficiency, Certainty, Simplicity, Effectiveness, Justice (equity) and Flexibility to tax the many operations that are increasingly being performed through the internet"[188].

A more radical suggestion of abandoning the PE principle as the leading condition for tax jurisdictions and introducing the system of source/state taxation of business profits, that is the location at which the profits were generated, was

186. United Nations : Report of the Secretary General in 10th Meeting of Ad Hoc Group of Experts on International Co-operation in Tax Matters, January 2002.
187. Australian Tax Office, Tax and the Internet : Discussion Report of the ATO Electronic Commerce Projects.
188. IFA 2001, SFO Congress.

discussed[189]. Following the suggestion of the tax base erosion concept, a levy of low withholding tax on all remittances claimed as tax deductible by enterprises in the source country was also thought of, which would take care of administration and enforcement issues[190]. As the consensus eluded the international community, different jurisdictions, whether developing or developed, resorted to unilateral measures to address base erosion. Therefore, we have seen countries such as Italy, the United Kingdom, Australia, Israel, Hungary, and India resorting to taxes such as web tax, diverted profit tax, advertisement tax, equalization levy, and the like. The challenge now for these countries is to subsume the unilateral levies, once the "Two Pillar Solutions" are embraced by these jurisdictions.

For the sake of completeness, Roy and Raghavendra have delved briefly into the ongoing work of the OECD BEPS initiative. They have elaborated the alternative UN approach of Article 12B within the UN Multilateral Tax Convention (MTC) for source state taxation rights on income earned from automated digital services (ADS). They have brought out the similarities and the contrasts between the ongoing OECD and the UN approaches with the limitations and the different ways their implementation is designed.

The authors conclude that "the modern notion of sovereignty will be influenced by comity and co-operation and taxation has evolved into more a conjunctive sovereign right than an insular one". The authors admit that the OECD approach is highly complex, however, has a higher degree of acceptance; the UN approach is simpler for adoption but makes no distinction between the large and small MNEs in terms of the threshold of revenues and profitability.

The authors have uniquely positioned their discussions on tax and sovereignty and concluded that a better approach should be the UN approach if accepted by all the stakeholders. It may be pertinent to note that the UN, inter-alia, has adopted "a blueprint to achieve a better and more sustainable future for all people and the world by 2030[191]". This global action plan on "people, planet and prosperity" would require significant investments and funding by territories, irrespective of whether they are developed or developing. his discussion on sovereignty and tax by the authors is of significance to achieving these universal goals.

While the OECD has moved at a fast pace and the members of its Inclusive Framework of 136 countries have agreed on a new, more realistic timeline to deliver a Multilateral Convention for the implementation of Amount A (defined in BEPS),

189. Arvind A Skaar, Permanent Establishment – Erosion Of A Tax Treaty Principle, 37.4 (Kluwer Law International Ed 1992).
190. Richard L Doernberg and Luc Hinnekens, Electronic Commerce & International Taxation 5.1.1.1.5 at 319-24 (Kluwer Law International Ed 1999).
191. Sustainable Development Goals (SDGs), set up by UN General Assembly in 2015 – 17 SDGs and 169 associated targets.

for the signing of MLC by mid-2023 and its entry into force by 2024, the UN tax committee is currently looking at developing a multilateral instrument that could help implement treaty based digital tax and minimum tax rules[192]. At the end of this long wait, what remains to be seen is how territories embrace a simple tax that is easy to implement, effective and fair and does not act as a dampener for the digital economy.

192. Bloomberg Tax – Daily Tax Report June 2022.

CHAPTER 4

TAXATION OF THE DIGITAL ECONOMY UNDER THE PRINCIPLE OF ECONOMIC ALLEGIANCE

Some Reflections on the Impact of Pillar One (and Pillar Two) on Developing Countries

Leandro M. Passarella[1]

I. Introduction

Internet and cyberspace have opened new showcases and shop windows to businesses around the world and are used to offer, both traditional and digital products and services to a broader clientele. The customer lists of these businesses have added new members, from near and afar, who have not set foot in their shops. Also, the mode of offering some intangibles such as music or video has changed, as it is no longer necessary to own the physical media used to store them until now. Rather, they are available and can be enjoyed any time by having them streamed or downloaded to our devices. In a way, CDs, vinyl, and DVDs have become collectible items simply because anything is just a click away from us.

The new technology has simplified activities and strategies of a business because there is no dire need to establish a physical presence outside their main territories to expand and sell their output.[2] It has also reduced their scope of concerns: They may no longer need to worry about overseas risks and costs of the realities of their market jurisdictions (*i.e.*, where their customers are located). An attractive website with products listed on it has been enough since then. Here, customers from around the world can access goods and services that may not be available in their home countries until then. In turn, from the customer's standpoint, niceties of foreign countries unavailable locally can now be enjoyed without crossing borders. In that sense, the digital economy has somehow faded away the territorial limits as we have known them.

---

1. J.D. Universidad de Buenos Aires (*cum laude*, 1995), LL.M./I.T.P. Harvard Law School (1998), Owner of Passarella Abogados, Professor of Universidad Torcuato Di Tella's Masters in Tax Law.
2. These territories are referred to as "residence jurisdictions" in this chapter. These jurisdictions include not only where digital businesses may be formally set up for purposes of their worldwide activities, but also where they have originated.

The surge of the digital economy (*i.e.*, the participation of a business in a different country's economy with no substantial presence therein) has impacted countries' tax revenues. Countries, where consumers are located, have seen their tax collections either dwindle or at least not increase because digital transactions have escaped taxation under current rules. At the same time, tax revenue collections in countries where the digital businesses' headquarters are based have not risen significantly (mainly, because of deferral strategies permitted under the same current rules). In simpler words, the digital economy's current "base erosion" (should this term apply to the digital economy) is the outcome of the current international tax system.

The OECD has been addressing the issue since 2013 through its BEPS initiative. Since then, and before a multilateral approach reached by consensus was *proposed*, several countries had already implemented unilateral solutions to these disparities through digital services taxes ("DSTs"). These DSTs are applied to certain specific transactions, such as online advertising, sales of user data, digital interface to buy or sell goods and services, audiovisual media services, or audiovisual commercial communications (the automated digital services, or "ADS").[3] Therefore, they look more like a patchwork to solve revenue losses, than a principled solution. In addition, the United States, where most digital companies (and the most successful ones) are headquartered, has seen DSTs as discriminatory because they ring-fence digital companies and treat them differently. In addition, because of their usual structure, DSTs are not income taxes *per se*, therefore, they cannot play a role to minimize double taxation. Instead, they create distortions.

In late 2020, the OECD disclosed its Two-Pillar approach to offer a solution to the matter. If implemented, Pillar One would give *some* taxing rights to market jurisdictions on income from ADS and consumer-facing businesses ("CFB"),[4] while Pillar Two would secure a minimum amount of tax to be collected by residence jurisdictions. Almost simultaneously, the UN—through its Department of Economic and Social Affairs—has come up with a different approach: introducing a new Article 12B in its Model Convention, which grants taxing powers only on payments for ADS to the country where payment is made from. CFB's income is outside the scope of Article 12B.

The proposals of both global tax policy drivers have something in common. They are not based on the long-standing principles of international taxation set out by the

3. In this chapter, "automated digital services" or "ADS" refers to services that "are provided on an automated and standardised basis to a large and global customer or user base and can do so remotely to customers in markets with little or no local infrastructure". Pillar One, p. 19.
4. In this chapter, "consumer facing businesses" or "CFB" refers to "traditional businesses that have been disrupted to a lesser degree by digitalisation, [which are] able to engage with consumers in a meaningful way beyond having a local physical presence and can thereby substantially improve the value of their products and increase their sales." Pillar One, p. 20.

Financial Committee of the League of Nations in 1923. The doctrine of economic allegiance seems irrelevant to them, as little or no reference is found in the documents published supporting these solutions.[5] In addition, they share a similar structure: their approach is top-to-bottom, in the sense that they are to be agreed upon at a high level among (or between) States, and then they must transpire to each jurisdiction's local legislation to become effective. Therefore, they might seem more like an *imposed* response to the matter, rather than one reached through *consensus*. In that sense, it could be argued that they share the same issues as the DSTs in that, at best, they are a compromise.

A Compromise is not inadequate or inappropriate if it is reached after adequate discussions on conflicting principles. However, this has perhaps not been the case, especially if the two most prominent global tax policy drivers offer almost contradicting solutions to the taxation of the digital economy. This may seem ill-founded with solutions appearing to be short-termed while creating inefficiencies and aggravating inequalities. The question, therefore, is whether existing or new principles can provide guidance to solve the issue of taxing the digital economy.

This chapter's objective is to propose a solution to the taxation of the digital economy based on the principle of the economic allegiance set by the Fiscal Committee of the League of Nations in 1923. For this purpose, four factors are considered.[6] The solution, which is presented in Section II, has been compared to the OECD and the UN proposals.

In this regard, two possible pitfalls that the OECD's Two-Pillar approach may present to developing countries are summarized. They refer to the potential limited extent of the market jurisdictions' taxing rights on the digital economy under both Pillars. Therefore, it may be necessary to reflect on whether the OECD's approach to taxing the digital economy implies a level playing field for all jurisdictions, or—instead—may result in an exacerbation of current disparities. It is anticipated that this approach is deemed respectful of the principle of economic allegiance following

5. A reference to the principle of economic allegiance is found only in the OECD's BEPS Action 1. *See* OECD (2015), Addressing the Tax Challenges of the Digital Economy, Action 1 - 2015 Final Report, OECD/G20 Base Erosion and Profit Shifting Project, OECD Publishing, Paris. http://dx.doi.org/10.1787/9789264241046-en (hereinafter, "BEPS Action 1"), p. 25. No reference to this principle is found in the document issued by the United Nations' Department of Economic and Social Affairs relating to its proposed Article 12B. *See* Article 12B and Commentary after 22nd Session Meetings 29 April 2021 (hereinafter "Commentary to Article 12B"), at https://www.un.org/development/desa/financing/sites/www.un.org.development.desa.financing/files/2021-09/Article%2012B%20and%20Commentary%20after%2022nd%20Session%20Meetings%2029%20April%202021.pdf (last visited on 29 May 2022).
6. They are (i) the origin of wealth or income, (ii) the situs of wealth or income, (iii) the enforcement of the rights to wealth or income, and (iv) the place of residence or domicile of the person entitled to dispose of the wealth or income. *See* BEPS Action 1, p. 25.

the interpretation provided in Section VI of this chapter. However, Pillar One does not have the principle of economic allegiance as its guiding light. Therefore, it may be a temporary solution, until a principled one is found and adopted.[7]

The pitfalls in the OECD approach should not be understood in the sense that the UN's approach outweighs the OECD's. On the contrary, it offers a pragmatic solution that is farther from international tax principles as well. Therefore, developed countries may be deterred to adopt it because of its inherent deviation from domestic tax laws and, most importantly, a potentially significant loss of tax revenues for them. Also, this proposal may create a loophole to avoid taxation all at once.[8]

Thus, the issue may be summarized in Prof. Parthasarathi Shome's words: Do the approaches to tax the digital economy currently discussed still reflect the "*pattern of the global colonial past*"?[9] It is anticipated that, although unwillingly, that might be the case. To express a contrarian view, recognizing *significant* taxing rights to market jurisdictions (as the UN's proposal may intend) may unwittingly prolong that pattern reflecting varying prevailing absorptive capacities of different countries. Could there be a reason, therefore, for those market jurisdictions to have limited taxing powers on income from the digital economy. Such a premise of leaving a significant exclusive right to residence jurisdictions could be hypothesized to comprise a step forward in the social development in a globalized environment. This interpretation presumes that residence jurisdictions are willing to assume a stronger and more active role in promoting global development. This could, however, imply some type of involvement or *intervention* in other States' internal affairs and could indeed create a conflict with current international law principles.

Because of this reason, this step forward, as it will be referred to in this chapter, may be rejected initially unless there is an understanding that it will imply substantial negotiations and mediations among States beyond taxation rights. The

7. *See* Kjærsgaard, L. F. (2021). *The Ability to Pay and Economic Allegiance: Justifying Additional Allocation of Taxing Rights to Market States. INTERTAX, 49*(8-9), 636-655 (hereinafter "Kjærsgaard"), in page 637 and its footnote 11.
8. *See* Commentary to Article 12B, pars. 10 and 11, in p. 5.
9. Shome, P. (2021), India in a Global Pandemic—Macro-economic and Tax Considerations. *Reimagining International Taxation. Navigating through the Crises of Pandemic, lack of consensus and Retrospective Taxation* (Parthasarathi Shome Ed.), Oakbridge Publishers, International Tax Research and Analysis Foundation, 2021, p. 15. Prof. Shome's position is that the international tax regime "was not fair over the past one century. This was because value added was not recognised as an appropriate criterion, but capital ownership was. That is, tax revenue never accrued to those countries *to which* capital was exported and where value added was created, but to those countries *from where* capital was exported. That convention and practice reflected the pattern of the global colonial past though, unfortunately, it continued even after colonies vanished. It reflected the predominance of OECD, an advanced economy group powerful in consolidating its interests. But the BEPS project is challenging and attempting that pattern due to G20."

digital economy may ultimately create a new form of allegiance between individuals and States, and we may be witnessing initial steps. Therefore, any intervention should be carefully considered, because it may have a significant impact on the future of society. Any such intervention by one State in the internal affairs of another, if it were to happen, should be pacific and voluntarily accepted, resulting in the recognition of what, perhaps, consumers around the world prefer: an efficient free-market economy, where goods and services are transacted at the lowest price possible based on the laws of supply and demand.

Inter-governmental intervention is, however, outside the scope of this analysis because it is not strictly tax-related. Still, it is discussed because it deals with the interpretation of the principle of economic allegiance. Therefore, it may have connections with the discussion on the taxation of the digital economy. It refers to how tax revenues are to be *used* by jurisdictions based on the economic allegiance that they may have with individuals residing elsewhere because *consumption* from the income generated is not unlikely to occur outside the territories where the digital economy is located. Until now, it may be argued that the principle of economic allegiance has been construed in a one-way direction: the allegiance that taxpayers have with the jurisdiction from where they derive their income, or where they reside or have a domicile.

The digital economy may have inadvertently expanded the need to interpret this principle both ways: States also have an allegiance with (and, perhaps, a duty to) individuals that consume their income (*i.e.*, enforce their rights on income) in their territories, even when they are not residents or have a domicile therein. Under this interpretation, double taxation arises in the context of the digital economy because rights on income can be deemed enforced in two different jurisdictions simultaneously.

To support this argument, this chapter is divided into five more Sections. Section II summarizes the proposed solution and its rationale based on an expanded interpretation of the principle of economic allegiance, arguing that it would be a step forward from the "*pattern of the global colonial past*". Section III presents the UN and OECD approaches to addressing the taxation of the digital economy. In Section IV, two pitfalls of the OECD's Two-Pillar structure are identified to explain why BEPS 2.0 may be viewed, unfortunately, as a continuation of the current situation, unless some additional non-tax measures are adopted. The core of this chapter's position is discussed in Section V, where it is stated why the principles of international taxation developed under the doctrine of economic allegiance are respected by sourcing the digital businesses' revenues or income both in residence and market jurisdictions. The argument, however, is that economic allegiance is two-fold: Digital businesses have an allegiance with market jurisdictions, while consumers also create an allegiance with digital businesses' residence jurisdictions. As a result, they may be entitled to claim the benefit of certain public goods and services rendered by those jurisdictions. This implies a limitation in their home countries' taxing rights. Section VI concludes the chapter and refers to additional issues that need to be addressed in regard to the relationship between customers and the digital businesses' home jurisdictions, which may result in an increased blur of territorial borders in the future.

II. A Principled Solution to Tax the Digital Economy

The proposals to tax the digital economy currently under discussion seem to subtly set aside the principles of international taxation. As a result, they may be destined to have short lives. In this chapter, a solution to support, as well as to limit, market jurisdictions' taxing rights on digital economy's participants is offered. The solution acknowledges some aspects of the OECD and UN proposals as starting points. The main difference, however, is that its goal is to provide a more general solution based on the principle of economic allegiance set in 1923.

In the Report on Double Taxation, Submitted to the Financial Committee of the League of Nations, it was concluded that the *economic allegiance* to a certain country or jurisdiction was due to "*certain economic interests in the place of (. . .) permanent residence or domicile, as well as in the place or places where (. . .) property is situated or from which (. . .) income is derived.*"[10] Thus, this or any other proposal may better stand the test of time, while providing a lasting solution, if the principle of economic allegiance (or any other principle, existing or to be developed) were to provide philosophical support.

Key elements in this solution are both digital businesses and consumers (*i.e.*, all participants of the digital economy), located in different jurisdictions. The proposed solution's rationale is two-fold: Digital businesses have an economic allegiance with market jurisdictions, while consumers have a similar allegiance with jurisdictions where digital businesses are based. In other words, both types of participants have a bond not only with their own jurisdiction but also with the other participant's. Since there is only a single item of income derived, it has to be split between both jurisdictions to be taxed properly, providing adequate revenues to provide public goods and services to those that should be deemed entitled to them.

The starting point for considering that digital businesses have an economic allegiance with market jurisdictions is the concession that they use intangibles located in market jurisdictions: their customers' personal data. They collect this intangible from their customers to provide them with better digital goods and

10. Bruins, G. W. J., et al. (1923), *Report on Double Taxation, submitted to the Financial Committee Economic and Financial,* Document E. F.S. 73. F.19 (hereinafter, the "Report on Double Taxation"), p. 20.

services. As a result, the *situs* of origin of these intangible assets' income should be deemed located where the data is produced. That is in the market jurisdictions. Thus, they should be given taxing rights.

From this point of view, it is not assumed that consumers are an active part of the digital businesses' production of wealth.[11] On the contrary, their participation is passive and inordinate, and many times without their conscious knowledge or consent. They just provide input to digital businesses. The latter have it adequately processed (whether directly or through third parties) for their direct or indirect benefit.

At the same time, it can be argued that consumers *enforce* property rights on their income in the jurisdictions where digital businesses are located. That is where the goods and services they are interested in are offered. Through the internet, they "travel" to foreign jurisdictions, where they consume their income while staying at home. Why could they be deemed to have such an economic allegiance with a foreign jurisdiction if they do not "earn" income therein? Because, following the Haig-Simons definition of "income", consumption is one of the representations of an individual's income.[12]

Through consumption, individuals enforce their property rights on income they earn (or have earned or will earn). This consumption occurs outside their home jurisdictions. That creates a bond between jurisdictions and foreign consumers, which needs careful attention. This bond is also two-fold: Consumers are a critical input for digital businesses because they provide key information on their needs and interests, which are used by these businesses to offer their goods and services. As such, it may be in the residence jurisdictions' interest to keep this asset (which is essential for digital businesses) properly protected and readily available. At the same time, consumers enforcing property rights on their income outside their home jurisdictions may be put in the position to be entitled to claim a right to receive *some* public goods and services from those foreign jurisdictions as well. In other words, it may be argued that residence jurisdictions have an economic allegiance with foreign consumers that spend their incomes in their territories.

In sum, under this proposal (which follows some features of the OECD's and the UN's proposals), the principle of economic allegiance is still useful to solve the conundrum of the taxation of the digital economy. It is not that the concepts of "source" and "residence" are to be discarded to determine how the digital economy is to be taxed because they are outdated. Rather, the scope of application may have

11. For the argument that consumers generate data for digital businesses, *see* Kjærsgaard, p. 648 and its footnote 109. Also, *see* Marian, Omri Y., *Taxing Data* (February 26, 2021). UC Irvine School of Law Research Paper No. 2021-17, BRIGHAM YOUNG UNIVERSITY LAW REVIEW, Vol. 47, No. 2, 2021, available at SSRN: https://ssrn.com/abstract=3793892 (last visited on 29 May 2022).
12. *See* Henry C. Simons, Personal Income Taxation 50 (1938).

to be reviewed and revised to have them updated (more specifically, to the new technological environment), simply because the factors that help to determine the economic allegiance of a person to a particular State for tax purposes may still be deemed as legitimate as in 1923.

Having summarized the rationale of the proposed solution, in Section III the OECD and the UN proposals are summarized, showing how they depart or set aside the economic allegiance principle.

III. The Current Multilateral Approaches: UN and OECD. A "Compromise"

Both global tax policy drivers, the UN, and the OECD have made proposals for the taxation of the digital economy. Although in different ways and with varying mechanisms, both have proposed to allocate taxing rights to market jurisdictions. Although there are disparities, both proposals share a common thread, and they provide pragmatic solutions to the issue. However, these solutions are deviations and do not pay much attention to the long-standing principles of international taxation - the principle of economic allegiance - set by the League of Nations in 1923. They are summarized below.

III.1. United Nations

The UN proposes a bilateral approach to solve the challenges of taxing the digital economy. Hence, it has developed Article 12B for its Model Convention, pursuant to which market jurisdictions are entitled to assess a withholding tax on payments for ADS rendered by residents in the other contracting jurisdiction. Under this new Article, companies providing ADS may also choose to be subject to tax on a net basis in the market jurisdictions, rather than through the withholding mechanism. For this purpose, a percentage of their qualified profits from ADS would be allocated to the market—source—jurisdiction.

This proposal results in taxing rights granted to the jurisdiction where the payer is a resident. In other words, income is sourced in the "place of payment". Although it may be a practical solution to the hurdles that the digital economy poses to the existing international tax rules, this criterion does not adopt any of the factors of the principle of economic allegiance. In addition, some significant issues may still be unaddressed. For instance, the case of "online advertising services" targets a specific market jurisdiction where the payer is not located. Therefore, income from ADS would still escape taxation.[13]

13. See (n 5) *supra*.

It may be argued that the UN's approach is in the right direction because it acknowledges that (i) market jurisdictions are entitled to collect tax on ADS, irrespective of the digital company's level of activity in the market jurisdictions, and (ii) digital businesses must have the option to be taxed on a net basis in market jurisdictions. However, its source rule may fall short of the objective of bringing equity to the international tax system, especially because it may create incentives to design structures to avoid taxation completely, and in addition, it does not provide any solution for CFB income.

III.2. Organization for Economic Co-Operation and Development

The OECD, before the UN, had already targeted the taxation of the digital economy as one of the main challenges to be addressed by tax policymakers. For instance, BEPS Action Plan No. 1 has turned into Pillar One. Unlike the UN proposal, Pillar One aims to attribute a portion of the *residual profit* of *certain* digital companies to *certain* market jurisdictions for taxing it at its usual corporate tax rates. Hence, the OECD recognizes the need for developing a new set of source rules. This "overlay of the existing nexus and profit allocation rules" is Amount A.[14]

Under this proposal, "market jurisdictions (which, for some business models, are the jurisdictions where the users are located)" would be granted taxing rights if "there is an active and sustained participation of a business in the economy of that jurisdiction through activities in, or remotely directed at, that jurisdiction".[15] The taxing rights would be applied to Amount A, which—from a quantitative standpoint—is defined as *residual profit.*

This residual profit is the excess of a profit-before-tax-to-revenue ratio.[16] OECD acknowledges that for the sake of, normal profit is a fixed percentage. In October 2021, the OECD announced that this threshold was set at 10%.[17] Thus, market jurisdictions would be granted taxing rights on 25% of the excess of the ratio over 10%. Therefore, if the relevant business has a pre-tax profit of 11% of its revenue, only 0.25% of 11-10% would be taxable by market jurisdictions.

14. OECD (2020), Tax Challenges Arising from Digitalisation – Report on Pillar One Blueprint: Inclusive Framework on BEPS (hereinafter, "Pillar One"), OECD/G20 Base Erosion and Profit Shifting Project, OECD Publishing, Paris, https://doi.org/10.1787/beba0634-en, Paragraph 1.2.1, p. 12.
15. *Id.*, Par. 1.2, p. 11.
16. *Id.*, par. 508-509, p. 123.
17. OECD, *Statement on a Two-Pillar Solution to Address the Tax Challenges Arising from the Digitalisation of the Economy*, 8 October 2021, p. 2, available at https://www.oecd.org/tax/beps/statement-on-a-two-pillar-solution-to-address-the-tax-challenges-arising-from-the-digitalisation-of-the-economy-october-2021.pdf (last visited on 28 May 2022).

In turn, not all digital businesses would be subject to tax where their customers are located.[18] Only those with a global turnover above EUR 20 billion would be subject to Pillar One rules. In addition, depending on whether their GDP is equal to or higher than EUR 40 billion or not, market jurisdictions would have the right to levy a tax on the selected digital businesses only if the amount of revenue from each of these businesses exceeds EUR 1 million or EUR 250,000, respectively. Therefore, a digital company subject to Pillar One may be in a position where it may not be required to pay taxes to all the market jurisdictions where its goods or services are sold but only to those where the relevant threshold is surpassed.

Last, but not least, the proposed sourcing rules deserve a special paragraph. Why? Because for the businesses to which Pillar One rules would apply, all profits that are not *residual* would continue to be sourced according to current international tax rules that follow the principle of economic allegiance. However, *residual profit* would be sourced pursuant to new rules, which in some cases, and depending on the type of ADS or CFB are the exact mirror of the current rules.[19] For instance, residual profit from consumer-facing goods sold directly to consumers would be fully sourced in the place of final delivery, rather than where the seller is located (*i.e.*, where income is originated under the principle of economic allegiance). But the question must be asked if the place of delivery of sold goods should be a factor to determine the economic allegiance of the digital business with the market jurisdiction? There is no clear answer. In some other cases (*e.g.*, the intermediation of tangible services, or intangible goods or services), Amount A's source is to be split between both jurisdictions into equal halves. What is the rationale for this split? Why should it be 50/50? In any event and most importantly, the first 10% of the ratio of digital businesses' profit-to-revenue, as well as at least three-quarters of any *residual profit*, would be sourced where the seller is located pursuant to Pillar One. Needless to say, digital businesses outside the scope of Pillar One would continue to be taxed under current international tax rules, which follow the economic allegiance principle.

Notwithstanding these aspects, Pillar One has at least one positive feature: It segregates different activities of the digital economy to establish the sourcing rules. This means, unlike the UN proposal that sets a single tax rate for all income from ADS, market jurisdictions would have different effective tax rates on incomes derived by digital businesses, depending on the type of activity they are engaged in.

Having presented these proposals, two possible pitfalls of Pillar One for market jurisdictions are identified and summarized in the next section. The focus is on Pillar One, rather than on the UN because it seems that its implementation would

18. *Id.*
19. *See* OECD, Pillar One Ch. 4.

be more plausible (in addition to the fact that it has already been *agreed upon*). Notwithstanding its flaws, Pillar One has a virtue: it recognizes a *limited* taxing right to market jurisdictions, which ultimately may be the right thing to do.

IV. Pillar One's Pitfalls (and One Benefit)

The OECD proposal, which is in the process of implementation at a fast speed, has several issues or shortcomings. This chapter identifies two.: its limited scope of application, and the limited taxing rights granted to market jurisdictions. Both are referred to below. Notwithstanding them, Pillar One implies a step forward: unlike the UN proposal, it recognizes that not all ADS are to be taxed in the same way. In other words, this hurdle is not solved by agreeing on a single withholding tax rate to be applied to income from ADS. Rather, each digital activity deserves its own tax treatment. In addition, it includes CFB in its consideration.

IV.1. Limited Scope

Compared to the UN proposal, Pillar One has a limited scope: First, it only applies to *residual profit*. Second, only a quarter of such residual profit is to be taxed, whether in full or in part, by market jurisdictions. Third, only certain digital companies are required to pay tax to market jurisdictions. Last, but not least, such payment would only be required to be made by those companies if they reach a specific level of revenue in each market jurisdiction. Therefore, it may be argued that companies that do not meet at least one of these requirements would be deterred from increasing their digital presence worldwide. Only those that already fall within Pillar One would be taxed in market jurisdictions. In that sense, Pillar One provides a safe harbour for companies that are still outside of its scope. This safe harbor may be advisable if Pillar One were to be an interim approach until a principled solution is in place. If not, this solution may not be positive for the world economy and its development in the long run.

IV.2. Market Jurisdictions' Limited Taxing Right

The BEPS 2.0 proposal may also create an additional issue regarding Pillar One, resulting from its interaction with Pillar Two. The global minimum tax is to be levied at a 15% rate on the full excess profits earned by a digital business, while market jurisdictions would only be entitled to assess their taxes on 25% of that digital business's *residual profit*. Therefore, Pillar Two may be viewed as granting more taxing powers to residence jurisdictions than to market ones, or at least as protecting most of the digital businesses' income (*i.e.*, the 10% normal profit, plus 75% of the residual one) from the market jurisdictions' taxing powers. There is no need to say that Pillar Two's sole implementation would secure revenues for residence jurisdictions that may be taxed by market jurisdictions only once Pillar One is in place.[20]

In that sense, it may be argued that the OECD proposal seems to be the continuation of the "*pattern of the global colonial past*". While trying to bridge gaps between residence and market jurisdictions, the ultimate result of Pillar One and Pillar Two may be the exacerbation of disparities. Nonetheless, such disparities may still be solved if residence jurisdictions were to recognize their economic allegiance with consumers located in market jurisdictions. This matter is addressed in the next section.

V. Taxation of the Digital Economy under the Principle of the Economic Allegiance

As already mentioned, both the UN and OECD proposals to tax the digital economy have their issues. Besides, they do not rely on international tax principles hence a long-term solution may be difficult to find.

V.1. The consequences

Finding a principled solution to address the issue of taxation of the digital economy has been a problem since the beginning. Rules applicable to traditional economy transactions are somehow bent to fit those of the digital economy. Thus, a fiction that digital companies are engaged in business activities or have a substantial presence in market jurisdictions has developed. This does not actually happen. Digital businesses are not located in market jurisdictions. They do not need to have any presence therein, not even digital.[21] Therefore, the fact that revenues flow from market jurisdictions to foreign digital businesses should not be the basis for those jurisdictions' claim to tax such businesses on the ground that they are deemed to be engaged in activities in their territories.

Nonetheless, digital companies do have an identifiable entity in the market jurisdictions: customers. To deal with them successfully, businesses should know—the tastes and interests of—their customers. For that purpose, digital businesses should get information from customers. Before the internet era, the customers

20. *See* International Bar Association's public comment on the Pillar Two Blueprint, par. 5.2.19 and 5.2.1.10, (published on 16 December 2020). It is available at https://www.dropbox.com/s/hevb3h13ckh1ppr/public-comments-blueprints-pillars-one-two-2020.zip?dl=0&file_subpath=%2FPublished+16+December+2020%2FInternational+Bar+Association+(IBA)+-+Pillar+Two.pdf (last visited on 29 May 2022).
21. On the contrary, *see* Y. Brauner & P. Pistone (2018), *Some Comments on the Attribution of Profits to the Digital Permanent Establishment* (hereinafter, "Brauner & Pistone"), 72 BULL. INTL. TAXN. 4a/Special Issue, Bulletin for International Taxation IBFD. In this paper, Professors Brauner and Pistone refer to the "significant presence of digital players in an economy".

would have (i) gone to a shop physically located in their territory (whether owned by the seller—*i.e.*, a related company—or not), (ii) talked to an individual face-to-face, who may have provided some tips or advice, (iii) chosen their products from those that were available in the store (or request one to be shipped to the store), (iv) paid for their purchase, and (v) left the shop with what they had purchased. Why would that have happened? Because sellers would have had a local physical presence. Steps (i) through (iv) can be obviated. In turn, step (v) can occur at a delivery kiosk or through the mail through the digital economy,.

It can be said that digital businesses have become closer to their customers. This is because, when making purchases online, consumers "basically have a decision assistant. [They] have somebody who seemingly works for [them] and tells [them] what would match [their] preferences pretty well."[22] In addition, "it comes as no surprise that companies use the data they obtain from [customer] online interactions and browsing habits to sell [them] different products."[23] In the digital economy, neither do customers need to move from their homes to get foreign companies' products or services. The COVID-19 pandemic has proven this statement right—again, territorial borders have faded away.

V.2. A proposal toward resolution

Based on these facts, a different approach is proposed for the analysis: let us leave digital companies and customers where they are, that is, in different territories or jurisdictions. At the same time, it should be acknowledged that digital business operations need some inputs that are available elsewhere, that is, where those businesses operate, namely, in the market jurisdictions. The inputs are the customer data, which include—among others—their tastes and interests. Digital companies collect the customer data from customers' visits to internet websites and/or consumption pattern. They can profile their customers through data analytics. Based on this profiling, digital businesses assist their customers or customers of other digital businesses. Without these inputs, digital companies may not be in a position to sell their products and services effectively or successfully to a larger and more diverse clientele. Those inputs, which are intangibles (but are not "marketing intangibles",[24]

---

22. Tharawat Magazine (9 May 2018), "The Rise of Data-Rich Markets. Interview with Prof. Viktor Mayer-Schoenberger, Professor of Internet Governance and Regulation at the Oxford Internet Institute at Oxford University", available at https://www.tharawat-magazine.com/big-data/rise-of-data-rich-markets/ (last visited on 29 May 2022).
23. Maia Levy Daniel (15 February 2022), "Online Ads Can Be More Harmful Than We Think", available at https://techpolicy.press/online-ads-can-be-more-harmful-than-we-think/ (last visited on 29 May 2022).
24. *See* OECD (2019), *Addressing the Tax Challenges of the Digitalisation of the Economy. Public Consultation Document*, p. 11, available at https://www.oecd.org/tax/beps/public-consultation-document-addressing-the-tax-challenges-of-the-digitalisation-of-the-economy.pdf (last visited on 29 May 2022).

as defined by the OECD), are in the market jurisdictions (*i.e.*, where the customers are).

An individual's data may be correctly deemed to be where that individual is based, regardless of how this data is used once it is "in the market". Why? Because the use of that data will be referred to the individual that has produced it. Thus, it should be acknowledged that digital businesses have an asset located in market jurisdictions (*i.e.*, the location from where the customer interacts with the relevant digital business). As a result, they create an *economic allegiance* with those foreign jurisdictions. With this starting point, a new approach may be developed. If we consider that revenues from the use of intangibles are to be sourced in the jurisdiction where those intangibles are located when used, taxation of the digital economy can still be established through the principles of international taxation set out by the League of Nations almost a century ago. Therefore, sourcing a portion of revenues therein may seem appropriate according to those principles. By making that sourcing possible, digital businesses "remunerate" market jurisdictions for their provision of an input: customer data. This remuneration is not paid to the owners of this input (*i.e.*, local customers) because they are the ones making payments to the digital businesses. Nonetheless, market jurisdictions should be entitled to assess their income taxes on this local source of income.

In the traditional economy as well, market jurisdictions provide this input (*i.e.*, data) to foreign businesses. However, such provision is made through the businesses' physical presence, as part of their local operations. Therefore, the provision of customer data is taxed in the form of profits earned by the local establishment. This no longer happens with the digital economy. Nonetheless, market jurisdictions may have a claim to tax a (still-to-be-determined) portion of the digital business income (or revenues, as a proxy to income) because customer data collected by the digital businesses should be deemed located where the customers are. In other words, that portion of income would be the market jurisdictions' remuneration for the use of assets located in their territories, rather than income from ADS or CFB. Therefore, it would not be necessary to apply different sourcing rules to the *same* item of income from the digital economy, which may not be in line with the principle of economic allegiance because the single item of income would be split with a portion of that income deemed derived by the market jurisdiction itself as remuneration for the use of an intangible located in its territory to exercise its primary taxing right thereon.

Under this approach, the issue that remains unresolved is how much that portion should be. In other words, how much of the income (or revenues) generated by digital businesses should be allocated to (*i.e.*, sourced in) the market jurisdictions. It has been proposed to apply the same elements considered for transfer pricing purposes: risk, functions, and people.[25] This may imply applying elements of the traditional economy to the digital economy, which may not be the most convenient approach.

Instead, this issue may be solved in the same way digital companies connect and deal with their customers—through available data and data analytics. Which data? The one that tax administrations (especially, those from developed countries where digital businesses are headquartered) have been collecting regularly from their taxpayers, as well as under their domestic transfer pricing rules from related-party transactions entered into by multinational companies of the traditional economy. This data is available and pertains to all industries. In other words, margins can be assessed for each activity that a multinational enterprise has been engaging in the traditional economy but is now carrying out online. This information has not been contested in general by tax authorities. And when it may have been contested, it could have been adjusted or, further still, be considered for adjustment or confirmation by the judiciary. Therefore, it can be argued that tax policymakers may have available information on the profit margins of the traditional economy's activities, which can be used for the purpose of the digital economy. Based on this information, a formulaic solution or a formulary apportionment of income could be discussed, negotiated, and reached.[26]

Data *from the past* can assist tax policymakers in solving *today* how much profit derived by digital businesses should be attributed to market jurisdictions. By crunching available numbers with artificial intelligence, tax authorities should be able to tell their tax policymakers how much a reasonable profit from the sale in the digital economy of a "comparable" product or service would have been on average in the traditional economy. With this information, an algorithm could be formulated to yield an average profit margin for each specific activity of the digital economy. This average profit margin, which should be subject to rebuttal by the relevant digital businesses, would set up the basis for sourcing a portion of revenues (as a proxy of income) in market jurisdictions. Through this approach, tax authorities and digital businesses would use the same tools—data—to target their customer base. In the case of tax authorities though, digital businesses are their customer base. The results from this algorithm, which would be based on verifiable data, should support a reasonable discussion to reach common ground in treaty negotiations.

---

25. *See* Brauner & Pistone in (n 22) *supra*.

26. A formulary apportionment solution had already been proposed by Prof. Reuven Avi-Yonah in his article *The Structure of International Taxation: A Proposal for Simplification*, Texas Law Review Vol. 74: 1301 (1996). There, Prof. Avi-Yonah already favored treating "the entire MNE as one unit and then [seeking] to apportion its income among taxing jurisdictions based on a formula." The issue with the digital economy is that it can be argued that MNEs continue to be "multinational" because they sell their goods or services to foreign market jurisdictions (*i.e.*, ultimately, they may no longer need to be based in more than one jurisdiction).

V.3. Advantages of the proposal

This approach considers two positive features of the OECD and the UN proposals. The first one is Pillar One's sourcing rules for Amount A based on the segregation of the digital economy's different activities, covering both ADS and CFB. This implies that revenues from the digital economy can be sourced in the market jurisdictions in different proportions, depending on the type of activity from which they are derived. This is not the case with UN's Article 12B, which proposes a single withholding tax rate for all ADS only. The second feature is the possibility to rebut the profit margin to be determined as a result of the analysis of past, comparable data. This rebuttal would imply the assessment of the tax liability on a net basis, as the UN proposes.

Also, a necessary consequence of this approach would be that any digital service tax (DST) however finally redesigned, may become a foreign tax creditable against domestic income tax on foreign source income. In sum, this solution would differ from the existing ones that have been implemented and/or proposed since it does not deviate from the *current* principles of international taxation. Therefore, they may not need to be set aside. Rather, this solution would put the available technology to work for the purpose of solving the issue of taxing the digital economy.

This proposal may be summarized as follows. Digital businesses collect personal data from their customers located in a specific market jurisdiction. The use of these data creates an allegiance between that market jurisdiction and the relevant digital business that uses this input located therein. The remuneration for the use of this asset is not paid to its direct owners in the form of royalties but, in the form of tax revenue, to the jurisdiction where they are resident (*i.e.*, located). How are these taxes going to be assessed? By sourcing a portion of the digital businesses' revenues in the market jurisdictions, where they can exercise their taxing rights, with the possibility that these businesses elect to be taxed on a net basis.

Having established the possibility to tax the digital economy according to the principle of economic allegiance, an issue remains to be considered. Should the profit margin attributable to market jurisdictions be comparable to that of a permanent establishment physically located therein? While the initial reaction would be in the affirmative, the OECD may be right in proposing a limited taxing right to market jurisdictions. To give a more comprehensive response to this question, the meaning of "economic allegiance" may need to be expanded to acknowledge that not only "an individual owes economic allegiance" to a jurisdiction (still like in 1923),[27] but also the jurisdiction (in this case, those where digital businesses are headquartered) owes the same *allegiance* to individuals and entities.

27. *See* Report on Double Taxation in (n 10) *supra.*

This view of economic allegiance is proposed because, in the case of the digital economy, foreign consumers spend their incomes buying goods and services from digital businesses located in foreign jurisdictions. Therefore, the question is whether residence jurisdictions should keep a substantial taxing right on income from digital businesses located in their territories, to be able to provide public goods and services not only to those digital businesses but also to their foreign customers. As this topic exceeds the scope of this analysis because it does not refer strictly to the taxation of the digital economy but the way that tax revenues from the digital economy are supposed to be used, is presented when concluding this paper, next.

VI. Conclusions: A New Approach to the Principle of Economic Allegiance

Solutions to tax the digital economy offered so far neither repeal the principle of economic allegiance that the League of Nations adopted almost a century ago nor propose new principles of international taxation. Rather, they bridge the gap between residence jurisdictions and market jurisdictions. Therefore, to tax the digital economy, it may be concluded that the principle of economic allegiance, which solved most double taxation problems in the 20th century, has been set aside to arrive at a new solution for revenue sharing from the digital economy among developed and developing countries. When the proposed solution fails to gather consensus it becomes necessary to look for a guiding principle to find a long-lasting solution.

According to the analysis of this chapter, the principle of economic allegiance should not be disregarded as a directive or instrument to solve the issue of taxation of the digital economy. It recognizes market jurisdictions' taxing rights on digital business income based on the fact that they generate such income using an asset located therein: the customer data. This intangible allows digital businesses to offer more personalized products and experiences to customers located in market jurisdictions.

Having established a connection between digital businesses and market jurisdictions, it is necessary to determine how taxes on these jurisdictions would be assessed because there is no distinguishable amount paid to or from market jurisdictions for the use of this intangible. Therefore, it is necessary to take a piece of the income (or revenues) obtained by digital businesses in market jurisdictions to source it therein. How would that be possible? The proposed solution looks to the past to offer today a solution for the future. It is argued that, by analyzing economic data from the traditional economy already available to tax authorities using digital business technology (*i.e.*, data analytics) and adjusting it to the current circumstances, tax policymakers can assess how much profit on average could be attributed to different activities of the digital economy in different jurisdictions.

Thus, the proposed solution would be based on an existing principle, as well as verifiable facts.

The issue that, nevertheless, remains open is the extent of market jurisdictions' taxing rights. Regarding this matter, Pillar One may be viewed as overly protecting digital businesses from market jurisdictions' taxing powers. The question is whether such protection is appropriate or not. While Pillar One—together with Pillar Two—is aimed at leveling the playing field in terms of taxing the digital economy, its proposal may be deemed initially contradictory to that goal because of the limited extent of market jurisdictions' taxing rights. Nonetheless, it should be acknowledged that, should market jurisdictions be granted any taxing rights on the digital economy such rights should not be equivalent or comparable to those that would have been in place if the digital economy had never emerged. Market jurisdictions should accept that what they provide to digital businesses is tantamount to consumers. Therefore, the economic allegiance of digital businesses with market jurisdictions is limited to that extent. The only asset at stake is the customer data. This is one of the arguments to support that those rights should be limited, or more limited than those that would apply to pre-digital, traditional businesses with a local physical presence.

Competing interests between residence and market jurisdictions as to how much income from the digital economy should be attributed to each should also consider that residence jurisdictions have taxing rights on digital business income because it is derived from sales that are closed in their territories. In this case, *situs* (of the sale) is also the factor to attribute taxing rights to residence jurisdictions. Therefore, both jurisdictions have similar rights on the same item of income, unlike income from the traditional economy, no solid arguments to make one jurisdiction concede to the other its right to tax. As a result, a Solomonic solution of splitting income between both jurisdictions, like Pillar One, may be the appropriate approach. The problem with Pillar One is that it is not based on principles, at least ostensibly.

In this regard, the lack of a physical presence in market jurisdictions is an argument to limit the portion of revenues to be attributed to these jurisdictions. In other words, the pro-rata portion of market jurisdictions' tax base should not be the same proportion that would have been derived in the scenario of the traditional economy. In the digital economy context, market jurisdictions only provide public goods and services to foreign digital businesses in the form of protecting their customers and their data. Thus, the margin that would have been so allocated had they had a physical presence therein should now be lower, mainly because of the lack of a local presence.

Besides this *situs* conflict, there is another reason to support a limited attribution of taxing rights to market jurisdictions: the subtle bond between residence jurisdictions and foreign consumers. This bond is created because of the place where the latter exercise their property rights on income. In other words, it may be argued that consumers not only have an *economic allegiance* with the jurisdiction where they are a resident, or they have their domicile but also with that jurisdiction where the digital business is located. Unlike wealth (*i.e.*, savings), the place of consumption has been considered a factor comprising economic allegiance in 1923 to a limited extent. This could be because at that time individuals consumed foreign products or services either by way of imports into their countries by local distributors, or consumers travelled to foreign countries to buy them. Therefore, there was no possibility of double taxation based on consumption. In addition, the jurisdiction in charge of providing the public goods and services to those consumers was the one where the consumption occurred.

This has changed with the digital economy. This *enforcement* factor, which also creates economic allegiance, should be considered at the time of attributing taxing rights to both jurisdictions. Thus, there may be an additional argument to limit the market jurisdictions' taxing rights because both jurisdictions can claim that consumption (*i.e.*, the enforcement of property rights on income) happened in their territories.

As a result, it can be argued that residence jurisdictions have an economic allegiance with digital businesses' foreign customers. Why? Because they are an asset, as well as a source of income, to those businesses. In other words, residence jurisdictions tax the income of foreign customers when they tax the profits of digital businesses. Therefore, it may be argued that the foreign customers also deserve to have some allegiance to residence jurisdictions, which may be in the form of public goods and services. In the words of the Fiscal Committee of the League of Nations, for foreign consumers, residence jurisdictions may be viewed as "countr[ies] of stable government[s] and laws which will render [them] those services without which [they] could not enter into the third stage of consumption with confidence".[28] Why? Because those jurisdictions provide them with some goods and services that, until the digital economy came into existence, were not available locally (or were inefficiently available). Therefore, they would be "countr[ies] to which [they owe] some economic allegiance."[29] Foreign customers can consume what is unavailable in their home countries. Since consumers would owe allegiance not only to the market jurisdictions where they live but also to residence jurisdictions. This is an additional argument for the former to have limited taxing rights on income from the digital economy.

Nonetheless, it may also be argued that residence jurisdictions owe economic allegiance to consumers located outside their borders because, without them, their digital businesses may not have succeeded as they currently do. In other words, foreign customers may not only be an asset to be protected by residence

28. Report on Double Taxation, p. 23.
29. *Id.*

jurisdictions, but also potentially the target of some of their public policies. Which public goods and services should residence jurisdictions provide to foreign consumers, if any? As mentioned in the Introduction, this is not a question related to the taxation of the digital economy. However, the surge of the digital economy brings the following issue to the forefront: if territorial borders fade away for economic purposes, why would they not blur for other reasons as well? In other words, why should residence jurisdictions not provide public goods and services to individuals that spend their income in the territories of those jurisdictions from abroad? This is an issue that, though it does not deal strictly with the taxation of the digital economy, arises as a consequence.

The digital economy has brought up not only the issue of fair collection of taxes among States but also—as the discussion continues—the issue of fair use of the tax revenues so collected. Granting taxing rights, whether limited or not, to market jurisdictions does not address this second issue. Nor is it solved if residence jurisdictions keep a substantial taxing right on the same digital income without recognizing this aspect. The issue of the fair use of tax revenues in the digital economy may imply the need for residence jurisdictions to acknowledge that they have an allegiance not only with the digital businesses headquartered in their territories but also with their foreign customers. Without them, digital businesses would not be as successful as they currently are. Therefore, when taxing the profits of those businesses, residence jurisdictions are also taxing foreign customers' income earned outside their borders. In other words, resources generated elsewhere flow to residence jurisdictions. Why could that happen? Because those States offer something that market jurisdictions do not. It can be just the goods and services, or perhaps, their economic and legal environment that makes the digital businesses flourish, and attract foreign customers. Or maybe it is both.

Therefore, it should be analyzed whether the issue of the taxation of the digital economy would be solved by just granting taxing rights to market jurisdictions, so that they have more tax revenues available to continue to provide the current (possibly, inefficient) public goods or services to their taxpayers. Perhaps, it may be necessary to analyze the issue from another standpoint: Should residence jurisdictions have to acknowledge that they owe something more to foreign consumers that help their digital businesses emerge based on their stable laws and governments? Currently, the issue of tax sovereignty and the competition among States to attract taxpayers (usually, wealthy) is being analyzed.[30]

This analysis though does not focus on whether foreign customers of the digital businesses are entitled to receive, or have a right to claim, public goods or services

30. *See* Tsilly Dagan, *Unbundled Tax Sovereignty: Refining Challenges*, Vogel Lecture 2021 (27 March 2022), available at https://papers.ssrn.com/sol3/papers.cfm?abstract_id=4067679 (last visited on 29 May 2022).

from the residence jurisdictions where those digital businesses are headquartered. This claim, if it were to arise, may also be a consequence of globalization and the digitalization of the economy.

If granting taxing rights to market jurisdictions does not solve the issue of the right to claim by third parties, it may imply that residence jurisdictions should adopt a different, more proactive, approach to deal with the digital economy. It may indicate that residence jurisdictions should adopt a more proactive approach, an approach that conflict with the principle of non-intervention (or non-interference of internal affairs).

Addressing the issue of the fair use of tax revenues by both residence and market jurisdictions may be a step forward from the pattern of the global colonial past, a step towards a more leveled playing field. While this issue is worth considering, it has remained outside the scope of this analysis, because—as previously stated—it does not deal strictly with the taxation of the digital economy but as its consequence. It is the result of blurring the territorial limits from an economic standpoint that the new technology has generated, and the COVID-19 pandemic may have corroborated. Solving this issue may prove harder than reaching a consensus as to how the digital economy should be taxed. But it may be a hurdle to tackle in the process of reaching the current goal of fairness and efficiency, especially if consumers no longer have boundaries to purchase goods and services (other than those that their governments can circumstantially impose and this may also be an issue for residence jurisdictions to consider).

REJOINDER

Hitesh Gajaria

OECD's Pillar One and Pillar Two—Conflicts for Developing Economies

1. Introduction

The Chapter by KR Girish reflecting on the OECD Pillar One and Pillar Two – Conflicts for Developing Countries is an earnest effort to bring to light the situation of developing countries, especially after the goal posts on significant aspects of the Two-pillar solution changed mid-way through the discussions. To recount, per OECD's October 2020 Blueprints, Pillar One's efforts were to deliver a new and sustainable taxation framework to adequately take care of the reality of today's increasingly digitalizing economy which the existing framework is unable to deal with. The promise was to achieve a fairer and more efficient allocation of taxing rights between source and residence countries. Pillar Two had sought to ensure that all large internationally operating businesses pay a minimum level of tax. The Two-pillar solution was the focus of attention for many developing countries since such nations often emphasized the importance of users/customers and their data in the entire value chain of digitalized businesses and claimed corresponding taxing rights.

One needs to decipher the outcome of the laborious discussions and whether the texts of both pillars will accomplish the desired objective of truly and fairly reallocating some taxing rights to the source jurisdictions and putting an end to the futile "race to the bottom" so far as tax rates are concerned.

2. Overhauled scope of the Two-pillar solution and impact on developing countries

After multiple rounds of negotiations among the members of the Inclusive Framework, the scope of Pillar One was drastically overhauled. The initial ambit of Pillar One was to include Automated Digital Services and Consumer-Facing Businesses, which, per the 8 October 2021 statement by the Inclusive Framework, has been replaced to cover almost all businesses, but with a higher consolidated revenue threshold of EUR 20 billion. As of the date of writing this note, details of the revamped Pillar One proposal are yet to be finalized by the Inclusive Framework and countries are keen to watch how the methodology to achieve this would be structured, especially concerning the final revenue sourcing rules.

Initially, the formulaic proposition to allocate a portion of taxing rights to market jurisdictions was seen by many developing countries as a shot in the arm since they have been long advocating the relocation of taxing rights based on the location of users /consumers. The revamped Pillar One appears to have dimmed that enthusiasm. With the revised economic impact assessment not yet published, it remains to be seen how much such countries will ultimately gain (or lose, for having already implemented certain unilateral levies) from the revised Pillar One proposals. As fittingly highlighted by Prof. Passarella, an important question worth considering in the context of Pillar One is *'are we putting the cart before the horse?'* i.e., formulaic allocation of taxing rights without agreeing on more fundamental issues such as locating the 'source' of activities undertaken in the digital economy?

In the context of Pillar Two, a crucial element from a developing country's perspective is the subject-to-tax rules ('STTR') which have the potential to boost their tax revenues. The final proposals for the STTR are yet to be released but developing countries are hoping to negotiate for the inclusion of a significantly higher number of payments to be within the ambit of the STTR. If STTR only covers interest and royalties, then it may not lead to any additional revenues for these countries already asserting a taxing right of more than 9 percent under their bilaterally negotiated tax treaties.

The concept of 'domestic minimum top-up tax' as envisaged in the GloBE model rules released in December 2021 could be pleasing for some developing countries, in the absence of which, a certain quantum of top-up tax could have been netted by the ultimate parent entity jurisdictions under the Income Inclusion Rule.

From the perspective of developing countries such as India, the focus will be on the implementation of Pillar One and the STTR which could have a salutary impact on boosting its tax revenues. The global minimum tax which was finalized as per the GloBE model rules may not be much of a concern from an Indian perspective considering that India has done away with most of its tax incentives and rationalized its corporate tax structure.

On the asynchronous implementation of Pillar One and Pillar Two, Prof. Passarella has appropriately raised a concern on the possible disparities that could arise when residence jurisdictions are allowed to collect taxes under GloBE Rules of Pillar Two while market jurisdictions are unable to do so due to it's the deferred implementation of Amount A. However, a point to note is that the statement on the Two-pillar solution, released on 8 October 2021, clarifies that till Amount A is implemented, countries can continue to levy unilateral Digital Services Taxes. So, in a way, market jurisdictions are not restricted from collecting taxes until Amount A is implemented. However, the concern remains valid for those developing countries, that have not implemented Digital Services Taxes or similar unilateral levies in their domestic tax laws, pending the consensus for the Two-pillar solution, in which case the asynchronous implementation could provide to be detrimental.

3. Conclusion

As stated earlier, the goal posts of Pillar One and Pillar Two have changed and could ultimately result in market jurisdiction countries being disgruntled and wanting more. In the opinion of some experts and commentators, the two-pillar negotiations may not have been the ideal solution that developing countries would have liked to see.

It now remains to be seen what the final rules will have for the developing countries, specifically concerning the revenue sourcing rules for determining Amount A, the scope of Amount B, and the ambit of the STTR. Further, the effective implementation of Pillar One in developing countries will eventually also decide the fate and relevance of Article 12B of the UN model.

As regards GloBE Rules, it ultimately boils down to whether countries will completely do away with incentives and levy a minimum tax of 15 percent. If this happens, the OECD would have achieved its objective of holding back the tax rates from racing to the bottom in most tax jurisdictions. Countries would then only be subject to the additional compliance requirements of the Two-pillar solution.

A key point in the implementation process would be assistance and training for taxpayers and tax administrations to understand and comply with the rules. It is likely to increase administrative costs for developing countries. Whether gains from the implementation of the Two-pillar solution would outweigh the costs is something on which the developing countries should keep a close eye.

Finally, to sum up, as paradoxical as it may sound, it may be apt to quote Dr Shome's comments (that were a part of last year's edition): *"A final question remains: e-commerce being mobile, where do 'mind and management' really reside (the principle behind residence-based taxation). It remains difficult to pin down, particularly in the digital economy context".*

CHAPTER 5

Tax Policies and The Emerging Challenges of Digitalization and Climate Change—Experience of Sweden[1]

Yvette Lind[2]

I. Introduction

Tax scholars have engaged in environmental aspects of climate change and, separately, taxation and digitalization. However, there is currently a gap in the tax literature when considering the intersection between taxation, digitalization, and climate change. This chapter addresses this gap by illustrating how these two topics, climate change, and digitalization, naturally merge when considering taxation.

The digital market demands a greater number of reliable power supplies for data centres as digital platforms continue expanding. Studies indicate that data centres used 1% of the world's energy consumption in 2019. Forecasts expect energy consumption to drastically increase over forthcoming years, placing additional strain on the environment through so-called digital pollution. Digital pollution is a more novel concept, encompassing the two ways digitalization contributes detrimentally to the environment through CO2 emissions: (i) the operation of digital services and devices which consumes electricity, and (ii) the production, rapid consumption, and disposition of digital devices.

Sweden's favourable electricity tax regime, and Facebook's consequent choice to build its first European data centre in Sweden, are illustrative examples of the differing dimensions national governments will need to consider in formulating present and future tax policies on digitalization and climate change. These dimensions include international tax competition, tax revenues, sustainability goals, balancing national and regional development, and tax fairness.

---

1. The author is grateful for the comments received at the 6th Annual Conference of the International Tax Research and Analysis Institute (ITRAF). A special thanks to Dr. Parthasarathi Shome and Dr. Nigam Nuggehalli.

2. Jur.dr. and Assistant professor in tax law at Copenhagen Business School. Email: yl.law@cbs.dk

The prevailing gap in the tax literature when considering the intersection between taxation, digitalization, and climate change is the focus of this chapter.

Forecasts expect the energy consumption of the digital market to drastically increase over the next couple of years.[3]

The power density of data centers has more than doubled over the last few years, allowing an increase in the data treatment capacity within the same space, while the availability of electric power is becoming increasingly constrained in metropolitan areas. More often, it becomes unrealistic to increase the power supply in larger cities as the power distribution infrastructure is already pushed to its limits.

Therefore, most of the new hyper-scale data centres are built in cold and remote areas where cooling naturally occurs and is thus at no cost. The Nordic countries (Sweden, Denmark, Norway, and Finland) have proven to be highly strategic locations for such data centres. This is not only because of the cold climate and rural remoteness but also due to the existence of renewable energy sources that primarily originate from wind and water. Over the past couple of years, these countries have managed to attract multinational tech giants such as Facebook, Microsoft, Amazon, and Netflix to build their data centres within their jurisdictions. Sweden's preferential tax treatment of data centres in combination with highly inexpensive pricing of electricity and modest costs for buying property combined with a property tax capped at a low level[4] provides a significantly favourable situation for multinational tech-companies to locate their data centres on Swedish soil.

Consequently, this study aims to provide the reader with an enhanced understanding of the intersection between taxation, digitalization, and climate change. The Swedish Facebook case is described and analyzed from two main lines of inquiry when fulfilling this aim:

1. a traditional tax law perspective where the Swedish tax regime is detailed and subsequently analyzed through a tax technical approach, and
2. a discussion on holistic sustainability and the political economy focusing on how national tax policies, such as the Swedish tax regime, may impact the

3. One of the most prevalent and most recent studies was conducted by IEA (International Energy Agency): George Kamiya, *Data Centres and Data Transmission Networks*, Tracking report by IEA June 2020. <https://www.iea.org/reports/data-centres-and-data-transmission-networks> Accessed 14 February 2021.
4. The property tax will have an effect on the operating costs of the data centre, and a low or non-existent property tax will naturally reduce the costs for the company. As a result, there will be an impact on their business strategy when choosing locations. The property tax is deductible as an operating cost for commercial properties. The current tax rate is 1% of the property value. Regulated in Ch 16 §17 SFS 1999:1229 Swedish Income Tax Act.

coherence of domestic tax systems and the balancing between differing political goals such as revenue generation, tax competition, fair taxation, and climate change.

The first line of inquiry is accomplished through a traditional tax technical study based upon Swedish legal sources (legislation, preparatory works, and administrative case law) and to some extent EU law (fundamental freedoms and state aid provisions). Exclusion criteria that, in practice, disadvantage domestic data centre companies are included in the description and analysis. The Swedish administrative clarification that excludes co-location centres[5] compared to those that are wholly owned would be one such example. In practice, such exclusion criteria result in a more inferior situation for domestic undertakings compared to multinational ones as the latter own their own data centres while the former consist of smaller domestic actors providing their facilities as services to other local consumers. Based upon the results of this initial analysis, the second line of inquiry is accomplished through a tax policy discussion in which differing policy objectives are discussed and measured against each other in this context. These policy objectives include international tax competition,[6] tax neutrality, tax sustainability, support of domestic businesses, and environmental priorities.

This chapter initially provides an extensive exploration of the Swedish Electricity Tax Act when providing the case study of Facebook's first data centre in Europe (Section II). This is followed (Sections III-V) by an analysis of how national tax policies, realized through the case of the Swedish electricity tax incentive, may impact different taxpayers and different industry sectors in addition to the balancing between regional and national needs and prioritizations. The Swedish political discourse, through an extensive amount of preparatory works linked to the design and introduction of the studied Swedish tax regime, is applied as a red thread to provide a more comprehensive understanding of the motives behind the tax regime, Sweden's current ambition to attract multinational enterprises (MNEs) to its jurisdiction and its failure to ensure a coherent environmental strategy despite its ambitious climate goals and green government. Section VI summarizes the discussions of the study and makes some tax policy considerations to be considered when individual jurisdictions proceed towards adapting their tax systems to digitalization and climate change.

5. A co-location center is any large data centre facility that rents out rack space to third parties for their servers or other network equipment. Common customers in the north would be local banks and smaller enterprises.
6. Further similar discussions have been done by others but in differing contexts. For instance, Schön compared company law and tax law when regulating competition in: W. Schön, *Playing Different Games? Regulatory Competition in Tax and Company Law Compared*, Common Market Law Review, vol. 42 issue 2, 2005, at 331-335.

II. Case Study: Facebook's First European Data Centre in Sweden

In 2018, Facebook announced that its first European data centre, with a capacity to serve more than 800 million Facebook users, would be built in Luleå, a northern city close to the Finish border. This decision was arguably based on several factors providing favourable conditions, such as cold, scalability, and affordable land. Yet one may also assume that the Swedish preferential tax treatment of data centres also played a significant role.

As of 2017, Sweden offered a reduced electricity tariff to data centres resulting in a reduction of electricity taxation by over 98% compared to the normal rate established in the Swedish Electricity Tax Act.[7] Later, in September 2018, the Swedish Tax Agency clarified the application of the tax reduction. Supporting themselves on EU state aid rules, the tax agency argued that only taxpayers that were considered end-consumers of the electricity could take advantage of the reduction and rebate.[8] As a result, many local data centres subject to so-called co-location[9] were found to be ineligible to benefit from the tax regime while data centres owned and operated by one single company, such as Facebook, Microsoft, or Google, are still able to utilize the favourable tax regime. This development has encouraged additional MNE tech companies to consider the potential of establishing their data centres in Sweden.

The Swedish electricity tax (SET) applies to the energy sector which, in practice, results in a taxation of the consumption of electricity. The tax is calculated per kWh and the same rate applies to all consumptions regardless of the primary energy source from which the electricity is generated. Stated differently, renewable energy sources are treated equally to conventional ones (power plant energy, etc.). The tax rate in 2020 was öre[10] 35,3/kWh (öre 44,13/kWh including VAT)[11]. As is standard within most systems, electricity exports are not subject to the Swedish tax but may (naturally) be subject to electricity taxes in the importing state.

There are some exemptions to the general tax rate that result in lower taxation, e.g. the residential and commercial sectors in certain municipalities in Northern

7. Swedish Electricity Tax Act (1994:1776).
8. Skatteverket Dnr: 202 321717-18/111 Den som förfogar över den utrustning i datorhallen som elen förbrukas i ska anses förbruka elen.
9. Colocation is the placement of enterprise-owned computers, storage, and networking assets in a third-party leased facility. Colocation facilities typically offer scalability, continuity, and security for applications, data, and systems, removing the need for companies to build, staff, and manage their own in-house server rooms or data centres.
10. The Swedish currency is SEK (kronor). There is 100 öre per SEK. 1 SEK is circa 0,099 Euro/8,2 INR and 1 öre is circa 0,00099 Euro. Öre is used instead of SEK as öre is used in the Swedish electricity act. Most likely because of simplicity and clarity.
11. Circa 0,034 Euro/kWH excluding VAT and 0,043 Euro/kWh including VAT.

Sweden are subject to lower taxation than those in other parts of the country (commonly referred to as the Northern Tax *Norrlandsskatten*).[12] The Northern Tax is designed to mitigate some of the disparities between the northern and southern regions of Sweden. The climate between the north and south differs considerably with the north suffering a significant cold (often reaching between -20 and -40 degrees Celsius) during large parts of the year in addition to being subject to few hours of sunlight during the winter. The residents of the north will therefore naturally need to consume more electricity than those in the south. The reduced electricity tariff subject to these residents is therefore a tax policy initiative aimed at mitigating regional disparities. This reduced tax rate for those in the north will be further referred to in this chapter.

However, for now, the present focus is on the reduced tax rate for data centres which was introduced in 2016.[13] As a result of the Swedish tax rebate, data centres pay öre 0,5/kWh (öre 0,63/kWh including VAT)[14] instead of the above-mentioned prices. This affords data centres the enjoyment of a tax reduction of more than 98% compared to the consumers or companies in the general sector.

The Swedish electricity tax defines a data centre as:

> ...a facility where a trader, who mainly carries out information service activities, information processing or rental of server space and related services, carries out such activities and whose total installed capacity amounts to at least 0,5 megawatts.[15]

The above-mentioned floor was implemented as a result of discussions during the legislative process.[16] A minimum electricity capacity of the business itself would arguably compel the company to have the data centre as their primary business rather than a part of the main business as a tax planning scheme. In practice, it is required for an installed electricity effect of at least 0,5 mW to qualify as a data centre and the tax regime. Later, in 2018, the floor for the "extensive energy consumption" criterion was lowered from a previous 0,5 mW to 0,1 mW in installed electricity effect.

In reality, a company that wishes to utilize the tax regime needs to register as a voluntary taxpayer (frivillig skattskyldig) with the tax agency to be eligible for repayment of the excess tax (difference between ordinary tariff and the reduced one).[17] The terminology is somewhat confusing. To clarify, the electricity tax is

---

12. Swedish Electricity Tax Act (1994:1776), Ch 11, §9, para 1 no. 8 and Ch 11, §4.
13. Swedish Electricity Tax Act (1994:1776), Ch 11, §9, para 1 no. 7.
14. Circa Euro 0,005/kWh excluding VAT and Euro 0,006/including VAT.
15. Swedish Electricity Tax Act (1994:1776),Ch 11, §10.
16. Lagrådsremiss, *Vissa frågor på elskatteområdet*, (9 June 2016), at 95.
17. *Ibid*, at 45f.

normally added directly to the electricity bill by the company providing the electricity. This facilitates the administration and tax collection. This would be why the company wishing to enjoy the tax rebate needs to register as a voluntary taxpayer as it would otherwise not be possible to administer the repayment of the tax.

Further, the SET proposed an assumption of "energy consumption in an extensive capacity" as a second qualification criterion which was initially assessed to 20 gWh (1 000 000 kWh) on an annual basis. At present, this assumption has been lowered to 10 gWh on an annual basis.[18]

Additionally, the company needs to be liable to pay a minimum of SEK 12 000 in electricity taxes in the fiscal year. The tax rebate only applies to the sum exceeding this threshold. This is a requirement that was established so that companies would not feel tempted to tax plan and use more electricity than needed simply to qualify for the tax regime. By implementing a threshold such as this one, there is an effective reduction in the number of taxpayers that qualify for the rebate. The Swedish government argued that this qualification amount is aimed to ease the administrative burden for the Swedish tax agency as there will be an excess of administration surrounding the favourable tax regime (registration of taxpayers, investigation into the fulfilment of the requirements, repayment of taxes, etc.). In reality, this is a requirement that favours significantly larger actors such as tech-MNEs compared to smaller domestic undertakings.

Of interest is the government's argumentation, when proposing the tax regime, of restricting eligibility for the tax reduction to a company's total electricity consumption and not parts of it.[19] The government made the argument that fragmentation would place an excessive administrative burden on the tax agency as they would need to go through the total electricity consumption and subsequently different parts of the consumption separately to examine whether the conditions for the refund were met. This may sound practical and reasonable while it factually acts as a way of excluding those consumers who are renting or acquiring services from co-location centres, e.g. banks and smaller companies.

III. Balancing the (Fiscal) Promotion of the Tech Industry versus Traditional Brick-and-Mortar Industries

Initially, the Swedish government ordered a preliminary consequence analysis during the legislative process when introducing the preferential tax treatment of the tech industry. The Swedish legislative process is known to be rigorous and prolonged compared to many other countries, including its Nordic neighbours, for instance,

18. Swedish Electricity Tax Act (1994:1776), Ch 11, §6 para. 1.
19. Lagrådsremiss, *Vissa frågor på elskatteområdet*, (9 June 2016) at 46.

Denmark, despite sharing a similar legal culture.[20] The inclusion of several actors such as governmental organs, academic institutions, and interest organizations contributes to a time-consuming and somewhat rigid process which arguably may hinder situations where there is a need for a hastier response. This has been apparent during the COVID-19 pandemic. The benefits, and underpinning reasons, for this protracted process comprise the upholding of the rule of law and democratic inclusivity. The comprehensive preparatory work attached to each legislative act in Sweden also provides the foundation for how the Swedish courts interpret the legislation.[21]

In the analysis of the Swedish electricity tax regime, the Swedish legislator placed a strong emphasis on tax neutrality, (international) competition, public finance, tax redistribution between aid receivers, and the impact on energy efficiency goals when designing the tax.[22] Compliance with EU state aid provisions was also expressed to be of particular importance as Sweden has a history of taxes, in particular environmental tax incentives, to be considered to be non-compliant with EU state aid law, e.g. the Swedish biofuel production tax incentive.[23]

In the preparatory works, the government argued that the decision to offer a tax reduction to data centres was aimed at placing these specific companies on an equal basis with the traditional industrial sector within Sweden and subsequently lay the foundation for a new tech industry.[24] Consequently, there was an ambition to establish tax neutrality between the traditional industrial sector (mainly the steel and forest industries) and the new tech industry as the former already enjoyed an identical electricity tax reduction. The traditional industry sector in Sweden benefits

---

20. Y. Lind, *Crossing a Border **a** Comparative Tax Law Study on Consequences of Cross-Border Work in the Öresund- and the Meuse-Rhine Regions*, Jure, 2017. For a more comprehensive description of the Swedish legislative process see P. Wahlgren, *Lagstiftning: rationalitet, teknik och möjligheter*, Jure, 2014.
21. Swedish courts are, compared to courts in other jurisdictions, weak and rarely go against the will and intention of the legislator. Preparatory works, therefore, hold a strong position within the Swedish sources of law. For a more comprehensive description see: Y. Lind, *Crossing a Border **a** Comparative Tax Law Study on Consequences of Cross-Border Work in the Öresund- and the Meuse-Rhine Regions*, Jure, 2017.
22. SOU 2015:87 Energiskatt på el – en översyn av nuvarande systemet, at 352.
23. See: State aid SA.48069 (2017/N) –Sweden –Tax reductions for pure and high-blended liquid biofuels, OJ C 380/1 (10 Nov 2017). Sweden has exempted liquid biofuels from energy and CO_2 taxation since 2002 under EU state aid rules. The reason for the tax exemption measure was to increase the use of biofuels and to reduce the use of fossil fuels in transport and the Commission investigated the measures under EU state aid rules. The European Commission has granted the continuation of tax exemption measures for biofuels in Sweden up until 31 December 2021 on the basis that the tax exemptions are important for stimulating the production and consumption of domestic and imported biofuels, without unduly distorting competition in the EU. Further, the scheme has also been deemed to assist both Sweden and the EU to deliver on renewables and CO_2 targets. The exemption can only be granted when operators demonstrate compliance with sustainability criteria as required by the revised Renewable Energy Directive.
24. Lagrådsremiss, *Vissa frågor på elskatteområdet*, (9 June 2016) at 95.

from several tax reductions, and the steel industry in particular is heavily promoted compared to other sectors within Swedish business life as it is subject to only the minimum level of electricity taxation and completely exempted from co2 taxation. The government argued that, with this new tax reduction, the two industries will be placed on an equal footing resulting in tax neutrality and an ability to compete on similar terms.

This reasoning is, in this author's opinion, flawed. The steel industry is not, nor should it be, the benchmark for competition or taxation. It is quite the opposite. It is an extreme case and, instead of arguing that other industries should be subject to the same conditions, the competitive advantage that is awarded to the steel industry should be acknowledged. A discussion should also probably ensue as to whether this advantage should be mitigated or completely removed instead of being extended to other sectors and industries.

In sum, national governments should take great care when extending preferential tax treatment to specific sectors or industries as this not only risks distorting market competition but also causes distortions within the overall tax system and tax policies previously implemented.

IV. International Tax Competition and the Consequences on Local Business Life when Offering Tax Incentives to the Tech Industry

Furthermore, it was argued that the companies that would be eligible to receive the tax relief would do so because they belong to industries that are indeed internationally competitive and, to a large extent, use electric power in their production processes.[25] Consequently, the design of the tax reduction (qualifications for receiving aid, minimum threshold for electricity consumption, etc.) was designed in accordance with the needs of larger and more energy-intensive corporations. The argument that other countries already have similar favourable tax regimes in place was proposed and, therefore, low taxation was necessary to be internationally competitive.[26]

It is true that, when reviewing neighbouring Nordic states, most of them have applied a strategy of lowering electricity taxes to attract tech-MNEs. Denmark and Finland are prominent examples of this. When reviewing Eurostat statistics on energy pricing for non-household consumption, it can also be seen that Swedish electricity pricing is currently among the lowest in Europe. This low pricing in combination with the tax reduction results in the lowest possible tax burden in accordance with the EDT and EU tax rules. This affords Sweden and its Nordic neighbours with an exceptionally competitive electricity tax.

25. *Ibid* at 47.
26. *Ibid* at 69.

Diagram 1. Electricity prices in Europe 2020

Electricity prices for non-household consumers, first half 2020 (EUR per kWh)[27]

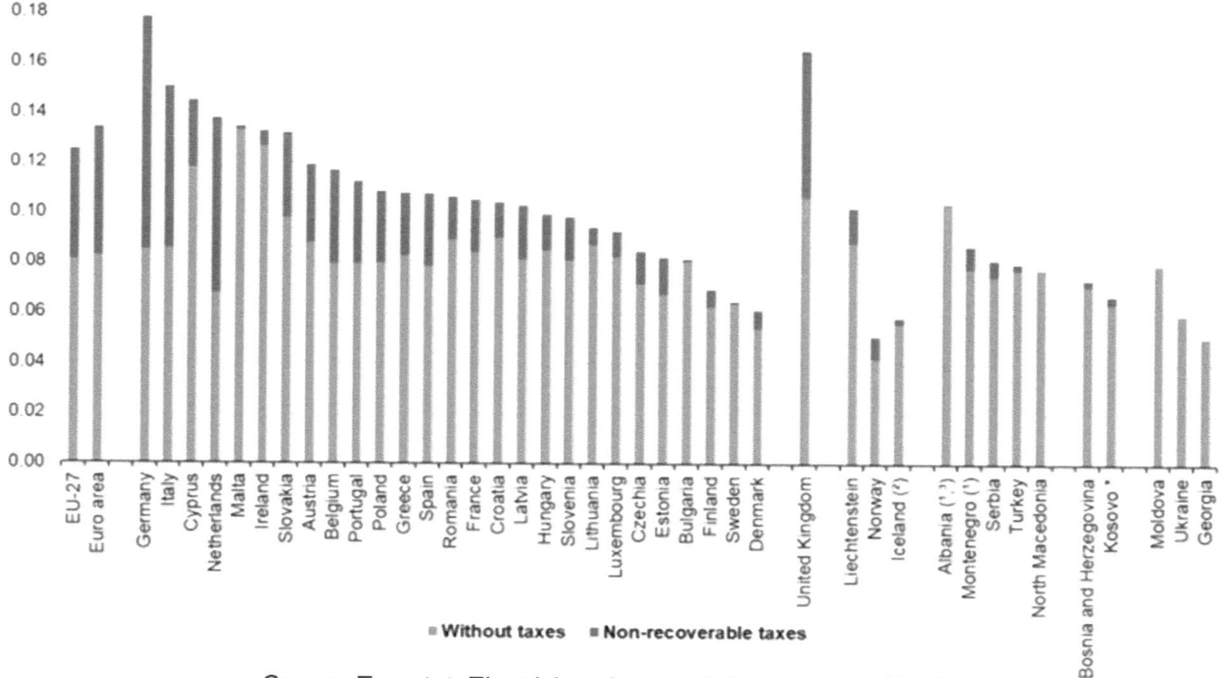

Source: Eurostat, Electricity prices statistics for 2020, (2020)

27. Eurostat, Electricity prices statistics for 2020, (2020), available at https://ec.europa.eu/eurostat/statistics-explained/index.php?title=Electricity_price_statistics &oldid=363293#Electricity_prices_for_non-household_consumers (accessed 29 Nov. 2020).

As initially mentioned, in 2018 the Swedish tax agency issued a statement that acts as administrative case law due to the necessity to clarify the application of the tax rebate.[28] At the core of it was the question of who was to be considered as the factual aid beneficiary of the tax regime. Stated otherwise, who is, *in practice,* consuming the electricity.

In the opinion of the Swedish tax agency, only those who possess the equipment for which the electricity is consumed can be considered as those who, in practice, consume the electricity. Therefore, a company renting space in a data centre is the end-consumer and the entity that is eligible to apply for the tax regime, clarifying that the tax regime would only apply to the end-consumer instead of, as had initially been the case, allowing the owner of the data centre to apply for the lower taxation through the tax rebate. Effectively, this does not allow the co-location centres themselves to take part in the regime of lower taxation.

The tax agency stated that there may very well be several companies that have equipment in the data centre in which the electricity is consumed. This assessment facilitates several companies being considered electricity consumers in the same data centre and, as a result, being eligible to apply for the tax rebate. For example, one company can be considered to consume the electricity that is used for operating fans and cooling systems while, at the same time, additional companies are considered to consume the electricity running individual servers.

In practice, the clarification had the following outcomes:

> *Example 1:* A data centre company rents out space in its facility to a banking company that stores data in its own server equipment in the data centre. In this case, it is the banking company that is considered to consume the electricity in the server equipment. The same applies if the banking company leases the server equipment from the data center company. This means that it is the banking company that must meet the requirements imposed on beneficiaries for the banking company to be able to receive the tax rebate. In assessing whether the data centre company itself is expected to consume enough electricity to be approved as a voluntary taxpayer, the consumption in this server equipment cannot be considered. Instead, the consumption is attributed to the banking company.

> *Example 2:* A data centre company stores data in its own server equipment on behalf of a banking company. In this case, it is the data centre company that is considered to consume the electricity in the server equipment. The same principle applies if the data centre company rents server equipment from someone else. This means that it is the data centre company that must meet

28. Skatteverket Dnr: 202 321717-18/111, Den som förfogar över den utrustning i datorhallen som elen förbrukas i ska anses förbruka elen.

the requirements imposed on beneficiaries for the company to be able to receive the tax rebate. Consumption of this server equipment may be considered when assessing whether the data centre company is expected to consume sufficient electricity to be approved as a voluntary taxpayer.

As a result, several individual customers/tenants of co-location centres will need to register as voluntary taxpayers and apply for the tax rebate and, by doing so, individually fulfil the qualifying criteria:

1. Passing the electricity taxation threshold of SEK 12 000/year in addition to having these electricity costs at a facility that fulfils the requirements for data centres.[29]

Not being one of the two excluded groups of aid receivers (in financial difficulty or subject to repayment of previous illegal state aid).

Larger corporations such as Facebook, Google, and Amazon were unaffected by the clarification as they operate their own data centres. However, domestic data centres for which their business plan was to offer their services to other (local) companies found themselves severely affected. Several data centres had to close down their businesses as they could not afford to pay the normal tax rate compared to the preferential tax regime to which they had previously been subjected (less than 2% of the normal electricity taxation). Neither could their customers, the end-consumers, enjoy the preferential tax regime as they did not fulfil the requirements, i.e. passing the SEK 12 000 threshold.

Administratively, the clarification and its subsequent changes place the burden of proof for the electricity usage on the end consumers when they are applying for the tax regime. It is a burden that is difficult to comply with as few data centres currently retain individual electricity records for their customers. Indeed, it will place an additional administrative burden on the tax agency as it will now have to administer 1400-1500 applications compared to a previous number of 50. This is contradictory to the many arguments initially put forward by the government when proposing the favourable tax regime.

To recall, the Swedish government discussed the option of restricting eligibility for the tax regime in accordance with the aid receiver's total electricity consumption.[30] This is a restriction that would have excluded those that are leasing or acquiring services from co-location centres, e.g. banks and smaller companies. The clarification from the tax agency results in a differing application of the tax regime as only end-consumers are eligible to apply for the tax regime., When doing so, they specifically involve the customers of co-location centres rather than the

29. Swedish Electricity Tax Act (1994:1776), Ch 11, §14.

30. Lagrådsremiss, *Vissa frågor på elskatteområdet*, (9 June 2016) at 46.

owners of them. Additionally, these customers will have to substantiate what parts of their electricity costs are directly linked to the data centre activity.

To sum up, the administrative case law issued by the Swedish tax agency clarifies who is to be considered as the actual state aid beneficiary as a precautionary measure, ensuring that the tax regime remains compliant with EU state aid provisions. This may very well be reasonable, especially when considering that Swedish environmental taxes have historically been, in many cases, considered incompatible with EU state aid provisions, e.g., the biofuel production tax incentive.[31] In practice, however, the clarification results in a delimitation of state aid receivers as data centres that were previously eligible are no longer so as an outcome of the end-consumer requirement. Customers who are now eligible to apply for the rebate, instead of the co-location data centres themselves, are excluded in some cases as their electricity consumption is too small to cross the SEK 12 000/year threshold. The administrative case law, therefore, excludes local actors while providing a beneficial tax treatment of MNE actors such as Facebook and others.

V. Socio-economic and Regional Considerations when Introducing Tax Incentives

In the preparatory works attached to the Swedish electricity tax regime, it was expressed that the new tech industry was expected to create new job opportunities which may be considered slightly contradictory as data centres employ a significantly smaller workforce than the traditional industry sector. For instance, a steel manufacturer that consumes the same amount of electricity as a data centre will have a considerably larger workforce compared to a data centre. Nonetheless, the government predicted that, for instance, Facebook's data centre would generate 260 new permanent employment opportunities and approximately 300 temporary ones as the data centre was built.[32] In hindsight, even this has not been realised. Municipalities in the north of Sweden have, after Facebook opened its data centre in Luleå, stressed that the data centre in question did not result in a wave of new

31. See: State aid SA.48069 (2017/N) –Sweden –Tax reductions for pure and high-blended liquid biofuels, OJ C 380/1 (10 Nov 2017). Sweden has exempted liquid biofuels from energy and CO_2 taxation since 2002 under EU state aid rules. The reason for the tax exemption measure was to increase the use of biofuels and to reduce the use of fossil fuels in transport and the Commission investigated the measures under EU state aid rules. The European Commission has granted the continuation of tax exemption measures for biofuels in Sweden up until 31 December 2021 on the basis that the tax exemptions are important for stimulating the production and consumption of domestic and imported biofuels, without unduly distorting competition in the EU. Further, the scheme has also been deemed to assist both Sweden and the EU to deliver on renewables and CO_2 targets. The exemption can only be granted when operators demonstrate compliance with sustainability criteria as required by the revised Renewable Energy Directive.
32. Lagrådsremiss, *Vissa frågor på elskatteområdet*, (9 June 2016) at 66-67.

employment. Instead, the news media have reported that merely 56 people received employment at the Facebook facility.[33]

As a result, the failure to create employment opportunities has subsequently led to these municipalities suffering tax revenue losses stemming from the tax rebate while not being able to collect income taxes from employees or corporate taxes from the data centre itself as Facebook does not fulfil the Swedish requirements for a permanent establishment.[34] Already financially weak municipalities are suffering while wealthy MNEs are receiving a more favourable tax treatment. This is an outcome that was both predicted and brought up by several external actors during the legislative process but ignored by the government.[35]

Moreover, though the Swedish government's consequence analysis did indicate considerable revenues losses with the implementation of the data centre tax regime, it was argued that these losses would be mitigated by a decrease in the northern tax reduction (Norrlandsskatten) through an increase in the electricity taxation on residents in the north of Sweden (currently enjoying a partial tax reduction due to longer winters and harsher climate compared to other parts of Sweden). The Government's risk assessment[36] indicated an increase in overall revenues.[37]

In this context, the socio-economic inequality between the north and south regions of Sweden should be considered. The north is generally considered a poorer region with high unemployment and ongoing urbanisation, a condition that is universal and not unique for Sweden in that region. The industries that employ northerners have traditionally been linked to the mining industry and the steel

33. J. Ekström, *Facebook fick 140 miljoner av svenska staten – ledde till 56 jobb*, Breakit, (17 Aug. 2020), available at https://www.breakit.se/artikel/25901/facebook-fick-140-miljoner-av-svenska-staten-ledde-till-56-jobb (accessed 29 Nov. 2020).
34. The author does not elaborate further in the question on PE in connection to data centres other than stating that, when considering present legal situation in Sweden, data centres do not as a general rule constitute PE. Permanent establishment (fast driftställe in Swedish) is regulated in Income Tax Act, Ch. 2, §29 (1999:1229). A data centre will need to be considered as the "core business for the corporation" for the requirements for PE to be fulfilled. Furthermore, according to the Swedish Tax Agency, a PE that has no staff and consists of only one server cannot be considered to have any significant people functions that can incur risks or decide on the use of the server. These significant people functions, and associated income, should instead be considered to go to the head office. However, the Swedish Tax Agency considers that the profit for the permanent establishment should reflect an arm's length compensation for the financial ownership of the server. According to the Swedish Tax Agency, the actual use of the server can be an alternative for allocating tangible assets. For more information on this discussion see: Skatteverkets ställningstagande dnr 202 493137-18/111.
35. Lagrådsremiss, *Vissa frågor på elskatteområdet*, (9 June 2016) at 66.
36. The Swedish legislative process is comprehensive and in connection to new taxes there are several risk assessments done in addition to gathering opinions from various external actors such as the courts, academics, interest organizations and municipalities.
37. *Ibid* at 354ff.

industry. This is an underpinning reason for the favourable tax situation currently applied to these industries.

The decision to remove the Northern Tax, i.e. the energy tax reduction for those in the North, has two major flaws. Firstly, the revenue increase has thus far not been realized, instead resulting in an overall revenue loss. Thus, the predicted and argued financial gains have not materialised. Secondly, placing an increased tax burden on the residents of the north only stresses the already detrimental development of the northern region and its municipalities. Not only would they suffer tax losses due to the preferential tax treatment of the data centres; but they would also experience an additional tax burden through increased energy taxation. To be able to attract and financially subsidize tech-MNEs while penalizing individual taxpayers in a region already suffering from higher unemployment and lower incomes compared to the national average does not result in a fair or sustainable tax policy.

To sum up, the Swedish case provides several valuable lessons applicable to other jurisdictions considering similar tax incentives. Depending on the design and implementation of such tax incentives there could be tangible effects, both positive and negative, on tax fairness not only among taxpayers but also between different regions within the overall tax jurisdiction.

VI. Conclusion

The case study concerned a Swedish tax regime though many of the findings are universal and applicable to other jurisdictions due to the essential mix of political economy with tax policy matters that tend to result in outcomes that are not necessarily economically beneficial in terms of employment generation or economic growth. For example, the north of Sweden has traditionally been subject to urbanisation, and the few jobs that exist there are linked to the traditional industrial sector. An establishment of the tech industry could, in theory, benefit this region just as it could benefit other regions. However, the risks associated with changing the north's sensitive environment, the thinness of population, and relatively high unemployment rates have to be kept in mind before undertaking sweeping policy changes without first analysing their likely beneficial impact.

It essentially concerns the transition from a traditional brick-and-mortar industry-based economy to a more digitalized business model. Most jurisdictions currently struggle with this transition, and it needs to be emphasized that such transitions should be deeply considered before policymakers employ tax policies that generate them. This pertains not only to a state such as Sweden but also has important ramifications for its regions and transcends to global considerations.

Additionally, it is appropriate to question the nature of implemented tax measures and how they impact other tax policy objectives for they are likely to perpetuate an incoherence within a tax system and cause an economic disequilibrium. To clarify, tax policy objectives such as the sustainability of the tax system and tax revenues, progressive climate goals, and the development (or at least preservation) of local business life. After all, most national governments are currently pursuing ambitious sustainability agendas that include the objective of relying completely on renewable energy by 2045.

The extensive electricity consumption of data centres has been linked to a threat of thinning energy supply not only at present but also in the long term, thus drawing concerns of increased digital pollution.[38] For ambitious climate agendas at both national and international levels to be achieved, countries will need to considerably expand their renewable energy sources while, at the same time, expanding their digital business sectors and collecting necessary revenues to support socio-economic welfare and infrastructure whose need can only increase in the future. These are complex policy goals that remain difficult to combine.

In conclusion, the findings in the study reveal that it is a difficult task for any jurisdiction to balance differing tax policy objectives when adapting to the emerging challenges of digitalization and climate change. Countries could, for instance, support several of the associated tax policy goals by expanding their energy supply chains which would create new jobs, provide additional (renewable) energy sources, and contribute, at the same time, to additional revenue sources for local municipalities and regions. Their revenue needs can be met through corporate taxes from the local businesses involved in energy supply expansion, income taxes, and social security contributions attached to their employees, in addition to increased consumption taxes and excise duties. That could occur only if local employment—both professional and blue-collar—expands and enables a more sustainable long-term growth in such regions. In turn, this analysis and its conclusions contain strong motivations and applications for developing economies.

38. T. Mossinge-Norhem, *Nätjättarnas serverhallar hotar elförsörjningen*, Aftonbladet (6 Oct. 2020), available at https://www.expressen.se/nyheter/natjattarnas-serverhallar-hotar-elforsorjningen/ (accessed 30 Nov. 2020).

REJOINDER

Parthasarathi Shome

On the Deleterious Ramifications of Tax Incentives

Yvette Lind's chapter has three characteristics that stand out. First, it deals with tax policy in Sweden, a hyper-advanced economy that has been admired for its fiscal policies for a considerable period. Second, it analyzes a particular tax policy on the information technology (IT) industry that has again been the beneficiary of high appreciation for its contributions in advanced and emerging economies alike, for example, through scientific advancements such as in the United States (US) and China, or stabilising a fledgling balance of payments through foreign exchange earnings. In the case of India and other similar economies, tax incentives have played important roles. Third, Lind takes up tax incentives for IT in Sweden and analyzes what impact it has had on the Swedish economy, in particular, on the region that was intended to benefit from the tax expenditure—or revenue loss—that government endured as a result.

A tax by itself has an opportunity cost on the economy in that it distorts the decisions made by consumers and consumers prior to the imposition of the tax, usually termed the efficiency costs from the introduction of any tax. In turn, this implies that tax incentives for some economic activities (and not for others) would further distort economic decisions in the economy.[39]

Lind's qualitative analysis of the issue is revealing. She finds that the incentives provided did not benefit the local population or increase local employment, an argument that was put forward by the policy authorities when the project was under consideration. Not only that but there has been an additional opportunity for local jurisdictions. This is because the electricity consumption of favoured IT companies has been very high, thus bringing on pressure for electricity rates to rise. She essentially concludes that the tax incentives did not intrinsically benefit the Swedish economy.

Lind's conclusion on the lack of societal benefits—or the lack thereof—of tax incentives mirrors several studies that have appeared in at least the previous five decades[40] for emerging economies such as in Asia, including by this author. To quote from his professional memoir where he refers to this work between 1976-78 for the World Bank,

39. See Shome, P. (2021), *Taxation: History, Theory, Law and Administration*, Springer, Cham, Switzerland, pages 81-90, for an elaboration.
40. Shome (2019), Parthasarathi, *Virtus in Arduis* (Virtue in Ardour), Orient Blackswan, Gurugram.

> I studied the role of tax incentives in India, Sri Lanka, Malaysia, the Philippines, and Singapore and became convinced even at that early stage about their pernicious effects, except in some restricted forms—such as incentives for capital investment—and only in strictly monitored environments. The analyses and results of the research were published in national journals of Malaysia, the Philippines, and Indonesia, and the World Bank's own republication programme.[41] (p.15)

Comparable experiences transpired across countries in Africa and Latin America in which the author provided technical assistance for the IMF and other organizations throughout 1983-2004. The derogatory conclusion regarding the sweeping use of tax incentives is universal. Yet governments adopt it as an instrument often because there is little monitoring and evaluation that is carried out and if at all, a routine one carried out in a bureaucratic fashion. Lind's study provides similar evidence from a case study of an advanced economy such as Sweden and, thus, adds to the earlier existing knowledge on the subject.

Indeed, the US Congress published data on the tax expenditure of the federal—central—government, thus divulging the revenue loss it incurs as a result. Following this pattern, the Union Budget of India introduced a similar exercise in 2006, publishing the findings annually. What is clear is that the vast majority of tax incentives favour a small segment of the productive sector at the cost of the vast majority, thus giving the former undeserved entitlements in the productive process. This carries distortionary ramifications across the economy and over a long period.

41. Shome (2019), Parthasarathi, *Virtus in Arduis* (Virtue in Ardour), Orient Blackswan, Gurugram.

CHAPTER 6

GIG ECONOMY – TAXATION AND BEYOND

Karnik Gulati

I. Introduction

The topic of this chapter is the taxation of the ever-growing gig economy and the challenges it presents in terms of the classification of gig workers. It further discusses the worldwide clamour about the gig economy, the mixed views of the judiciary, and the administrative response in the advanced economies to the classification of gig workers. After an introduction to the nature of services that comprise the gig economy, issues relating to its taxation around the world are discussed, including how to bring gig workers into the tax ambit, the head of income under which such income may be taxed if not treated as full-time employment income, cross border tax issues, and how India taxes the gig economy. The focus is on high-skilled gig activities, or what is called white-collar jobs, which are borderless and can easily be rendered from anywhere across the globe[1].

The term 'gig economy' was first coined in 2009 by the former *New Yorker* editor, Tina Brown. Its history is as old as the formal economy. Early on, it was word of mouth through which the gig workers could source work, whereas now it has evolved from the word of mouth to a click of a button due to advancements in technology leading to the introduction of a plethora of platforms through which work can be sourced.

A primary reason why some businesses have come to prefer a gig structure is that it is beneficial to not always have full-time employees and rather deploy gig workers as freelancers. This helps them avoid fixed salary costs and absolves them from complying with withholding tax (WHT) obligations and various social contributions and other benefits to which a full-time employee is entitled.

In recent years, the gig economy has started growing rapidly, and given the ongoing trend, this is likely to continue in the future as well. The Great Resignation[2] is a prime example of this trend where people have left their jobs *en*

1. I intentionally chose to use the term 'universe' instead of 'world' given that it's a matter of time that humans make a habitat on other planets, and the term 'world' usually only covers planet earth whereas the term 'universe' is much broader covering all planets. Who knows one of us starts rendering services from some other planet in the future?
2. *https://en.wikipedia.org/wiki/Great Resignation [Last accessed on 5 March 2022].*

masse. However, not all of them are leaning toward freelancing, which implies that the gig economy is not the only reason for the 'great resignation'. It is much more than that - a fundamental shift in professional preferences and behavior that was triggered, *inter alia,* by the Covid-19 pandemic. During the pandemic, people got an opportunity to pause and reflect on their priorities. This compelled some professionals to realign their career choices and, perhaps, seek more flexibility in the form of work timings, remote working, and reduction in transport costs.

There is little doubt that with the rapid advancements in technology, the business model has already been heading towards newer styles of working, but one would agree that the pandemic forced economies to adopt newer ways more swiftly. This holds not only for employees or workers but also for employers who appear to rapidly shift their workforce composition from largely full-time employees to a mixture of full-time employees and freelancers.

II. What Exactly is the Gig Economy?

The term 'gig' is often used to cover a wide range of activities and work arrangements, including part-time employment, freelancers, contract labour, and on-demand staffing services. However, it is important to note that there is no standard or universally accepted definition for the gig economy. The gig economy exists not only in white-collar jobs but also in blue-collar jobs.

The fact that there is no single or standard definition of the gig economy has led to numerous interpretations and multiple definitions. However, gig work has certain features that are universal and are discussed below.

II.1. Characteristics of gig work

- Temporary and transactional;
- Time-based or task-based payment;
- Flexibility of choosing work and time of work; and
- Individual worker

II.2. Evolution of phases of work

The work trend has evolved over time. It has moved from the turtle era to the goldfish era to the centipede era.[3] The diagram below attempts to explain the same.

3. *The credit for these terminologies goes to the Economist, Mr. Andreas Hatzigeorgiou, who used them in his Ted Talk. The video can be found here: https://www.youtube.com/watch?v=ewelBy30PZ8 [Last accessed on 6 March 2022].*

Diagram 1. Evolution of Gig Economy

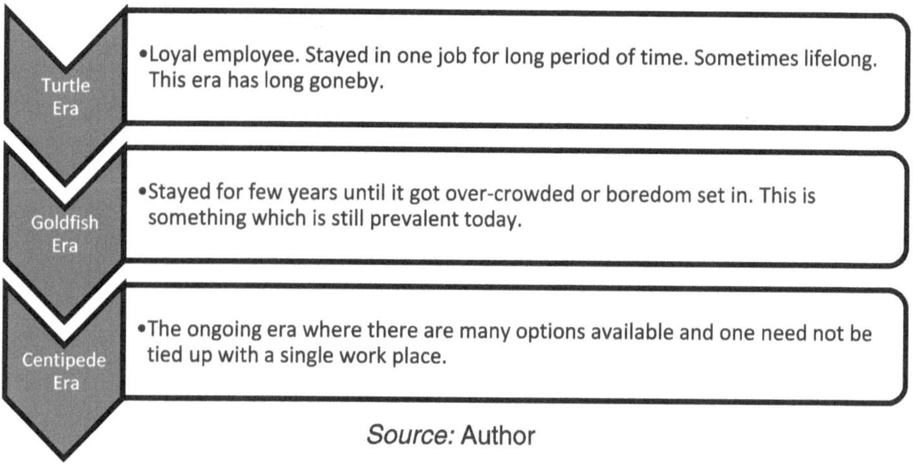

Source: Author

II.3. Factors behind the proliferation of gig economy

While the pandemic played a role in the rise of the gig economy, one cannot deny that three additional factors that will continue to propel the gig economy include digitization, millennization, and growing opportunities.

III. Traditional Employment versus Gig Work

The broad difference between traditional employment and gig work is generally known. Tabulated below the broad differences between the two are elaborated:

Table 1. Factors Differentiating Traditional Employment from Gig Work

Factors	Traditional Employment	Gig Work
• Employer-employee relationship	• Yes	• No
• Degree of control	• Yes – what to do, how to do, when to do. Fully dependent	• Yes – what to do. Varies according to the bargaining power
• Timing of work	• Employee has zero control other than in Flexi-hour arrangements	• Gigger has full control (except in some cases)

Factors	Traditional Employment	Gig Work
• Bargaining power	• Nil to very low	• Usually yes. Higher for skilled work. Much less for semi-skilled. Least for unskilled.
• Social benefits	• Yes	• No
• Resources to carry out work	• Provided by employer	• Gig worker uses his own
• Relationship	• Principal-Agent	• Principal-Principal, usually but not always. Ex – Uber-Driver relationship; it's complicated.
• Vicarious Liability	• Yes	• No
• Contract	• Contract of service	• Contract for service
• Risk & Reward	• With employer	• With hirer/gigger – depends

Source: Author

IV. Cross-country Information

Diagram 2. Gig Work as Primary Source or Secondary Source of Income

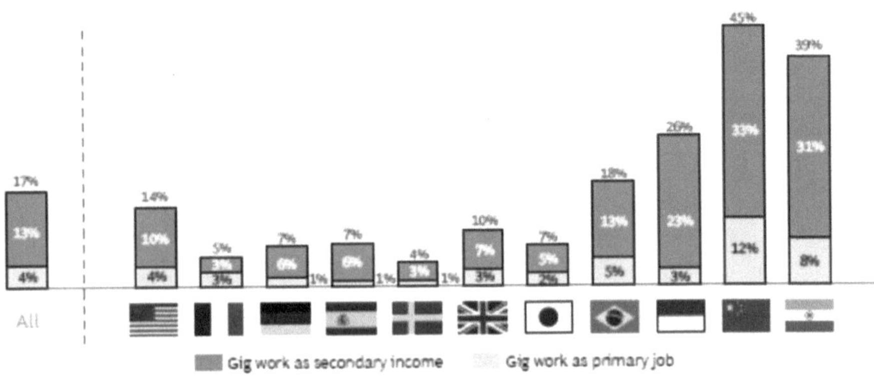

Source: https://media-publications.bcg.com/India-Gig-Economy-Report.pdf

If one were to examine Diagram 2 for the split between primary and secondary gig work in selected countries, it may be observed that China leads the pack, followed by India. What is surprising is that gig work participation is higher in emerging countries compared to advanced countries. That is perhaps mainly due to having comparatively higher unorganized sectors in emerging countries rather than a more intrinsic reason.

Diagram 3 demonstrates that India leads the pack in high-skill gig work. This is where the problem lies for tax administrations to bring such transactions under the tax ambit since high-skill gig work is easily rendered without any physical presence in the source or market jurisdiction. Though for service-exporting countries with residence-based taxation systems, this may not pose a threat, since it is the export of services for them, and the resident service provider is taxable on his global income. However, for the service-importing nation, it becomes relevant to ensure how to tax such peer-to-peer or non-business transactions.

Diagram 3: Gig work across various skillsets

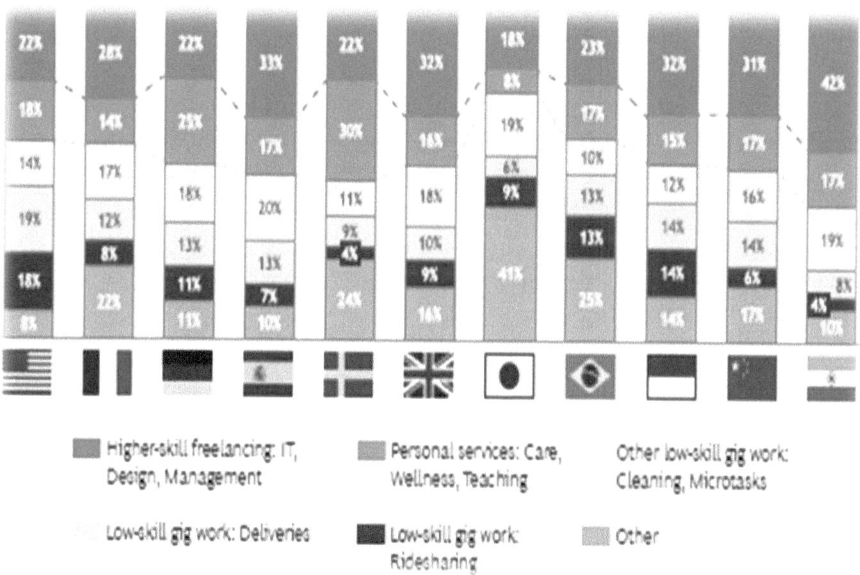

Source: https://media-publications.bcg.com/India-Gig-Economy-Report.pdf.

Diagram 4 suggests that people prefer to work independently than having a full-time job to the extent that it reflects choices that they make.

Diagram 4: Percentage of work population choosing to work independently or as full-time employee

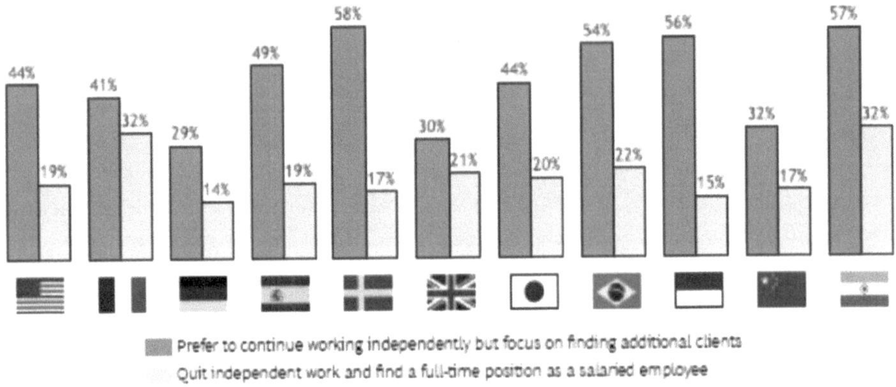

Source: https://media-publications.bcg.com/India-Gig-Economy-Report.pdf.

However, it is pertinent to note that the above analysis is based on a survey undertaken in 2018, i.e., pre-Covid. One can safely say that the data might undergo a major change post the pandemic. However, a post-pandemic shift cannot be guaranteed, as independent workers would have taken a financial hit due to loss of work depending on the nature of their work. Also, they might have had second thoughts preferring to have a full-time job, where a regular income to meet rising expenses may be earned.[4]

However, the trend of the recent Great Resignation that started in 2021 suggests completely the opposite as this is not only about money but much more than that.[5] This shift in trend towards independence reflects that more opportunities are available due to rapid change as well as speedy adoption of technology during Covid combined with the realization that remote work is possible and acceptable. Perhaps there was also a change in philosophy towards a better work-life balance.

4. There is mixed feedback on whether the Great Resignation subsided post-pandemic. No doubt that some people who were part of the Great Resignation regret leaving their previous job in search of either doing their own gig or find a better job but, at the same time, there are people who are actually happy with their decision. Having said that, the ongoing fear of recession hitting all around, the trend of Great Resignation seems to be waning.
5. *https://www.fastcompany.com/90727646/its-not-just-money-this-is-whats-still-driving-the-great-resignation.*

V. Classification: A Plaguing Issue

A major issue that plagues the gig economy and its workers is classification. There is a worldwide clamour on the classification of gig workers whether they should be considered as full-time employees who usually receive full social protection benefits, or as independent contractors (self-employed) who do not receive it. Or should a new category called 'workers with limited benefits' where they receive limited social protection benefits, be introduced for gig workers.

Misclassification, or incorrect categorization, implies a full-time worker being classified as a freelancer or vice-versa. In practical terms, the incentive to misclassify exists since it is a win-win situation for both the employer and the worker to misclassify. For the employer, the incentive is to avoid numerous compliances required under labour or related laws, and to avoid other compliance requirements under tax laws such as withholding tax requirements and submitting return forms. On the other hand, workers have an incentive to misclassify themselves as freelancers as usually there are no withholding tax requirements applicable to freelancers.

In a nutshell, this could be viewed as a collusion between the employer and worker leading to misclassification. Nevertheless, even though the mutual arrangement may look like a win-win situation for both stakeholders, the win is likely to be tilted more towards the employer, as the employee loses out on social benefits entitlements of a full-time employee. The typical structure operated under the guise of an independent contractor even though a worker is a full-time employee. For the hirer, it saved on fixed costs and social obligation costs, and the hiree got away with no WHT or a relatively small percentage of the correct WHT and no filing of an income tax return.

Until recently, all was good for the workers as they were often not concerned about the benefits from which they are excluded. However, with the increase in platform operators and untenable work conditions offered, there was a gradual shift towards recognizing the importance of obtaining the right to benefits. This holds especially for low-skill workers such as drivers, riders, and delivery staff reflecting the exploitation they encountered in terms of working hours and work conditions. It is not surprising that they have realised the importance of social benefits. A movement may have started with Uber drivers knocking on the doors of the courts with petitions across the world. This is discussed in detail later.

The fatalities during the pandemic were also one reason why the lack of benefits has come to the fore. Workers were left in the lurch without any rights to claim benefits due to the nature of classification and were found to want to receive appropriate rights. Governments had to bear the needed resource costs of financing benefits in some advanced economies. But it was challenging for gig workers operating in emerging economies, as governments could not afford to foot the bill due to the existence of a large gig economy that involves a large segment of their populations.

V.1. Mixed views of judiciary on classification

Around the world, a plethora of platform companies are locked in legal battles on the classification issue. Uber is at the forefront of all this. For almost all platform companies, the crux of the issue around the world, is whether its workers are entitled to the same rights and benefits as full-time employees. The answer to this question depends on the definition of the term 'worker' in the respective labour laws of various countries. Mostly, the laws, in their current shape and form, are archaic and need to be aligned with today's reality.

There is no clear answer from the courts around the world because there is no straight jacket formula to determine the answer, and a lot depends on the facts of each case. Until now, the courts have a divided opinion on the classification issue. Below, several instances of what the judiciary of major countries has had to say on the classification issue are reviewed.

V.1.1. United Kingdom

Uber BV and others (Appellants) v Aslam and others (Respondents) – Supreme Court of the United Kingdom **[19 February 2021][6]**

This is a very interesting landmark ruling delivered by [a] six-member bench.[7] It fundamentally discusses the rights and obligations of Uber drivers and the overall relationship between Uber and its drivers. Captivating findings have been made by the appellate authorities in the form of how Uber actually operates and the influence it has on its so-called independent drivers.

The seminal question before the Hon'ble Supreme Court was whether the Uber drivers, who are freelancers or contractual workers, are entitled to statutory rights like minimum wages, annual paid leave, and other similar rights available to full-time employees in the UK. Before moving on to the observations made by the Hon'ble Supreme Court, it is important to understand the definition of 'worker' in the labour law of the United Kingdom.

The term "worker" is defined under section 230(3) of the Employment Rights Act, 1996. The relevant definition of "worker" is reproduced as under:

> "an individual who has entered into or works under (or, where the employment has ceased, worked under) –
>
> (a) a contract of employment, or
>
> (b) <u>any other contract</u>, whether **express or implied** and (if it is express) whether **oral or in writing, whereby the <u>individual undertakes</u>** to do or perform **<u>personally</u> any work or services for another party** to

6. [2021] UKSC 5.
7. *Originally presided by seven-members but due to illness of one of the members, it was finally delivered by the remaining six members.*

the contract whose status is not by virtue of the contract that of a client or customer of any profession or business undertaking carried on by the individual;

and any reference to a worker's contract shall be construed accordingly."

[*Emphasis supplied*]

The Supreme Court was unanimous in upholding the findings of the Court of Appeals and other lower forums that the Uber drivers are not at all independent and the so-called independence was only disguised by Uber to avoid certain obligations that it must keep if the drivers are assigned any kind of rights and benefits. The findings were made based on the following observations:

- Remuneration paid to drivers for the work they do is fixed by Uber and the drivers have no say in it (other than by choosing when and how much to work).
- The notional freedom to charge a passenger less than the fare set by Uber is of no possible benefit to drivers.
- Uber also fixes the amount of its own "service fee" which it deducts from the fares paid to drivers.
- Contractual terms on which drivers perform their services are dictated by Uber.
- Although drivers have the freedom to choose when and where (within the area covered by their PHV licence) to work, once a driver has logged onto the Uber app, a driver's choice about whether to accept requests for rides is constrained by Uber by imposing penalty and other restrictions. This is done by Uber in two ways:
    - One is by controlling the information provided to the driver i.e. limited passenger information shared with the driver (only name and user rating are shared)
    - Second is exercised by monitoring the driver's rate of acceptance (and cancellation) of trip requests.

The above factors do place drivers in the position of subordination to Uber.

- Uber exercises a significant degree of control over the way in which drivers deliver their services. The use of the rating system whereby passengers are asked to rate the driver after each trip and the failure of a driver to maintain a specified average rating will result in warnings and ultimately in termination of the driver's relationship with Uber.
- Uber restricts communication between passenger and driver to the minimum necessary to perform the trip and takes active steps to prevent drivers from establishing any relationship with a passenger capable of extending beyond an individual ride.
- Inability of drivers to offer a distinctive service or to set their own prices and Uber's control over all aspects of their interaction with passengers - mean

that they have little or no ability to improve their economic position through professional or entrepreneurial skills. In practice, the only way in which they can increase their earnings is by working longer hours while constantly meeting Uber's measures of performance.

In a nutshell, the Hon'ble Supreme Court upheld the principle of substance over form and highlighted the importance of the actual conduct of the parties. The Court further went on to reiterate the principles of contract and agency law, and the role that the bargaining power of parties played in this case. Based on the observations of the Court, it was always one-way traffic with Uber being the traffic controller.

Interestingly, the Hon'ble Supreme Court did not comment on the dissenting member's view. One of the three judges of the Court of Appeal dissented with the majority view.

The dissenting member chose to give a literal interpretation of the existing employment-related legislation. He consciously chose not to apply the common law approach wherein the judicial precedents make the law. His straight answer was that if the current legislation, in plain letters, does not protect the drivers then the only way is for the Parliament to amend the legislation. He specifically pointed out that the existing agreements between the stakeholders do not misstate the true relationship but that the relationship created by them is one that the law does not protect[8].

Deliveroo – Court of Appeals of the United Kingdom **[24 June 2021]**[9]

In this case, the Court of Appeals unanimously held that the riders were self-employed.

This ruling stands in opposition to the landmark gig economy ruling in the case of Uber (supra). It concluded by saying that the fact that Deliveroo's riders did not have an obligation to provide services 'personally' was a material factor to reach this conclusion. This is based on the definition of 'worker' discussed in Para 7.1.1 above.

It will be interesting to see the fate of this case if this case reaches the Supreme Court

Pimlico Plumbers and another (Appellants) v Smith (Respondent) – Supreme Court of the United Kingdom **[13 June 2018]**[10]

Similar to what the Hon'ble Supreme Court held in the case of Uber (*supra*), it was concluded that the plumber was not self-employed but a worker under the prescribed definition of 'worker' discussed in Para 7.1.1 above.

---

8. *https://www.karnikgulati.com/a-rap-on-the-knuckles-for-uber-by-the-uk-supreme-court-what-it-means-for-the-gig-economy-and-its-potential-impact-in-the-indian-context/*
9. *The Independent Workers Union Of Great Britain (Appellant) and The Central Arbitration Committee (Respondent) and Roofoods Ltd T/A Deliveroo (Interested Party) [(2021) EWCA Civ 952]*
10. [2018] UKSC 29.

V.1.2. Australia

Ms. Amita Gupta v. Uber Eats – Fair Work Commission (Full Bench ruling) [21 April 2020][11]

This case involves an unfair dismissal claim of an employee who was minutes late in delivering an order.

The fair work commission ('FWC'), in this case, held that the rider is not an employee. It acknowledged that Uber does have control over the rider but only soft control. The key factors considered while reaching this conclusion include own assets like vehicle and personal phone.

After this ruling, many believed that the bench missed the chance to dig deep and look through the arrangement between Uber Eats and its drivers. However, as expected, aggrieved with this ruling, the gig worker approached the Federal Court of Australia (FCA) where Uber Eats faced certain uncomfortable questions. It is believed[12] that the FCA has concluded hearing the matter and reserved its judgment, but Uber Eats played smart and decided to settle this matter out of court with the driver rather than fighting it further and risking a negative ruling that could be used as a precedent in other similar cases.

Rajab Suliman v. Rasier Pacific Pty Ltd (Fair Work Commission) [12 July 2019][13]

This case also involved an unfair dismissal claim wherein the petitioner's access to the Uber platform was revoked. The petitioner argued that he was a casual employee, not a permanent employee, but nevertheless entitled to an unfair dismissal claim.

The FWC applied a multi-factor test as tabulated in Table 1 above and concluded that the petitioner is not an employee of Uber.

Klooger v. Foodora Australia Pty Ltd (Fair Work Commission) [16 November 2018][14]

This case also involved an unfair dismissal claim whose contract was terminated with immediate effect. In this case, FWC by applying the multi-factor test as tabulated in Table 1 above concluded that the petitioner is an employee.

---

11. [2020] FWCFB 1698.
12. *https://www.theguardian.com/technology/2020/dec/30/uber-eats-avoids-landmark-ruling-on-workers-status-by-settling-case-with-delivery-rider*
13. [2019] FWC 4807.
14. [2018] FWC 6836.

V.1.3. Canada

***Canadian Union of Postal Workers (CUPW) v. Foodora Inc* (Ontario Labour Relations Board) [25 February 2020][15]**

The Canadian Union of Postal Workers filed an application to be the exclusive bargaining agent for the couriers of Foodora Inc. in Toronto and Mississauga. The question was whether the couriers were dependent contractors, and thus covered by the Labour Relations Act, or independent contractors, who would be ineligible to be represented by a union.

Canadian law provides that individuals may be entitled to collective bargaining even if they are not common law employees but are instead dependent contractors.

The Board found that the couriers were dependent contractors and thus able to join a union.

V.1.4. France

***Mr. X v. Uber France and Uber BV* (Labour Chamber of the Court of Cassation) [4 March 2020][16]**

Mr. X, the driver for Uber BV since October 12, 2016, was permanently de-platformed in April 2017. He filed a claim seeking to reclassify his contract as an employment contract and sought back pay and termination indemnities.

The decision of the court turned on the question of whether the driver was in a relationship of permanent legal subordination with regard to the principal. This is demonstrated when there is "the performance of a job under the authority of an employer who has the power to give orders and instructions, to oversee performance thereof and to sanction the subordinate for any breaches." The court further explained that working within an organized service may constitute subordination where the employer unilaterally determines the terms and conditions of performing the job.

This case was decided in favour of the driver holding him to be an employee of Uber. The factors considered by the tribunal in arriving at this conclusion are similar to the ones discussed by the Hon'ble Supreme Court of the UK in the case of Uber (*supra*).

V.1.5. USA

***Dynamex Operations W., Inc. v. Superior Court* (Supreme Court of California) [30 April 2018][17]**

This case was related to minimum wages wherein the Hon'ble Supreme Court of California proposed the ABC Test which puts the onus on the hirer to prove that

15. *Case No: 1346-19-R.*
16. *Ruling No. 374.*
17. (2018) 4 Cal. 5th 903.

the hiree is not an employee. The ABC test is a three-pointer test wherein all the following conditions must be satisfied.

- The worker is free from control and direction;
- The worker performs work that is outside the usual course of the hiring in the entity's business; and
- The worker is customarily engaged in an independent business of the same nature

V.1.6. India

The Officer In-Charge, Sub-Regional Appellants Provident Fund Office & Anr. v. M/s. Godavari Garments Limited **(Supreme Court) [24 July 2019][18]**

This case was to decide whether the women workers engaged by the respondent who used their own sewing machines and worked from home to prepare garments, would qualify as employees under the Employees Provident Fund and Miscellaneous Provisions Act ('EPF Act').

Contentions of the respondent

- It did not exercise any supervisory control over the workers.
- Sewing machines used by the female workers were owned by the workers themselves.
- The women worked from their homes and not at the production centers of the respondent.
- Work to be performed by the workers could be done by their relatives or any other person on their behalf.

Decision of the Court and reasoning

- Definition of an employee under the EPF Act is wide enough to include any person engaged, either directly or indirectly, in connection with the work of the establishment.
- The respondent had the absolute right to reject the garments, in case of any defects, and thus, it was held that the control and supervision test was met.
- The fact that the workers stitched garments at home or were paid wages by the respondent on a per-piece basis was held to not result in any difference to the arrangement.

---

18. Civil Appeal No. 5821 OF 2019.

The Indian Federation of App-based Transport Workers (IFAT) v. Union of India[19]

A petition has been filed by IFAT in the Supreme Court urging the Court to direct the Central Government to extend social security benefits to gig workers and platform workers engaged by aggregators like Uber, Swiggy, Zomato, and other similar aggregators.

The matter is still pending before the Court and is listed for the next hearing on 11 April 2022.[20]

Table 2. Summary of Case Law Discussed

Country	Issue	Parties Involved	Date	Ruling	Forum
United Kingdom	Equal rights such as minimum wages, annual paid leaves, and other similar benefits	Uber BV and others	19 February 2021	Worker with limited rights.	Supreme Court
	Misclassification	Deliveroo	24 June 2021	Self-employed	Court of Appeal
	Unfair dismissal claim	Pimlico Plumbers	13 June 2018	Worker with limited rights.	Supreme Court
Australia	Unfair dismissal claim	Uber Eats	21 April 2020	Not an employee	Fair Work Commission (Full Bench ruling)
		Rasier Pacific Pty Ltd	12 July 2019	Not an employee. Applied multi-factor test.	Fair Work Commission
		Foodora	16 November 2018	Employee. Applied multi-factor test.	Fair Work Commission
Canada	Dependent contractor or independent contractor	Foodora	25 February 2020	Dependent contractor	Ontario Labour Relations Board

19. *Diary No.- 22576 – 2021 filed on 20 September 2021.*

20. *As per the website of The Supreme Court of India [Last accessed on 18 March 2022].*

Country	Issue	Parties Involved	Date	Ruling	Forum
France	Principle of subordination	Uber	4 March 2020	Employee	Labour Chamber of the Court of Cassation
USA	Minimum wages	Dynamex Operations	30 April 2018	Employee. Introduced ABC test.	Supreme Court of California
India	Application of EPF	Godavari Garments	24 July 2019	Employee.	Supreme Court
	Social security benefits to gig workers and platform workers	Indian Federation of App-based Transport Workers	Still pending before the Court	N.A.	Supreme Court

Closely observing the above, it may be concluded that, while low-skilled workers have higher chances of being classified as employees or workers with limited benefits, high-skilled workers/freelancers are more likely to fall under the self-employed category.

V.2. Authorities' response on classification/benefits[21]

Across the globe, various efforts are being made to respond to the growth of gig work and the corresponding worker protection and classification issues. The efforts range from classifying gig workers as almost full-time employees to not adequately recognizing gig work in those terms. Many countries are inclined to treat gig workers as employees with limited benefits, while only selected workers are recognized as full-time. What emerges is that there are no straight jacket formula to distinguish between a full-time worker and a gig worker. The distinction continues to evolve as various relevant issues continue to be identified with consequent policy measures varying accordingly. Some of these are illustrated below.

V.2.1. USA

US Labour Secretary indicated a shift in stance towards gig workers and treating them as employees.[22]

The ABC test proposed by the California Supreme Court in the case of Dynamex (supra) was codified in September 2019 in California. However, the companies like

21. *https://media-publications.bcg.com/India-Gig-Economy-Report.pdf.*
22. *Reuters: 29 April 2021.*

Uber, Lyft, and other similar companies continued to misclassify workers. For reasons unknown, such companies succeeded in getting Proposition 22 ('Prop 22') passed in terms of which workers are treated as independent contractors. However, Prop 22 was recently struck off by the local court in 2021.

V.2.2. UK

The UK stresses the responsibility of employers to provide benefits and provides rights to gig workers to request permanent roles and paid time off.

V.2.3. China

China does not formally define or recognize gig workers in its employee classifications.

V.2.4. Australia

Introduced the Fair Work Amendment to ensure that all workers are protected under the Fair Work Act, 2009 in terms of labor standards, minimum wages, and conditions established under the act. The Making Australia More Equal Bill, 2018 (which includes the Fair Work Amendment), would enable the Fair Work Commission to apply certain wages, terms, and conditions to workers, even where they are not classified as 'employees'.

V.2.5. Canada

Ontario is expected to introduce a bill granting relevant rights and protections to gig workers - considering introducing the ABC test proposed by California SC.

V.2.6. India

India introduced the Code on Social Security 2020, which provides that gig and platform workers, albeit not employees, may be provided with certain social security benefits, including life and disability cover, accident insurance, health and maternity benefits, old age protection, crèche and childcare services, and other benefits.

It further provides that the Central Government will constitute a Social Security Fund for gig and platform workers, and aggregators will contribute to such fund between 1% to 2% of their turnover with a ceiling of 5% of the amount paid to gig and platform workers.

Gig and platform workers have been defined separately and they fall outside the traditional employer-employee relationship.

V.2.7. Other countries

Countries like Denmark, Italy, and Spain have also recognized gig workers as employees.

VI. The Tax Conundrum

While it took more than two decades for organizations like the OECD and the United Nations to reach a global consensus on how to tax the digital economy, it is only a matter of time that taxation of the gig economy becomes a challenge for policymakers worldwide. What may be said is that the taxation of the digital economy, in its current shape, is work-in-progress, and the proposed solutions are generally too complex to understand, leave alone comply with or administer. Only time will tell how effective the proposed solutions are.

Selected issues that could potentially pose major challenges for the policymakers are discussed below.

VI.1. How to bring a gig worker into the tax ambit

The above discussion on the misclassification of gig workers points towards how gig-related income should be taxed under the income tax law. It is straightforward to bring gig workers under the tax ambit if they are considered employees under the tax laws since the employers are usually responsible for withholding tax on salaries. The challenge occurs when gig workers are not considered employees under the tax laws but self-employed. Who, in that case, should be made responsible for withholding tax, or will the tax authorities rely solely on self-assessment reporting and payment? Should platforms be responsible for withholding tax in such a case? The answer may be in the affirmative in theoretical terms, but what happens if there is no platform involved at all, that is, what happens if it is a peer-to-peer transaction?

These alternatives may be summarised as follows:

(i) If a gig worker is considered an employee, the Employer will be responsible for WHT.

(ii) If a gig worker is not considered an employee, the question arises as to how do we ensure WHT? If a platform is involved, then should the platform be responsible for WHT?

Further complications may arise. For example, while a platform could be made responsible for withholding tax, what happens if the platform is a non-resident? How can one enforce compliance with WHT provisions on a non-resident? This aspect has been discussed later under cross-border considerations.

Alternatively, can platforms be asked to collect relevant information from sellers/service providers registered on their platforms? This way the tax authorities can send notices and reminders to the relevant sellers/service providers to ensure compliance with the tax law.

(i) If no platform is involved, can a banking transaction tax be explored?

A case study considered below may be useful to understand such cases in which an alternative solution may be required. Also, a solution is proposed below to address such transactions.

(ii) What happens when it is a peer-to-peer transaction?

While a transaction between a gig worker and an entity (company, firm, any other non-individual entity) may be subjected to a WHT mechanism, but what happens when a peer-to-peer transaction takes place and there is no platform involved at all. Different scenarios and their implications from an Indian perspective have been captured below and, thereafter, potential solutions to bring them into the tax ambit have been discussed.

VI.1.1. Head of income

The fundamental challenge is to decide the head of income under which gig-related income should be chargeable to tax. Based on the above discussion on misclassification, it is worth considering classifying gig workers for the purposes of labour and allied laws differently from tax laws. This reflects the fact that income is generally taxed under a category or head of income.

For example, in India, there are five heads of income under which incomes are classified. The income heads are income from salary (employment income), income from house property (rental income), income from profession or business (business or professional related income), income from capital gains (sale of immovable property, securities, and other assets) and income from other sources (residuary head). They differ from definitions under the labour or allied laws. Therefore, for income tax purposes, gig income must be classified differently. The gig income classification under income tax should depend on whether gig income comprises a primary or secondary source of income for the gig worker. Thus,

Gig Work	Head of income
Primary source of income	Business income
Secondary source of income	Business income or Income from other sources(?)

Assuming that a gig worker's primary source of income is income from full-time employment, and gig-related income is only a secondary source of income, can his/her employer be made responsible for withholding tax on the side-hustle?[23] This could be done by mandating disclosure from employees about their income from gig work.

VII. Cross-border Tax Issues

Cross-border tax issues pose a real challenge. Gig work-related taxation within the domestic borders is at a nascent stage but could at least be addressed through the WHT mechanism. When a transaction is cross-borders and, more so, when it is a peer-to-peer transaction, the correct tax treatment becomes more complex. Some of the issues that a cross-border transaction presents in the case of the gig economy are discussed below.

23. *Side-hustle means a piece of work or a job that you get paid for doing in addition to doing your main job.*

VII.1 Relevance of physical presence or fixed base in the extant OECD and UN Model Tax Convention (MTC)

The extant OECD MTC 2017 does not have a separate article for independent personal services since it considers it to be covered by Article 7 (Business Profits)[24]. The OECD endorses the concept of necessarily having a physical presence/fixed base to tax independent personal services. However, in some countries, including India, the payer's residence or utilization of service is the deciding factor to tax services. In India, therefore, the location of the service provider is not relevant for taxability under the Indian tax laws.

On the other hand, UN MTC 2021 continues to have a separate article for independent personal services (Article 14). While the UN acknowledges the view of certain emerging economies to consider source-based principle for taxing services, it continues to have the requirement of physical presence/fixed base.

Given that the OECD and UN have acknowledged the challenges presented by the digital economy from the perspective of businesses mainly comprising corporates, it is time to accept that, with the rise of the gig economy, the relevance of having a physical presence/fixed base is diminished.

VII.1.1. Using freelancers to avoid PE exposure

Businesses use freelancers to avoid PE exposure in the garb of disguised independence of freelancers. This has been a common phenomenon wherein businesses, instead of sending their full-time employees, use freelancers to avoid potential PE exposure in the source jurisdiction. They can claim a lack of control over the disguised freelancers, hence, the absence of a PE.

VII.1.2. Making platforms operating across borders without physical market presence responsible for WHT compliance

It is difficult to enforce legislative requirements in markets with no physical presence without international cooperation. Furthermore, data protection guidelines will also come into play if the platforms are required to maintain the details of sellers/service providers using their platforms.

VII.1.3. Invoking the GAAR (substance over form) principle

An entity that is disguising a full-time worker as an independent contractor, or where businesses are using freelancers to avoid PE exposure in the source jurisdiction, whether and how GAAR or the "substance over form" principle could be invoked on such entities needs consideration.

24. *Until 2000, the OECD MTC had a separate article for independent personal services (Article 14).*

VIII. How Tax Administrations are Approaching the Gig Economy

Given that the gig economy's rise is relatively recent, it is crucial that the stakeholders, including gig workers themselves, the platforms and intermediaries, the direct payer (in the case of peer-to-peer transactions) are made aware of the tax implications of the income derived therefrom. Furthermore, it is also important for the stakeholders to recognize their responsibility to pay the final taxes due, either through self-assessment by the gig workers themselves or through the tried and tested WHT mechanism wherein the payer or platform/intermediary is responsible for withholding the applicable tax and deposit it with the tax authorities.

VIII.1. Country practices

Various countries have been taking measures to bring the gig economy under the tax ambit. Examples are:

- Countries like India, Italy, and Mexico have already made platforms/intermediaries responsible for withholding tax on the service providers/sellers using their platforms.
- Countries like Denmark, France, Greece, Hungary, Ireland, Spain, and the USA have a practice of educating and engaging with the stakeholders.
- Countries like Australia, Greece, Italy, Japan, and Norway run awareness campaigns to make the gig workers aware of their responsibilities of reporting appropriate gig-related income and paying applicable taxes.
- Countries like France, Norway, and Spain also collect relevant information from platforms. This could be quite challenging in the case of non-resident platforms/intermediaries. Challenges include data protection, dealing with unstructured data, and last, but not least, such efforts are a resource-intensive exercise.
- For cross-border transactions, relevant information may be collected from a counterpart tax administration through the exchange of information (EOI) clause in tax treaties or separate tax information exchange agreements (TIEA). However, reflecting current practices in EOI or TIEA, no roving inquiry can be made, and the information sought should also be justifiably relevant.

VIII.2. Indian approach

India has been proactive when dealing with the taxation of emerging bases and it is no different in the taxation of the gig economy. Two new sections, namely section 194-O and section 194M, were introduced in the Indian Income Tax Act, 1961 ('IITA') to, *inter alia*, deal with the taxation of the gig economy.

However, the aforesaid WHT provisions only address the taxation issue for resident service providers/sellers, as WHT on gig workers providing services to business entities is taken care of by the existing WHT provisions, enshrined in section 195 of the IITA read with section 40(a)(i), wherein the relevant expenditure is disallowed for tax purposes unless the applicable withholding tax is deducted and deposited with the Indian government. For non-resident (individual) service providers, a peer-to-peer transaction is a matter that requires attention.

In what follows, we discuss existing WHT provisions, substantive tax provisions for the taxability of gig-related income, and a case study summarizing the Indian tax landscape for gig workers.

VIII.2.1. Withholding taxes

If the transaction involves e-commerce platform [Section 194-O]

Features of Section 194-O:

- Obligates the e-commerce platform operator to withhold tax at source at the rate of 1% on the gross amount (sales/service consideration).
- In the case where there is no PAN, the rate is increased to 5%.
- The platform can be a resident or a non-resident.
- The service provider/seller can only be a resident.
- Amount paid directly to service provider/seller deemed collected by the platform for the purpose of WHT.
- This section is not applicable where the seller/service provider is an individual or a HUF and the gross amount of sales or services or both is up to INR 0.50 million (approx. USD 7,000) and the recipient has furnished his PAN or Aadhaar number.

It may be important to highlight a pending Writ Petition in this section. This section has a deeming fiction that deems that the platform has collected the sales consideration even though it has been directly collected by the seller/service provider. This has created havoc since it is a practical challenge to comply with this deeming fiction where a platform has not collected any sales consideration. Due to this practical challenge, one of the platform taxpayers has approached the Hon'ble Calcutta High Court through a Writ Petition[25] on this issue.

---

25. *MJunction Services Ltd. and Anr. (WPO/441/2021) – Calcutta High Court [Last accessed on 18 March 2022] [https://services.ecourts.gov.in/ecourtindiaHC/cases/display_pdf.php?filename=QnBUxJ6a3gIx%2B5SFrUiAoPAbwETTGASAznoLQJYoJyN69%2FzN%2FyQrhGJCTp0B15qz&caseno=WPO/441/2021&cCode=1&appFlag=].*

If the transaction does not involve any e-commerce platform [Section 194M]

Features of Section 194M:

- Applicable only to individual or HUF payers where the payee is a resident. The payee could be an individual or a non-individual. Since this chapter is about the gig economy, the service provider will always be an individual.
- WHT rate is 5% on the entire gross amount.
- Minimum threshold prescribed is INR 5 million, i.e., no WHT if the payment is up to INR 5 million.

This section intends to cover peer-to-peer transactions; however, the minimum threshold seems to be a little too high to cover "side hustlers" or small operators. Furthermore, this section is only applicable to resident service providers and not to non-residents. This could be because the existing section 195 is potentially wide enough to cover any payments made to a non-resident. However, section 195 is usually not applied to individual service recipients since it will put an undue burden on individuals to comply with WHT provisions. With the rise of the gig economy, this aspect must be examined further to avoid tax leaks on peer-to-peer transactions.

VIII.2.2. Final tax liability

While WHT should ensure that the gig economy transactions are brought into the tax ambit, it is also important to provide a simplified tax reporting structure for individuals who want to file their return of income. In this section, we discuss the options available to individuals for computing their income.

Section 44AD and section 44ADA are presumptive sections for computing income from business and profession, respectively.

Section 44AD is applicable to business income wherein a flat 6% or 8% (depending on the fulfilment of prescribed conditions) of gross receipts is deemed to be the income of the taxpayer. This presumptive section is only applicable where the turnover or gross receipts do not exceed INR 20 million.

Section 44ADA is applicable to professional income wherein a flat 50% of gross receipts is deemed to be the income of the taxpayer. This presumptive section is only applicable where the turnover or gross receipts do not exceed INR 5 million.

There are no audit obligations unless the income is claimed to be lower than the limit prescribed under section 44AD or 44ADA.

VIII.2.3. Case study

Table 3. Case study on the taxability of gig workers in India

Service Provider/ Seller	Mode	Service Recipient/ Buyer	Legal status of Service Recipient/ Buyer	Implications
Resident Individual	Platform *(R/NR – Indifferent)*	R/NR – Indifferent	Individual	Platform responsible for WHT under the new regime (194-O)
			Non-Individual	Platform responsible for WHT under the new regime (194-O)
	Direct	R/NR – Indifferent	Individual	Services (Various sections) – Recipient liable to WHT only if recipient's turnover exceeds specified limit (INR 10 mn - USD 0.14 mn/INR 5 mn - USD 0.07 mn). Transaction amount limits are separate. Exception in certain cases if services are for personal consumption. Could lead to litigation in the Gig economy? What is personal consumption? I take content writing services for my personal website. No revenue was generated. Just a knowledge-sharing platform. Goods (194Q) – Recipient liable to WHT only if recipient's turnover exceeds the specified limit (INR 100 mn - USD 1.40 mn) and

Service Provider/ Seller	Mode	Service Recipient/ Buyer	Legal status of Service Recipient/ Buyer	Implications
				purchase value exceeds the specified limit (INR 5mn ~ USD 0.07 mn).
			Non-Individual	Services (Various sections) – Liable to WHT subject to transaction amount limits. Goods (194Q) – Same as for individuals above.
Non-Resident Individual	Platform	Resident	Individual	Payment to platform *Platform = Resident* → New regime (194-O) NOT APPLICABLE. Are other WHT sections applicable? Depending on goods/ services. *Platform = Non-Resident* → New regime (194-O) NOT APPLICABLE. Section 195 shall be applicable? Depending on goods/ services. Treaty applicable. Payment directly to service provider/seller Section 195 shall be applicable? Treaty applicable.
			Non-Individual	New regime (194-O) NOT APPLICABLE. Section 195 shall be applicable? Treaty applicable.

Service Provider/ Seller	Mode	Service Recipient/ Buyer	Legal status of Service Recipient/ Buyer	Implications
		Non-Resident	Either	No nexus. Can nexus be established if the platform is R in India?
	Direct	Resident	Individual	New regime (194-O) NOT APPLICABLE. Section 195 shall be applicable? Treaty applicable. Can banking transaction tax be explored in this case?
			Non-Individual	New regime (194-O) NOT APPLICABLE. Section 195 shall be applicable? Treaty applicable.
		Non-Resident	Either	No nexus.

Source: Author

Overall, India seems to have covered reasonable ground to bring the gig economy under the tax ambit at least for residents. A lot of work needs to be carried out in the case of non-residents.

IX. OECD and European Union's (EU) Work on Gig Economy

The OECD, of late, has circulated certain model rules for reporting by platform operators with respect to sellers in the sharing and gig economy[26]. In light of the above, the OECD has developed a transparency framework consisting of the following components:

26. A sharing economy refers to an economy based on the sharing, acquiring and providing goods and services through the facilitation of an online platform. *https://www.oecd.org/tax/exchange-of-tax-information/model-rules-for-reporting-by-platform-operators-with-respect-to-sellers-in-the-sharing-and-gig-economy.htm [Last accessed on 15 March 2022].*

IX.1. OECD Model Rules for reporting by platform operators with respect to sellers in the sharing and gig economy [published on 3 July 2020][27]

These model rules require digital platforms to collect information on the income realised by those that offer accommodation, transport, and personal services through platforms and report the information to tax authorities. These rules are designed to help taxpayers to comply with their tax obligation while ensuring a level playing field for traditional businesses in the key sectors of the sharing and gig economy.

By providing a standardised reporting regime, these model rules help to minimise burdens on platform sellers and digital platform operators, which might be high in jurisdictions with multiple requirements.

IX.1.1. Code of Conduct [published on 3 July 2020][28]

A draft model code of conduct was originally included in the OECD's The Sharing and Gig Economy: Effective Taxation of Platform Sellers (OECD, 2019[29]) and subsequently revised after further consultation. The Code of Conduct intends to facilitate a possible standard approach of cooperation between administrations and platforms on providing information and support to platform sellers on their tax obligations while minimising compliance burdens published by the OECD Forum on Tax Administration, the Code of Conduct aims to supplement the model reporting rules for sellers in the sharing and gig economy in instances where sellers are not subject to reporting under the model rules, for example, where the transactions are out of scope, or the jurisdiction has not yet implemented the model rules.

IX.1.2. Model Reporting Rules for Digital Platforms: International Exchange Framework and Optional Module for Sale of Goods [Published on 22 June 2021][30]

Reflecting the interest of several jurisdictions in permitting the extension of the scope of the Model Rules to the sale of goods and rental of means of transportation, the OECD has developed an optional module allowing such jurisdictions to implement the Model Rules with an extended scope. Exchange of the information

---

27. *https://www.oecd.org/tax/exchange-of-tax-information/model-rules-for-reporting-by-platform-operators-with-respect-to-sellers-in-the-sharing-and-gig-economy.pdf [Last accessed on 15 March 2022].*
28. *https://www.oecd.org/tax/forum-on-tax-administration/publications-and-products/code-of-conduct-co-operation-between-tax-administrations-and-sharing-and-gig-economy-platforms.pdf [Last accessed on 15 March 2022].*
29. *https://www.oecd.org/ctp/the-sharing-and-gig-economy-effective-taxation-of-platform-sellers-574b61f8-en.htm [Last accessed on 15 March 2022].*
30. *https://www.oecd.org/tax/exchange-of-tax-information/model-reporting-rules-for-digital-platforms-international-exchange-framework-and-optional-module-for-sale-of-goods.pdf [Last accessed on 15 March 2022].*

under the Model Rules is operationalised by an international legal framework in the form of the Multilateral Competent Authority Agreement.

IX.2. European Union work on gig economy[31]

On 22 March 2021, the Council of the European Union ('the Council') adopted new rules revising the Directive on Administrative Cooperation in the Field of Taxation ('Council Directive 2011/16/EU' or 'DAC') to extend the EU tax transparency rules reporting by digital platforms on their sellers ('DAC7').

It obliges digital EU and non-EU platform operators that facilitate the provision of relevant domestic and cross-border activities to collect and share data about the sellers to which they offer their facilitation services. This data includes the seller's name, registered office address, tax identification number, VAT number, date of birth, residence country of the seller, the sales price, and the amount(s) retained by the platform. The relevant activities in scope include the letting of immovable property, personal services (e.g., babysitting), sales of goods, and renting out any mode of transport.

X. Conclusion

The effects of the gig economy — on all stakeholders including workers, customers, taxpayers, and governments —continue to be more widely understood., Hopefully, as the gig economy grows, clearer rules, regulations, tax policies, and better compliance will emerge.

The topmost issue to address is misclassification which is mainly due to outmoded laws that are insufficient to deal with the evolving work trend. It is essential to ensure that the relevant laws are amended to provide equal protection to gig workers and create a level-playing field through tax provisions (including WHT provisions) whether it is income from employment or gig-related income. This change will leave no incentive for the stakeholders to misclassify. Another solution that could be adopted, at least in the short run, is the intensification of judicial activism – a plethora of court actions addressing the issue of misclassification to replicate what is happening currently.

Having said that, it is important for the administrative authorities to balance their acts to ensure no unnecessary burden is placed upon the hirers who help generate much-needed employment in the economy and upon hirees who will pay tax on gig-related income. Not letting the workers be oppressed by the hirers or letting stakeholders negatively impact the tax revenue are also major cautions to keep a vigil over.

31. *http://kluwertaxblog.com/2021/04/16/the-global-tax-reporting-framework-for-digital-platforms-in-the-sharing-and-gig-economy-importance-for-tax-administrations/ [Last accessed on 15 March 2022].*

It is important to have easy-to-understand and easy-to-implement procedures to ensure higher compliance. Concepts like deemed income, used by India, or standard deductions will ensure higher compliance and greater tax revenue.

Before implementing any solution, it is important to ensure that the monetary and cognitive resources required to bring the gig economy under fair taxation are commensurate with the benefits expected from it by the tax administrations.

Going forward, several other issues remain to tackle. For example, it is critical to ensure uniformity across jurisdictions. The work done so far by the OECD and EU perhaps needs to be sharpened. First, it is worth exploring whether the classifications for labour and tax laws should be the same. Second, while countries such as India, Italy, and Mexico have taken relevant steps to bring the gig economy under the tax ambit, they currently address only the local gig economy,[32] and, need to bring in cross-border transactions.

Third, an effective method of covering cross-border peer-to-peer transactions should be explored. Can a Banking Transaction Tax (BTT) be explored? Not to replace the income tax with a BTT but to apply a 'modified BTT' on all international transactions. In short, this will be an improvised WHT which the banks would be responsible for withholding.

One eye of the policymakers, tax administrations, and the tax fraternity, concerned with the low tax contribution of the digital economy should be open to keep the Pillar One and Pillar Two concerns alive to ensure and raise global tax participation by the digital economy. Indeed there is the 135-member country grouping called the Inclusive Framework (IF) of the OECD that could do that. The other eye should be on newly emerging, dynamic sectors such as the gig economy and artificial intelligence before they too become out of reach. The global tax community was slow in dealing with the digital economy. It should not repeat such tendencies for the emerging future challenges of international taxation.

32. *The Author acknowledges that he is unaware of the exact tax provisions applicable on platforms in Italy and Mexico and, hence, would abstain from commenting on it.*

REJOINDER

Krupa Venkatesh

India's Gig Economy – Current Outlook and Potential

India's job data on the gig sector has long remained outdated and inadequate. The data for about 25% of the workforce employed in the formal sector is readily available from sources such as provident fund and pension registrations and reports filed by employers. However, for the 75% of the workforce employed in the informal sector, data points are sketchy. The need to collect data had accentuated during the pandemic when out-of-job migrant workers had to leave cities because there was no mechanism to bring them under government support programs.

To collect data on workers in the informal sector, the Indian government launched the 'E-SHRAM' portal in August 2021 and offered insurance and other social security benefits to those signing in. This should help the government to devise targeted social security programs and ensure that the benefits reach the correct beneficiaries. So far, 249 million workers have registered on the portal[33].

The gig economy is not new to India; contract labourers in the construction industry, and self-employed semi-skilled workers have always been around. However, the digitalization of services has changed its composition and increased participation in the gig economy. A 2021 BCG-Dell Foundation report pegs the potential of non-farm sectors to provide about 90 million jobs and add about 1.25% ($ 250 bn) to India's GDP[34]. The adoption of technology-based ride-hailing, food delivery, and logistics apps has contributed in large measure to the growth of the gig economy, especially during the pandemic that made heroes of delivery boys in urban areas. The pandemic and the work-from-home culture, followed by the hybrid work culture have contributed, in no small measure to altering the composition of the gig economy. The constituents of the economy are no longer delivery boys or drivers but also include white-collared professionals. As Gulati shows in his chapter, China and India are leaders in the gig sector in a cross-country comparison.

In the US, a record number of professionals have quit their office jobs beginning in early 2021, prompting economists to call the phenomenon the Great Resignation or the Big Quit. According to the Bureau of Labor Statistics, about 33 million people or a fifth of the US workforce have quit since April 2021. Reasons cited are early retirement, better jobs, moving to jobs offering flexibility, caregiving responsibilities, investing in reskilling, and better work-life balance. There are differing perspectives on whether the Great Resignation is truly all that 'Great' since

33. *https://www.eshram.gov.in/.*
34. *https://www.bcg.com/en-in/unlocking-gig-economy-in-india.*

large numbers of US workers have been 'quitting' for years. The highest percentage of quits of 6.4% is in the leisure and hospitality sector which, in any case, has endured the pandemic and will probably be amongst the last sectors to recover. Regardless, the flexibility offered by the work-from-home (WFH) policies that corporates were forced to adopt is certainly a major factor influencing workers to move jobs. It could mean that workers favour similar jobs that offer flexible hours or work environments such as WFH over regular go-to-office jobs; This could be more attractive than job security alone. The growth of platforms like Upwork in the US stands testimony to the changing definitions of fulfilment in careers, especially among young millennials.

The gig economy in India can be broadly represented as follows:

Diagram 1.

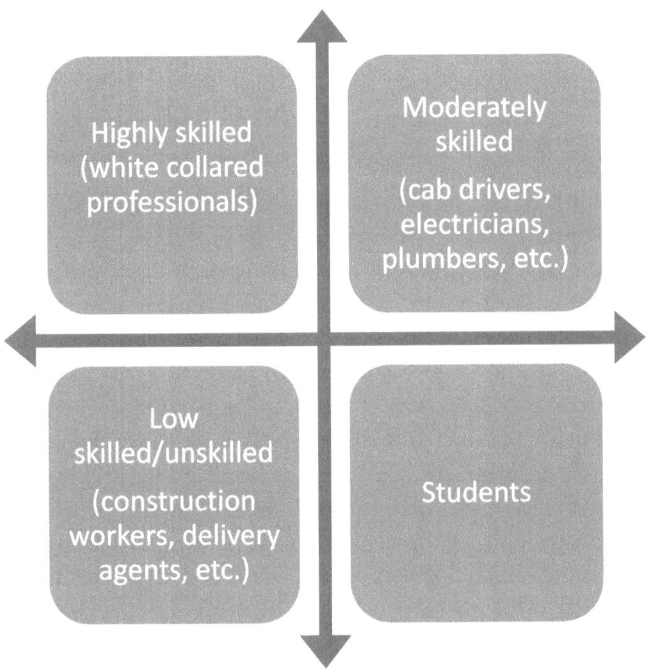

Source: workflexi.in

ASSOCHAM has predicted that the gig economy will grow at a CAGR of 17% to $ 455 billion by 2023. Experts believe that for most organizations, conventional hiring may be outdated and that they may increasingly prefer having a pool of gig workers, which can be more cost-effective. Start-ups have shown the way in drawing white-collar talent from the gig economy; they prefer to hire even critical resources like CFOs on a contract or on a 'virtual' basis as it is now termed until they reach the desired scale. It is not uncommon for corporations to hire special talent for niche operations on contract.

Women looking to get back to work after a break or looking for flexi-options are likely to drive the growth of the gig economy in the white-collar segment. The emergence of app-based services has increased customer confidence in the quality of services in the segments that employ moderately skilled and low-skilled gig workers, not just because of a certain level of perceived accountability but because it also offers features like background verification and service ratings, such information being critical for this sector. The migrant urban population that does not speak the local language or is not familiar with the local landscape, may also use these services confidently. Typical examples are ride-hailing applications, or aggregators that offer home or personalized service enablers. These tech-based services have completely altered the way these services are rendered in Tier I metros and now in Tier II cities and offer a safety net for local users of the services. They are useful even for settlers who do not speak the local language or even senior citizens since the aggregators or platforms collect complete background information from service providers before signing them on. This is generally not the case if an individual were to employ these services on his own. For those registering on these platforms, the reach is wider, and they gain access to a larger base of customers, in contrast to the traditional modes of seeking work largely confined to a local area or word-of-mouth references.

An Aon survey[35] revealed that 49% of the 145 companies surveyed had already employed gig workers and 65% planned to increase hiring gig workers in the next 2-5 years. Table 1 shows sector-wise trends in gig hiring.

Table 1. % of companies looking to hire gig workers – by sector

Industry	2020	Future (2-5 years)
FMCG – Pharma	15%	69%
BFSI	32%	56%
Manufacturing	35%	65%
Technology & BPO	57%	60%
Services	47%	76%

Source: AON-'Decoding the Gig Economy'

35. 'Decoding the Gig Economy'.

In sectors such as technology, BPO, and services that can be performed remotely, hiring from the gig economy can be borderless and could represent the true democratization of contractual employment. It is not a surprise, therefore, that the number of freelancing platforms has significantly increased – from 80 in 2009 to 330 in 2021 and not just start-ups, but also Fortune 500 companies among their clientele.

As the gig economy absorbs those that lost their jobs due to the pandemic and continues growing, it is crucial that the government protects the interests of gig workers by providing healthcare benefits, and insurance covers – life, accidental, and disability via the Social Security Code, the initial steps for which were taken in 2019. The key is to balance the regulation – too much of it can destroy the attractiveness of hiring from the gig economy, and too little can lead to exploitation of the gig workers – especially those in the blue-collar, or low and unskilled segments and those where intermediaries are involved. But this tightrope must be walked, since this is too big a constituent of the workforce to be ignored, and there is potentially too much to lose.

PART B

CONTINUING CHALLENGES IN TAX STRUCTURE AND ADMINISTRATION IN INDIA

CHAPTER 7

Tax Challenges from Financial Innovations: A Case Study of Special Purpose Acquisition Companies (SPACs)

Suranjali Tandon

I. Introduction

In recent years, traditional initial public offerings (IPOs) have given way to special purpose acquisition companies (SPACs) and direct listings. It is noteworthy that in 2021, SPACs based issues surged to $170 billion[1] and the money raised by SPACs in the US market was 76% of the IPO market[2]. Many companies choose a SPAC over a traditional IPO for reasons such as better price discovery and access to finance in international capital markets. Indian companies have also been listed through SPACs. This was driven by the consideration that regulations in India do not permit companies to directly list their shares in the foreign stock markets[3]. Therefore, the SPAC allows a company to merge with a listed entity abroad. The most prominent example is the SPAC-based indirect listing of Renew Power. The restriction posed by the current regulations on Indian entities from listing in a foreign market was bypassed via the merger of Renew Energy, a UK-based holding company of Renew Power, with the US-based SPAC RMGII[4].

Companies also prefer to access finance through SPAC as better valuations are available to a company for a SPAC unlike the traditional IPO route[5]. Therefore, the

1. Patturaja Murugaboopathy, *Global spac deal volumes This Year surpass total for 2020*, Reuters, (9 March 2021). https://www.reuters.com/article/us-usa-markets-spac-idUSKBN2B11UU.
2. *Ibid.*
3. Although in 2020 the Ministry of Finance announced its intent to allow direct listing, the legal amendments giving effect to the same have not yet been released.
4. *ReNew Power lists in US via SPAC, m-cap hits $4.5 billion*, The Times of India, (21 August 2021), https://timesofindia.indiatimes.com/business/india-business/renew-power-lists-in-us-via-spac-mcap-hits-4-5bn/articleshow/85607683.cms.
5. Siri Bulusu, *India's 'buoyant' startup culture shut out of global SPAC hunt*, The Economic Times, (24 April 2021), https://economictimes.indiatimes.com/markets/stocks/news/indias-buoyant-startup-culture-shut-out-of-global-spac-hunt/articleshow/82226538.cms?from=mdr.

use of SPACs in a jurisdiction will depend on the regulatory environment, including the prevailing tax system where the company operates Jurisdictions such as Cayman Islands, Luxembourg, Netherlands, and, British Virgin Islands are popular among companies looking to list a SPAC[6]. This is possible since certain international stock exchanges such as the NYSE allow foreign entities to directly list. Therefore, a SPAC provides access to capital while making it possible to locate the company in a tax-efficient jurisdiction. Thus, it is anticipated that with their growing prevalence SPACs may present tax and regulatory challenges. In recent times there has been growing concern regarding the due diligence of the sponsors[7]. The Securities Exchange Commission (SEC) launched an inquiry into SPAC deal fees, volumes, and controls banks have in place to vet the deals[8].

This chapter considers the key issue of the implications of SPAC on tax policy. As will be discussed in detail, there are emerging concerns, especially with the proposals such as Pillar two, shifts in residence through the reverse merger. To address the challenges of the complicated structure of SPAC, countries such as the United States have introduced anti-inversion rules. These rules act as a backstop to corporations shifting their residence to low-tax jurisdictions. However, like any tax provision, there are exclusions or exceptions. Regardless, the market for SPACs has thrived. In India, the application of capital gains to the offshore indirect transfer of shares adds a layer of complication. So even where the SPAC is in a low-tax jurisdiction, it is possible that the exchange of shares held by Indian residents upon the merger may be treated as capital gains taxable in India.

This chapter includes a review of the nature and lifecycle of SPACs. While doing so, it reviews the regulatory factors that encourage companies to list via SPAC while trying to understand if tax is among their main considerations. Thereafter the chapter identifies the key challenges in taxation of the gains arising from the transactions and suggests a way forward.

II. What is a Special Purpose Acquisition Company (SPAC)

The non-traditional route to raising capital is a reverse merger[9]. That is, the company does not offer an IPO but instead merges with a listed natural or cash shell

6. Cayman Island exempted companies are particularly popular among SPACs. Moreover there is no tax on capital gains, income, corporation or withholding taxes. The Use Of Cayman Islands Structures For SPAC IPOs - Corporate and Company Law - Cayman Islands (mondaq.com)
7. *2021 Report on FINRA's Examination and Risk Monitoring Program*, Financial Industry Regulatory Authority, (February 2021).
8. *SEC opens inquiry into Wall Street's blank check IPO frenzy: Reuters, citing sources*, CNBC, (24 March 2021), https://www.cnbc.com/2021/03/25/sec-opens-inquiry-into-wall-streets-blank-check-ipo-frenzy-reuters.html.
9. Going public via special purpose acquisition companies: Frogs do not turn into princes.

company[10]. Natural shells are listed companies that have gone bankrupt or have sold a large part of their assets. Cash shell companies or blank check companies do not have business operations and do not possess assets other than cash and limited investments[11]. To get investors to buy into an entity that does not have a declared investment plan, institutional investors with a successful track record are involved as sponsors who also usually manage the SPAC.

II.1. Formation of SPAC and IPO

Sponsors form a SPAC which raises capital through an IPO of the SPAC shares. The sponsors contribute a fraction of the total capital, usually around a fifth of the shares, and pay a nominal price for it.

In the US, sponsors typically receive 20% of the shares for the payment of 2.5-3% of funds or for as low as $25,000[12]. Similarly, in a SPAC issuance in Frankfurt, a sponsor receives 20% of the shares by paying EUR 136,000 for founder shares. In Amsterdam, the sponsor pays EUR 1533-90,000 for founder shares and receives anything between 10-30% of the shares[13]. Shareholders buy each unit for $10, with 20% of the shares owned by sponsors.

The SPAC is registered with the securities market regulator in the jurisdiction where it is listed. Unlike the regular IPO, SPACs do not have to undergo the kind of due diligence required of listed companies[14], this is so since SPACs do not have an operating business or tangible assets at the time of IPO[15]. However, the nature of disclosures and the regulatory environment for SPACs are evolving. For example, in the US the SPACs disclose information such as: "i) the mechanics of the securities being issued by the SPAC; (ii) the expertise of the SPAC's directors and officers; and (iii) the potential conflicts between the SPAC's sponsor and the other equity holders in the SPAC that are inherent in all current SPAC structures"[16]. This is light touch in comparison to the expansive set of disclosures that companies must make for

10. David N. Feldman, *Reverse Mergers: And Other Alternatives to Traditional IPOs*, (Bloomberg Press, 2010).
11. *What You Need to Know About SPACs – Updated Investor Bulletin*, U.S. Securities Exchange Commission, (25 March 2021), https://www.sec.gov/oiea/investor-alerts-and-bulletins/what-you-need-know-about-spacs-investor-bulletin.
12. The Spac sponsor bonanza | Financial Times (ft.com).
13. *Update: SPAC Momentum Continues in Europe with Further Listings in Amsterdam and Frankfurt and Reform in London*, Freshfields Bruckhaus Deringer LLP, (September 2021).
14. *Guidance on Special Purpose Acquisition Companies,* Regulatory Notice 08-54, FINRA, (n.d.), https://www.finra.org/rules-guidance/notices/08-54.
15. *Changes to SPACs regulation will impact European tech M&A, Out-Law Analysis,* (19 October 2021), https://www.pinsentmasons.com/out-law/analysis/changes-spacs-regulations-european-tech-ma.
16. Jonathan Milne et al., *SPACs: Disclosing Before Closing*, International Finance Corporation Review, (19 November 2021), https://www.ifcreview.com/articles/2021/november/spacs-disclosing-before-closing/.

IPOs. This has drawn the attention of the SEC, as in some cases plaintiffs claimed that SPACs have not carried out adequate due diligence on de-SPAC[17] targets and have not made adequate disclosure to shareholders[18].

At the moment, different countries have varying formal regulatory frameworks for SPACs. Apart from Singapore, the US, UK, Germany, and the Netherlands mentioned above, even India's offshore financial centre -- the International Financial Services Centre (IFSC) -- has proposed to introduce a separate regulation for SPACs[19]. These regulations specify the minimum capital requirements, reporting requirements pre- and post-merger, retail investment[20], liquidation requirements,[21] and compliance upon merger. While the US is a preferred jurisdiction for SPACs, there has been growing interest in the European market wherein Netherlands and Germany have remained significant recipients of funds[22]. The preference for the Netherlands is attributed to the regulatory flexibility, which allows SPAC shareholders to trade even after the deal is announced[23].

The clampdown by the SEC on SPACs for misclassifying the warrants as equity[24], and the growing conflict of interest between the SPACs and the underwriting or deal advising banks also contributed to the reason for the shift in SPACs to the EU[25]. Therefore, for investors, regulatory control is a significant motivation to opt for a SPAC in a particular jurisdiction. Owing to the ease of regulation, the US possessed the first mover advantage. Between 2003 and 2021 there was a massive increase in SPACs issuances in the US. The issuances increased particularly after 2016 and, in 2021, it was on account of a growth in merger activity post-Covid-19.

---

17. De-Spac is the merger between the SPAC and the company that the SPAC seeks to acquire.
18. *Id.* at 16.
19. *Consultation Paper on Proposed International Financial Services Centres Authority (Issuance and Listing of Securities) Regulations, 2021,* Press Information Bureau, (10 March 2021), https://pib.gov.in/PressReleasePage.aspx?PRID=1703854.
20. Kiyuan Wong, *Hong Kong Plans to Limit Retail Investor Access to SPACs,* Bloomberg Wealth, (10 September 2021), https://www.bloomberg.com/news/articles/2021-09-10/hong-kong-plans-to-limit-access-for-retail-investors-to-spacs.
21. Guide to Special Purpose Acquisition, Clifford Chance, (3 September 2021).
22. Tomás de Heredia et al., The SPACs Boom, Deloitte Insights, (14 July 2021), https://www2.deloitte.com/xe/en/insights/industry/financial-services/spacs-in-europe.html
23. *European SPACs Data Hub*, White and Case, (January 2021), https://www.whitecase.com/publications/insight/european-spacs-data-hub.
24. Adam Lewis, *Will private equity get caught up in a SPAC showdown with regulators?, Pitchbook,* (18 April 2021), https://pitchbook.com/news/articles/SPACs-private-equity-SEC-regulations.
25. Anirban Sen & Chris Prentice, U.S. *SEC focuses on bank fee conflicts as it steps-up SPAC inquiry - sources,* Reuters, (13 July 2021), https://www.reuters.com/business/exclusive-us-sec-focuses-bank-fee-conflicts-it-steps-up-spac-inquiry-sources-2021-07-13/.

Be it value or volume, the US leads the SPAC market. SPACs in the US raised \$13.9 billion in 2019 and \$80.4 billion in 2020[26]. In fact, in 2021 these represented 55.7 percent of all IPOs[27].

Figure 1. Number of US SPAC IPOs

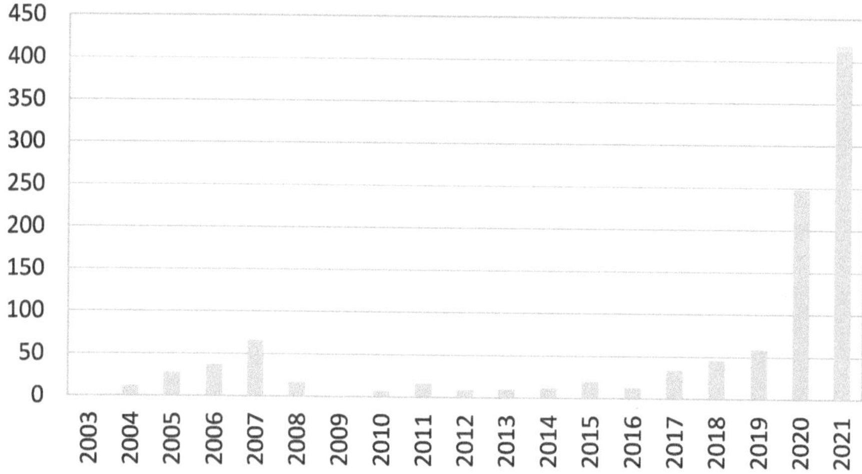

Source: Number of SPAC IPOs in the U.S. 2003-2022 | Statista

After a SPAC is formed in the US, the SPAC registers, with the SEC, the offer and sale of redeemable securities for cash through conventional underwriting. The SPAC sells them primarily to hedge funds and other institutions, and places the proceeds in a trust for future acquisition of a private operating company[28]. NYSE, NASDAQ, and SGX SPAC frameworks require that 90 percent of the gross proceeds be parked in the trust fund[29]. The proceeds parked in the trust fund may be invested in Treasury Bills[30]. In lieu of the proceeds received from the investors the

26. Tomás de Heredia et al., The SPACs Boom, *Deloitte Insights,* (14 July 2021), *https://www2.deloitte.com/xe/en/insights/industry/financial-services/spacs-in-europe.html.*
27. Sara B. Potter, *U.S. IPO Market: SPACs Continue to Dominate in the first quarter of 2021*, Factset, (17 May 2021), https://insight.factset.com/u.s.-ipo-market-spacs-continue-to-dominate-in-the-first-quarter-of-2021.
28. John Caotes, *SPACs, IPOs and Liability Risk under the Securities Laws,* U.S. Securities Exchange Commission, (8 April 2021), https://www.sec.gov/news/public-statement/spacs-ipos-liability-risk-under-securities-laws.
29. Guide to Special Purpose Acquisition, Clifford Chance, (3 September 2021).
30. Chris Bryant, *Hedge Funds Love SPACs But You Should Watch Out,* Bloomberg Opinion, (9 December 2020), https://www.bloomberg.com/opinion/articles/2020-12-09/hedge-funds-love-spacs-but-retail-investors-should-watch-out#footnote-3.

SPAC issues a unit. Each unit is made up of a public share and may include a warrant, or some fraction, that is exercisable at the time of the merger.

That is, when a target company is announced, a warrant allows investors an option to buy more shares at a pre-determined price that is slightly above the price of a share. Therefore, if the target company is expected to do well, the stock price of the merged entity may rise to $15. At this point, the warrant holder can exercise the right to purchase additional shares typically at $11.5. For this reason, it is often argued that investors earn profits from investment at the expense of SPAC shareholders or target shareholders[31]. Retail investors are also permitted to invest via market purchases or purchases from an underwriter in certain jurisdictions prior to the merger. This has been a cause of concern for regulators in the US and Hong Kong that see this as potentially problematic from the point of investor protection. The European Securities and Market Authority has also expressed the need for investor protection through better disclosures[32]. Hong Kong, on the other hand, is considering limiting the participation of retail investors, unlike US and Singapore. The Chair of the House Financial Services Committee in the US expressed concerns that "SPAC mergers are structured to ensure Wall Street insiders receive huge profits and retail investors pay the cost"[33].

The costs include dilution costs and fees associated with the various stages of capital raising in a SPAC's lifecycle[34]. The underwriters are paid 2% as commission upfront and a deferred commission of 3.5% is paid when the de-SPAC transaction or business combination with private company is complete. This is relatively lower than a traditional IPO, for which the fees are approximately 7 %[35]. In cases where the shareholders choose to redeem their units prior to the de-SPAC, the commission charges can be in fact comparable of the proceeds[36]. Therefore, the structure of the SPAC raises valid regulatory concerns regarding the profit incentives of sponsors and costs to retail investors. While, for any financial market, the depth is achieved through wider participation, the opacity in SPACs limits the symmetry in information.

---

31. Michael D. Klausner et al., *A Sober Look at SPACs*, 39 Yale Journal on Regulation 1, (December 20, 2021), https://ssrn.com/abstract=3720919 or http://dx.doi.org/10.2139/ssrn.3720919.
32. *SPACs:* prospectus disclosure and investor protection considerations, European Securities and Market Authorities, (15 July 2021).
33. *Maxine Waters opening statement at hearing on SPACs, direct listings and public offerings*, U.S. House Committee on Financial Services, (May 24, 2021), https://financialservices.house.gov/news/documentsingle.aspx?DocumentID=407916.
34. *Gary Gensler, Testimony before the Subcommittee on Financial Services and General Government*, U.S. House Appropriations Committee, (26 May 2021), https://www.sec.gov/news/testimony/gensler-2021-05-26
35. Robert Armstrong, *SPACs Fee Problem,* Financial Times, (30 September 2021), https://www.ft.com/content/6b1d70db-edae-474c-bd6f-bb60dfa99c51
36. *Ibid.*

On the flipside, by their very design, investor participation in SPACs remains concentrated. Klausner et al. (2021) find that the median large institutional ownership of SPAC shares after IPO was 85%[37]. In recent times, the ownership of shares has diversified with interest from family offices and sovereign wealth funds[38]. Among these hedge funds are an important class of investors in the SPAC market. They own more than a quarter of all SPAC securities, and the top 75 investment managers hold almost 70%[39]. They are interested in SPACs because they perceive SPAC investments as substitutes for fixed income instruments with limited downside risks. Large investment banks have been involved and well-known investors and private equity funds have acted as sponsors. These include TPG Capital, Apollo, Third Point, Blackstone, Fortress, and Pershing Square. The size of SPAC IPO equity raised has increased, with several being over US$1 billion. The largest SPAC IPO to date was conducted by Pershing Square in July 2020, raising US$4 billion alongside forward purchase commitments by affiliates of the sponsor of up to US$3 billion[40]. From the profile of investors in the US, it seems that the market is dominated by large institutional investors, while the risk to retail participants as minority shareholders may remain. Furthermore, this concern may be relatively pronounced in jurisdictions such as the Netherlands where SPACs receive a large share of investments from households. In August 2021, households invested Euro 134 million in SPACs compared to institutional investors who invested Euro 159.2 million[41].

II.2. Post IPO and merger

After an IPO is complete, the units become tradable. In the US, 52 days after the listing of the SPAC unit, they become separable. That is, shares trade alongside whole warrants separately while the unseparated units[42] also continue to trade. Note that the warrants become exercisable upon the completion of the merger or a year from the formation of SPAC, whichever is later[43]. The funds raised by the SPAC are

37. Michael D. Klausner et al., *A Sober Look at SPACs*, 39 Yale Journal on Regulation 1, (December 20, 2021), https://ssrn.com/abstract=3720919 or http://dx.doi.org/10.2139/ssrn.3720919
38. Chris Bryant, *Hedge Funds Love SPACs But You Should Watch Out*, Bloomberg Opinion, (9 December 2020), https://www.bloomberg.com/opinion/articles/2020-12-09/hedge-funds-love-spacs-but-retail-investors-should-watch-out#footnote-3.
39. The SPACresearch.com analysis compared the value of SPAC holdings with the cash held in SPAC trust accounts. While not an exact measure of proportional SPAC ownership, it's a decent approximation.
40. *Guide to Special Purpose Acquisition*, Clifford Chance, (3 September 2021).
41. *Institutional investors increasingly investing in SPACs*, De Nederlandsche Bank, (15 November 2021), https://www.dnb.nl/en/actueel/statistical-news-releases/statistical-newsreleases-2021/institutional-investors-increasingly-investing-in-spacs/.
42. *Guide to Special Purpose Acquisition*, Clifford Chance, (3 September 2021).
43. Ramey Layne et al., *Special Purpose Acquisition Companies: An Introduction*, Harvard Law School Forum on Corporate Governance, (6 July 2018), https://corpgov.law.harvard.edu/2018/07/06/special-purpose-acquisition-companies-an-introduction/.

then employed to acquire shares of one or more businesses. Any expenses incurred for offering, underwriting discount as well as working capital are met by the sponsors[44]. The businesses are not pre-identified, although the industries or sectors may be pre-specified. The acquisition is to be executed within a time frame specified in the Charter[45] and mandated by regulations. For example, in the US, the SPAC must acquire a business within 18-24 months from the date of registration. In Germany and Amsterdam, the SPAC receives a maximum of 24 months to complete the deal, although extensions are available under certain circumstances. The investor funds are held in escrow until invested and a fixed percentage of the funds (80%) must be utilised at the time of acquisition. In case, at the time of acquisition, the funds raised are inadequate, the sponsor may loan funds.

Further, before the signing of the acquisition, the SPAC will arrange committed debt or equity financing. The latter includes private investment in public equity (PIPE) commitment to finance a portion of the purchase price for the business combination and thereafter publicly announce both the acquisition agreement and the committed financing[46]. Therefore, PIPE investors have an advantage over others that they can assess a deal before the information becomes publicly available[47]. Usually, PIPE investors pay a discounted price for the shares and receive warrants[48].

Thereafter shareholders are required to vote on their preference for the potential businesses. The minimum number of votes required for approval varies across jurisdictions. There are some jurisdictions where the required number is a simple majority (the US, Germany, the Netherlands, and the Cayman Islands); in others, a two-third majority is necessary (Luxembourg, Jersey); then there is the British Virgin Islands (BVI) where the transaction may be approved by a simple majority but there is no pre-condition for special or supermajority[49]. If the investors agree to the investment proposition, the SPAC merges with the entity at a 1:1 share exchange or stock for a stock merger, also known as de-SPAC. At this point, shareholders in the SPAC can choose to redeem their shares plus interest, and the sponsor can choose to cancel its shares or earn out.

---

44. *Id. Supra* n. 43.
45. This can be between 18-24 months in the US.
46. *Id., Supra* n. 6.
47. Dmitri Batsev & Jason C. Katz, *How SPAC Skepticism Has Given PIPE Investors an Edge*, Lazard Insights, (May 2021), https://www.lazardassetmanagement.com/us/en_us/research-insights/lazard-insights/spac-skepticism-pipe-edge#!
48. Christopher S. Auguste, *SPACs And PIPEs: A User's Guide*, Corporate Council Business Journal, (1 February 2008), https://ccbjournal.com/articles/spacs-and-pipes-users-guide
49. *Update: SPAC Momentum Continues in Europe with Further Listings in Amsterdam and Frankfurt and Reform in London*, Freshfields Bruckhaus Deringer LLP, (September 2021).

II.3. Unsuccessful merger

If the investors do not vote in favour of the combination then the SPAC may proceed to identifying an alternative investment. The investors who are not in favour of the investment may choose to convert shares into a pro-rata portion of the IPO proceeds. In the case of an unsuccessful merger, the SPAC may liquidate. Different country regulations restrict the payment made to founders and management on liquidation. For example, Singapore Exchange (SGX) allows the deduction of taxes and direct expenses related to liquidation. Whereas the US exchanges allow deduction of taxes and working capital paid to management[50]. Therefore, upon liquidation, sponsors lose value on account of the costs.

Diagram 1. Sequence of Events for SPAC Investment

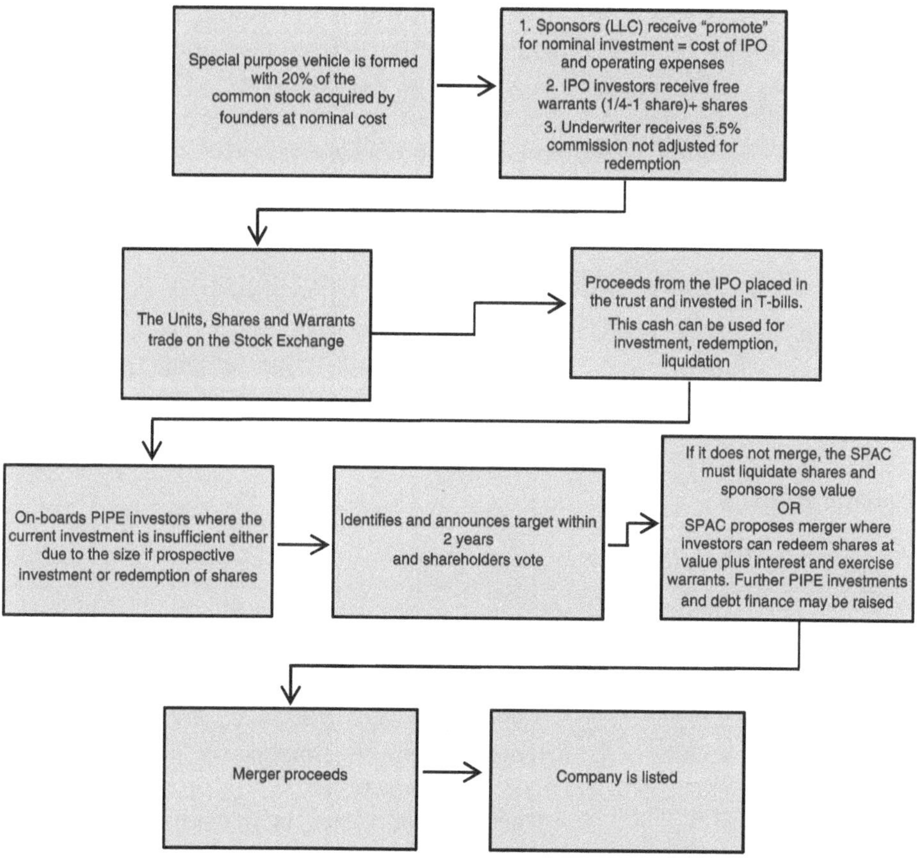

Source: Author

50. *Guide to Special Purpose Acquisition,* Clifford Chance, (3 September 2021).

III. Taxable Events in a SPAC

Based on the description of the SPAC process, the taxable events should be easily identifiable. The investor who is not a promoter but has invested money in the SPAC can exercise the right to redeem the share.. This may be carried out by relinquishing rights after the announcement of the deal or at the time of the sale of shares. On redemption, the investor receives IPO price less pro rata cost in taxes plus pro rata interest. Moreover, opportunity is there for converting the warrants and swapping shares of the SPAC with that of the merged entity. On the other hand, the promoter converts his units to shares in the new company. Further, PIPE investors acquire the shares at a discount.

Besides the aforesaid transactions, the merger transaction between the SPAC and the target company is also a taxable event. There are three kinds of taxes that can arise for each transaction. A capital gains tax will arise on investors and promoters, a tax on the company on the transfer of assets, and a tax on the future financial flows of the company. The jurisdictions where these taxable events will arise are also a function of the transaction structure, i.e., where the SPAC, target company, and the investors are located for tax purposes i.e., the residence countries. The table below provides a quick summary of taxable events arising from each transaction.

Table 1. List of Taxable Event

Event	Nature of income tax or other tax applicable
Redemption of shares of SPAC by shareholders	The tax treatment of interest accumulated
Cancellation or earn out of Sponsor shares	Capital loss
Sale of units/Shares/Warrants on the stock exchange	Capital gains
Commission to manager	The manager's income will be subject to tax in the residence country. However, one challenge remains where the key decisions or the management is undertaken in India—in a SPAC transaction the residence of the SPAC may be considered in the jurisdiction of the manager owing to the definition of place of effective management. As a result, the SPAC's global income will be taxable in India.

Event	Nature of income tax or other tax applicable
Merger of companies	- Offshore indirect transfer on capital gains - Calculation of gains for sponsors with nominal investments - Calculation of gains for non-redeeming shareholders - Calculation of gains for PIPE investors
Profits of SPAC	Income *less* costs
Target company	Gains on share swap or exchange

Source: Author

While most of the tax issues are fairly straightforward, there are certain issues that complicate the taxation of SPACs such as the taxation of de-SPAC. This is based on the target country, is the location of the SPAC, taxation of income of sponsors, and the residence of the SPAC. To add to this where the underlying shares of the SPAC derive value from assets in another jurisdiction, the transfer of such shares will be subject to capital gains tax in the latter. This is further subject to the inclusion of offshore indirect transfers within the scope of capital gains and the treaties allowing for the same. In addition, the nature of this merger, whether it is outbound, inbound, or a share swap, will also determine the nature of income. Each of these events will trigger tax treatment specific to the jurisdiction. These are discussed in some detail below.

III.1. Taxation of the sponsors

First, the structure of a SPAC is important from the tax perspective. For example, if a SPAC is structured as a transparent entity, i.e., it is a pass-through such as a partnership, then the returns will be taxed as the sponsor's gains or capital gains. In this case, the tax residence of the sponsor and the source of the income will matter. Whereas if the SPAC is not structured as a transparent entity, income tax will be paid on the distribution of profits to the sponsors.

As has already been mentioned, the founder/sponsor shares are acquired at a price lower than their value of $10. These shares are then converted into shares of the target company. As a result, the phenomenal gains arising to sponsors that may from the merger are not realised until the sponsors sell their shares. The taxable event, therefore, is the swap of shares. The taxability of the swap will then depend on the domestic laws applicable.

There is a conflicting response to the treatment of these gains from two different aspects. The first relates to the cost of acquisition and if it is ascertainable pre-IPO. It could either be a nominal investment or if shares are issued around the time of the

IPO, their cost would be pegged at the face value of shares at $10. The second aspect is whether the gains on the sponsor shares are to be taxed as entrepreneurs' income or returns[51] (fair market value minus investment), akin to a start-up. These gains arise from share swaps or stock for stock exchange. This is particularly important in the case of the UK, where the tax treatment of sponsor shares held directly as securities is interpreted as employment-related securities.

Typically, the SPAC is structured as a transparent entity that in turn is held by another pooling vehicle. The risk in case where the sponsor shares of the SPAC are directly held by a UK resident. Where the sponsor takes on employment or management roles, subject to the timing of taking on such roles, the exchange may be treated as employment-related securities (ERS). A similar risk arises for share warrants that are convertible to shares by exercising an option. In such a case[52], where the investments are demonstratedly undertaken at 'arm's length', the tax implications may not be less favourable and capital gains tax would be charged at 20% in the UK. But where this cannot be proven, the applicable tax rate is 45%[53]. Therefore, with the characterization of gains and the structure of the SPAC can significantly alter the tax implications.

Indian investors can also participate as founders or sponsors of SPACs. The tax treatment will depend on the tax residence status and FEMA regulations that permit foreign investment of $250,000 per year as per the Liberalised Remittance Scheme (LRS). When a foreign SPAC invests in an Indian target, approvals must be sought from the Reserve Bank of India (RBI) that the transaction is not merely roundtripping. Therefore, while there are checks in India to ensure that the SPAC is not used to channel funds through low tax jurisdiction, similar controls may not exist The lack of such controls would allow a shift of residence of companies. As will be discussed herein, the US applies anti-inversion laws to check for the same.

In the event of a de-SPAC, capital gains tax applies to the taxpayers, irrespective of the fact that the shares have been monetised. The tax rates applicable depend on the period of holding and are considered as an off-market transaction thus attracting 20% tax as per the statute[54].

---

51. Joyce Beebe, *SPACs and Select Tax Considerations*, Baker Institute Blog, (29 April 2021), https://blog.bakerinstitute.org/2021/04/29/spacs-and-select-tax-considerations/.
52. *Article: Taxation of Founders Shares in a SPAC,* Binder Dijker Otte, (22 April 2021), https://www.bdo.co.uk/en-gb/insights/tax/global-employer-services/taxation-of-founders-shares-in-a-spac.
53. *Ibid.*
54. Pranav Sayta & Pavan Sisodia, *Special purpose acquisition company (SPAC) likely to boost inflow of foreign investment in India,* Ernst & Young, (10 May 2021), https://www.ey.com/en_in/tax/india-tax-insights/special-purpose-acquisition-company-likely-to-boost-inflow-of-foreign-investment-in-india.

Under India's Income Tax Act 1961, the transfer of shares is a taxable event. Therefore, where an Indian target company chooses to swap shares for the shares in SPAC, capital gains tax applies to the swap[55]. Whereas in countries such as Ireland, participation exemption is available. Mergers in India are tax-neutral events but not in the case of outbound mergers. That is, where an Indian entity merges with a foreign SPAC and the latter survives, tax is applicable, and, as per section 47(vii) of the ITA, the merger becomes a taxable event for the investors and the SPAC. It is possible to list using a subsidiary in a foreign jurisdiction that does not apply similar taxes but the risk of capital gains tax on offshore indirect transfer remains.

In the US, a de-SPAC transaction is tax-free for the target shareholders in the US, so long as the transaction meets certain requirements: (i) The target company's shareholders exchange control stock of the target company for voting stock of the SPAC; (ii) At least 80% of the total consideration paid to the target company's shareholders is SPAC voting stock; and (iii) After the merger, the target company holds "substantially all" of its assets. In addition, the merger must meet a certain continuity of shareholder interest, continuity of business enterprise, and business purpose.

It is seen that the taxation of the sponsor's from the transaction, that account for a large part of the transaction, is, in turn, dependent on (i) the nature of the merger, (ii) the residence of the sponsor, and (iii) the holding structure. Given that large institutional investors are typically the sponsors of SPACs, it is possible for them to pool resources in an offshore jurisdiction in which case the income can remain untaxed in a high tax jurisdiction where the SPAC is not a transparent entity.

III.2. Taxation of the SPAC and target entity

It is estimated that, in 2020, of the 240 SPACs created, 94 were registered in the Cayman Islands, and BVI[56] and used for non-US SPAC acquisition. These two countries do not apply a withholding tax, capital gains tax, or stamp duty. Tax-exempt companies are used for setting up a SPAC[57]. Thus, even though regulatory concerns may dominate the preference for SPAC, one of the key considerations when deciding the domicile of a SPAC is taxation.

The US leads the SPAC deals globally. One of the reasons for this has been that the US permits non-resident entities to list in the US. Thus, SPACs have been

55. Rise of SPACs: An Indian Perspective, PricewaterhouseCooper, (May 2021).

56. Murray Roberts & George Weston, *De-SPAC' Transactions: A Cayman Islands and British Virgin Islands Perspective*, Business Law Today, (15 June 2021), https://www.americanbar.org/groups/business_law/publications/blt/2021/06/de-spac-transactions/.

57. David Bulley & Dean Bennett, *The use of Cayman Islands Structures for SPAC IPOs,* Appleby Global, (27 July 2020), https://www.applebyglobal.com/publications/the-use-of-cayman-islands-structures-for-spac-ipos/

structured as corporations domiciled in Delaware, the Cayman Islands, Jersey, the Netherlands, and Luxembourg[58]. Typically, SPACs that are domiciled outside the US are considered more convenient than those residents in the US because it is more difficult to offshore a domestic SPAC, where the target entity is foreign[59] than the other way around. This is because if the SPAC merges with a foreign entity, then the Controlled Foreign Company (CFC) rules would apply, and the foreign income of the SPAC would be subject to the US tax. Further, the US SPAC would have to pay withholding taxes in the US on foreign incomes.

There are anti-inversion rules in the US. This prevents a US firm from moving its headquarters to another jurisdiction through a merger with a foreign entity[60] after which the US entity becomes a subsidiary of a foreign entity. Yet, there are instances where the residence of the company was shifted to a foreign jurisdiction because of the specific threshold exemptions available. This trend is not nascent; companies such as Ingersoll-Rand, Tyco, the PXRE Group, Foster Wheeler, Nabors Industries, and Coopers Industries[61] have used inversions in the past. In recent times, the trend of inversions is observed to be picking up in the US, with companies like Burger King moving their headquarters to Canada. In 2012, Wall Street Journal reported that companies were moving their headquarters to jurisdictions such as the Cayman Islands and Switzerland[62]. A similar trend was observed in the UK in 2008 when companies began inverting their residence to low tax jurisdictions such as Luxembourg[63]. This motivated high corporate tax rate (28%) and the application of the worldwide system of tax although, the UK shifted to a territorial tax structure and lowered its corporate tax rates. The UK could not implement an anti-inversion rule like the US because of its EU membership. That is by virtue of its membership it could not restrict business activity by the legislation of inversion rules. Hence the UK introduced CFC rules[64].

---

58. Brenda Lenahan et al., *Update on Special Purpose Acquisition Companies,* Harvard Law School Forum on Corporate Governance, (17 August 2020), https://corpgov.law.harvard.edu/2020/08/17/update-on-special-purpose-acquisition-companies/
59. Marcus Mick et al., *SPAC Transactions: Trends and Key Tax Issues,* Taxand, (29 April 2021).
60. Kyle Pomerleau, *The United Kingdom's Experience with Inversions, Tax Foundation, (5 April 2016), https://taxfoundation.org/united-kingdom-s-experience-inversions/*
61. *While Companies Shift Addresses to Tax Havens, CEO's Stay Put,* Bloomberg Visual Data, (May 4, 2014), http://www.bloomberg.com/infographics/2014-05-04/companies-shift-addresses-abroad.ht ml.
62. John D. McKinnon & Scott Thurm, *U.S. Firms Move Abroad to Cut Taxes: Despite '04 Law, Companies Incorporate Overseas, Saving Big Sums on Taxes,* Wall Street Journal, (28 August 2012), https://www.wsj.com/articles/SB10000872396390444230504577615232602107536.
63. Julia Werdigier, *British Companies Emigrating Over Taxes,* New York Times, (4 September 2008), http://www.nytimes.com/2008/09/05/business/worldbusiness/05tax.html.
64. *Corporate Inversions: The UK Perspective, National Law Review, (12 November 2014), https://www.natlawreview.com/article/corporate-inversions-uk-perspective.*

There are two interesting fallouts of the process. One is that the inversion of the corporate holding structure is easily possible through the SPAC. As the international tax rules close in on avoidance practices, it is possible for companies to explore this route to minimise their taxes. While this would be difficult for US-based companies that face anti-inversion, it is not impossible, for example, Aon, ENSCO, and Rowan moved to the UK[65]. Similarly, it remains a viable option for corporations headquartered in other countries.

The UK has attracted businesses looking to invert but there are challenges regarding stamp duty and transaction tax on the transfer of shares[66]. Because the stamp duty legislation only applies where the company is UK-incorporated, some inverting groups have adopted the simple expedient of establishing a holding company that is managed and controlled (and thus tax resident) in the UK but incorporated in Jersey or other similar jurisdictions that do not impose a corporate income tax. Also, where a UK-incorporated company is used, it is often possible to obtain a ruling from the HM Revenue & Customs (HMRC) that the reorganization will not attract a significant stamp duty charge[67].

Backstops are in place in the US legislation to prevent inversions. First, any gain that arises to shareholders on the stock conversion[68]is recognized and computed as the difference between the fair market value of the foreign corporation shares received and the adjusted basis of the domestic corporation stock exchanged[69]. Second, there could be tax consequences from the transfer of other assets. Third, foreign subsidiaries are also taxable in the US. Fourth, if the US shareholders receive more than 80% of the shares of the new foreign parent's stock, then the new foreign parent is a deemed inverted corporation and taxed as a US corporation. Fifth, if at least 60 percent but less than 80 percent of the new foreign parent's stock is acquired by the shareholders of the US parent, the foreign parent will be treated as a "surrogate foreign corporation," resulting in "inversion gain". Being recognized by an "expatriated entity" in the expatriation transaction from the transfer of stock (or other property or from a license), it is fully taxable without offset by credits, losses, or other tax attributes and, for the following ten years, the expatriated entity's gain on transfers (excluding sales of inventory in the ordinary course of business) or

65. Corporate Expatriation, Inversions, and Mergers: Tax Issues, Congressional Research Service, (17 June 2021).
66. *Corporate Inversions: The UK Perspective,* 12 National Law Review 43, (12 November 2014), https://www.natlawreview.com/article/corporate-inversions-uk-perspective.
67. *Ibid.*
68. Anthony Diosdi, *Introduction to Corporate Cross-Border Transfers, Recognizations, and Inversions Part 3*, SF Tax Council, (06 May 2021), https://sftaxcounsel.com/introduction-to-corporate-cross-border-transfers-reorganizations-and-inversions-part-3-the-anti-inversion-rules-its-not-just-for-large-multinational-corporations-anymore/.
69. *Ibid.*

licenses to a "foreign related person also is taxable without offset." For these purposes, an expatriated entity (that is subject to these special tax rules) is a US parent (or a US partnership) and any "related person."[70]

The implication is that, in a SPAC transaction, there are risks that the inversion rules will apply and, even though a US SPAC merges with a foreign entity, or a US entity merges with a foreign SPAC, the ownership of the stocks will determine the tax treatment. Nevertheless, there are exceptions to the application of inversion rules based on a substantial activity test that includes (i) employees in the foreign corporation are at least 25% of the group employees; (ii) employee compensation in the foreign jurisdiction is 25% of group compensation; (iii) group assets located in the foreign jurisdiction are 25% of the group assets, and (iv) group income in the foreign jurisdiction is at least 25% of the total group income. Therefore, there is room to avoid tax to the extent that substantial activity is reported.

Where a foreign SPAC is merged with a domestic entity in the US, then the income of the SPAC may become taxable in the US because it may be classified as a Passive Foreign Investment Company (PFIC)[71], in which case the domestic transaction is subject to tax. Although there are exceptions to this rule for start-ups and QEF, except for in the case of PFIC warrants.

On the other hand, in the case of other popular destinations for SPACs- Ireland, Germany, and Spain- a merger may be tax-neutral where the merger is in the EU/EEA area. As for combinations that are with entities outside the EU, the tax would depend on the form of merger. However, there are no inversion rules.

An important consideration when determining the tax treatment of a SPAC is to determine its place of tax residence or place of effective management. In the case of India, if key management and commercial decisions are taken in the jurisdiction, the place of effective management ("POEM") of the SPAC may be regarded to be in India and the SPAC could be subject to Indian taxes on its global income. Even after the de-SPAC when the entity acquired folds in as a subsidiary, it may constitute a PE or branch in India, thus leading to issues of attribution of profits and taxation. It could be similar in some other tax jurisdictions as well.

Last but not the least, currently 35% of the tax treaties in the world allow for capital gains tax to apply to offshore indirect transfers. While some countries such as India do not have a similar provision within their tax treaties, nevertheless, wherever the tax law permits India to tax as per its domestic tax law, this may apply. For example, say a target entity is located in India and the foreign entities hold a substantial interest (greater than 50%) in the Indian target entity and the assets held are more than INR 100 million. In

70. *Ibid.*
71. If a foreign corporation generates at least 75% of its income as passive income (such as from investments), or if 50% of its assets generate passive income or are held for generating passive income.

case the investors of SPAC sell their shares on a foreign exchange or redeem their shares after the target is announced, capital gains tax on offshore indirect transfer would arise. This is applicable where a treaty permits the domestic tax law of the treaty partner with a tax on the offshore indirect transfer to apply.

IV. Conclusion

The discussion in this chapter sheds light on the growing complexity in financial transactions that in turn complicates the application of tax. In the years after SPACs became popular, it is observed that tax laws were enacted to ensure that the flexibility of companies was tamed, for example, in the choice of their residence. Despite such constraints, investors can exploit differences in legal provisions across jurisdictions, such as the qualifying exemptions for the substantial activity or the constraints on the application of tax given that it works counter to the freedom of movement of capital in the EU. Therefore, financial innovations such as the SPAC can slip through the cracks in cross-border taxation. As a result, there has been an increase in revealed preference of companies to shift their headquarters to jurisdictions with lighter tax treatment. For example, Cayman Island, Jersey, Luxembourg, and the Netherlands were among the preferred destinations for inversions including SPACs. As has been observed, exempt companies in the Cayman Islands and BVI remain popular. Nearly 55% of the listings in HKex were Cayman companies in 2020[72]. As per another estimate, a third of all SPACs launched were incorporated in Cayman[73]. Therefore, foreign target companies can be acquired via and can shift residence to low tax jurisdiction.

It is further possible for the offshore SPAC to acquire a US target company via Delaware[74]. An example of such a transaction is Cayman Islands-incorporated SPAC Social Capital Hedosophia Holdings Corp. II acquired San Francisco's Opendoor at an enterprise value of $4.8 billion. [75]It is seen that in fact domestic SPACs or mergers with domestic target companies are typically undertaken via Delaware[76].

Therefore, even though regulatory controls have given an impetus to the market for SPACs making it an alternative for IPOs, tax considerations remain important.

72. *SPACs and traditional IPOs: An offshore perspective,* Carey Olsen, (23 June 2021), https://www.careyolsen.com/articless/spacs-and-traditional-ipos-offshore-perspective.
73. *Ibid.*
74. Murray Roberts & George Weston, *De-SPAC' Transactions: A Cayman Islands and British Virgin Islands Perspective*, Business Law Today, (15 June 2021), https://www.americanbar.org/groups/business_law/publications/blt/2021/06/de-spac-transactions/.
75. Alex Wilhelm & Natasha Mascarenhas, *Opendoor to go public by way of Chamath Palihapitiya SPAC,* Techcrunch (15 September 2020), https://techcrunch.com/2020/09/15/opendoor-to-go-public-by-way-of-chamath-palihapitiya-spac/
76. *SPACs and traditional IPOs: An offshore perspective,* Carey Olsen, (23 June 2021), https://www.careyolsen.com/articless/spacs-and-traditional-ipos-offshore-perspective.

Source countries such as India and China have also taken measures to ensure where SPAC transactions occur and gains derived from related assets are situated in their jurisdictions. Capital gains taxation in the case of an offshore indirect transfer can be challenging where there are layers of entities through which these assets are owned. However, it is possible to a limited extent that such transactions get taxed. It makes one consider if the growing complexity is viable for tax administrations in emerging economies. Would it not be more practical for such countries to consider a financial transactions tax (FTT) that affords simplicity while compensating—through an appropriate tax rate—for any narrowing of the tax base. This route may be useful especially since SPACs, although registered in low-tax countries, must trade their units in international markets.

The ongoing discussions in international taxation focus specifically on MNEs that operate without sufficient nexus. The need to tax these companies, under the Pillar One proposal has preoccupied experts. It has been suggested that a specific exclusion be made for regulated financial services[77] which include banking, insurance, and asset management[78]. Pillar Two reform seeks to raise the overall effective tax rates, subject to substance-based carve-outs. Moreover, bilateral treaty treatment of capital gains is still under consideration. Therefore, to the extent that there are treaty-based preferential treatment and that domestic tax law is not reformed, SPACs can continue to be used to effectively shift the residence of the corporation and for lowering tax incidence of corporate restructurings.

While the income inclusion rule seeks to end the search for a new residence, over the past decades companies have undertaken innovations to bypass domestic tax changes by inverting the corporate structures. Such incentives may exist due to not just the headline corporate tax rates but also because of participation exemptions to dividends, capital gains, and other shareholder incomes. For example, Tax Foundation summarises the exemption of foreign sourced dividends and capital gains. This can encourage the setting up of a SPAC in a jurisdiction with such exemption to lower tax outgo upon the merger. In the past, anti-inversion rules have been applied, as was discussed in the case of the United States, that prevent companies from shifting their residence. As per the rules, there is minimum activity, assets, and income test as well as a shareholding requirement. Therefore, so long as there are threshold-based exemptions, whether for anti-inversion rules or offshore indirect transfers SPACs can be used to avoid paying taxes on mergers and transfers of shares. This presents a new tax challenge for authorities as financial markets become more sophisticated.

77. *Addressing the Tax Challenges of the Digitalisation of the Economy – Policy Note*, page 2, OECD/G20 Base Erosion and Profit Shifting Project, OECD, (2019), https://www.oecd.org/tax/beps/policy-note-beps-inclusive-framework-addressing-tax-challenges-digitalisation.pdf.
78. *Tax Challenges Arising from Digitalisation – Report on Pillar Two Blueprint: Inclusive Framework on BEPS,* OECD/G20 Base Erosion and Profit Shifting Project, 51, OECD, (2020), https://doi.org/10.1787/abb4c3d1-en.

Figure 3 Territoriality of tax systems in Europe

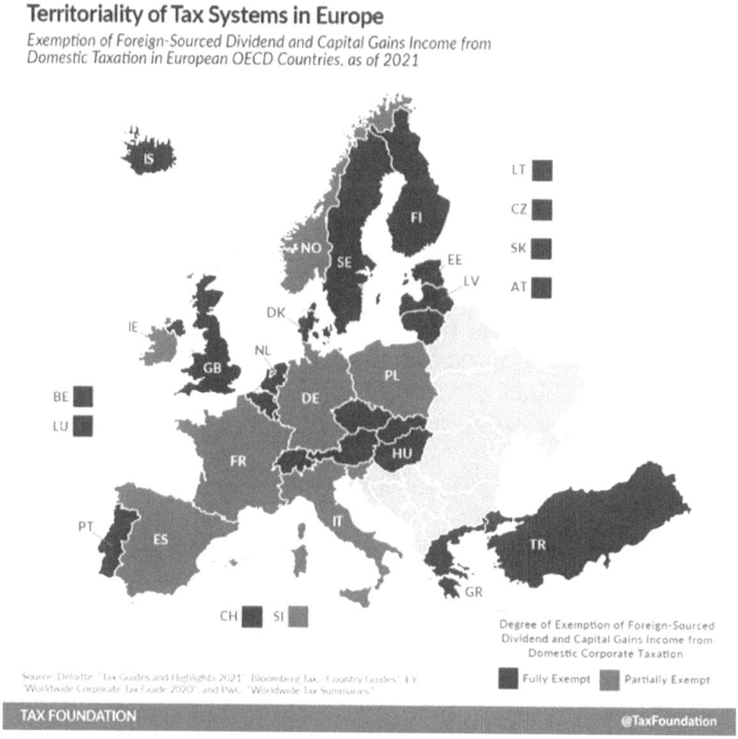

Source: Tax Foundation

The anti-inversion rules have been made more stringent over years to restrict companies from relocating their headquarters. But substance requirements or dilution of shareholding can allow companies to continue to invert. Moreover, there are many countries that do not have inversion rules thus allowing them to seek residence abroad. It may be plausible that with Income Inclusion Rule under Pillar 2 and anti-inversion, the tax base would be relatively secure for the US. However, the fact that companies continue to use the Cayman Islands for forming SPACs with foreign targets, due to relatively easy exchange controls, no income taxes, and an easy merger regime[79], indicates that the inversion rules may not provide absolute cover. Pillar two, with its substance-based carve-outs may not be useful.

Other than the characterisation of incomes that can be complicated in the case of SPACs, as shown in the case of the UK, there is also the issue of tax residence of the SPAC investor.

79. David Bulley & Dean Bennett, *The use of Cayman Islands Structures for SPAC IPOs,* Appleby Global, (27 July 2020), https://www.applebyglobal.com/publications/the-use-of-cayman-islands-structures-for-spac-ipos/.

REJOINDER

K.R. Sekar

SPAC - Challenges in the Revised Landscape

1. Introduction

The chapter by Suranjali Tandon introduces SPAC, a financial innovation, and addresses the challenges that have emerged in taxing it. SPAC as a concept has caught the attention of various investors/unicorns to access Overseas Capital Market. Suranjali Tandon in her Paper "Tax Challenges from Financial Innovations-A Case Study of Special Purpose Acquisition Companies (SPACs)" has detailed various tax issues relating to setting up of SPAC and merger of SPAC. The paper deals with both the tax and regulatory perspectives from India and International perspectives.

2. Special Purpose Acquisition Companies (SPACs)

The concept of SPAC (Special Purpose Acquisition Companies) was primarily used as a vehicle to access Overseas Capital Market by companies to circumvent the regulatory/valuation challenges in India. Special Purpose Acquisition companies are shell companies that raise money by listing shares on a stock exchange. SPACs have no operating business model or business revenue either from sale of goods or services but choose to go public only with the objective of finding the right private company to merge with.

A SPAC uses the route of merger of Target company once it is found, with the already public SPAC and through this merger the private business goes public and gets listed on the stock exchange.

A SPAC keeps the money raised in an interest-bearing trust account till SPAC finds target companies. Once the SPAC completes the acquisition of the target company, investors get the option to swap their existing shares for the shares of the merged company upon completion of the merger process.

In the event a SPAC is unable to complete an acquisition within the stipulated time, the money is returned to the investors along with the interest earned.

3. SPAC- Is it the right concept to access capital markets?

Suranjali, in her paper, has detailed the tax challenges faced by a SPAC and has discussed the legislative provisions of other countries also in addition to the Indian legislation. The concept of SPAC though practiced in a newer form, the model itself is not alien to the traditional businessmen of yesteryears. Until 1980, Income-tax Act in India had two rates; a lower rate for companies in which public are substantially Interested (PSI Companies)[80] along with such companies being exempted from Wealth Tax; and another with a higher rate for companies in which the public are not substantially interested (Non PSI Companies) along with such companies being subject to Wealth Tax. PSI companies are those, which are listed on the stock exchanges in India or where 40% of the shares are held by Listed Companies. Many companies instead of going to the public would form a dormant company which is listed on the stock exchange in India to hold the company shares with the aim to become a PSI company. This route was used not only as a tax planning measure but also as a route to access the stock market. SPAC operates in a little different manner but with the same objective of accessing the capital market.

SPAC, though a beneficial route to Unicorns/Start-ups to get listed on the stock exchanges, in the long run may not be advantageous given the absence of a business model to go public. Further, any failure of a business model or failure on the part of the SPAC to identify target companies will lead to erosion of the investor's confidence.

4. SPAC-Challenges in India

Under the Indian company law, a company may be formed for a business objective as stated in the objects clause in its memorandum of association. Investment could also be one of the business objectives. In the case of SPAC, the objective is to identify a company, acquire it and merge with it. Where merger should be objective of the business, under the present Indian law, whether a mere acquisition without any business is sufficient for compliance is a matter of debate.

Moving on to eligibility criteria for the listing of companies, SEBI has prescribed certain eligibility criteria. For listing purposes a company must have (i) an operating profit of INR 15 crores, net tangible assets of at least INR 3 crores and net worth of at least INR 1 crore, respectively, for the last three years; or (ii) a company which is not satisfying the above mentioned conditions at (i) would be eligible to make an IPO only if the issue is made through the book-building process, the company undertakes to allot at least 75% of the net offer to qualified institutional buyers and to refund the full subscription money if it fails to do so. At this point it remains to be seen whether SPACs would meet these conditions.

Further under the Indian context, the SPAC will have the following challenges:

- The Indian Companies Act does not expressly permit Cross-Border Mergers and one needs to follow the subsidiary model or create a holding company outside India for the purpose of merger with SPAC.
- Mergers will be tax neutral in India only on satisfaction of certain conditions.
- The Indian company merging with the overseas SPAC will face challenges in carrying forward their tax losses, despite being approved by the

80. Section 2(18) of Income-Tax Act 1961.

regulators, unless the company model/business model is allowed to be tweaked in order to enable it to do so.

- SEBI allows the listing of Indian companies outside India but without the corresponding listing in India, it may pose challenges for the Indian investors and create issues around valuation.
- The disinvestment by investors in the SPAC entity after the merger will attract capital gains tax as it will be treated as an indirect transfer.
- Tax laws in India do not deal directly with SPAC type of transactions. Therefore, it is important for the companies to structure SPAC transaction to be able to avail any benefits arising from tax without coming under scrutiny by the tax authorities.

Considering the challenges faced by and also the opportunities created by SPACs, the Government needs to amend the SEBI Laws, Corporate Laws, Income-Tax Act, and FEMA to facilitate SPAC related transactions.

According to news reports SEBI represented before the Parliamentary standing committee stating that "The sub group of the primary market advisory committee (PMAC) is in the process of finalising the report on SPACs. Subsequently, a consultation paper for public comments may also be issued on the matter. Steps regarding SPACs framework may be taken only after consultation with PMAC. The company law committee report of the Ministry of Corporate Affairs (MCA) of February 2022, recommended introducing an enabling provision to recognize SPAC under the Companies Act and allowing a SPAC incorporated in India on domestic and global exchanges."[81]

5. Conclusion

SPAC provides opportunities for Indian companies to list outside India and access the capital markets outside India. Few Indian companies have also benefited out of SPAC. But for SPAC to be a successful model, it is important that Government makes changes to the Indian law to make it investor-friendly. Further, with the rise of Unicorns in India, amendments to Indian regulations are critical to make SPACs more effective. Finally, in the new business environment, accessing the capital market may be one of the objectives but running the business and making it profitable is equally important. Hence, SPACs can be effective only if careful governance is ensured through legislative measures failing which, it may adversely impact and lead to erosion of investor confidence.

81. https://www.thehindubusinessline.com/markets/sebi-readies-framework-for-spac-listing-in-india/article65430748.ece- Published on May 19, 2022.

CHAPTER 8

TAX-RELATED INVESTMENT ARBITRATION – THE INDIAN EXPERIENCE

Aditya Vora*

I. Introduction

India's experience with tax-related investment arbitration has been dramatic. This chapter critically evaluates that experience, particularly the publicly available *Cairn Award*, its aftermath, and lessons for the future.[1] The author's analysis accepts the argument in the *Cairn Award* that the retroactive tax legislation enacted by India were in violation of the international standards of protection that it promised.

To contextualise, the *Cairn Award* dealt with the question whether the retroactive tax amendments enacted by India to tax offshore indirect transfers (OIT) were in breach of the United Kingdom–India Bilateral Investment Treaty (UK–India BIT).[2] OITs are transactions involving sale of shares or other instruments of a foreign company overseas, where the value of the shares or other instruments is substantially derived from assets situated in India. Such a transaction becomes an offshore sale of shares rather than an onshore sale of assets.

The Supreme Court of India, in the case of *Vodafone International Holdings B.V. v Union of India* (*Vodafone (SC)*),[3] held that OITs are not taxable in India on the basis of law that existed in 2012.[4] This position was overruled by way of an

---

* An earlier version of this Chapter was published by Thomson Reuters, trading as Sweet & Maxwell, 5 Canada Square, Canary Wharf, London, E14 5AQ, in the British Tax Review as Aditya Vora, *Cairn Energy Plc and Cairn UK Holdings Private Limited v The Republic of India*: retroactive tax legislation when it ceases to meet the fair and equitable treatment standard, (2021) 3 British Tax Review 287 and as Aditya Vora, The Indian Taxation Laws (Amendment) Act, 2021: a commendable change of policy or simply an offer for settlement? (2021) 5 British Tax Review 521.

1. *Cairn Energy Plc and Cairn UK Holdings Private Limited v the Republic of India* (*Cairn Award*) PCA Case No. 2016-7
2. Agreement between the Government of India and the Government of the United Kingdom for the Promotion and Protection of Investments dated 14 March 1994 (enforced 6 January 1995) (UK–India BIT), *https://dea.gov.in/sites/default/files/United%20Kingdom.pdf* [Accessed 15 February 2022].
3. *Vodafone International Holdings B.V. v Union of India* (*Vodafone (SC)*) (2012) 6 SCC 613.
4. Finance Act, 2012 No. 23 of 2012 s. 4 (2012 Amendment).

amendment through the Finance Act, 2012 (2012 Amendment), making OIT transactions taxable in India with retroactive effect from 1962.[5] Using the 2012 Amendment as justification, the Indian Revenue initiated proceedings against 17 taxpayers, most notably against Vodafone International Holdings B.V. (Vodafone) and Cairn Energy Plc and Cairn UK Holdings Private Limited (collectively, Cairn) levying a total charge of INR 1.10 lakh crore (approximately GBP 11 billion in 2021).[6]

This move of retroactively amending section 9(1)(i) of the Income-tax Act, 1961 (ITA 1961) was heavily criticised.[7] For fear of a similar override by the Indian Parliament, the various foreign investors chose the remedy through investment arbitration under the relevant Bilateral Investment Treaty (BIT) over litigation in the Indian courts.

As a result, investment arbitration was initiated by Vodafone and Cairn and the tribunals rendered their final awards in late 2020.[8] The *Cairn Award* is used as an example to highlight the concerns with the 2012 Amendment and its impact on the arbitration.[9] In the *Cairn Award*, the Arbitral Tribunal established by the Permanent Court of Arbitration (the Tribunal) was asked whether the 2012 Amendment was in breach of India's obligation under the UK–India BIT, particularly the fair and equitable treatment (FET) standard. The Republic of India (India) argued, first, that the Tribunal lacked the jurisdiction to hear the dispute as fiscal measures fell within its sovereign functions and hence were not amenable to arbitration. In any case, India argued that the matter would be covered under the UK–India Double Tax Convention (UK–India DTC). And second, on merits, India justified the 2012 Amendment by arguing that it was merely clarificatory, and even if retroactive, it did not violate the FET standard.

Reflecting that the Award was against India, it is interesting to look at the facts of the case and the analysis of the Tribunal, which, in a jurisprudential exposition, lays down the rule on the interplay between double taxation conventions and bilateral

5. Income-Tax Act, 1961, No.43 of 1961 (ITA 1961) s.9(1)(i).
6. Press Trust of India, "India asks US court to reject Cairn Energy's $1.2 billion suit" (18 August 2021) *Business Standard*, *https://www.business-standard.com/article/companies/india-asks-us-court-to-reject-cairn-energy-s-1-2-billion-suit-121081700956_1.html* [Accessed 15 February 2022].
7. See P. Ranjan and K. Duggal, "The 2016 Model Indian Bilateral Investment Treaty: A Critical Deconstruction" (2017) 38(1) *Northwestern Journal of International Law & Business* 1; S. Mysore and A. Vora, "Tussle for Policy Space in International Investment Norm Setting: The Search for a Middle Path?" (2016) 7(2) *Jindal Global Law Review* 135, 143.
8. *Cairn Award* PCA Case No. 2016-7 and *Vodafone International Holdings B.V. v Government of India* PCA Case No. 2016-35 (*Vodafone Award*) (collectively, the Awards).
9. Arbitral tribunals under BITs, including the tribunal in *Cairn Award* PCA Case No. 2016-7, do not have jurisdiction to rule conclusively on the interpretation of Indian domestic law but may interpret Indian law to determine whether or not the BIT is breached.

investment treaties. For the first time the Tribunal also considered whether retroactive taxation breaches investment obligations. This is discussed in Part II of the chapter. Next, in Part III, the chapter discusses the post-Award phase where the Award was challenged and subsequently India revoked the retroactive element of the 2012 Amendment. It is recommended and hoped that India makes it a policy decision to not enact retroactive legislation that violate the vested rights of taxpayers in order to increase the tax base. India's revamp of its investment obligations and the author's comment on the Tribunal's analysis, including the subsequent events are elaborated in Part IV.

II. The *Cairn* Award

II.1. Background facts

Cairn sought to consolidate all its Indian assets into one holding company and list it on the Bombay Stock Exchange (BSE).[10] First, new entities were incorporated. Cairn India Holding Company (CIHL) was incorporated in Jersey,[11] Cairn UK Holding Company (CUKHL) was incorporated in the UK, and Cairn India Limited (CIL) was incorporated in India.[12] CIL would be listed on the BSE. CUKHL was the 100 per cent parent of CIHL and CIL. Secondly, all of Cairn's India holdings (accounting to 27 operating subsidiaries) were transferred first to CIHL. Later, the ownership of CIHL was transferred from CUKHL to CIL.[13]

This transfer from CUKHL to CIL was divided into four tranches. These four tranches were the subject of the *Cairn Award*. In the first step, CIL acquired, in two tranches, 21.8 per cent of CIHL. To finance this acquisition, Cairn Energy Plc (CEP) took a daylight loan. The loan was transferred to CUKHL through an intra-group loan.[14] CUKHL used that money to subscribe to additional shares of CIL.[15] CIL used the proceeds from the subscription to purchase shares of CIHL from CUKHL. This occurred in two tranches of 16.5 per cent and 5.3 per cent for a total of 21.8 per cent of CIHL, as pictorially represented below in Diagram I.[16]

10. *Cairn Award* PCA Case No. 2016-7 at [27]; a separate option of listing on the London Stock Exchange was considered by the CEP Board and was rejected.
11. *Cairn Award* PCA Case No. 2016-7 at [36].
12. *Cairn Award* PCA Case No. 2016-7 at [34] and [38].
13. *Cairn Award* PCA Case No. 2016-7 at [57-78].
14. *Cairn Award* PCA Case No. 2016-7 at [58].
15. *Cairn Award* PCA Case No. 2016-7 at [59].
16. *Cairn Award* PCA Case No. 2016-7 at [60] and [63].

Diagram 1. First two tranches of CIHL Acquisition

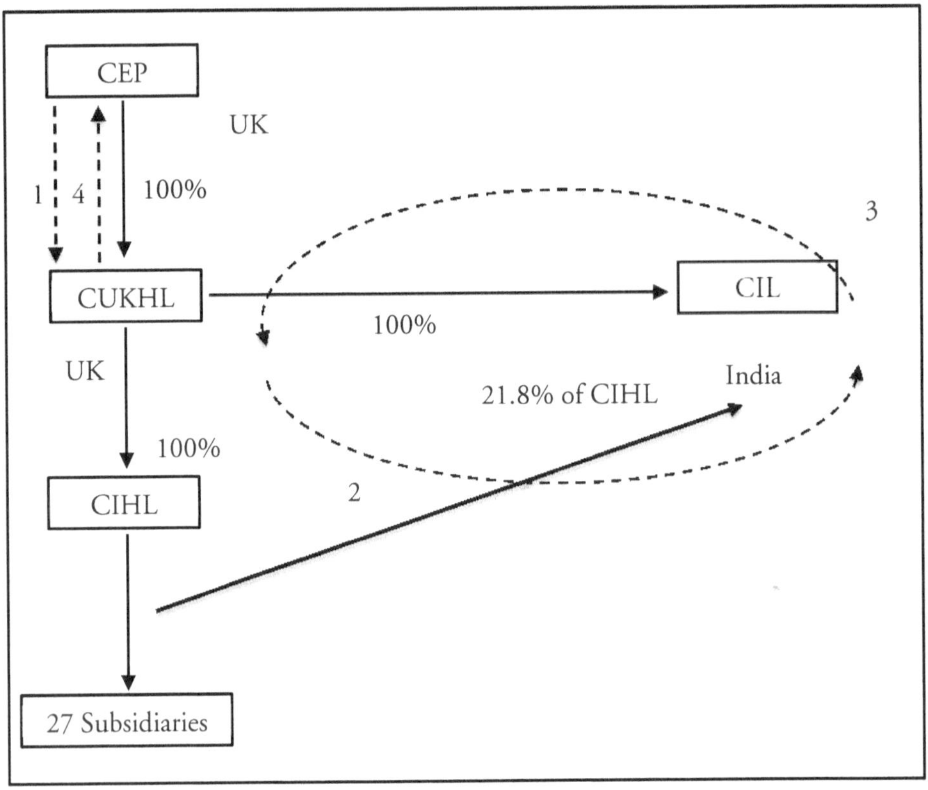

Dashed arrows show flow of money, thick arrow shows the transfer of shares:

Jersey 1 – Intra-group loan from CEP to CUKHL

2 – CUKHL subscribes for shares in CIL

3 – CIL used the amount subscribed to acquire 21.8% shareholding of CIHL from CUKHL

4 – CUKHL uses the proceeds to pay back CEP

As a result, 21.8% of CIHL was transferred from CUKHL to CIL

Source: Author

In the second step, post Indian regulatory approvals, CIL was listed on the BSE. In the third step, CIL acquired the remaining 78.2 per cent (in two tranches) of CIHL, through a share swap and using proceeds from the public listing. As a result of transfer, CIHL became a 69% subsidiary of CIL with 31% of it owned by the public (2006 Transactions). The 2006 Transactions are the subject of the *Cairn Award.*

Diagram 2. Final Shareholding pattern post 2006 Transactions

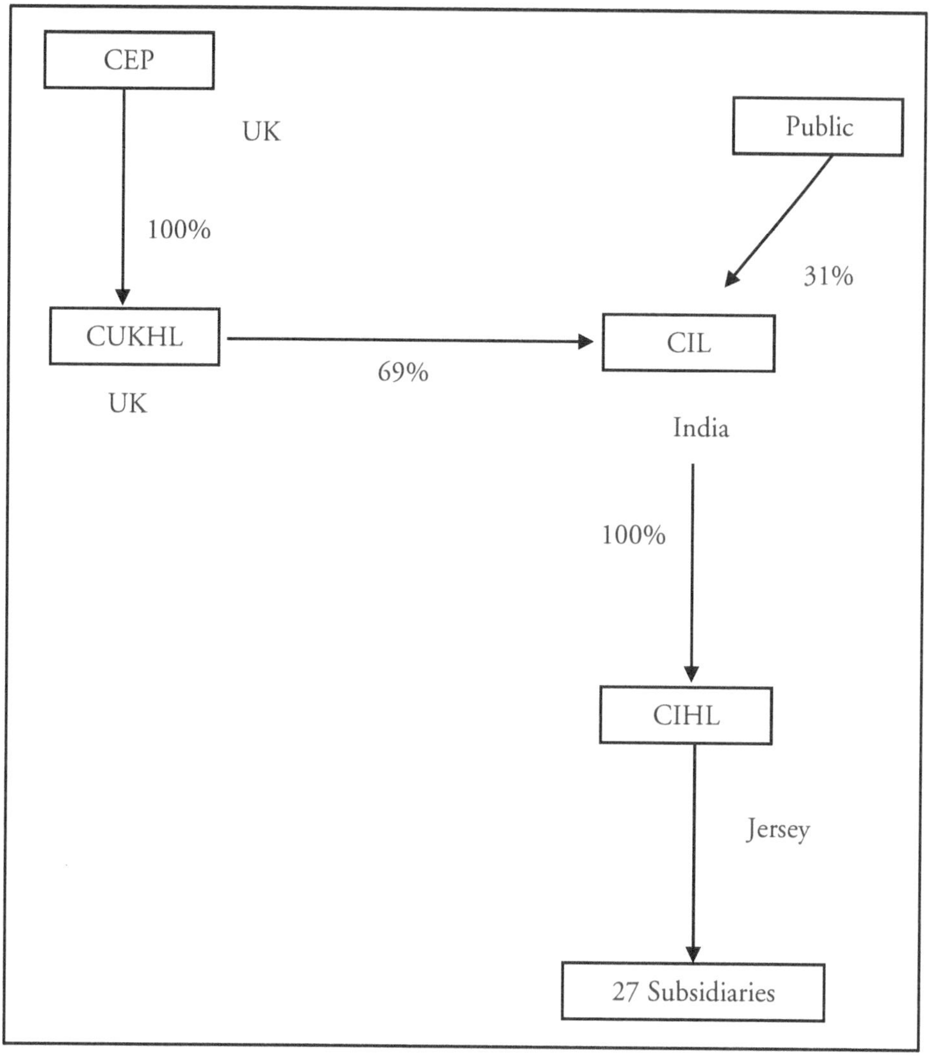

Source: Author

Through the 2006 Transactions, the ownership of CIHL was transferred to CIL, leading to a capital gain. To tax the 2006 Transactions, the Indian Government argued that the value of the shares of CIHL (the capital good transferred) was substantially derived from the underlying Indian assets (the 27 operating Indian subsidiaries). The 2006 Transactions were OITs and thus, as per the retroactive 2012 Amendment, India had the right to tax the 2006 Transactions.

II.2. Analysis of the Tribunal

The Tribunal's analysis can be divided into two parts. First, on India's jurisdictional objection that the matter was a tax dispute and hence was excluded from the scope of the UK–India BIT. Second, on India's breach of FET standard to Cairn.

II.2.1. India's jurisdictional objection

First, India claimed that tax disputes were incapable of resolution through investment arbitration. It was argued that tax disputes must be resolved through the UK–India DTC with the implied exclusion of the UK–India BIT.[17] The BIT too, contained a tax-exclusion clause. Secondly, India made a broader argument that Cairn's challenge to the 2012 Amendment falls within India's sovereign authority to tax and thus it is not arbitrable under international law, Dutch law (being the seat of arbitration) or as a matter of Indian public policy.[18]

Before proceeding with India's objections, the Tribunal clarified that Cairn's case was a "tax-related investment dispute" and not a "tax dispute" *simpliciter*. Cairn's allegation was denial of substantive protection offered under the BIT that resulted from India's 2012 Amendment. This is different from a tax dispute *simpliciter*, where the issue would be the application of the fiscal measure itself to determine whether a particular transaction is taxable and to what extent. This is a significant distinction. The challenge does not concern India's sovereign right to impose a tax. However, it alleges that India's exercise of legislative authority in the field of taxation is in breach of the substantive protection India offered to its investors under the UK–India BIT.[19]

Regarding India's first objection, the Tribunal held that the dispute resolution clause under the UK–India BIT contained no carve-out for tax-related investment disputes.[20] The tax carve-out was rather contained only in the Most-Favoured Nation and the National Treatment clauses, which according to the Tribunal favoured Cairn's position.[21] The limited tax carve-out meant an implied acceptance to arbitrate tax-related disputes for other protections offered under the UK–India BIT.[22] India took objection to such an interpretation.

Additionally, India argued that the BIT and the DTC dealt with the same "subject-matter" and the more specific treaty, the DTC, superseded the BIT

17. *Cairn Award* PCA Case No. 2016-7 at [763]–[764].
18. *Cairn Award* PCA Case No. 2016-7 at [792].
19. *Cairn Award* PCA Case No. 2016-7 at [793].
20. UK–India BIT art. 9.
21. UK–India BIT art. 4.
22. *Cairn Award* PCA Case No. 2016-7 at [799].

following Article 32 of the Vienna Convention on the Law of Treaties (VCLT).[23] The Tribunal rejected this argument, holding that the DTC covers aspects of avoidance of double taxation and the prevention of fiscal evasion.[24] The BIT, on the other hand, offered protection to the investments made by nationals of the other contracting party.[25] Thus it can very well be that a tax measure otherwise governed by the DTC denies legal certainty or right to a fair trial and therefore violates the treatment guaranteed under the BIT.[26] The non-discrimination clause or the dispute resolution clause under the DTC do not create sufficient overlap so as to exclude the application of the BIT. The two treaties deal with different protections and are not exclusive of each other.[27]

The Tribunal also rejected India's second jurisdictional objection, noting that there was nothing in international public policy, let alone Dutch public policy, to support India's stance that tax-related investment disputes are not arbitrable.[28] Hence, the Tribunal concluded that it had jurisdiction to adjudicate the dispute.

II.2.2. Liability of India under the FET standard

The innovative question before the Tribunal was whether tax legislation could undermine the substantive protection offered to an investor under the BIT. On merits, the Tribunal first determined whether the 2012 Amendment was "retroactive". Secondly, the Tribunal analyzed whether the FET standard was breached as a result of the retroactive 2012 Amendment.

1. Whether the 2012 Amendment was retroactive

First, the Tribunal considered whether the 2006 Transactions resulted in a capital gain. The Final Assessment Order (FAO) issued by the Indian Revenue alleged that the 27 subsidiaries were valued originally at book value but were sold to CIL at market value. This gain in value, the Tribunal held, was a rational basis for India to tax.[29] This, however, did not make the 2006 Transactions taxable as the issue was on what basis under Indian tax law would these gains be taxable. The FAO relied heavily on the 2012 Amendment as a basis of levying the tax on capital gains, concluding that the 2006 Transactions were OITs of assets situated in India.[30]

23. Vienna Convention on the Law of Treaties, 1155 UNTS 331, entered into force on 27 January 1980, art.32 (VCLT).
24. UK–India BIT Preamble.
25. *Cairn Award* PCA Case No. 2016-7 at [803].
26. *Cairn Award* PCA Case No. 2016-7 at [808(b)].
27. *Cairn Award* PCA Case No. 2016-7 at [808].
28. *Cairn Award* PCA Case No. 2016-7 at [823]–[836].
29. *Cairn Award* PCA Case No. 2016-7 at [1042(b)].
30. *Cairn Award* PCA Case No. 2016-7 at [1049]–[1050].

Regarding the temporal application of the 2012 Amendment, the FAO held that it was "clarificatory" and hence applicable to the 2006 Transactions. The Tribunal questioned this reasoning in the FAO and the position of the Indian Government. The Tribunal relied on various factors such as the intent of the ITA 1961, reports of special tax committees, and the *Vodafone (SC)*[31] judgment to conclude that the 2012 Amendment expanded the tax base and thus was "retroactive" and not "clarificatory" as held by the FAO.[32]

Primarily, the Tribunal relied on two Reports of Special Tax Committees constituted by the Indian Government and headed by Dr Parthasarathi Shome: the *Report on Retrospective Amendments Relating to Indirect Transfer* (the Shome Committee Report)[33]; and the *Report of the Tax Administration Reform Commission* (the TARC Report).[34] The Shome Committee Report concluded that the 2012 Amendment, "…[was] not clarificatory in nature…[and] should be applied prospectively".[35] Further, the TARC Report dealt with the issue directly to state that the 2012 Amendment overruled the *Vodafone (SC)* judgment. The TARC Report noted that such an "overnight change in the interpretation of a provision" is "deeply harmful" to investor sentiments and the Indian economy.[36]

Further, the Tribunal attached much weight to the *Vodafone (SC)* judgment, being the only authoritative ruling on the application of section 9(1)(i) of the ITA 1961 pre-2012 Amendment.[37] The Supreme Court handed down a clear ruling—for section 9(1)(i) of the ITA 1961 to apply, there must be a capital asset situated in India, which should be transferred leading to a gain.[38] The Supreme Court further held that section 9(1)(i) of the ITA 1961 to include OITs would amount to "changing the content and ambit" of the section.[39] Further, since the words "situate in India" could be found in the section, to interpret it to include OITs would render that phrase nugatory.[40] At the arbitration, India tried to dismiss the Supreme Court's judgment as incorrect. However, the Tribunal noted that though the

31. *Vodafone (SC)* (2012) 6 SCC 613.
32. *Cairn Award* PCA Case No. 2016-7 at [1060]–[1251].
33. Expert Committee, *Report on Retrospective Amendments Relating to Indirect Transfer* (the Shome Committee Report) (2012), *https://qc.incometaxindia.gov.in/Lists/Press%20Releases/Attachments/21/Draft_Report.pdf* [Accessed 15 February 2022].
34. *First Report of the Tax Administration Reform Commission* (the TARC Report) (2014), *http://www.nadt.gov.in/writereaddata/MenuContentImages/First_report_TARC635480254365343004.pdf* [Accessed 15 February 2022].
35. Shome Committee Report (2012), p. 34.
36. TARC Report, p. ii.
37. *Vodafone SC* (2012) 6 SCC 613.
38. *Vodafone SC* [2012] 6 SCC 613 at [164].
39. *Vodafone SC* [2012] 6 SCC 613 at [71].
40. *Vodafone SC* [2012] 6 SCC 613 at [71].

judgment was not binding on it, it would be "an extraordinary step" to not give the judgment the "weight it commands".[41]

For the above reasons, the Tribunal concluded that the effect of the 2012 Amendment was to "render taxable transactions that were previously not taxable" and hence was retroactive and not clarificatory in nature.[42]

II.2.3. Whether 2012 "retroactive" Amendment breached FET standard

The final leg of the analysis was whether the 2012 Amendment violated the FET standard. India argued that there was no rule of customary international law that prohibited retroactive legislation. With such an absence, India's authority to enact retroactive legislation was only subject to the Indian constitutional limitations.[43] The Tribunal accepted that Indian law may permit retroactive tax legislation, but the question remained whether the "core principles of fairness" prohibit such tax legislation.[44] On this issue, the Tribunal realised that it was treading on new ground.[45] The Tribunal looked at the general principle of legal certainty and its determination by investment tribunals.

The Tribunal's analysis was two-pronged: first, it determined whether tax legislation by being retroactive violated the principle of legal certainty; secondly, whether there was an equally countervailing and proportional public policy justification for such legislation to be enacted. This justification would need to be such that it could not have been attained by legislating prospectively.[46]

The Tribunal began its analysis by laying the contours of legal certainty. Fundamental to the rule of law is that taxpayers must be able to understand the obligations of their conduct.[47] Legislation must cater to future transactions and not past conduct, failing which, it would undermine legal certainty and legitimate expectation. Thus, retroactive laws that change the legal consequences of past transactions are inimical to this norm.[48] By way of corollary, the law must permit the taxpayers to transact in accordance with the law as it existed at the time of the transaction. Thus, the law must, as a general rule, operate prospectively.[49] The Tribunal noted, however, that this is not without exceptions.

41. *Cairn Award* PCA Case No. 2016-7 at [1228].
42. *Cairn Award* PCA Case No. 2016-7 at [1737].
43. Constitution of India [As on 9 September 2020], *https://legislative.gov.in/sites/default/files/COI.pdf* [Accessed 15 February 2022], Pt III.
44. *Cairn Award* PCA Case No. 2016-7 at [1732]–[1733].
45. *Cairn Award* PCA Case No. 2016-7 at [1734].
46. *Cairn Award* PCA Case No. 2016-7 at [1790].
47. *Cairn Award* PCA Case No. 2016-7 at [1750].
48. *Cairn Award* PCA Case No. 2016-7 at [1750].
49. P. Baker, "Retrospective Tax Legislation and the European Convention on Human Rights" [2005] B.T.R. 1.

The question then was, when would it be permissible to legislate retroactively and whether India met that standard with the 2012 Amendment. The Tribunal relied on the Shome Committee Report and two of Professor Philip Baker QC's articles. The Shome Committee Report divided retroactive tax legislation into four parts based on its effect. Such legislation could 1) remove apparent errors or mistake, 2) remove procedural defects, without affecting the substance, 3) prevent erosion of substantive tax provisions through highly abusive tax practices, or 4) expand the tax base.[50] The Shome Committee Report concluded that the first two types of legislation are necessary. The Report also noted that the third type of retroactive legislation would still be justifiable as "any avoidance of tax through exploitation of any loophole in the system means a windfall to a dishonest taxpayer at the cost of general body of the taxpayers".[51] For the fourth type of retroactive legislation, the Report held it to be "against the basic tenet of the law as it affects the certainty of law".[52] Therefore, without justifiable exception (such as to prevent tax avoidance), retroactive legislation would be "an affront to the principle of legal certainty and runs afoul of the guarantee of predictability of the legal environment".[53]

The Tribunal further relied on Professor Philip Baker QC's arguments against retroactive tax legislation.[54] Baker argues that as a rule, the legislation must be prospective as the taxpayer has a legitimate expectation that the tax would be levied as anticipated. This is true of both retrospective and retroactive legislation.[55] For retroactive legislation to be condoned, it must be "zealously scrutinised" and the state concerned must prove why "the objective could only be attained by introducing retrospective provisions".[56] If the taxpayer participates, Baker argues, in highly tax abusive structures then it is a possible justification for retroactive legislation.[57] Specific to the Cairn Award, Baker argues, retroactive legislation that override binding and final court decisions are a "clear breach of human rights norms".[58] Such legislation would, apart from violating legal certainty, also take away the right of the taxpayer to a fair trial. Though the second leg may be more relevant for Vodafone, the law laid down by the Supreme Court in *Vodafone (SC)* would be applicable to Cairn as well.[59] Thus, if such retroactive legislation fails to exclude the

50. Shome Committee Report (2012), p. 30.
51. Shome Committee Report (2012), p.30, accepting the position in *R. v HMRC* [2011] EWCA Civ 893.
52. Shome Committee Report (2012), p.30.
53. *Cairn Award* PCA Case No. 2016-7 at [1757].
54. P. Baker, "Retroactive Tax Legislation" (2012) 6(48) *International Taxation* 780; Baker, "Retrospective Tax Legislation and the European Convention on Human Rights" [2005] B.T.R. 1.
55. Baker, "Retroactive Tax Legislation" (2012) 6(48) *International Taxation* 780, 781.
56. Baker, "Retrospective Tax Legislation and the European Convention on Human Rights" [2005] B.T.R. 1, 8.
57. Baker, "Retroactive Tax Legislation" (2012) 6(48) *International Taxation* 780, 781.
58. Baker, "Retroactive Tax Legislation" (2012) 6(48) *International Taxation* 780, 781.
59. *See,* Constitution of India [As on 9 September 2020], Article 141, *https://legislative.gov.in/sites/default/files/COI.pdf* [Accessed 15 February 2022].

decision it seeks to overrule, or any pending litigation already initiated or right already accrued (as in Cairn's case), it will violate the right to fair trial, a core element of the FET standard.[60]

For these reasons, the Tribunal proceeded to determine whether there was any specific public policy justification (such as to prevent tax abusive practices) which allowed India to enact the 2012 Amendment retroactively. Undertaking this balancing exercise, the Tribunal looked at possible reasons to enact the 2012 Amendment.[61] Cairn conceded that combating tax abuse was a valid justification.[62] However, India could not show that the 2012 Amendment was meant specifically to combat the tax abuse by Cairn, as the FAO did not make any allegation of tax avoidance.[63] Thus, India was restricted to arguing that the 2012 Amendment was enacted to counter widespread tax avoidance through OITs. Even there, India could not show systemic abuse by foreign investors using OITs to erode the Indian tax base. Rather, on India's own submission, OITs were "rarely seen".[64] To make it worse, India had argued that it has always had the basis to combat tax avoidance through the substance over form principle in its domestic laws.[65] This would negate the purpose of enacting the 2012 Amendment retroactively.

In conclusion, the Tribunal noted that while India had the sovereign right to enact the 2012 Amendment, it was not entitled to do so retroactively and especially not without excluding the decision it sought to overrule and any pending litigation.[66] Thus, the 2012 Amendment violated the principle of legal certainty and was in breach of the FET standard under the BIT.

III. Post-Award Phase

Post the *Cairn Award*, India sought to challenge it in Netherlands (the seat of the arbitration).[67] Additionally, the award in *Vodafone International Holdings B.V. v Government of India* (*Vodafone Award*) was also not in India's favour and challenged in Singapore (its seat of arbitration).[68] On the other hand, Cairn sought to enforce the *Cairn Award* in various jurisdictions, like France and the US. This is permissible

60. Baker, "Retroactive Tax Legislation" (2012) 6(48) *International Taxation* 780, 784.
61. *Cairn Award* PCA Case No. 2016-7 at [1796]–[1800].
62. *Cairn Award* PCA Case No. 2016-7 at [1812].
63. *Cairn Award* PCA Case No. 2016-7 at [1812].
64. *Cairn Award* PCA Case No. 2016-7 at [1813].
65. *Cairn Award* PCA Case No. 2016-7 at [1813].
66. *Cairn Award* PCA Case No. 2016-7 at [1816].
67. *Cairn Award* PCA Case No. 2016-7.
68. *Vodafone Award* PCA Case No. 2016-35.

under the New York Convention on the Recognition and Enforcement of Foreign Arbitral Awards (New York Convention).[69]

At the enforcement proceedings, India maintained, amongst other things, that it had the sovereign right to enact the 2012 Amendment and that tax measures were outside the jurisdiction of the Tribunal. Hence, the Awards ought not to be enforced under the New York Convention. India's argument was not received well by the French Court that ordered seizure, in July 2021, of real estate holdings situated in Paris.[70] Further, in May 2021, Cairn had approached the US courts with a view to seizing Air India airplanes claiming Air India (India's national carrier) to be an "alter ego" of the government.[71]

Mindful of the global enforcement proceedings and potentially the reasoning of the Tribunal in the *Cairn Award*,[72] the Government of India introduced a Bill to amend section 9(1)(i) of the ITA 1961[73] in the Indian Parliament on 5 August 2021.[74] The Bill was passed by both Houses of Parliament in four days and received Presidential assent on 13 August 2021 to become the Taxation Laws (Amendment) Act, 2021 (the 2021 Amendment Act).[75] The 2021 Amendment Act nullifies the taxability of income resulting from an OIT that took place before 28 May 2012.[76] This is a significant policy change because, as noted above, on the basis of the retroactive aspect of the 2012 Amendment, the OIT transactions were made taxable with effect from 1962.[77]

With the 2021 Amendment Act, India has sought to 'undo' the retroactive effect of the 2012 Amendment. In the 2021 Amendment Act's Statement of Objects and Reasons, the Honourable Finance Minister, Ms Nirmala Sitharaman, referred to 17 cases that the 2021 Amendment Act is specifically intended to address.[78]

---

69. Convention on the Recognition and Enforcement of Foreign Arbitral Awards, entered into force 7 June 1959, 330 UNTS 3 (New York Convention) Art. V. The Awards can be enforced in any country that is party to the New York Convention where India has assets. India is a party to the New York Convention.
70. David Sheppard, Amy Kazmin and David Keohane, "Cairn Energy freezes Indian state-owned properties in Paris" (8 July 2021) *Financial Times*, *https://www.ft.com/content/ac0e2c3d-e50c-418e-a43a-5a8ca2c803ad* [Accessed 15 February 2022].
71. Ammar Zaidi, "Cairn CEO says $1bn refund offer acceptable to firm, to drop cases within days" (7 September 2021) *Outlook*, *https://www.outlookindia.com/newsscroll/cairn-ceo-says-1bn-refund-offer-acceptable-to-firm-to-drop-cases-within-days/2155380* [Accessed 15 February 2022].
72. As reflected in the Statement of Object and Reasons of the 2021 Amendment Act.
73. Income-Tax Act, 1961, No.43 of 1961 (ITA 1961).
74. Taxation Laws (Amendment) Bill, 2021, No. 120 of 2021.
75. Taxation Laws (Amendment) Act, 2021, No. 34 of 2021 (2021 Amendment Act). Introduced Lok Sabha 5 August 2021; passed Lok Sabha 6 August 2021; passed Rajya Sabha 9 August 2021.
76. To provide context, OITs transactions involve a sale of shares or other instruments of a foreign company overseas, where the value of the shares or other instruments is derived substantially from assets situated in India.
77. Finance Act, 2012, No. 23 of 2012 s. 4 (2012 Amendment).
78. Taxation Laws (Amendment) Bill, 2021, No. 120 of 2021, Statement of Objects and Reasons.

III.1. 2021 Amendment Act

The 2021 Amendment Act reverses the retroactive effect of the 2012 Amendment. The Objects and Reasons (O&R) of the 2021 Amendment Act are:

> "2. As the verdict of the Supreme Court was inconsistent with the legislative intent, the provisions of the Income-tax Act, 1961 were amended by the Finance Act, 2012 with retrospective effect, to clarify that gains arising from sale of share of a foreign company is taxable in India if such share, directly or indirectly, derives its value substantially from the assets located in India....
>
> 3. Pursuant thereto, income-tax demand had been raised in seventeen cases....
>
> 4. The said clarificatory amendments made by the Finance Act, 2012 invited criticism from stakeholders mainly with respect to retrospective effect given to the amendments. It is argued that such retrospective amendments militate against the principle of tax certainty and damage India's reputation as an attractive destination....
>
> 5. The Bill proposes to amend the Income-tax Act, 1961 so as to provide that no tax demand shall be raised in future on the basis of the said retrospective amendment for any indirect transfer of Indian assets if the transaction was undertaken before 28th May, 2012 (i.e., the date on which the Finance Bill, 2012 received the assent of the President)...."[79]
>
> (*Emphasis supplied*)

The O&R proceed on the basis that the 2012 Amendment was "*clarificatory*" though it is acknowledged that the 2012 Amendment is "*argued*" to be against "*the principle of tax certainty*".[80] This admission is significant. With the reasons to remedy the retroactive effect of the 2012 Amendment, the 2021 Amendment Act was enacted.

The 2021 Amendment Act inserts three provisos into section 9(1)(i) of the ITA 1961.[81] The 2021 Amendment Act can be divided into two heads: where an order of assessment is "to be passed" and where an order of assessment "has been passed" under the 2012 Amendment.[82]

---

79. Taxation Laws (Amendment) Bill, 2021, No. 120 of 2021, Statement of Objects and Reasons, emphasis added.
80. Taxation Laws (Amendment) Bill, 2021, No. 120 of 2021, Statement of Objects and Reasons, para. 4.
81. 2021 Amendment Act s. 2.
82. 2021 Amendment Act s. 2. The Act uses the phrase "(i) an assessment or reassessment to be made under section 143, section 144, section 147 or section 153A or section 153C; or (ii) an order to be passed enhancing the assessment or reducing a refund already made or otherwise increasing the liability of the assessee under section 154; or (iii) an order to be passed deeming a person to be an assessee in default under sub-section (1) of section 201". For the present purposes, the phrase is shortened to "assessment".

First, through the fourth proviso (Section 9(1)(i) of the ITA 1961 already contained three provisos), in the case where the order of assessment '*is to be passed*', the 2021 Amendment Act excludes the application of the 2012 Amendment. That is, the OIT must have been "*made before the 28th day of May, 2012*".[83] This makes the 2012 Amendment prospective legislation. India appears to have accepted the analysis of the Tribunal in the *Cairn Award* that the object of 2012 Amendment was "*a valid policy justification for prospective taxation, [but] it is insufficient to justify retroactive legislation*".[84]

Secondly, through the fifth proviso, the 2021 Amendment Act deals with cases where the order of assessment has already been passed in a case where the OIT took place before 28 May 2012. In such cases, if certain "specified conditions" are fulfilled, then that order of assessment "*shall be deemed never to have been passed or made*".[85] Since the order would become nullified, any tax collected under that order would be rendered nugatory. For this, the sixth proviso requires that the government refund the taxes so collected, without any interest.[86]

Further, the "specified conditions" for the fifth and sixth provisos to apply are mentioned in the explanation to the proviso. It requires that the taxpayer, "withdraw" (i) "any appeal before an appellate forum or any writ petition", (ii) "any proceeding for arbitration, conciliation or mediation" and (iii) "[waive] his right" to any future litigation.[87] The 2021 Amendment Act also gives delegated authority to the Indian Revenue to prescribe other conditions.

The Indian Revenue exercised this right and released a draft notification on 28 August 2021 (Draft Rules),[88] inviting comments and suggestions from stakeholders. The final rules were released on 1 October 2021 *(Rules)*.[89] The Rules insert Rule 11UE and Rule 11UF into the Income Tax Rules, 1962 (ITR 1962).[90] Rule 11UE prescribes the "Specified conditions under *Explanation* to fifth and sixth proviso…" to avail the benefit of the 2021 Amendment Act.[91]

---

83. 2021 Amendment Act s. 2.
84. *Cairn Award* PCA Case No. 2016-7 at [1732]–[1750], [1814].
85. 2021 Amendment Act s. 2.
86. 2021 Amendment Act s. 2.
87. 2021 Amendment Act s. 2, "Explanation".
88. Ministry of Finance, *Inviting comments on the draft notification for framing rules for implementing the amendments made by the Taxation Laws (Amendment) Act, 2021* (28 August 2021), *https://incometaxindia.gov.in/Lists/Latest%20News/Attachments/449/Inviting-comments-on-the-draft-notification-dated28-08-2021.pdf* [Accessed 15 February 2022].
89. Ministry of Finance, Income-tax (31st Amendment) Rules, 2021 (1 October 2021), *https://www.incometaxindia.gov.in/news/notification_no_118_2021.pdf* [Accessed 15 February 2022] ["Rules"].
90. Income-Tax Rules, 1962 (ITR 1962).
91. ITR 1962 r. 11UE.

First, the taxpayer must submit an undertaking under Form No. 1 and append undertakings from all 'interested parties'.[92] Post submission of the undertaking, the jurisdictional Principal Commissioner or Commissioner (Commissioner) would "grant a certificate in Form No. 2 accepting such undertaking".[93] The Commissioner has discretion to reject the undertaking after hearing the taxpayer.[94] After grant of the above certificate, additional conditions such as indemnity against any future claims and public notice of waiver of any claims, under Rule 11UE(2) must be fulfilled.[95] This is an additional condition not under the 2021 Amendment Act.[96]

The rule explains that the "interested party" is, amongst others, "all companies...in the entire chain of holding...till the ultimate holding company..."[97] or "any person who has initiated proceedings" against a "relevant order".[98] A "relevant order" is explained as a specified order[99] in respect of income "arising through or from the transfer of an asset or capital asset situate in India in consequence of the transfer of a share or interest in a company or entity registered or incorporated outside India made before the 28th day of May, 2012..."[100] This is an extremely broad requirement and with many investors having holding companies across the world, the requirement becomes extremely cumbersome as well.

Interestingly, if there is any dispute under the Rules, for instance basis a rejection of undertaking under Form No. 1, such dispute "shall be governed by the relevant Indian laws...under the exclusive jurisdiction of the...courts in India".[101]

IV. Conclusion

Before dealing with the impact of the 2021 Amendment, it is pertinent to analyze the *Cairn Award* and its impact. Though the 2021 Amendment nullifies the retroactive application of the 2012 Amendment, it does not negate the Award itself. The *Cairn Award* is valid and enforceable subject to the New York Convention.[102] The 2021 Amendment Act does not in any way impact the enforceability of the Award. It may be argued that the relief granted by the Tribunal is satisfied by the 2021 Amendment Act (*albeit* without costs and interest). Thus, its reasoning still stands and is worth analysing.

92. ITR 1962 r. 11UE(1).
93. ITR 1962 r. 11UF(2)(a).
94. ITR 1962 r. 11UF(2)(b), read with r. 11UE(2).
95. ITR 1962 r. 11UF(3)
96. ITR 1962 r. 11UE(2), read with 2021 Amendment Act, "Explanation" cl. iv to fifth and sixth provisos.
97. ITR 1962 r. 11UF, "Explanation" cl. (c)(i).
98. ITR 1962 r. 11UF, "Explanation" cl.(c)(iv).
99. ITR 1962 r. 11UF, "Explanation" cl.(f).
100. ITR 1962 r. 11UF, "Explanation" cl.(e).
101. ITR 1962 r. 11UF(17).
102. See, New York Convention, art. V.

The Tribunal's analysis is commendable in that it clarifies the law on the general approach to retroactive legislation. It also showcases investment arbitration as a more efficient alternative to domestic courts or dispute resolution under the DTC.[103] Cairn could have approached the Indian domestic courts, as Part III of the Indian Constitution lays down similar rules against retroactive legislation.[104] There is a probability that the Indian courts would have struck down the 2012 Amendment for violating the Indian Constitution. However, this alternative was presumably not favoured for fear of a similar override by the Indian Parliament.

The *Cairn Award* is pioneering in that it has suggested the solution to various debates on the interplay between the investment arbitration regime and the international tax regime. In a clear, structured, and logical exposition, the Tribunal concludes that investment disputes, which irrespective of their root in taxation, would be amenable to arbitration under the BIT. The Award's reasoning stems from the difference in the scope of the BIT and the DTC. Tax disputes are not reserved for dispute resolution under the DTCs, to the implied exclusion of the BIT. If the dispute also raises issues of violation of the FET standard or other protections offered under the BIT, it can be subject to a BIT arbitration.[105]

The determination that substantial rights guaranteed under the BIT are breached is exclusive of whether the measure under scrutiny is a tax measure. Therefore, there is no reason why tax matters should be excluded, unless specifically stipulated under the BIT. Consequently, the Tribunal was correct to note that tax-related investment disputes are within the scope of its jurisdiction. Further, the Tribunal admits that India has the sovereign power to enact the 2012 Amendment.[106] However, in exercising its power to legislate, India cannot breach the rights that it has guaranteed under the UK–India BIT.

The Tribunal's analysis, however, is no longer tenable under India's current investment framework. Mindful of the potential reasons, India amended its Model Bilateral Investment Treaty in 2015 (2015 Model BIT) and cancelled almost all of its existing BITs in 2017. Currently[107], only four pre-2015 BITs, with Senegal, Latvia, Lithuania, and Libya are in existence. Further, only six countries (Bangladesh, Belarus, Columbia, Taipei, Kyrgyzstan, and Brazil) have signed the 2015 Model BIT. Apart from Bangladesh, India has no existing investment treaty

103. See *LSF-KEB Holdings SCA v Republic of Korea* ICSID Case No. ARB/12/37, where Belgium MAP proceedings were sought to be initiated but Korea rejected the proposal.
104. Constitution of India [As on 9 September 2020], *https://legislative.gov.in/sites/default/files/COI.pdf* [Accessed 15 February 2022], Pt III.
105. See K. Perrou, "Tax Law Disputes before Investment Arbitration Panels: Practical Experience" (2016) 56(10) *European Taxation* 451.
106. *Cairn Award* PCA Case No. 2016-7 at [1805].
107. As of February 2022.

with its major trading partners.[108] This is pertinent because the 2015 Model BIT contains an explicit carve out for all taxation measures. In the India-UK BIT that the Cairn Tribunal dealt with, there was only a limited tax carve-out that was restricted only to the National Treatment and Most Favoured Nation protections. The Tribunal had interpreted the limited carve-out to hold it as inapplicable for FET protection. The 2015 Model BIT now makes it clear that this carve-out is applicable for all the BIT protections. If this was not sufficient, the 2015 Model BIT gives the power to the State requiring that:

> "For greater certainty, it is clarified where the State in which investment is made decides that conduct alleged to be a breach of its obligations under this Treaty is a subject matter of taxation, such decision of that State, whether before or after the commencement of arbitral proceedings, shall be non-justiciable and it shall not be open to any arbitration tribunal to review such decision".[109]

As a result, the Tribunal's reasoning on its jurisdiction may not be applicable to a subsequent Tribunal interpreting a BIT based on the 2015 Model BIT.

On merits too, the Tribunal has laid down general principles that transcend the *Carin Award.* In a pure jurisprudential exposition, the Tribunal considers whether retroactive tax legislation could breach substantial protections offered under the BIT. Being mindful that it was in unchartered territory, the Tribunal went the extra mile to elaborate circumstances in which retroactive legislation would be permissible.[110]

The reasoning of the Tribunal is clear. Retroactive tax legislation would violate a State's obligation under the BIT unless there exist compelling reasons that warrant the legislation to be enacted retroactively. India's sovereign authority to enact the 2012 Amendment retroactively was subject to it providing justifiable cause. The purpose behind such an evaluation is to balance the violation of legal certainty for the taxpayer and the State's power to enact legislation in the public interest. Thus, the State must show that there was a public policy justification that outweighed the taxpayer's legitimate expectation for legal certainty. This balance, the Tribunal ruled, is achieved by Baker's test – "no reasonable taxpayer, properly advised, could have had a legitimate expectation of enjoying the fruits of the avoidance".[111] The Tribunal left the public policy justification to the State and thus went beyond the

108. As per Ministry of Commerce Data, *https://dashboard.commerce.gov.in/commercedashboard.aspx*, India's top 5 trading partners (in descending order) are: United States, United Arab Emirates, China, Bangladesh and Hong Kong.

109. 2015 Indian Model BIT, *https://dea.gov.in/sites/default/files/ModelBIT_Annex_0.pdf* [Accessed 15 February 2022].

110. *Cairn Award* PCA Case No. 2016-7 at [1734].

111. Baker, "Retroactive Tax Legislation" (2012) 6(48) *International Taxation* 780, 781.

limited justification of countering tax abuse argued by Shome and Baker. The State must show that the legislation could not have been enacted prospectively. What may cause the State to legislate retroactively is for the State to decide. Albeit the justification must be proportional and have a causal link with the legislation. Having failed to meet this test, the Tribunal concluded that India had breached the FET standard.

Presently in India, OITs are taxable, and the OECD has acknowledged that such transactions should be taxable.[112] Thus, it can be argued that there was justifiable cause to enact the 2012 Amendment. Faced with such a scenario, the State must retain the power to remedy court judgments that counter the State's tax policy. Baker accepts that this is not unusual.[113] However, to overrule judgments retroactively, by negating the judgment itself denies the taxpayer the right to a fair trial and legal certainty. Particularly in India's case, there was no existing policy of India to tax OITs and it could not show systemic tax avoidance or its inability to deal with them. Thus, on this argument as well, the Tribunal ruled that India breached the FET standard.

Potentially due to the sound reasoning of the Cairn Award and possibly the enforcement and seizure of Indian assets abroad, India enacted the 2021 Amendment Act. The Act is a commendable step, but it is recommended that India make it a policy decision not to enact retroactive legislation. India must appreciate that retroactive legislation is problematic, independent of the Awards. India has enacted other retroactive amendments, which the 2021 Amendment Act does not deal with. Apart from the OIT retroactive amendment, the definition of royalty was also expanded retroactively from 1976 pursuant to section 4(b) of the Finance Act, 2012 (Royalty Amendment).[114] Similarly, this expansion was also claimed to be a clarificatory amendment to section 9(1)(vi) of the ITA 1961.[115] It is recommended that India make it a policy decision to withdraw all retroactive legislation and provide reassurance that it will not enact such legislation moving forward. Some relief in relation to the Royalty Amendment was granted by the Indian Supreme Court in *Engineering Analysis Centre of Excellence Private Ltd v Commissioner of Income Tax*.[116] The court held that the Royalty Amendment expanded the definition of royalty unilaterally and would not apply to cases where the definition under the

112. The Platform for Collaboration on Tax, *The Taxation of Offshore Indirect Transfers—A Toolkit*, available at: *https://www.tax-platform.org/sites/pct/files/publications/PCT_Toolkit_The_Taxation_of_Offshore_Indirect_Transfers.pdf* [Accessed 15 February 2022].
113. Baker, "Retroactive Tax Legislation" (2012) 6(48) *International Taxation* 780, 785.
114. Finance Act, 2012, No. 23 of 2012 s. 4(b).
115. ITA 1961 s. 9(1)(vi) explanations 4–6.
116. *Engineering Analysis Centre of Excellence Private Ltd v Commissioner of Income Tax* [2021] 432 ITR 471 (SC).

relevant double tax convention is more favourable to the taxpayer. But the ruling would not apply to cases involving countries with which India does not have a double tax convention.

Nevertheless, the 2021 Amendment Act re-establishes faith in Indian tax laws, furthering India's reputation as a tax-friendly nation. It is undoubtedly a welcome step. The swiftness shown, be it in enacting the legislation itself or in the timeline under the ITR 1962, showcases India's desire to deliver quickly. The willingness of the government to refund the INR 8,100 crores collected is commendable. Almost all the refund – INR 7,900 crores – is due to Cairn.[117] Senior officials have been quoted in the media saying that all the 17 taxpayers are accepting the 2021 Amendment Act.[118] As the phrase goes, "all's well that ends well", the Revenue Secretary has been quoted saying that the "government is well on course to settle nearly all" of the payments due under the 2021 Amendment Act.[119] Thus, the book may soon be shut on the 2012 Amendment.

117. ANI, "Govt will refund Rs 8000 crore to four companies once new taxation laws come into effect: CBDT Chairperson" (10 August 2021) *Economic Times*, *https://economictimes.indiatimes.com/news/ economy/policy/govt-will-refund-rs-8000-crore-to-four-companies-once-new-taxation-laws-come-into-effect-cbdt-chairperson/articleshow/85199595.cms* [Accessed 15 February 2022].

118. Gireesh Prasad, "Cairn Energy sees near term solution to India tax dispute" (7 September 2021) *Mint*, *https://www.livemint.com/companies/news/cairn-energy-sees-near-term-solution-to-india-tax-dispute-11631000923081.html* [Accessed 15 February 2022].

119. Rituraj Baruah and Ravi Dutta Mishra, "Govt to settle almost all retrospective tax cases in February: Revenue Secretary" (4 February 2022) *Mint*, https://www.livemint.com/economy/govt-to-settle-almost-all-retrospective-tax-cases-in-february-revenue-secretary-11643988459447.html [Accessed 15 February 2022].

REJOINDER

Hans Mooij

The *Cairn* Arbitration Award – On Abusive Tax Avoidance

1. Introduction: Abusive Tax Avoidance, Retroactive Taxation, and the FET standard

The *Cairn* arbitration, next to its 'twin' the *Vodafone* arbitration, made history for its decision to disallow retroactive taxation. There will be only a few who had anticipated a different outcome. Fortunately, the full text of the decision in *Cairn* is now public[120], including the parties' submissions and the arbitral Tribunal's considerations – unlike *Vodafone* of which only the brief award is available. In the meantime, the *Cairn* award has been formally annulled by the decision of The Hague Court of 21 December 2021, with consent from the Cairn companies, following the new Indian Tax Rules 2021 which provide for partwise elimination of the retroactive taxation, and the agreed settlement between the Indian Government and the companies based thereon. But the decision and considerations in *Cairn* retain their relevance, of course, as guidance for future cases.

On the examination of the *Cairn* decision, the Indian Government, while losing the final award, appears to have made a considerable gain in advancing the argument that retroactive taxation would be applicable under the India/UK BIT for the reason of abusive tax avoidance. In the end, the Indian Government lost this argument as well, because, in the view of the Tribunal, it failed to produce the evidence that there had been abusive tax avoidance and not because the argument as such was void.

2. Justification

The Tribunal accepted the argument of abusive tax avoidance as a possible justification for breaching the Fair and Equitable Treatment (FET) standard under the BIT. To be specific, the Tribunal at first considered that:

> ...[it] agrees that [the Indian Government's] two primary defences (tax avoidance and ...), if successful, could potentially defeat an FET claim.[121]

While further elaborating, however, the Tribunal opined more specifically that:

> ...the question that the Tribunal must answer is whether [the Indian Government] had a specific justification for enacting retroactive tax legislation

120. Final award of 21 December 2020, PCA Case No. 2016-7.
121. §1018.

> and applying it to [the Cairn companies], i.e., beyond the legitimate purpose of providing revenues for India's general budget.[122]

And that:

> A major justification in respect of retroactive taxation is the State's power to combat tax abuse.[123]

This raises the question whether the Tribunal meant to recognize the justification of abusive tax avoidance only in the narrow context of retroactive taxation or more generally to the effect that the presence of abusive tax avoidance will also be recognized to justify other breaches of the FET standard. The difference between these two readings, obviously, is substantial since abusive tax avoidance as an occurrence is far more regular than retroactive taxation.

The decision is very summary in explaining where the Tribunal derived its view from. There is only a brief reference to the European Commission of Human Rights[124] having expressed similar views when scrutinizing the permissibility of retroactive taxation by the UK of certain abusive transactions.[125] Perhaps the Tribunal simply thought that an elaborate explanation is not necessary, since Cairn, too, had conceded that the need to combat tax abuses would be a recognized justification.[126]

A similar ambiguity can be found where the decision analyzes the breach of an investor's 'legitimate expectation' as part of the FET standard. The Tribunal's source is equally limited, consisting of a mere quotation from an article by -Philip Baker[127]:

> Noting that retroactivity and retrospectivity in tax legislation "both undermine legitimate expectations where the taxpayer has either anticipated a particular tax outcome for previously earned income, or, in the case of retrospective legislation, anticipates a particular future outcome," Baker accepts that neither is objectionable "where the taxpayer, viewed realistically, had no legitimate expectation of the previous outcome", i.e., "where the avoidance was so abusive that no reasonable taxpayer, properly advised, could have had a legitimate expectation of enjoying the fruits of the avoidance."[128]

Despite the focus of this quotation being on retroactive taxation, as is the entire article from which it was derived, it is difficult to see why the understanding that a

122. §1808.
123. §1796.
124. *A, B, C and D v the United Kingdom*, Application No. 8351/79, (1981) 23 D.R. 203.
125. §1797.
126. §1812.
127. Philip Baker QC, *Retroactive Tax Legislation,* 6(48) International Taxation 780 (June 2012), CLA-60, p 781.
128. §1775.

legitimate expectation cannot be claimed in a case of abusive tax avoidance might not apply more broadly to any kind of taxation whether retroactive or not.

If investors are denied protection by the FET standard in each case where there is abusive tax avoidance, this would bring BITs in line with tax treaty and EU tax law. The OECD Commentary clearly stipulates that States do not have to grant the benefits of a tax treaty where arrangements that constitute an abuse of the provisions of the treaty have been entered into.[129] The European Court of Justice considers tax avoidance an abuse of EU law that must be stricken down even in the absence of any express provision to that effect in either an EU Directive or implementing domestic law.[130] These latter provisions may be regarded as expressions of the general 'abuse of rights' principle, which stems from civil law but has occasionally also found application under common law and public international law and aims to prevent the exercise of a right in a harmful manner which is arbitrary or unjustifiable or not in accordance with the reason for which the right was conferred.[131]

It may serve as an excuse that the Tribunal, as it admitted itself, was "trading new ground".[132] There does not appear to be any precedent under the investment arbitration. Due to BEPS and the MLI, there is a growing awareness of international tax avoidance among authorities and an increase of legal instruments to combat it, including in developing countries. This may easily cause authorities to clash with foreign investors enjoying the special protection of BITs. Before long more cases must therefore be expected to emerge in BIT arbitration wherein the right to investor protection is challenged on grounds of abusive tax avoidance – either established or alleged.

3. Reference to Indian Court Decisions

In *Cairn*, no prior determination had been made by the Indian tax authorities of any specific abusive tax avoidance. In taking their position, the authorities had merely referred to the application of the GAAR. At the time, the Tribunal cast its decision, legal proceedings before the Delhi High Court against the assessment imposed were still pending. The Tribunal, however, did not want to wait for that the decision, as it had made clear:

---

129. §60 of the Commentary on Art 1, 2017 OECD Model Tax Convention on Income and on Capital.
130. CJEU decisions of 26 February 2019, C-116/16, C-117/16, C-115/16, C-118/16, C-119/16 and C-299/16 ("Danish cases").
131. See, for instance, A. Kiss, *Abuse of Rights*, in: R. Bernhardt, ed., *Encyclopedia of Public International Law*, vol. 1 (Amsterdam: North-Holland, 1992); and more specifically regarding arbitration, Ahmed El Far, *Abuse of Rights in International Arbitration* (Oxford University Press, 2020).
132. §1734.

> The Tribunal cannot anticipate what the Indian courts might or might not do.[133]

Why not, the Tribunal did not explain. It appears, in any event, neither the Indian Government nor Cairn had asked the Tribunal to delay its decision. However, the question remains if the Indian courts had determined a specific abuse would the Tribunal have accepted such determination as an established fact to take stock of in its own decision? Or would it, notwithstanding, have still examined for the presence of abusive tax avoidance, if any?

In defining abusive tax avoidance, the Tribunal referred to a wide range of relevant Indian court decisions over time, including, for instance, *Duke of Westminster* (1936), *Calcutta Chromotype* (1998), *Azadi Bachao* (2003), *Aditya Biria Nuvo* (2011), and, of course, *Vodafone* (2012). The sole explanation provided by the Tribunal was that the Indian Government had proposed so:

> The Tribunal agrees with the [Indian Government] that the applicable standard to determine whether there was tax avoidance is to be found in Indian law. The Parties do not appear to dispute this.[134]

Thus, this appears to have been a mere matter of convenience. But a more principled underpinning might have been possible with the application of the *lex fori* rule of international law. It must be noted that there is no internationally agreed definition of what constitutes abusive tax avoidance, neither under the OECD Model Tax Convention and its Commentaries nor in the MLI. Instead, the international courts leave it primarily to domestic law and practice to determine if a particular case is abusive.

Be it with some hesitance, the Tribunal, from the range of general rules and approaches developed by the Indian courts, opted to apply the 'dominant purpose' test:

> In arriving at a view on the law, although the Tribunal is not fully convinced that the "dominant purpose" test which [the Indian Government] has sought to impress upon it is what has emerged from Vodafone (in that on one reading of the Chief Justice's reasons it might be said that a colourable device is required to demonstrate tax avoidance), the Tribunal has opted to accept the dominant purpose test as being the applicable one.[135]

Yet, further in its decision the Tribunal inconsistently referred to the 'substance over form' principle[136] being the one it applied, seemingly unaware that in the

133. §1436.
134. §1298.
135. §1424.
136. §1591.

common tax language 'substance over form' implies an essentially different test than that for 'dominant purpose'. The 'dominant purpose' test which the Tribunal said to have opted for, rather resembles in wording the 'principal purpose' test under the MLI[137]. But this is not to say that both would necessarily share the same concept. In any case, the Tribunal did not attempt to develop a definition of abusive tax avoidance of its own invention independent from familiar tax practices. This must be considered a fortunate thing.

With abusive tax avoidance thus defined, the Tribunal proceeded by examining the transactions of Cairn, not only for the avoidance of Indian tax but foreign tax as well, including UK corporation tax and UK stamp duty.[138] The Tribunal even examined for any breaches of Indian security and exchange laws, in search, so it seems, of any kind of abuse or illegality.[139] This appears strange and pointless, considering that the Indian GAAR serves only to protect Indian revenue interest and the Indian authorities applied it for no other reason than that. Did the Tribunal misunderstand the objective and functioning of the GAAR? Its broad examination makes more sense, however, if the Tribunal believed, as discussed above, that any abuse or illegality irrespective of its nature and location, including the other treaty partner or perhaps even third countries, disqualifies an investor for protection under a BIT.

4. Matter of Proof

The Tribunal upon examination found the transactions by Cairn "not avoidant" in any event.[140] What eventually seems to have tipped the balance in favor of Cairn, however, was that the Indian Government had itself failed to produce any evidence of tax avoidance. As the Tribunal observed:

> ...the [tax authorities] did not tax [Cairn] on a theory of tax avoidance. It has not been suggested that the 2012 Amendment was enacted to sanction [Cairn] for their specific abuse.[141]

The Tribunal, again with reference to Indian case law, showed firm determination in holding the Indian Government accountable for this failure:

> The Vodafone judgment is crystal clear that the burden of proving tax avoidance is on the Revenue.[142]

137. Art 7(1) Multilateral Convention to Implement Tax Treaty Related Measures to Prevent Base Erosion and Profit Shifting (MLI)
138. §1647.
139. §1647.
140. §1812.
141. §1812.
142. §1424.

Indeed, while a GAAR typically, with a general scope, can strike any type of tax avoidance, tax authorities in applying a GAAR nevertheless must specify which type of avoidance they allege a taxpayer has committed and which transactions or entity structures, to enable a taxpayer to properly defend itself. The predominant question, ordinarily, is how much proof authorities must provide. Particularly, the presence of genuine business reasons or the absence of abusive intent are things that a taxpayer can best prove because these things relate to circumstances or a mindset known only to that taxpayer. Under the principal purpose test of the MLI, for instance, the burden of proof is therefore allocated reversely to the taxpayer, who must prove that granting a treaty benefit in their case was in fact intended.[143] In *Cairn*, however, it was not necessary for the Tribunal to dive this deep into the matter since the Indian authorities did not even produce a little evidence in support of abusive tax avoidance.

5. *Prima facie* Abuse?

In the hearings, the Indian Government finally argued that indirect transfers should be regarded prima facie as a 'systematic abuse':

> [The Indian Government's] argument appears to be that it passed the 2012 Amendment to combat systematic tax abuse by foreign investors engaging in indirect transfers "and not paying tax anywhere in the world."[144]

In comparison, under the OECD Model, indirect transfers of shares in the immovable property are subject to source country taxation equally as direct transfers[145], and under some bilateral tax treaties, the same even applies to indirect transfers of shares generally. It is obvious that without this provision source country taxation might easily be frustrated by interposing a foreign entity and thus transforming a direct transfer into an indirect one. The relevant OECD Commentary, however, is silent on the purpose of the provision, particularly whether it is meant to prevent tax avoidance or simply generate more source country revenue. The Tribunal, in any case, was little convinced of any anti-avoidance motive:

> The 2012 Amendment does not target foreign investors who evade or wrongly avoid taxes; it applies to any indirect transfer, whether tax abusive or not. Its goal is to tax transactions which indirectly involve the transfer of assets situated in India, regardless of whether they have been taxed elsewhere.[146]

143. Art 7(1) MLI.
144. §1813.
145. Art 13(4), 2017 OECD Model.
146. §1815.

In the specific case of Cairn, whether the Tribunal would have been more responsive to this argument of 'systematic abuse' by resolving the need to identify abusive tax avoidance if the 2012 Amendment had stated its goals more precisely, is anybody's guess.

6. Cause for Specialized Tax Arbitrators

It seems that the Tribunal was not very comfortable dealing with the case. It may explain that all three arbitrators were generalist arbitration experts and not tax experts. The Tribunal expressed in honesty that it had difficulty tracing the development of the law of India on the distinction between legitimate tax planning and abusive tax avoidance, as it did so:

> ...with full knowledge that [the Tribunal] is not an Indian court and that the exercise ... is not as comprehensive as the Tribunal believes the briefing of the law would be, were an allegedly tax avoidant transaction to once again go before the Supreme Court or the Constitutional Court.[147]

The comparison with the Indian Supreme Court (which, I believe, also acts as Constitutional Court) is not too far-fetched if one considers the measure of the impact of the Tribunal's decision. But in terms of tax expertise, a judgment from the Delhi High Court as is currently pending would seem more trustworthy already. It may be questionable that the Tribunal did not bother to consult any independent expert evidence. Apparently, to excuse itself, the Tribunal observed:

> ...it merits clarifying that the present dispute is a tax-related investment dispute, not a tax dispute.[148]

This distinction between a tax-related dispute and a tax dispute may be argued from an institutional point of view. *Cairn*, however, was dominated by pure tax issues such as retroactive taxation and abusive tax avoidance, rather than the issues of investment or arbitration law, although line between the two was only thin.

Identifying abusive tax avoidance is an arbitrary matter by its very nature. Its dependence on factual circumstances, individual motives of taxpayers, and their appreciation inevitably cause it to have a high degree of subjectivity. The *Cairn* award, likewise, is an arbitrary decision. Identifying abusive tax avoidance, either to combat it or to prevent it, is a typical tax technical expertise and nowadays almost a daily concern for tax experts globally. This is not to say that true tax experts would have decided differently than the present Tribunal, but with tax experts aboard the Tribunal, its decision would in any case have been less arbitrary and better trusted. The standard rule must simply be that tax experts arbitrate on tax issues. To this

147. §1424.
148. §793.

end, arbitration institutes should acknowledge the need and value of specialized tax arbitration and start with including an offer of qualified tax experts on their lists. Eventually they may proceed to creating entirely specialized tax panels. And disputing parties, of course, should care in the future not to select any others but tax experts.

CHAPTER 9

India's Change in Position on the Application of Retroactive Taxation

Philip Baker

I. Introduction

This chapter focuses on the Vodafone[1] and Cairn[2] arbitration cases, in the broader context of India's change in position on the application of retroactive taxation. That is the change that took place in August 2021 when the Indian Government announced[3] that it was going to reverse the legislation that retroactively introduced a tax charge on offshore indirect disposals. As a consequence, India settled the cases with Cairn and with Vodafone, and others.

Personally, it is something of an end of a long journey. It was probably 2007 or 2008 that I was first approached by the internal tax advisors at Vodafone about the tax charge that they were potentially facing in India. I was engaged as an expert witness in the domestic litigation that went through to the Indian Supreme Court[4] and then again as an expert in the arbitration in the Vodafone case.

This chapter will consider first the background (though it is well known), then the Cairn arbitration award and its discussion of retroactive legislation.[5] Then I am going to pick up on the August 2021 change, and finally say something about the future.

II. The Background

In terms of the background, there is sometimes a distinction made between retroactive and retrospective taxation. Retroactive taxation is where a tax charge is

1. PCA Case No. 2016-35, Vodafone International Holdings BV v The Republic of India (award of 25th September 2020).
2. PCA Case No. 2016-7, *Cairn Energy Plc and Cairn UK Holdings Limited v The Republic of India* (award of 21st December 2020).
3. Legislation was introduced on the 5th August 2021 and became law on 13th August 2021 in the form of the Taxation Laws (Amendment) Act, 2021. This reversed the effect of the retroactive tax charge with regard to offshore indirect disposals that took place before 28th May 2012.
4. The Supreme Court decision is reported at *Vodafone International Holdings B.V. v Union of India* (*Vodafone (SC)*) (2012) 6 SCC 613; (2012) 14 ITLR 431 (Sup Crt India) 20th January 2012.
5. The Vodafone award is not publicly available, but in any event it does not go into the same detail as the Cairn award on retroactive legislation.

imposed on events that have already occurred and which would not previously have been taxable, or a higher tax is imposed than would otherwise have been the case. Retrospective taxation is sometimes distinguished, and that is where the tax applies to the future but on the income flowing from an event that has already occurred and cannot be changed. For example, if I have put money aside into my pension fund expecting that in the future it will be taxed at a lower rate. If a change is made such that my expectations about future taxation are different, that is not quite the same as retroactively imposing a tax charge on something that was not taxable at the time. From the point of view of the taxpayer, both types of change in the tax law depart from the expected tax treatment and may conflict with the taxpayer's legitimate expectation.[6] Both retroactive and retrospective tax legislation undermine confidence in the stability and certainty of the tax system.[7]

The focus of this chapter is on retroactive taxation - a tax charge that would not previously have existed. Broadly, one can divide countries into three groups so far as retroactive tax is concerned. There is a large group of countries where, by their constitution or by their law on taxation, retroactive tax legislation is simply banned.[8] They do not permit any retroactive tax legislation at all. There is then a group of countries where retroactive legislation is only permitted in limited circumstances. The constitution or the tax law may identify specific situations where that is permitted. Then there is a final group of countries where there are no restrictions; in

6. Of course, the degree to which a taxpayer has a legitimate expectation may depend upon the history of retroactive / retrospective tax changes in that particular jurisdiction, as well as the issue whether the taxpayer has engaged in aggressive tax planning that may have taken advantage of weaknesses in the tax system. In that respect, as explained below, India has something of a history of retroactive tax legislation, and tax advisors may well have brought this to the attention of companies investing in India. Even in those circumstances, however, it would have contravened expected practice for India to have taken away from a taxpayer the results of successful litigation to the Supreme Court (though there were examples of that previously).
7. Retroactive / retrospective tax legislation has been the subject of discussion in several cases of the European Court of Human Rights. See especially: *ABCD v. UK* (application no. 8531/79 - ECnHR) – s. 31 FA 78 was retrospective for 2 years; *M.A. and 34 others v. Finland* (27793/95) – retrospective change to tax; *SB v. Finland* (30289/96) – retrospective change to tax; *Joubert v. France* (30345/05) – retrospective validation of administrative action while litigation under way – breach; *Di Belmonte v. Italy* (72638/01) – 20% withholding tax imposed during delay in paying compensation; *Agurdino SRL v. Moldova* (7359/06) – retrospective legislation to override final decision of Supreme Court; *Arnaud v. France* (36918/11 and Ors) (retrospective taxation of Monaco residents); and *Huitson v. UK* (50131/12) (retrospective change in law on avoidance schemes). See also Melvin Pauwels, *Retroactive Tax Legislation in view of Article 1 First Protocol ECHR* (2013) EC Tax Rev 268 – 281.
8. For information on countries that ban retroactive tax legislation, see IFA, *The Practical Protection of Taxpayers' Fundamental Rights* (2015, 100B Cahiers de Droit Fiscal International) – General report by P Baker and P Pistone, and for updates see IBFD, Observatory on the Protection of Taxpayers' Rights – available at *https://www.ibfd.org/Academic/Observatory-Protection-Taxpayers-Rights*

principle, the government could introduce retroactive legislation as it wanted. In some countries, it is more widely used than in others.

India has been in the past the outlier among those groups of countries. India is in the third group, and retroactive legislation has in the past been used far more widely in India than in any other country that I am aware of. The current government of India has indicated that it does not intend to use retroactive legislation so widely, and I am not aware that there has been any retroactive tax legislation since the current government took power. Previous governments have not been so conservative in their view on the point.

It was said a number of times during the Vodafone litigation that the United Kingdom also adopted retroactive tax legislation, and that is true. We do not have a constitutional or legal restriction in the UK on retroactive tax legislation, save insofar as there are restrictions indirectly through the European Convention on Human Rights. That being said, the UK rarely uses it, and there are no more than about 20 examples since the Second World War. There have also been principles enunciated as to when retroactive legislation will be permitted and they are set out in a UK government statement that is monitored by a committee in the UK (of which I happen to be one of the members).[9] So the UK is not comparable to India's historical practice in this area.

III. Vodafone and Cairn

The particular issue of retroactive legislation came to the fore with the Vodafone case. Vodafone acquired indirect control over the Indian-based telecoms activities that had been established by Hutchison. The Indian Revenue Service came after the transaction and asked why Vodafone, as the purchaser, had not withheld 25% of the purchase price. Vodafone denied that they had a legal obligation to do so, and many Indian advisers had said there was no obligation to withhold. The Indian Revenue pursued Vodafone as an assessee in default, and the matter went ultimately to the Indian Supreme Court. In January 2012 the Indian Supreme Court came down unanimously in favour of Vodafone that the legislation did not permit the Indian Revenue to impose this tax withholding on Vodafone.

The ink was hardly dry on the judgment when one Friday morning in March 2012, less than two months after the judgment, the Indian Government announced that it was going to reverse the decision by retroactive legislation. This was the most surprising feature: to see a government not just adopting retroactive legislation but doing so to reverse a unanimous decision of its Supreme Court. It is said that there were probably about 17 companies affected by this, that had carried out transactions

9. This is the Protocol on Unscheduled Announcements of Changes In Tax Law, available at Tackling tax avoidance (publishing.service.gov.uk), page 17.

prior to the change in the law and that were going to be taxed. The total amount of tax that is said to have been involved is a large amount: it is roughly 500 billion rupees or US $6-7 billion, of which the claims against Vodafone and Cairn were a substantial part.

Vodafone, having already litigated to the Indian Supreme Court and won, did not go back to the Indian courts. Instead, they took the case to international arbitration, as did Cairn. As explained, the Vodafone tribunal decision is not publicly available, so I am not going to comment on it. The Cairn decision was publicly available and though it is a long decision – more like a small book – it is very well worth the read. Indeed, it refers to wide-ranging literature on the matter including seven times to Baker's work and 15 times to the analysis and conclusions of the committee—commonly known as the Shome Committee—on retroactive taxation that the Government of India itself set up in 2012.[10]

The arbitral tribunal consisted of Mr. Laurent Lévy (Presiding Arbitrator), Mr. Stanimir A. Alexandrov, and Mr. J. Christopher Thomas QC. None of them were tax specialists. I tend to rather disagree with those who suggest that the decision would have been any different if the panel had been tax experts, or that it would have been desirable to have had tax experts on the panel. This is not a case that turned on a detailed understanding of difficult issues of tax law, including the interpretation of tax treaties (for which I strongly agree that a panel with tax expertise is not only desirable but essential). This was not a case that involved any question of deliberate tax avoidance. The Vodafone case concerned a commercial acquisition, while the Cairn case involved internal reorganizations. Sometimes it is quite refreshing to have non-tax experts looking at what the tax authorities get up to, with a sense perhaps of greater shock that a tax authority might have done what the Indian authorities did here.[11]

In the Cairn matter, of course, Cairn had not litigated the dispute through to the Supreme Court and did not have a Supreme Court decision in their favour. However, the background was that Vodafone had taken a case through litigation, and there was a binding Supreme Court judgment denying the power to impose the withholding tax obligation. The 2012 legislation was not just retroactive but it was overriding the Supreme Court, and that raises major issues about respect for the courts and the rule of law in a country. I would have been very surprised if any tribunal would have decided this case differently from the arbitral tribunal in Cairn.

---

10. For an analysis, see Parthasarathi Shome, 2021, "Rejoinder on Retrospective Taxation to Nigam Nuggehalli," in P. Shome ed., *Reimagining International Taxation*, Chapter 4, pp. 71-94, Oakbridge Publishers, New Delhi.
11. The reader may be interested to see the view expressed by Mooij on this matter in his rejoinder to Vora's chapter in this volume on the Cairns matter.

The Cairn arbitration award case is considered elsewhere in this volume (see the chapter by Vora). I would like to focus specifically on what the tribunal said about retroactive tax legislation. The key passages include the following:

> 1791. In the context of fiscal measures, this means that a public purpose that typically justifies prospective tax measures, such as increasing the taxable base and fiscal income, does not in and of itself suffice to justify the measure's retroactive application. The goal of protecting and enhancing the public treasury is present in any attempt by a government to raise revenue. Instead, there must be an identifiable and specific public purpose justifying why it would not suffice to apply the measure prospectively, and why the State has deemed it necessary to apply it to past transactions.
>
> 1792. This is the approach towards retroactive taxation under Article 1 of Protocol 1 of the ECHR. The Baker article[12], to which the Tribunal has previously referred, concludes, after analysing the ECHR's jurisprudence on retroactive taxation, that:
>
>> Such [retroactive tax] legislation is not *per se* an infringement of the Convention. However, it will be zealously scrutinized to ensure that it can be justified. *The government concerned will need to show why the objective could only be attained by introducing retrospective provisions.* (emphasis added)

What the tribunal emphasises here is the obligation of a state to justify not just the tax measure, but why that measure must be applied on a retroactive basis. This is a very important element in the decision. The tribunal was, for the first time trying to put flesh out the "fair and equitable treatment" ("FET") obligation in the bilateral investment treaty by reference to general principles of law. As a general principle, they stated that legal certainty requires that legislation should be prospective in its application. A government that wishes to apply legislation retroactively has to justify that. They took part of the reasoning for this from the case law on the European Convention on Human Rights, which I had summarised in the article that they cited.

Going on from that point the tribunal discussed the practice of various jurisdictions that have grappled with the balancing exercise in the context of retroactive taxation:

> 1793. The practice of various jurisdictions that have grappled with the same balancing exercise in the context of retroactive taxation supports this conclusion. While that practice is not uniform as to the specific occasions at

12. Note: two articles were referred to in the arbitral award: Philip Baker QC, "Retroactive Tax Legislation", 6(48) International Taxation 780 (June 2012), and Philip Baker, "Retrospective tax legislation and the European Convention on Human Rights", (British Tax Review, 2005).

> which retroactive taxation is allowed, the general rule is that retroactivity should be specifically justified by a compelling public purpose.
>
> 1795. Turning now to the specific public purposes that could justify retroactive taxation, the practice of various municipal jurisdictions points to the following non-exhaustive circumstances:
>
> 1796. *Combatting abusive practices:* [this is merely the heading for the discussion in the award, but the heading will suffice for this purpose]
>
> 1798. Correcting inadvertent technical errors:
>
> 1800. *Avoiding the "announcement effect":*
>
> 1801. While it is not realistic to list all possible scenarios in which retroactive taxation may be justified, the above examples from the jurisprudence of municipal and international courts demonstrate that <u>the appropriate balance between the individual's interests of legal certainty / stability / predictability, on the one hand, and the State's power to regulate in the public interest, on the other, should be struck by reference to the principles of reasonableness and proportionality,</u> bearing in mind that the Tribunal is *ad hoc*, not part of the judicial machinery of the State, and not vested with a legislative or policy-making power. (emphasis added).

The tribunal explains that it falls to the government to justify retroactive tax legislation by reference to a specific public purpose. The tribunal goes on to consider certain specific purposes and provides a non-exhaustive list of specific purposes that might justify retroactive legislation. Thus, the tribunal mentions "combatting abusive practices" and discusses what is meant by that. I suspect we would probably all agree that if there is very clear abuse – not just avoidance, but actual abuse – with significant adverse revenue consequences, then a government may be able to justify retroactive tax legislation. Similarly, and less controversial, "correcting inadvertent technical errors in the legislation": I do not think anyone would have particular problems with that. They also mention the particular issue of avoiding the announcement effect where the mere fact that a government has announced that it will be legislating may affect conduct, and the government needs to have forestalling legislation to stop taxpayers from carrying out transactions to avoid a tax charge.

The tribunal made it very clear that they could not possibly list all the scenarios, but they did set out a general principle (underlined in the quotation). The appropriate balance between the individual's interest in legal certainty, stability, and predictability on the one hand, and the state's power to regulate the public interest on the other, should be struck by the reference to the principles of reasonableness and proportionality. Those are all general principles of law recognized by all nations, and the tribunal draws upon those to give substance to the FET obligation.

IV. The Indian Change in Practice

How was this taken in India? Litigation was commenced after the award, with Cairn seeking to enforce the decision against Indian assets, and India starting to bring a challenge to the arbitral award. Then, perhaps unexpectedly, in August 2021 the Government of India announced that it was to back away from the retroactive legislation. They would withdraw the retroactive legislation, and it was open to the companies that were affected to withdraw their claims against India. It is understood that both Cairn and Vodafone have withdrawn any claims and the issues have now been settled.

What is perhaps less clear is whether that is a general statement of Indian Government policy on the practice of retroactive tax legislation. The circumstances of the Cairn and Vodafone cases were special – there was the overturning of a Supreme Court case, and it did affect very large investments into India – and the current Indian Government has made it clear that it does not intend to use retroactive legislation very actively.

Pausing there, the tribunal in the Cairn arbitration has formulated an approach to Fair and Equitable Treatment in the context of retroactive tax legislation in an extremely persuasive fashion. It is difficult not to agree with the general principle set out in the award, and with the specific circumstances identified as justifying retroactive tax legislation. It is reasonable to assume that subsequent tribunals, engaged in applying the FET principle in the context of bilateral investment treaties and retroactive tax legislation, will follow this guidance (even though arbitral awards are not strictly speaking of a binding nature). The principles quoted above are highly persuasive. It is hoped that India might apply these principles more generally towards retroactive tax legislation if it is contemplated in the future.

V. The Future

So what does going to the future hold? One would like to think that going forward the Indian Government and other governments will follow the criteria in the Cairn award. The tribunal is very persuasive on this point. In keeping with other countries, for example, the tribunal's position is very similar to the criteria that are applied in the UK to justify the occasional retroactive tax measure. It does recognize that retroactive tax legislation is highly problematic: it undermines legal certainty, and any undermining of certainty increases costs and deters investment. If an investor is told: you may have a tax charge; you may have to litigate for ten years; you may face retroactive tax legislation even if you win your litigation, then the potential investor may not go ahead, or may look to invest in another country. If they try to take out insurance against the risk (if it is available) that will be a cost that they will have to incur.

Not adopting retroactive tax legislation, except in very limited circumstances, is clearly part of a stable environment for investment. In the Cairn and Vodafone cases, there was a very specific circumstance of the overturning of a Supreme Court judgment. As the tribunal acknowledged, that fundamentally undermines the rule of law and confidence in a government's respect for the rule of law. One may contrast that with other investment destinations where perhaps the rule of law is not part of the general atmosphere under which investments take place, but the more that one is seen to secure for investors (and for domestic taxpayers as well) a respect for the rule of law in tax matters, the more attractive an environment is likely to become.

VI. Concluding Remark

It was an important decision that the Indian Government took, ultimately and effectively, to uphold the decision of the Supreme Court. Mr. Justice Kapadia, the Chief Justice, of course, sadly died after the case and before this legislative amendment. However, there is an element here of respecting his memory by stepping back from the reversal of his judgment in 2012.

REJOINDER

Parthasarathi Shome

India's Modified Stance on Retroactivity

Philip Baker's chapter is a *tour de force* on India's journey in legislating retroactive taxation, his discussion focussed on Vodafone and Cairns, two multinational companies, versus the Government of India. To begin with, he makes a nuanced distinction between retrospective and retroactive taxation. The former enacts legislation today that affects existing businesses who may have made business decisions earlier but the new legislation affects their income streams going forward.[13] The latter affects the taxability of events that occurred even prior to the legislation. In that sense, he correctly uses the phrase retroactive taxation in the case of India though the common parlance has been to use retrospective taxation.

Another aspect to think of when considering retroactivity or even retrospectivity is that, while a business may have invested reflecting its own 'risk' evaluation, by facing new legislation that affects that earlier basis of expected income streams, the business enters a realm of business 'uncertainty'. This, in turn, renders the business 'impossible to perform'. This author has emphasised the point time and again beginning with the report on retrospective taxation of the Government of India that he had chaired and in subsequent analysis.[14]

In this volume, there is a rich discussion on the arbitration award of Cairn rather than on Vodafone since the former is available to public view while the latter is not. These analyzes have been carried out by Vora (Chapter 8) and Baker (Chapter 9) as well as a Rejoinder by Mooij to Vora. Essentially what emerges is a congruence in the views of international tax experts in that the "fair and equitable treatment" (FET) obligation in the bilateral investment treaty was not followed by the government of India in either of the taxation cases cited here.

---

13. Baker elaborated with an example, "Retrospective legislation is where a transaction takes place on the basis that the tax treatment of future income is expected to be in a particular form, and the tax treatment is changed when the transaction can no longer be altered or reversed, for example, a taxpayer invests in a pension fund expecting the pension payments to be tax free, but the government subsequently changes the rules s the payments become taxable." Electronic correspondence, 10 June, 2022.
14. See Shome, Parthasarathi (2021), "Rejoinder" to Nigam Nuggehalli's chapter, "Retrospective Taxation and the Vodafone Case," in *Reimagining International Taxation*, Oakbridge Publishers, Gurugram, Chapter 4, p.80.

    Shome (2021) also addresses the issue in the textbook, *Taxation History, Theory, Law and Administration*, Springer, Cham: Switzerland, p. 341.

Indeed, Baker alludes to the "shock" of the original 2012 legislation overturning the Supreme Court decision that Vodafone had no obligation to undertake a 25% withholding when it acquired the assets of Hutchison. While it took almost a decade for the government to step back from retroactive taxation, he applauds the August 2021 announcement that they "would withdraw the retroactive legislation, and it was open to the companies that were affected to withdraw their claims against India. It is understood that both Cairn and Vodafone have withdrawn any claims and the issues have now been settled."

Baker recommends that the FET principle must be strictly followed by the government when enacting legislation. To conclude, governments must also keep in mind the enormous financial and opportunity costs to both government and the productive sector of the government introducing legislation negligent of its long-term consequences. A bureaucracy that is blindly protected may not directly bear such costs but they certainly trickle down to the rest of society whose effective costs can be staggering in an economy such as India.

CHAPTER 10

Faceless Assessment in India

S. Krishnan

I. Introduction

India introduced faceless assessment to significantly reduce the physical interaction between the taxpayer and the tax officers and to mitigate abuse of power by the tax officers resulting in harassment, corruption, and unmanageable litigation. Under the faceless assessment procedure, a tax officer does not have jurisdiction over any taxpayer, so much so that the identity of the taxpayer and the tax officer is not known to each other. An income-tax return is allocated to an assessment unit dynamically through an automated allocation system, in a jurisdiction different from the taxpayer's location.

The Indian authorities launched a platform for 'Transparent Taxation-Honouring the Honest' on 13th August 2020, on the eve of India's 74th Independence Day. This platform comprising of three reforms -- faceless assessment, faceless appeals, and the Taxpayers' Charter is aimed at providing "Painless Tax Regime and Seamless Tax Compliance". It was launched through a video conference that symbolically depicts the assessment and appeal procedure in India in the future. While faceless assessment and taxpayers' charter are effective from 13th August 2020, the faceless appeal services came into effect on 25th September 2020.

Before we examine the features and procedure of faceless assessment, it would be appropriate to examine the face-to-face assessment procedure, its shortcomings, and the need for a faceless assessment scheme.

II. Procedure and Shortcomings of Face-to-Face Assessment

II.1. Face-to-face assessment procedure in India

Every taxpayer in India is required to furnish the details of their income to the Income Tax Department (ITD) by filing a return of income. The ITD would examine the income tax return for its correctness. The process of examining the income tax return by the ITD is called "Assessment". Under the Income-tax Act, 1961 ("Income-tax Act" or "Act"), there are four major types of assessments:[1]

1 https://www.incometaxindia.gov.in/Tutorials/33-various%20assessments.pdf.

- Assessment under section 143(1), i.e., Summary assessment without calling the assessee
- Assessment under section 143(3), i.e., Scrutiny assessment
- Assessment under section 144, i.e., Best judgment assessment
- Assessment under section 147, i.e., Income escaping assessment

Summary assessment:

Assessment under section 143(1) is a preliminary assessment and is referred to as a "Summary assessment". At this stage, the assessee (i.e., the taxpayer) is not required to be present, no detailed scrutiny of the income tax return is carried out and the total income or loss is computed after making the following adjustments (if any), namely:

(i) any arithmetical error in the return; or

(ii) an incorrect claim, if apparent from any information in the return; or

(iii) disallowance of the previous year's carry-over loss which is set off against the current year's income, if the previous year's income tax return was furnished beyond the due date specified; or

(iv) disallowance of deduction claimed if the current year's return is furnished beyond the due date specified; or

(v) disallowance of expenditure indicated in the audit report but not taken into account in computing the total income in the return.

However, no such adjustment shall be made unless an intimation is given to the assessee of such adjustment either in writing or in electronic mode. Further, the response received from the assessee, if any, shall be considered before making any adjustment, and in the case where no response is received within 30 days of the issue of such intimation, such adjustments shall be made. An intimation will be generated and sent to the taxpayer specifying the sum to be payable by, or the amount of refund due to the taxpayer.

II.1.1. Scrutiny assessment

An assessment made under section 143(3) is a detailed assessment and is referred to as a "Scrutiny assessment" or "Regular assessment". The objective of the Scrutiny assessment is to confirm that the taxpayer has not understated the income or computed excessive loss or underpaid the tax in any manner. The criteria and process of Scrutiny assessments have evolved over a period of time. Initially, all returns filed were taken up for scrutiny. Subsequently, returns showing income above a certain monetary limit were taken up for scrutiny. After that, returns for scrutiny assessment were picked up on a random basis. With the progressive increase in the workload of the ITD, scrutiny assessment in a few selected cases became the accepted norm.

The finance minister in the year 2003 announced a basket of reforms in the area of tax administration on the basis of the recommendations of the Task Force on Direct Taxes. The concept of risk analysis in the selection of taxpayers was introduced for the first time.

II.2. Broad criteria for selection of cases for scrutiny[2]

Cases are selected for scrutiny based on risk analysis conducted through the computer-assisted programme and also manually with reference to broad parameters decided every year for the entire taxpayer population. Two types of selections for scrutiny emerged:

- Computer Assisted Selection of cases for Scrutiny (CASS)
- Manual Selection of cases for Scrutiny

Compulsory Computer Assisted Selection of cases for Scrutiny (CASS): CASS is a system-based method for scrutiny selection that identifies the cases through data analytics and 360-degree data profiling of taxpayers and in a non-discretionary manner. A risk-based intelligent criterion was introduced for CASS and the first cycle was run in November 2004.[3] Selection of cases under CASS is generally made under two categories: (a) Compulsory, and (b) Score based selection.

Manual Selection of cases for Scrutiny: Similar to CASS, manual scrutiny is performed under two parameters:

- Compulsory selection
- Other than the compulsory selection

Cases for scrutiny are selected manually based on directions/parameters finalized by the Central Board of Direct Taxes (CBDT) every year.

Apart from compulsory manual selection, assessing officers (AOs) may select any case after recording reasons and obtaining approval of the Chief Commissioner of Income Tax (CCIT)/Director General of Income Tax (DGIT). Cases under this category are selected if there are compelling reasons and the case is not selected under CASS. Such cases are monitored by CCIT/DGIT in respect of the quality of the assessment.

II.3. Shortcomings in Face-to-Face Assessment

The Tax Administration Reform Commission (TARC) was constituted in August 2013 to recommend reform exclusively in tax administration. It was specifically mandated "to review the application of tax policies and tax laws in the context of

---

2 Income Tax Department press release.
3 AST Instruction No. 35.

global best practices and to recommend measures for reforms required in tax administration to enhance its effectiveness and efficiency." It recommended a complete overhaul together with detailed recommendations. In five volumes, and reflecting consultations with trade bodies and visits to tax offices all over the country, the TARC reports comprise the most voluminous assessment of India's tax administration at a commission level, including taxpayer (customer) treatment, risk-based assessment, the administration's trust in tax officers, strong repudiation in case of corruption and tax evasion, and various other aspects. In its first report, the TARC made the following observations regarding the income tax assessments.

II.3.1. Infructuous tax demands on the taxpayer

The risk-averse behaviour of the tax administration has routinely led to infructuous tax demands on the taxpayer, often with the full knowledge that eventually such demands would not be able to withstand or pass the judicial process. The resultant number of disputes and the time taken to resolve these have surpassed heights that are globally incomparable. A high proportion of cases that end in eventual defeat have led to a minuscule proportion of recovery compared to demand. Yet there is no accountability regarding recovery for the concerned officer. While raising demand is praised, there is no punishment for infructuous demands. The loser is the taxpayer in terms of time lost, advance payment required of the disputed amount resulting in deleterious effects on the cash flow of business, and the length of staff time and expenses associated with a long-drawn-out dispute resolution process.

II.3.2. Quality of assessments[4]

Framing of assessments by tax officials, the inadequacy of time for taxpayers to respond to the notices, and not dealing adequately with evidence on record have also been significant contributors to the logjam at various stages in dispute resolution. The substandard quality of assessments (whether in the form of non-speaking order or lack of judicial discipline or misinterpretation of judicial precedents) can be partly attributed to inadequate training/industry experience of tax officers and the practice of taking up assessments at the tail-end of statutory timelines. This also results in taxpayers not getting adequate time to respond to queries raised during the assessment.

II.3.3. Arbitrary/aggressive additions[5]

It has been widely claimed by taxpayers represented by major chambers during stakeholder consultations held by the TARC in the five metros that revenue authorities have been making arbitrary/irrational demands because of the revenue target-linked performance evaluation and incentive policy for tax officers. While

4 First Report of TARC.
5 First Report of TARC.

such an evaluation policy encourages revenue collection, the policy cuts both ways – from the tax administration's standpoint, it creates undue pressure on tax officials to augment revenues leading to arbitrary/frivolous demands in certain cases; from taxpayers' standpoint, it casts doubt on the sanctity of the entire tax administration, reducing the taxpayer's willingness for compliance, thus indirectly creating incentives for non-compliance.

In the absence of a reliable economic model capable of making meaningful revenue projections, budget revenue targets are set in the most rudimentary fashion and, subsequently, not revised to reflect the changing performance of the economy. Consequently, there is immense pressure on the tax administration to collect (non-existent) revenue, which results in the extortive behaviour of the pressured tax officer.

II.3.4. Excessive litigation by way of appeals[6]

A direct consequence of the lack of objectivity and fairness in the original decision is that far too many cases get into tribunals and courts. These needlessly add to administrative and compliance costs and add uncertainty to the tax environment. The tendency to file appeals against orders in favour of taxpayers, without giving due importance to the merits of the case, is pronounced. Although both departments (Central Board of Direct Taxes and Central Board of Excise and Customs) have come out with guidelines for litigation to control the practice, it appears to have had little effect. Apart from this, there is currently no time limit prescribed for the disposal of cases. In places where such a time limit is prescribed, it is not adhered to. In cases where there is the closure of cases, detailed reasons before closure are not provided, which consequently leads to appeals and counterappeals being filed.

II.3.5. Moral hazard[7]

Taxpayers openly complained during the TARC's consultations about their helplessness against demands for bribes to make refunds, to hold back infructuous demands, or to speed up processes from dormancy. Even senior officers admitted their ineffectiveness in controlling this growing phenomenon.

II.3.6. Taxpayer unfriendly approach – the absence of trust and collaboration[8]

Currently, the process of engagement with the taxpayer where there is a potential or existing dispute is primarily adversarial and lacks trust or openness. Besides, there is neither a conscious effort on the part of tax administrators to establish facts nor an effort to understand the position of the taxpayer in an open and collaborative

6 First Report of TARC.
7 First Report of TARC.
8 First Report of TARC.

manner. This leads to an unsatisfactory outcome in a large number of cases and escalates them to higher levels of formal disputes. The overall perception that is generated is that the existing system is not taxpayer-friendly and taxpayers' submissions do not affect the eventual decisions. In general, therefore, taxpayers do not have confidence that they would get justice at the hands of departmental officers. Thus, the first level where they can expect a fair order is the tribunal. The entire process thus functions in an adversarial environment.

III. E-initiatives to Reduce Human Interface with Taxpayers

The Indian Ministry of Finance undertook various steps to reduce the human interface between the taxpayer and the tax administration by using information technology to provide increased consistency, transparency, and efficiency in tax administration.

III.1. E-Sahyog

As a part of its "Digital India" initiative, the Indian government launched an e-platform to enable the ITD to correspond with taxpayers electronically. The "e-Sahyog" project launched on a pilot basis in October 2015, was aimed at reducing compliance cost especially for small taxpayers[9]. Traditionally, income tax returns were selected for scrutiny when the ITD found a mismatch in the information shown in the income tax return with the information submitted from third parties in the form of Annual Information Return (AIR), TDS statement, etc. The objective of "e-Sahyog" was to provide an online mechanism to resolve mismatches in income tax returns of taxpayers, without visiting the income tax office. Under this initiative, the ITD intended to provide an end-to-end e-service using SMS and emails to inform the taxpayers of the mismatch. The taxpayer was required to log in to the e-filing portal to view the mismatched information and provide an online response. The responses submitted online by the taxpayers would be processed and if the response and other information were found satisfactory as per automated closure rules, the issue would be closed. The taxpayers could check the updated status on the e-filing portal.

The CBDT notified the usage of emails as the new mode of communication with the taxpayers, as part of the government's e-initiative to reduce human interface and complaints of harassment and corruption in conducting tax-related jobs[10].

As a part of the e-governance initiative to conduct assessment proceedings electronically, the ITD launched 'E-Proceeding' facility. Under this facility, the tax officer is required to communicate with the taxpayers through the e-filing website of

9 CBDT press release dated 27 October 2015.
10 CBDT Notification No. 2/2016 dated 03 February 2016.

the ITD.[11] The taxpayers are required to submit the responses along with attachments and evidence (as applicable) on the e-filing website, without the need to visit the Income Tax Office. The response submitted by the taxpayer will be viewed by the tax officer electronically.

In the case of time-barring scrutiny cases pending as on 1st October 2017 in seven metro cities namely Ahmedabad, Bengaluru, Chennai, Delhi, Hyderabad, Kolkata, and Mumbai, where assessment proceedings were already underway through 'email-based communication' and the assessee was having 'e-Filing' account, proceedings in such cases were migrated to the 'e-Proceeding' facility, under intimation to the concerned assessee by the AO.[12] An option was provided to the assessee to opt out from this scheme at a subsequent stage after intimating the AO. In respect of time-barring 'Limited Scrutiny' cases pending with AOs, an option was provided to the concerned assessees having an 'e-Filing' account to furnish their consent to the ITD for the conduct of assessment proceedings through the 'e-Proceeding' facility. The CBDT mandated e-proceedings for all regular assessment cases from the year 2018-19, with certain exceptions.[13]

In order to transform the age-old conventional method of manual assessments, and ensure greater transparency, accountability and curb undesirable practices in the tax administration system, the Finance Act, 2018 inserted three new sub-sections (3A), (3B) & (3C) in section 143 (titled Assessment) of the Income-tax Act, which stipulate that the Central Government may introduce a scheme for making assessment so as to impart greater efficiency, transparency, and accountability by:

a. eliminating the interface between the AO and the assessee in the course of proceeding to the extent technologically feasible;
b. optimising utilisation of resources through economies of scale and functional specialisation;
c. introducing a team-based assessment with dynamic jurisdiction.

III.2. E-assessment Scheme, 2019

The CBDT notified the E-assessment Scheme in September 2019. E-assessment means the assessment proceedings conducted electronically in 'e-Proceeding' facility through the assessee's registered account on an e-filing portal termed as 'designated portal' by the Principal Chief Commissioner or Principal Director General, in charge of the National e-assessment Centre;

11 CBDT Notification No. 4/2017 dated 03 April 2017.
12 CBDT Instruction No. 8/2017 dated 29 September 2017.
13 CBDT Instruction no. 3/2018 dated 20 August 2018.

To implement the e-assessment scheme, the CBDT changed the assessment procedure and set up the following units:

(i) A National e-assessment Centre (NeAC) to facilitate the conduct of e-assessment proceedings in a centralised manner, which shall be vested with the jurisdiction to make assessments in accordance with the provisions of the E-assessment Scheme, 2019.

(ii) Regional e-assessment Centres (ReAC) to facilitate the conduct of e-assessment proceedings in the cadre controlling region of a Principal Chief Commissioner, which shall be vested with the jurisdiction to make assessments in accordance with the provisions of the E-assessment Scheme, 2019. Under each ReAC, there will be an assessment unit, a verification unit, and a review unit.

(iii) Assessment units to perform the function of making assessment which includes identification of points or issues material for the determination of any liability (including refund), seeking information or clarification on points or issues so identified, analysis of the material furnished by the assessee or any other person, and such other functions as may be required for the purposes of making an assessment. Currently, 95 assessment units are established in India.

(iv) Verification units to perform the function of verification which includes enquiry, cross verification, examination of books of accounts, examination of witnesses and recording of statements, and such other functions as may be required for the purposes of verification. Currently, 35 verification units are established in India.

(v) Technical units to perform the function of providing technical assistance which includes any assistance or advice on legal, accounting, forensic, information technology, valuation, transfer pricing, data analytics, management, or any other technical matter which may be required in a particular case or a class of cases, under this Scheme. Currently, 4 technical units are established in New Delhi, Mumbai, Calcutta, and Chennai.

(vi) Review units to perform the function of the review of the draft assessment order which includes checking whether the relevant and material evidence has been brought on record and whether the relevant points of fact and law have been duly incorporated in the draft order, whether the issues on which addition or disallowance should be made have been discussed in the draft order, whether the applicable judicial decisions have been considered and dealt with in the draft order, checking for arithmetical correctness of modifications proposed, if any, and such other functions as may be required for the purposes of review. Currently, 20 review units are established in India.

The NeAC is the only unit that virtually connects with assessees and various other units. It will identify the assessees for assessment, send notices, and receive responses from them. It will assign tasks to required units and will facilitate the conduct of proceedings in a centralised manner. All the communication among the different units will be done by the NeAC. Each ReAC comprising of an assessment unit, a verification unit, a technical and a review unit, and reports to NeAC.

III.3. Faceless Assessment Scheme, 2019

The CBDT made amendments to the E-assessment Scheme by a notification dated 13th August 2020[14] to introduce faceless assessment. The name of the Assessment Scheme was changed from E-assessment Scheme, 2019 to Faceless Assessment Scheme, 2019, and the 'Procedure for assessment' was modified.

The introduction of faceless assessment is a significant tax reform, aimed at reducing the scope for corruption and harassment by tax officials. Launching the Faceless Assessment Scheme on 13th August 2020, India's Prime Minister said, "Till now, all tax-related matters in a city are dealt with by the Income Tax Department of that city and IT officers of that city play the main role. Now on, using technology, scrutiny will be done by a randomly chosen IT officer anywhere in the country." Under the new mechanism, the identity of the taxpayer and the assessing officer will remain unknown to each other. Notices, if any, will be sent only by a centralised computer system, and the taxpayer can respond to them electronically without the requirement of visiting a tax office or meeting any official. This, according to the Prime Minister, would end the era of "*jaan pehchan*" (acquaintance) to get scrutiny or notices settled.

IV. Highlights of Faceless Assessment Scheme

The faceless assessment scheme was expected to bring about a paradigm shift in the assessment and scrutiny of income tax returns and the functioning of the ITD. It is important to consider the features mentioned below to be able to assess its success.

IV.1. Pillars of Faceless Assessment Scheme[15]

1. The scheme promises a team-based assessment unlike an individual-driven activity under manual assessments (non-faceless assessments). Multiple units such as the verification unit and technical unit may assist in the assessment procedure. The verification unit performs the function of enquiry, cross verification, examination of books of accounts, examination of witnesses, recording of statements, and such other functions as may be required for the

14 CBDT Notification nos. S.O. 2745 (E) and S.O. 2746 (E), dated 13 August 2020.

15 See Annexure 1 for the language of the Scheme.

purposes of verification. The technical unit is required to provide technical assistance such as advice on legal, accounting, forensic, information technology, valuation, audit, transfer pricing, data analytics, management, or any other technical matter which may be required in a particular case or a class of cases. This results in functional specialization and optimising the utilisation of resources through economies of scale.

2. Under the faceless assessment procedure, an AO does not have jurisdiction over any assessee, so much so that the identity of the assessee is not even disclosed to an AO (hence faceless). A case is allocated dynamically through an automated allocation system to an assessment unit, in a jurisdiction different from the taxpayer's location. There is no need for a taxpayer or his authorised representative to appear in person before any AO at the National Faceless Assessment Centre (NaFAC), Regional Faceless Assessment Centre (ReFAC), or an assessment unit regarding his assessment. In case a modification is proposed in the draft assessment order, the taxpayer or his authorised representative may request a personal hearing to make their submissions. If the request is granted, such a hearing also shall be conducted exclusively through video conferencing. There is electronic communication with the assessee at every stage of assessment and an opportunity is provided to the assessee to respond. This is expected to bring about transparency, efficiency, and standardisation of procedures.
3. The faceless assessment procedure centralises the assessment procedure at the NaFAC and removes the power of the AO at a local jurisdictional level, to issue assessment orders. The NaFAC will be the focal point of the faceless assessment procedure and the sole point of interaction with the taxpayer. The interaction between an AO and a taxpayer is eliminated except where complexity is involved. In such circumstances, the NaFAC may transfer the case to the AO having jurisdiction over such case, if considered necessary. Faceless assessment is expected to eliminate the possibility of taxpayer overreach and corruption since there is no physical interface between tax officers and taxpayers.
4. The faceless assessment procedure involves multiple layers of evaluation by different units. The assessment unit can only make a draft assessment order and send it to the NaFAC. Any errors or biases of the AO in the drafting of assessment orders would be mitigated when the NaFAC examines the draft assessment order in accordance with the risk management strategy specified by the CBDT, including by way of an automated examination tool. It may decide to assign the draft assessment order to a review unit in any ReFAC through an automated allocation system, for a review of the same.

The review unit is required to review the draft assessment orders, which includes checking whether the relevant and material evidence has been brought on record, if the relevant points of fact and law have been duly incorporated in the draft order, whether the issues on which addition or disallowance should be made have been discussed in the draft order, if the applicable judicial decisions have been considered and dealt with in the draft order, checking the arithmetical correctness of variations proposed, if any, and such other functions as may be required for the purpose of review. The review unit may suggest such variation as it may deem fit in the draft assessment order and send it to NaFAC, which will then assign the case through an automated allocation system to an assessment unit, other than the assessment unit which prepared the draft assessment order.

The second layer of review will not only ensure that all the contentions of the taxpayers including papers on record are duly considered by the review unit but also ensures that no mistake apparent on record is made while passing the order. This will not only reduce the scope for rectification but also potential litigation. The new multi-layered procedure of issuing an assessment order reduces the scope for arbitrariness by an AO. Consequently, high-pitched assessments and taxpayer harassment can be largely eliminated.

5. The faceless assessment procedure envisages the use of automated examination tools, artificial intelligence, and machine learning, which will reduce the scope of discretion of AOS. The allocation of a scrutiny assessment to an assessment unit, the conduct of enquiry or verification by the verification unit, and seeking technical assistance from the technical unit will be made through an automated allocation system. Better assessment orders may be generated due to the use of technology in analysing data.
6. All communication amongst the NaFAC, ReFACs and various assessment units and with the taxpayers will be exclusively done by electronic mode. This would deny an opportunity to the AOs to pass an order favouring the taxpayer in return for a pecuniary gain.
7. The turnaround time for completing faceless assessments is expected to be lower than under manual assessment as each process would be documented with a date and time stamp on it. This would put the onus on the teams to explain the pendency, which each official can see on the department's portal.

IV.2. Changes to E-assessment Scheme resulting in Faceless Assessment Scheme

1. The name of the Assessment Scheme was changed from E-assessment Scheme, 2019 to Faceless Assessment Scheme, 2019.

2. The scope of 'assessment' in the Faceless Assessment Scheme 2019 was expanded to include 'Best Judgment Assessment' under section 144 of the Act, in accordance with the amendments introduced by Finance Act, 2020.
3. The Faceless Assessment Scheme, 2019 modified the 'Procedure for assessment'.
4. The CBDT issued an order[16] effective 13th August 2020 that all the assessment orders shall hereafter be passed by NaFAC through the Faceless Assessment Scheme 2019 except assessment orders in cases assigned to Central Charges (such as serious frauds, major tax evasion, sensitive and search matters, black money and benami cases) or International Taxation. The Order further states that any assessment order which is not in conformity with this order shall be treated as "*non est*" (meaning non-existent) and shall be deemed to have never been passed. Consequently, all assessments pending as on 13th August 2020 will be concluded under the Faceless Assessment Scheme, 2019.

   Sub-section (9) of section 144B (titled Faceless Assessment) states, "Notwithstanding anything contained in any other provision of this Act, assessment made under sub-section (3) of section 143 (Assessment) or under section 144 (Best judgment assessment) in the cases referred to in sub-section (2), (other than the cases transferred to an AO by the Principal Chief Commissioner or the Principal Director General in charge of NaFAC), on or after the 1st day of April 2021, shall be non-est if such assessment is not made in accordance with the procedure laid down under this section."
5. The NaFAC, upon receiving suggestions for variation from the review unit, shall assign the case through an automated allocation system, to an assessment unit, other than the assessment unit which made the draft assessment order.

   Under the E-Assessment Scheme, the NeAC was required to communicate the suggestions for modifications from the review unit to the same assessment unit which made the draft assessment order.
6. The Faceless Assessment Scheme permits an assessee to seek an extension of the time limit from the NaFAC, to file a response.
7. Under the E-Assessment scheme, the assessee or his authorised representative was entitled to seek a personal hearing so as to make an oral submission or present his case before the income-tax authority in any unit.

   Under the Faceless Assessment Scheme, the assessee or his authorised representative can only request for a personal hearing to make his oral submission or present his case before the income-tax authority in any unit. The

16 CBDT Order F No. 187/3 /2020-ITA-I dated 13 August 2020.

Chief Commissioner or the Director General, in charge of the ReFAC, under which the concerned unit is set up, may approve the request for a personal hearing under certain circumstances (to be announced by the Principal Chief Commissioner or the Principal Director General of the NaFAC).

8. The Faceless Assessment Scheme permits the filing of an appeal against a penalty order made by the NaFAC.
9. Under the Faceless Assessment Scheme, the Principal Chief Commissioner or the Principal Director General in charge of NaFAC, may at any stage of the assessment, if considered necessary, transfer the case to the Assessing Officer having jurisdiction over such case, with the prior approval of the CBDT. Under the E-Assessment scheme, prior CBDT approval was not required.
10. The E-Assessment Scheme provided for the exchange of all the communication exclusively by electronic mode. The Faceless Assessment Scheme gives an exception to this requirement in case of enquiry or verification conducted by the verification unit under certain circumstances (to be announced by the Principal Chief Commissioner or the Principal Director General of the NaFAC).

IV.3. Faceless assessment under the Income-tax Act

The Government of India enacted the Taxation and Other Laws (Relaxation and Amendment of Certain Provisions) Act, 2020 (TOLA) which came into force on 31st March 2020. TOLA legislated the Faceless Assessment Scheme, 2019 into the Income-tax Act by inserting section 144B with effect from 1st April 2021. The provisions of section 144B of the Income-tax Act reflect the provisions of the Faceless Assessment Scheme, 2019 and the Faceless Assessment (1st Amendment) Scheme, 2021 with the following changes/additions –

- The National e-Assessment Centre has been renamed as National Faceless Assessment Centre (NaFAC) and the Regional e-Assessment Centre (ReFAC) as Regional Faceless Assessment Centre.
- The authorities to be assigned to the assessment unit, verification unit, technical unit, and review unit have been specified.

TOLA has amended certain other provisions of the Income-tax Act to enable faceless jurisdiction of income-tax authorities (section 130), faceless collection of information (section 135A), faceless inquiry or valuation (section 142B), faceless assessment of income escaping assessment (section 151A), faceless rectification, amendments and issuance of notice or intimation (section 157A), faceless collection and recovery of tax (section 231), faceless revision of orders (section 264A), the faceless effect of orders (section 264B), faceless approval or registration (section 293D) and determination of the arm's length price in relation to the international transaction or specified domestic transactions with associated enterprises [section 92CA(8)].

The Principal Chief Commissioner or the Principal Director General, in charge of NaFAC may at any stage of the assessment, if considered necessary, transfer the case to the AO having jurisdiction over such case, with the prior approval of the CBDT.

IV.3.1. Exchange of communication exclusively by electronic mode

For the purposes of this Faceless Scheme, all communications between the NaFAC and the assessee, or his authorised representative, or any other person shall be exchanged exclusively by electronic mode. Similarly, all internal communication between the NaFAC, ReFAC, and various units shall be exchanged exclusively by electronic mode. Exchange of communication exclusively by electronic mode shall not apply to the enquiry or verification conducted by the verification unit under certain circumstances (to be announced by the Principal Chief Commissioner or the Principal Director General, in charge of the NaFAC).

IV.3.2.No personal appearance in the Centres or Units

A person shall not be required to appear either personally or through authorised representative in connection with any proceedings under the Faceless Assessment Scheme before the income tax authority at the NaFAC or ReFAC or any unit set up under the said Scheme.

IV.3.3.Personal hearing to be conducted exclusively through video conference facility

In a case where a variation is proposed in the draft assessment order or final draft assessment order or revised draft assessment order, and an opportunity is provided to the assessee by serving a notice calling upon him to show cause as to why the assessment should not be completed as per such draft or final draft or revised draft assessment order, the assessee or his authorised representative may request for a personal hearing so as to make his oral submissions or present his case before the income tax authority in any unit under this Scheme.

The Chief Commissioner or the Director General, in charge of the ReFAC, under which the concerned unit is set up, may approve the request for a personal hearing, under certain circumstances (to be announced by the Principal Chief Commissioner or the Principal Director General of the NaFAC). This indicates that such approval may also not be approved.

If the request for a personal hearing has been approved by the Chief Commissioner or the Director General, in charge of the ReFAC, such hearing shall be conducted exclusively through video conferencing or video telephony, including the use of any telecommunication application software which supports video conferencing or video telephony, in accordance with the procedure laid down by the CBDT.

Other than an enquiry or verification conducted by the verification unit, any examination or recording of the statement of the assessee or any other person (other than a statement recorded in the course of survey under section 133A of the Income-tax Act) shall be conducted by an income-tax authority in any unit under the Faceless Assessment Scheme, exclusively through video conferencing, including use of any telecommunication application software which supports video conference or video telephony in accordance with the procedure laid down by the CBDT.

The CBDT should establish suitable facilities for video conferencing including telecommunication application software that supports video conference or video telephony at such locations as may be necessary, so as to ensure that the assessee, or his authorised representative, is not denied the benefit of this Faceless Scheme merely on the consideration that such assessee or his authorised representative, or any other person does not have access to video conferencing at his end.

IV.3.4. Penalty proceedings for non-compliance

1. In the course of assessment proceedings, any unit may, if it considers necessary or expedient to do so, recommend to the NaFAC to initiate any penalty proceedings under Chapter XXI of the Act (titled Penalties imposable), against such assessee or any other person, for non-compliance of any notice, direction or order issued under this Scheme by the assessee or any other person.

2. The NaFAC shall, on receipt of such recommendation, serve a notice on the assessee or any other person, as the case may be, calling upon him to show cause as to why penalty should not be imposed on him under the relevant provisions of the Act.

3. The response to the show-cause notice furnished by the assessee or any other person, if any, shall be sent by the NaFAC to the concerned unit which made the recommendation for a penalty.

4. The said unit shall, after taking into consideration the response furnished by the assessee or any other person, as the case may be,—

- make a draft penalty order and send a copy of such draft to NaFAC, or
- drop the penalty after recording reasons, under intimation to the NaFAC.

5. The NaFAC shall levy the penalty as per the said draft penalty order and serve a copy of the same along with demand notice on the assessee or any other person, as the case may be.

6. The NaFAC shall thereafter transfer electronic records of the penalty proceedings to the AO having jurisdiction over the said case for such action as may be required under the Act.

IV.4. Allocation of resources to implement Faceless Assessment Scheme

In order to implement the Faceless Assessment Scheme, the CBDT has diverted over two-thirds of its existing workforce at all levels of the ITD to the Faceless Assessment centres. The overall manpower strength of NaFAC and the ReFACs consists of 30 Chief Commissioners of Income Tax, 154 Principal Commissioners of Income Tax, 565 Additional/Joint Commissioners of Income Tax, 645 Deputy/Assistant Commissioners of Income Tax, and 2,830 Income Tax Officers and attendant staff.

IV.5. Field functions outside the faceless assessment centres

The field formations outside the hierarchy of faceless assessment centres will perform in a faceless manner to the extent possible, functions such as demand management, collection and recovery of taxes, rectification proceedings, taxpayer outreach, education and facilitation, grievance handling, and judicial functions including giving effect to the appellate orders of Commissioners of Income-tax (Appeals), Income Tax Appellate Tribunals, High Courts, Supreme Court, and Settlement Commission, preparing scrutiny reports and filing of appeal wherever considered necessary, defending writ petitions, prosecution and compounding proceedings and related court matters, custody, and management of case records, administrative, HRD and cadre control matters, management and control of infrastructure.

Table 1. Differences between Manual (non-faceless) Assessment and Faceless Assessment

Manual assessment	Faceless assessment
Cases are assigned to a single territorial jurisdiction. An AO had jurisdiction over a defined number of cases in a defined territory and is responsible for all types of work relating to those assessments such as processing, scrutiny, and assessment and also tasks related to the post-assessment period such as recovery, filing appeals, and sending remark reports. This overburdened the AOs compromising the quality of the assessments.	Cases are assigned to any faceless team anywhere in the country comprising 95 assessment units (dynamic jurisdiction) through an automated allocation on a random basis. An AO is only required to focus on assessment, assisted by a team performing different focused functions such as verification, review, and technical assistance.
Physical meetings between the taxpayer and the officers. All the assessees in a particular jurisdiction were assessed by the AOs in	No physical meeting with any officer. The assessee and the AO become anonymous in the assessment process eliminating the scope for over-reach

Manual assessment	Faceless assessment
that jurisdiction. The identity of the assessee was therefore known to the AO. The law required the taxpayer either to attend the office of the AO or, to produce or cause to be produced before the AO any evidence on which the assessee may rely in support of the return. This gave the opportunity to the AOs to harass the taxpayers and compromise on the assessment process giving scope for corruption. High-pitched assessments were issued to meet the high tax collection targets set for the tax officers resulting in a high level of litigation.	and high-pitch assessments. The cases will be randomly allocated to various assessment units using an automated allocation system. In addition, there is no direct contact between the AO and the assessee since the NaFAC in New Delhi works as a nodal office to communicate with the taxpayers, ReFACs, and the various units such as the assessment unit, verification unit, technical unit, and review unit. In addition, different units may be engaged in various aspects of the assessment of a particular assessee.
Case selection through a. System b. Manual c. Tax evasion information Taxpayers would be subject to compulsory scrutiny based on pre-defined parameters such as an addition in an earlier assessment year in excess of a defined threshold amount, on a substantial and recurring question of law or fact pending before an appellate authority. Consequently, the same taxpayers may be subject to compulsory scrutiny every year. Taxpayers who have indulged in incorrect transactions or in transactions meant to avoid tax may not be picked up for scrutiny, indicating that the case selection is not scientific and is not based on a proper risk matrix.	1. No discretion to any officer in selection of assessment cases. 2. No selection of cases except through system red alerts 3. No selection of cases other than information based Cases will be randomly allocated to various assessment units based on algorithms, data analytics, machine learning, and artificial intelligence. After the initial assessment, the NaFAC shall examine the draft assessment order in accordance with the risk management strategy specified by the CBDT, including by way of an automated examination tool. The NaFAC may decide to assign the draft assessment order to a review unit in any one ReFAC through an automated allocation system for conducting a review of such order. In case the review unit suggests any modification to the draft assessment order, the NaFAC will reassign it to a

Manual assessment	Faceless assessment
	new assessment unit. This process eliminates the individual and team-level discretions completely.
Issue of notices both manually and on system	Notices are to be issued electronically and centrally, only from the NaFAC in New Delhi (single point of faceless contact)
Assessment orders are passed by the AOs. Wide discretion provided to officers leads to subjective assessment and varying interpretations amongst AOs of various jurisdictions.	All the assessment orders are passed by NaFAC except assessment orders in cases assigned to International Tax Charges and Central Charge. 1. Team-based assessment and review 2. Drafting of assessment order in one city, review in another city, finalisation in the third city 3. Objective, fair and reasonable order

Source: Author.

V. Shortcomings in Faceless Assessment

Despite the good intentions of the government, several shortcomings prevail in practice. They have also been pointed out by some associations/ chambers.[17] They may be enumerated as follows.

V.1. Faceless Assessment Scheme has been mired in litigation since its announcement

Surprisingly, NaFAC which is the focal point of the faceless assessment procedure and the sole point of interaction with the taxpayer has identified 9 commonly occurring procedural lapses in faceless assessment proceedings based on an analysis of writ petitions filed in various courts against faceless assessments between April to December 2021[18]. These commonly occurring procedural lapses are:

17. 1. Suggestions from Bangalore Chamber of Industry and Commerce (BCIC) to Finance Minister to improve faceless assessment and appeal process, submitted on 10.12.2021.
 2. Representation by Direct Taxes Professionals' Association to CBDT dated 28.09.2021 regarding problems in Faceless Assessments.
 3. Article published in The Bombay Chartered Accountant Journal in July 2021 on Faceless Regime: Some Issues and the way forward, authored by Sanjay Sanghvi /Mr. Raghav Bajaj/Ujjval Gangwal.
18. NaFAC, Delhi, F No. NaFAC/Delhi/CIT-3/2021-22/340/148 dated 31-12-2021.

i. Assessment order has been passed even before the due date for reply allowed in the show cause notice/draft assessment order.

ii. Order has been passed without serving a draft assessment order/show cause notice

iii. Order has been passed without giving the opportunity of personal hearing (video conference) to the assessee

iv. Reasonable time has not been allowed to respond to notices

v. Order has been passed without taking cognizance of the response uploaded by the assessee

vi. Order passed beyond scope of scrutiny.

vii. Order passed without disposing of objections / grounds of reopening challenged

viii. Order passed before directions issued by Dispute Resolution Panel

ix. Order passed without considering adjournment application

NaFAC has requested Chief Commissioners of Income Tax (ReFAC) to sensitise the assessment units under their charge so that such lapses are not repeated, and the unit heads may also be directed to check upon such issues before approving the final assessment order. The commonly occurring procedural lapses identified above clearly indicate an implementation failure of the faceless assessment procedure by NaFAC since the faceless assessment procedure centralises the assessment procedure at the NaFAC.

V.2. Technical glitches on the income-tax e-filing portal

Under faceless assessment, all submissions and responses to notices can only be filed online on the e-filing portal. Taxpayers are facing the following issues while trying to respond online –

- Notices are issued to taxpayers to respond within a specific due date. Taxpayers are unable to upload their responses within the due date due to technical glitches on the portal.
- While uploading the attachments to the submission on the e-filing portal, some taxpayers received an error message stating "Error: File is not getting uploaded due to internal server issue". In some instances, the said issue lasted for several days thereby preventing the taxpayer from filing the response within the due date.

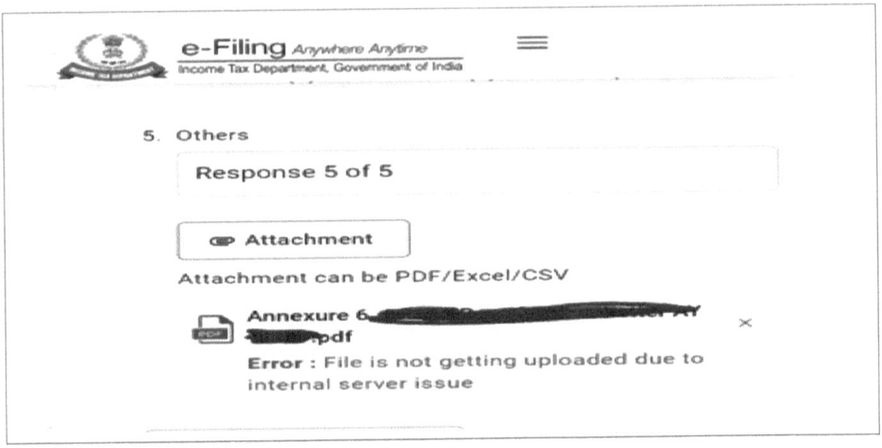

Source: Representation from Bangalore Chamber of Industry and Commerce to Finance Minister to improve the faceless assessment process

- While taxpayers filed grievances to address the above issues, they did not get resolved in a timely manner. Consequently, taxpayers were unable to furnish responses to the notices within the due date and the assessment units passed assessment orders considering the taxpayer to be non-compliant.
- In some instances, taxpayers were unable to file adjournment requests on the portal due to technical glitches and hence appearing as if they have not complied with the notice.
- While uploading documents, the session timed out frequently and the taxpayers were forced to repeat the process all over again.

V.3. Capacity constraints on the e-filing portal to upload attachments

- The ITD has set a limit to the size of taxpayer response to notices under e-Proceeding.[19] The response should be provided in less than 1,000 characters in the 'Response/ Remarks' field. The maximum size permitted for uploading each attachment is 5 MB and a maximum of 10 PDF attachments can be submitted in a single response submission. In case a taxpayer has more than 1 document to upload, he has to put them together in a zipped folder and upload the folder. The maximum size of all attachments in a zipped folder should be 50 MB. If the size of the single document or the zipped folder exceeds the permitted limit, the taxpayer has to optimize the document or the folder by reducing the file size.

19. e-Proceedings FAQ | Income Tax Department.

- In the notices issued to some taxpayers, a large amount of information and documents were sought. Due to capacity constraints for uploading the attachments, some taxpayers were unable to upload all the data sought from them, resulting in providing incomplete information in response to the notice. Some taxpayers were unable to provide the appropriate response due to size limitations. Consequently, inappropriate assessment orders were passed by the AOs.
- Due to the size limitations on the e-filing portal, taxpayers are forced to split their submission into multiple parts while uploading large files, resulting in the taxpayer spending a large amount of time in uploading documents on the e-filing portal.

V.4. Inadequate time given to taxpayers to respond to notices

- In the notices issued to taxpayers where a large portion of information, data, and documents was sought, inadequate time was given to taxpayers to respond to the notices. Further, some of the notices also stated that part compliance of the notice will be treated as non-compliance. Since a large number of documents were sought, taxpayers were required to spend a lot of time scanning documents and uploading them in multiple batches, given the capacity constraints for uploading attachments on the portal.
- During the prevalence of the Covid pandemic, many taxpayers were unable to respond within the time provided, due to constraints caused by lockdowns, curfews or unavailability of staff. This resulted in the issue of inappropriate assessment orders by the ITD.

V.5. Repeated notices issued to taxpayers ignoring the earlier submission filed by the taxpayers

- Assessment orders were passed without considering the submissions filed by taxpayers, or without providing the basis for not accepting taxpayers' submission
- There have been instances where follow-up notices were issued to taxpayers stating that the first notice has not been responded to, despite the taxpayer responding online to the earlier notice.
- In some cases, assessment orders were passed making adjustments stating that no response was filed by the taxpayer even though detailed submissions were filed by the taxpayer.
- Further, in certain cases, assessment orders did not mention the reasons why the taxpayer's submission was not accepted.

V.6. Arbitrary assessment orders passed without regard to the nature of the taxpayer's business or industry

- The faceless assessment as the name suggests is an assessment of a taxpayer whose identity is unknown to the AO. Oftentimes, the AOs may not have any knowledge or understanding of the taxpayer's business. Their ability to assess the corporate taxpayers in such circumstances is inadequate.

  The Madras High Court while reviewing a writ petition[20] in February 2020 made the following observation, "The Government of India has introduced E-Governance for the conduct of assessment proceedings electronically. It is a laudable step taken by the ITD to pave way for an objective faceless E-assessment without human interaction. At the same time, such proceedings can lead to erroneous assessment if officers are not able to understand the transactions and statements of accounts of an assessee without a personal hearing." A discussion-based assessment will enable the income tax officers to understand the nuances of the business or restructuring events and in analysing a large volume of transactional data.

V.7. AOs sometimes seek irrelevant and voluminous information from corporate taxpayers

- Some companies whose accounts are audited have been asked to provide copies of all bank statements, copies of all sales invoices, purchase invoices, freight bills, etc. Companies are unable to provide all the data sought from them due to the capacity constraints on the portal for the upload of information.
- In some of the notices, the following vague allegations were made:

  "As per the information available with the tax office, the purchases are bogus."

  "Custom duty paid as shown in the ITR is less than the duty paid as per Export Import data."

  When the taxpayer requested the AO to provide the source or basis for these statements, the taxpayer did not receive any response to the request.

V.8. Assessment orders passed without providing the opportunity of personal hearing through video conferencing

Under the manual assessment procedure in India, a taxpayer was provided an opportunity either to attend the office of the AO or to produce or cause to be produced before the AO, any evidence on which the assessee may rely in support of the income-tax return.

---

20. *Salem Sree Ramavilas Chit Company Pvt Ltd v. DCIT, Salem* (Madras High Court), dated 04-02-2020.

Under the E-assessment Scheme, 2019, if a modification is proposed in the draft assessment order, the assessee or his authorised representative, as the case may be, was entitled to seek a personal hearing so as to make oral submissions or present his case before the income-tax authority in any unit under this Scheme, and such hearing was to be conducted exclusively through video conferencing.

However, under the faceless assessment procedure, the assessee or his authorized representative may request a personal hearing so as to make oral submissions or present his case before the income-tax authority in any unit. The Chief Commissioner or the Director General, in charge of the ReFAC, under which the concerned unit is set up, may approve the request for a personal hearing, under certain circumstances (to be announced by the Principal Chief Commissioner or the Principal Director General of NaFAC). This indicates that such approval may also not be approved. CBDT issued a Standard Operating Procedure (SOP)[21] for personal hearing through video conference under the Faceless Assessment Scheme, 2019. According to the SOP, the CCIT ReAC may allow a personal hearing through Video Conference, after considering the facts and circumstances of the case, as below:-

i. The assessee has submitted written submission in response to the Draft Assessment Order.

ii. The video conference will ordinarily be of 30 minutes duration. It may be extended at the request of the assessee or authorized representative.

iii. The assessee may furnish documents/ evidence, to substantiate points raised in the video conference during the session or within a reasonable time allowed by the assessment unit, after considering the facts and circumstances of the case

All these issues lead to the passing of inappropriate assessment orders. In order to obtain relief at the appellate level, the taxpayer has to incur additional costs. In some instances, the taxpayers settle the demand amount where the cost of litigation is higher than the demand amount, causing grave hardship to the corporate taxpayer.

V.9. A large number of writ-petitions were filed at various high courts when taxpayers were not granted a personal hearing

The ITD presented the following views in response to the writ petition:

a. The grant of personal hearing in a routine and mechanical manner would not only frustrate the entire concept of the Faceless Assessment Scheme but would also defeat the very purpose for which this Scheme was introduced.

21. CBDT Circular F.No.Pr.CCIT/NeAC/SOP/2020-21 dated 23.11.2020.

b. The personal hearing is discretionary. The taxpayer does not have a vested right to a personal hearing and the same could be granted depending upon the facts of each case and on fulfilling the conditions laid down in SOP dated 23.11.2020.

The High Court held that a taxpayer has a vested right to a personal hearing and the same has to be granted if an assessee asks for it. The right to a personal hearing cannot depend upon the facts of each case.

V.10. Conduct of tax officials during the personal hearing through video conferencing

Few taxpayers received messages asking them to request video-conferencing by a particular date, but before that date, they received their final assessment orders.

When the taxpayer was explaining the case on a video conference and clarifying the issues raised by the AO in the draft assessment order, there was no response from the AOs as to whether they were satisfied with the taxpayer's explanation and if they required any further details or information. It was more of one-way communication.

During the video conference, in some instances, the AO's camera was switched off. Consequently, the taxpayer was unable to determine if the AO was present in the video conference and hearing the responses provided by the taxpayer since there was no response from the AO.

The AO's comportment during the video conference gave an impression that the personal hearing through video conferencing was more of a formality and only one-way communication and did not serve the purpose it was intended for

V.11. On uploading of notice or assessment order, no alerts are provided to taxpayers on their registered mail ID and mobile number

As per CBDT Notification No. 61/2019 dated 12th September 2019 issued under the E-assessment Scheme, 2019, every notice or order or any other electronic communication under this Scheme shall be delivered to the addressee by sending an authenticated copy thereof to the registered email address of such person, followed by a real-time alert.

The scheme defines "real-time alert" to mean any communication sent to the taxpayer, by way of a Short Messaging Service on his registered mobile number, or by way of an update on his Mobile App, or by way of an email at his registered email address, so as to alert him regarding the delivery of electronic communication.

In certain instances, notices were uploaded by the tax office on the income-tax portal without providing any intimation to the taxpayer through SMS or email. The taxpayer was thus unaware of the notices issued or orders passed and hence unable to respond to the same within the deadline.

V.12. Use of manpower having technical/specialised knowledge

A technical unit under the Faceless Assessment Scheme is required to provide assistance or advice on legal, accounting, forensic, information technology, valuation, audit, transfer pricing, data analytics, management, or any other technical matter in a particular case or a class of cases. Most of these functions require subject matter or technical matter expertise, specialised knowledge, and training. The Supreme Court of India (SC) acknowledged the role of technical experts while deciding on tax issues arising from complex technical matters[22]. It directed the CBDT to issue directions to ITOs to seek the opinion of technical experts in cases involving complex technical issues and substantial revenue, and to bring on record technical evidence in addition to the evidence placed before the tax authorities. The CBDT accordingly issued an instruction[23] in March 2011 to all its officers to use the opinions of technical experts in assessment proceedings.

The Internal Revenue Service, the tax department of the United States of America employs economists, statisticians, lawyers, information technology professionals, and other technical researchers. Lack of technical expertise is the bane of the ITD. The CBDT has transferred two-thirds of its existing workforce at all levels of the ITD to the Faceless Assessment units including the technical units. Unless the CBDT recruits the appropriate workforce having the required expertise, specialised knowledge, skills, and training to staff the technical units, the existing non-specialised workforce would be forced to undertake these functions, defeating the purpose of creating technical units.

V.13. Communication in the English language only

India is a country with many languages. Many of the taxpayers communicate, both orally and in writing, in a regional language. The Faceless Assessment Scheme is presently enabled to correspond in the English language only. It will be a challenge for regional language taxpayers to provide responses in English, forcing them to seek professional help from a service provider who can correspond in English. This will increase their cost of response, during an assessment. Similarly, many legal documents such as contracts that are generally required to be submitted and examined during assessment proceedings may be in a regional language. When the assessment case is assigned to an assessment unit in another ReFAC, the team of tax officers in that assessment unit may not be able to understand the documents submitted, creating challenges in the assessment process. If an English translation of these documents is sought, it will not only increase the compliance cost for the taxpayers but also the timeline to submit the documents. The exclusivity of the use of English in the correspondence associated with faceless assessment is no less a

22. In the case of *CIT, Delhi v. Bharti Cellular Ltd,* dated 12-8-2010.
23. CBDT instruction no. No. 5/2011 [F.No. 225/61/2011-IT(A-II)], dated 30-3-2011.

lacuna in the Prime Minister's stated goals. Thus, regional languages should be included in the faceless assessment process.

VI. Amendments to Section 144B (Faceless Assessment) in Finance Act, 2022

The following amendments were made to section 144B of the Income-tax Act to streamline the process of faceless assessment and to prevent avoidable litigation between taxpayers and the ITD. It addresses some of the shortcomings highlighted earlier.

VI.1. Mandatory personal hearing

The taxpayer did not have a right to a personal hearing under section 144B and the same could be granted depending upon the facts of each case and on fulfilling the conditions laid down in CBDT Standard Operating Procedure dated 23.11.2020. Many High Courts had held that a personal hearing is an assessee's vested right and cannot be denied under any circumstances, and any order passed without granting such an opportunity would be in violation of principles of natural justice.

Under the amended section 144B, if a taxpayer requests a personal hearing, the income-tax authority of the relevant unit shall allow such a hearing, through NaFAC. It shall be conducted exclusively through video conferencing or video telephony, including the use of any telecommunication application software which supports video conferencing or video telephony, to the extent technologically feasible, in accordance with the procedure laid down by the CBDT.

VI.2. Modification/elimination of certain functions

a. NaFAC was created to facilitate the conduct of faceless assessment proceedings in a centralised manner and was vested with the jurisdiction to make a faceless assessment.

   Under the amended section 144B, NaFAC is only tasked to facilitate the conduct of faceless assessment proceedings in a centralised manner. It is no more vested with the jurisdiction to make a faceless assessment.

b. Assessment Units (AUs) were originally created to facilitate the conduct of faceless assessment, to perform the function of making assessments which includes identification of points or issues material for the determination of any liability (including refund) under the Act, seeking information or clarification on points or issues so identified, analysis of the material furnished by the assessee or any other person, and such other functions as may be required for the purposes of making a faceless assessment.

Under the amended section 144B, the role of AUs has been significantly enhanced as they are no more required to 'facilitate' but 'conduct' the faceless assessment. For example, the AU shall serve upon an assessee, who has failed to provide further information, documents or evidence sought from such assessee, a notice, through the NaFAC, under section 144, giving him an opportunity to show cause on a date and time as specified in such notice as to why the assessment in his case should not be completed to the best of its judgment. Similarly, the AU shall serve show-cause notice on the assessee, through the NaFAC.

Further, the term "assessment unit" shall refer to an AO having powers so assigned by the CBDT.

c. The amended section 144B does not make any reference to ReFAC. Consequently, one administrative layer has been eliminated and henceforth, NaFAC will facilitate the conduct of faceless assessment proceedings in a centralised manner.

d. Under the amended section 144B, Technical Units are also required to provide technical assistance on Double Taxation Avoidance Agreements entered into by the Indian government with the Government of any country outside India or specified territory outside India.

e. NaFAC shall, upon receiving suggestions for variation from the Review Unit (RU), assign the case to an AU, other than the AU which made the draft assessment order, through an automated allocation system.

   Under the amended Faceless Assessment Scheme, NAFAC shall forward the review report to the same AU which had proposed the income or loss determination proposal.

f. The AU was originally required to consider the variations suggested by the RU and send the final draft assessment order to NaFAC.

   Under the amended section 144B, the AU shall accept or reject some or all of the modifications proposed in the review report and after recording reasons in case of rejection of such modifications, prepare a draft order and send it to NaFAC. Under the amended faceless assessment, the power of the AU is enhanced at the cost of overriding the functions of a RU.

VI.3. Provision for review of the draft assessment order

An assessee was provided multiple opportunities to respond to a draft assessment order (DAO) or final DAO or revised DAO in case any variation prejudicial to the interest of assessee is proposed in such orders.

Under the amended faceless assessment, the assessee is provided only one opportunity to respond to a show-cause notice that states the variations proposed to be made to the income of the assessee. In particular, the assessee is not provided an opportunity to respond to the final assessment order even if the order is prejudicial to the interests of the assessee. This may result in litigation on the grounds of violation of principles of natural justice.

VI.4. No specific time limit is mentioned for filing the response to a notice issued under Section 143(2)

A taxpayer was provided a timeframe of 15 days to file a response to a notice issued under section 143(2). Under the amended section 144B, a taxpayer is required to file a response to NaFAC within the date specified in the notice.

VI.5. Deletion of provisions declaring assessment proceedings as "*non est*" in case of non-observance of the prescribed procedure

Section 144B provided that a faceless assessment shall be "*non est*" (meaning non-existent) if such assessment is not made in accordance with the procedure laid down under this section. Consequently, many courts had set aside the assessment orders passed when the prescribed procedure was not followed such as not granting a personal hearing, not serving the draft order and show cause notice, etc.

Under the amended section 144B, the said provision is deleted with retrospective effect from April 1, 2021 to save the assessment proceedings from being declared *non-est* due to technical glitches. There would be no recourse to the assessee if arbitrary assessments are issued without following the procedure of section 144B.

VI.6. Scope of faceless assessment widened to include reassessment under Section 147 (titled Income escaping assessment)

To remove any ambiguity, reassessment under section 147 has been specifically included under faceless assessment.

VI.7. Draft Assessment Order replaced by an Income or Loss Determination Proposal (ILDP)

Reference to the draft assessment order has been removed under the amended section 144B. The AU is now required to prepare an ILDP where no variation prejudicial to the assessee is proposed and send it to NFAC. In cases where a variation prejudicial to the assessee is proposed, a detailed procedure is proposed before a draft order is prepared and sent to NFAC by the AU.

VII. Conclusion

India is a frontrunner in introducing faceless assessment in order to significantly reduce the physical interaction between the taxpayer and the tax officers and to mitigate abuse of power by the tax officers resulting in harassment, corruption, and unmanageable litigation. To accomplish this, the assessment procedure is moving away from a territorial jurisdiction to a randomised allocation of cases by using suitable technological tools, including artificial intelligence and machine learning, with a view to optimise the use of resources. It is moving away from a single assessment officer to a team-based assessment. The faceless assessment procedure is expected to bring about transparency, efficiency, and standardisation of procedures.

Based on an evaluation of the implementation of faceless assessment since August 2020, it appears that some aspects of the faceless assessment should be modified, the manner of its implementation should be vastly improved and the technical infrastructure should be enhanced. The Finance Act, 2022 has proposed changes to faceless assessment in terms of the right of a taxpayer to be provided an opportunity for a personal hearing, similar to what prevailed in manual and E-assessments. If this right was provided to the taxpayer under the faceless assessment earlier, a large number of writ petitions could have been avoided. The customer-friendliness of the tax officials during the personal hearing through video conference should be ensured for a meaningful implementation of the faceless assessment.

The success of faceless assessment depends on its effective implementation and the onus falls on the tax officials in charge of NaFAC since it plays a very important role in every stage of the faceless assessment procedure and is the final authority to issue the assessment orders. Staffing of appropriate manpower is critical to ensure proper implementation of faceless assessment. The TARC made the following observations on the quality of manual assessment procedure, "Framing of assessments by tax officials, the inadequacy of time given to taxpayers to respond to the notices and draft assessment orders, not dealing adequately with evidence on record have also been significant contributors to the logjam at various stages involved in dispute resolution. The substandard quality of assessments (whether in the form of non-speaking order or lack of judicial discipline or misinterpretation of judicial precedents) can be partly attributed to inadequate training/industry experience of tax officers and the practice of taking up assessments at the tail-end of statutory timelines. This also results in taxpayers not getting adequate time to respond to queries raised during assessment."

The shortcomings in manual assessment as highlighted by TARC Reports are repeated in the faceless assessment, as indicated in the analysis of writ petitions filed in various courts between April to December 2021. It is surprising that these procedural lapses have occurred since the faceless assessment scheme was specifically introduced to avoid these kinds of issues. This shows the ability of the tax officials to sidestep the procedure with impunity even under faceless assessment and the inability of the CBDT to implement it effectively.

Section 144B provided that a faceless assessment shall be "*non est*" if such assessment is not made in accordance with the procedure laid down under this section. This provision has been removed by the Finance Act, 2022 with retrospective effect, from the date it came into force on 1st April 2021. The faceless assessment procedure was specifically designed to involve multiple layers of evaluation by different units, thereby providing checks and balances to eliminate errors and biases of the AO in the drafting of assessment orders. The removal of "*non-est*" is retrograde since there are no negative consequences such as setting aside the assessment order if the faceless assessment procedure as originally envisaged is not followed. This may result in the issue of substandard assessment orders and harassment of taxpayers.

The role of NaFAC has been significantly curtailed by the amendments introduced by Finance Act, 2022 and the powers for an assessment unit have been significantly enhanced so much so that it now has the responsibility to implement the faceless assessment unlike in the past where it was a facilitator. Under the modified faceless assessment procedure, the assessment unit has the power to either accept or reject some or all of the modifications proposed in a review report and after recording reasons in case of rejection of such modifications. Thus, the crux of the usefulness of faceless assessment in assigning a definitive role to the conclusion of a review now appears to have been removed. The importance of the functions of a verification unit and a technical unit is also not clear since the modified faceless assessment procedure does not specifically mention that the assessment unit should consider all the inputs provided by the verification unit or the technical unit.

The faceless assessment involves significant use of technology during the entire assessment procedure -- from the filing of income tax returns, selection of cases for scrutiny, uploading of documents by the taxpayer in response to notices and draft assessment orders, to issue of assessment orders. Concerns were expressed about the ability of the CBDT to create appropriate information technology infrastructure to support big data submissions, process assessments of a large volume, and archive the entire assessment documents of all the taxpayers over a period of time. This concern emanates from the taxpayer experience with the GST filings and the quantum of e-assessments finalized in the pilot project launched in September 2019.

Since the launch of the faceless assessment in August 2020, some taxpayers were unable to upload documentary evidence or seek adjournments due to the inept functioning of the designated portal and were penalised with inappropriate assessments. The ITD should invest adequately to create the appropriate technology infrastructure so that there are no glitches in the functioning of the designated portal and the taxpayers are not inconvenienced or even penalised in the process.

The faceless assessment scheme may be apt for individuals, partnership firms, and small and medium enterprises where the volume of data submission and complexity in tax issues may be low. It may not be appropriate for large companies for multiple reasons. A faceless assessment provides an opportunity for a discussion only after the assessment is completed. Whereas in the case of large companies, it is important for the AOs to be aware of the company's industry attributes and the nuances of the company's business model before commencing the assessment.

The Madras High Court while reviewing a writ petition[24] in February 2020 made the following observation, "The Government of India has introduced E-Governance for the conduct of assessment proceedings electronically. It is a laudable step taken by the ITD to pave way for an objective faceless E-assessment without human interaction. At the same time, such proceedings can lead to erroneous assessment if officers are not able to understand the transactions and statements of accounts of an assessee without a personal hearing."

Submission of a large volume of transactional data is another challenge for large companies and the ITD. More so, when there are capacity constraints on the e-filing portal to upload attachments. Many companies may also not have the required IT infrastructure to submit a large volume of data. Since tax audits always examine data from past periods, tax divisions of large companies often find it difficult to retrieve and provide documentary evidence and tax-relevant data within a short period of time, mainly due to the lack of dedicated personnel for this exercise. To avoid the submission of a large volume of transaction-level data during corporate tax audits, the tax authorities in many countries require corporate taxpayers to provide them access to their IT systems for an online audit. The CBDT should create teams of IT experts at technical units who could support AOs in online data evaluation and analysis.

An assessment involving human interface through a video conference may be appropriate for companies that are large, or which operate globally or undertake different types of businesses or have engaged in activities like mergers and acquisitions, restructuring, or have overseas transactions involving transfer pricing or Foreign Tax Credit. Instead of a faceless assessment, a multi-member team from an assessment unit, verification unit, and technical unit should conduct the assessment through video conference, to prevent instances of taxpayer harassment and high-pitch assessments.

The success of the faceless assessment depends on the quality of assessment orders which is eventually measured by the number of assessment orders litigated and the amount of litigation. The faceless assessment is expected to improve the quality of assessments by using an algorithm for standardized examination of draft orders, with a view to reducing the scope of discretion. To improve the robustness of assessment

---

24. *Salem Sree Ramavilas Chit Company Pvt Ltd v. DCIT*, Salem (Madras High Court), dated 04-02-2020.

orders issued, the existing staff should be supported by a workforce from various faculties such as accounting, taxation, valuation, law, economics, statistics, data analysis, and information technology, who can provide the required subject matter expertise in the assessment process. The faceless assessment should also ensure that the inputs provided by the verification and technical units are appropriately considered by the AOs and reflected in the assessment orders.

At the launch of the faceless assessment scheme in August 2020, the Prime Minister said that an attempt has been made to make the tax system seamless, painless, and faceless. While seamless means tax administration does not complicate, painless means simple rules and technology. He further remarked that "the tax system may be turning faceless but it promises fairness and fearlessness for taxpayers" and added that the focus was on making the tax system "people-centric and public-friendly rather than power centric". The implementation of the faceless assessment so far has belied the expectations set by the Prime Minister at the launch.

Annexure 1

Procedure[25]

Faceless assessment procedure under Section 144B (titled Faceless Assessment) of the Income-tax Act, 1961

The assessment, reassessment or recomputation under section 143(3) or section 144 or section 147 of the Income-tax Act, as the case may be, shall be made in a faceless manner as per the following procedure, namely:—

(i) The NaFAC shall assign the case selected for the faceless assessment to a specific assessment unit (AU) through an automated allocation system. "Automated allocation system" means an algorithm for randomised allocation of cases, by using suitable technological tools, including artificial intelligence and machine learning, with a view to optimise the use of resources;

(ii) The NaFAC shall intimate the assessee that assessment in his case shall be completed in accordance with the procedure laid down under section 144B of the Income-tax Act;

(iii) The NaFAC shall serve a notice on the assessee under section 143(2) or under section 142(1) of the Income-tax Act, 1961 and the assessee may file his response to such notice within the date specified therein, to the NaFAC which shall forward the same to the AU;

(iv) The AU may make a request to the NaFAC for -

  (a) obtaining such further information, documents or evidence from the assessee or any other person, as it may specify,

  (b) conducting of certain enquiry or verification by a verification unit (VU),

  (c) seeking technical assistance in respect of determination of arm's length price, valuation of property, withdrawal of registration, approval, exemption or any other technical matter by referring to the technical unit (TU).

(v) If the AU has requested

  (a) for conducting of enquiry or verification by the VU, the NaFAC shall assign the request to a VU through an automated allocation system; or

  (b) for reference to the TU, the NaFAC shall assign the request to a TU through an automated allocation system.

25. Section 144B of the Income-tax Act, 1961, as amended by Finance Act, 2022.

The NaFAC shall send the report received from the VU or the TU to the concerned AU.

(vi) The NaFAC shall issue appropriate notice or requisition to the assessee or any other person for obtaining the information, documents or evidence requisitioned by the AU.

The assessee or any other person, as the case may be, shall file his response to such notice within the time specified therein (or such time as may be extended on the basis of an application in this regard) to the NaFAC which shall forward the reply to the AU.

(vii) If the assessee fails to comply with the notice issued under clause (*vi*) above or a notice issued under section 142(1) or section 143(2), the NaFAC shall intimate such failure to the AU;

(viii) The AU shall serve upon such assessee, a notice through the NaFAC, under section 144, giving him an opportunity to show-cause on a date and time as specified in such notice as to why the assessment in his case should not be completed to the best of its judgment

(ix) The assessee shall, within the time specified in the notice referred to in clause *(viii)* above or such time as may be extended on the basis of an application in this regard, file his response to the NaFAC which shall forward the same to the AU;

If the assessee fails to file his response to the notice served under clause *(viii)* above within the time specified therein or within the extended time, if any, the NaFAC shall intimate such failure to the AU;

(x) The AU shall, after taking into account all the relevant material available on the record, prepare, in writing,—

(a) an income or loss determination proposal, where no variation prejudicial to assessee is proposed and send a copy of such income or loss determination proposal to the NaFAC; or

(b) in any other case, a show-cause notice stating the variations proposed to be made to the income of the assessee, that are prejudicial to his interests and calling upon him to submit as to why the proposed variation should not be made. The AU shall serve such show-cause notice on the assessee, through the NaFAC;

(xi) The assessee shall file his reply to the show-cause notice served under clause *(x)* above on a date and time as specified therein (or such time as may be extended on the basis of an application made in this regard) to the NaFAC, which shall forward the reply to the AU;

If the assessee fails to file his response to the show-cause notice within the time specified therein or within the extended time, if any, the NaFAC shall intimate such failure to the AU;

(xii) The AU shall, after considering the response received or receipt of intimation under clause *(xi)* above, as the case may be, and taking into account all relevant material available on record, prepare an income or loss determination proposal and send the same to the NaFAC;

(xiii) On receipt of the income or loss determination proposal, as referred to in clauses *(x)(a)* or *(xii)* above, the NaFAC may, on the basis of guidelines issued by the CBDT,—

  (a) convey to the AU to prepare draft order in accordance with the income or loss determination proposal, which shall thereafter prepare a draft order; or

  (b) assign the income or loss determination proposal to a review unit (RU) through an automated allocation system, for conducting review of such proposal;

(xiv) The RU shall review the income or loss determination proposal assigned to it by the NaFAC, whereupon it shall prepare a review report and send the same to the NaFAC.

The NaFAC shall, upon receiving the review report, forward the same to the AU which had proposed the income or loss determination proposal;

(xv) The AU shall, after considering such review report, accept or reject some or all of the modifications proposed therein and after recording reasons in case of rejection of such modifications, prepare a draft order;

(xvi) The AU shall send such draft order prepared under sub-clause (*a*) of clause *(xiii)* or under clause *(xv)* to the NaFAC;

(xvii) In case of an eligible assessee, where there is a proposal to make any variation which is prejudicial to the interest of such assessee, as mentioned in section 144C(1), the NaFAC shall serve the draft order referred to in clause (*xvi*) above, on the assessee;

"eligible assessee" means,—

  (i) any person in whose case the variation which is prejudicial to the interest of such assessee arises as a consequence of the order of the Transfer Pricing Officer passed under section 92CA(3); and

  (*ii*) any non-resident not being a company, or any foreign company.

(xviii) In any other case, the NaFAC shall convey to the AU to pass the final assessment order in accordance with such draft order, which shall thereafter pass the final assessment order and initiate penalty proceedings, if any, and send it to the NaFAC;

(xix) Upon receiving the final assessment order, the NaFAC shall serve a copy of such order and notice for initiating penalty proceedings, if any, on the assessee, along with the demand notice, specifying the sum payable by, or refund of any amount due to, the assessee on the basis of such assessment;

(xx) If a draft order is served on the assessee as referred to in clause *(xvii)* above, such assessee shall,—

(a) file his acceptance of the variations proposed in such draft order to the NaFAC; or

(b) file his objections, if any, to such variations, with the Dispute Resolution Panel and the NaFAC, within the period specified in section 144C(2);

(xxi) The NaFAC shall,—

(c) upon receipt of acceptance from the eligible assessee; or

(d) if no objections are received from the eligible assessee, within the period specified in section 144C(2),

intimate the AU to complete the assessment on the basis of the draft order.

(xxii) The AU shall, upon receipt of intimation under clause *(xxi)*, pass the assessment order, in accordance with the relevant draft order, within the time allowed under section 144C(4) and initiate penalty proceedings, if any, and send the order to the NaFAC;

(xxiii) If the eligible assessee files objections with the Dispute Resolution Panel, under sub-clause *(b)* of clause *(xx)*, the NaFAC shall send such intimation along with a copy of objections filed to the AU;

(xxiv) The NaFAC shall, upon receipt of the directions issued by the Dispute Resolution Panel under section 144C(5), forward such directions to the AU;

The AU shall, in conformity with the directions issued by the Dispute Resolution Panel under section 144C(5), complete the assessment within the time allowed in section 144C(3) and initiate penalty proceedings, if any, and send a copy of the assessment order to the NaFAC;

(xxv) The NaFAC shall, upon receipt of the assessment order referred to in clause *(xxii)* or clause *(xxiv)*, as the case may be, serve a copy of such order and notice for initiating penalty proceedings, if any, on the assessee, along with the demand notice, specifying the sum payable by, or the amount of refund due to, the assessee on the basis of such assessment;

(xxvi) The NaFAC shall, after completion of assessment, transfer all the electronic records of the case to the Assessing Officer having jurisdiction over the said case for such action as may be required under the provisions of this Act;

(xxvii) If at any stage of the proceedings before it, the AU having regard to the nature and complexity of the accounts, volume of the accounts, doubts about the correctness of accounts, multiplicity of transactions in the accounts or specialised nature of business activity of the assessee, and the interests of the revenue, is of the opinion that it is necessary to do so, it may, upon recording its reasons in writing, refer the case to the NaFAC stating that the provisions of section 142(2A) may be invoked and such case shall be dealt with in accordance with the provisions of section 144B(7).

REJOINDER

P.V.S.S. Prasad

Faceless Assessment

1. Introduction

The Indian authorities launched a faceless assessment scheme under its Direct Tax Laws on 13th August 2020 with the objective of facilitating tax compliance by honest taxpayers. This has replaced the erstwhile manual assessment system which was in existence since tax administration was established in India. The objective of the scheme is to avoid the interface between an Assessing Officer (AO) and the taxpayer. Unlike the manual system where assessments were made on territorial jurisdiction, the faceless system is a dynamic jurisdiction concept on the basis of which a team-based assessment is expected to occur in a seamless manner. The objective is laudable and well taken by tax experts and taxpayers alike. However, numerous practical issues are being faced by the taxpayers as have been enumerated by S. Krishnan. In what follows, a view is taken on some of the prevailing characteristics and flaws of the system as it is being practiced currently.

2. Salient Features of the Scheme

The procedure of the Faceless Assessment Scheme is depicted in a nutshell in the diagram below.

Diagram 1. Procedure

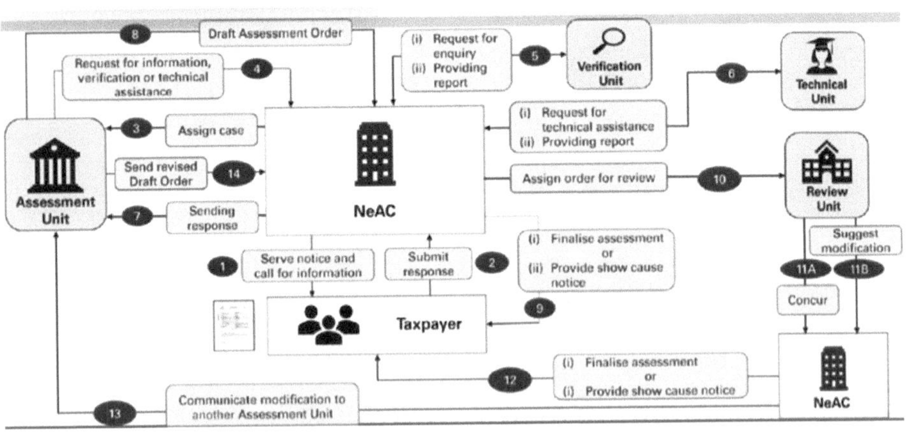

Source: Kariya, Jayesh. "Presentation on Technical Aspects of Representations under Faceless Assessment Scheme," slide presentation

- Using data analytics and artificial intelligence, cases for scrutiny will be selected by the National Faceless Assessment Centre (NaFAC).
- A selected case for scrutiny is allotted to an Assessment Unit (AU) in a dynamic manner through an automated allocation system (in a jurisdiction different from the taxpayer's location).
- Centralized system of issue of notices to taxpayers through electronic modes using Unique Document Identification Number (UDIN).
- The response by taxpayers should be made through electronic modes without an interface with tax officials.
- NaFAC shall provide an opportunity to the assessee in case an adjustment is being proposed to the income returned.
- An assessee can seek adjournment/extension of time on filing a response.
- In case an adjustment/modification is proposed in the Draft Assessment Order, the taxpayer (or) his authorized representative can request for personal hearing to make their submissions.
- This request may be accepted by the head of the Regional Faceless Assessment Centre (ReFAC). If granted such hearings shall be conducted exclusively through video conferencing.
- Taxpayers may receive notices digitally signed by an NaFAC officer in their r e-filing portal.
- The entire communication between the taxpayer and the NaFAC is through electronic mode which provides transparency and efficiency.
- The process is based on a team-based assessment unlike in the past when an individual AO drove the whole assessment process.
- The NaFAC is the focal point of the faceless assessment procedure in respect of communication and finally passing the Assessment Orders.
- Different units operate in the assessment process till the final order is passed. The Assessment Units (AU) can only make a Draft Assessment Order and send it to the NaFAC.
- On examining the Draft Assessment Order in accordance with the Risk Management Strategy specified by the CBDT, it may assign the Draft Assessment Order to a Review Unit (RU) in any other ReFAC through an automated allocation system. In the same manner, a Verification Unit (VU) and Technical Unit (TU) would also contribute to finalizing the assessment by the NaFAC.

3. Paramount Need for IT Infrastructure

The Faceless Assessment Scheme succeeds on the basis of the robust and efficient IT infrastructure of the CBDT. The present IT portal is bogged down with many technical glitches and the representative taxpayer finds it difficult to upload returns and specific forms. It is of paramount importance that the portal works smoothly without any glitches. Otherwise, the success of the scheme would remain questionable. In view of huge data being called for by the NaFAC, the taxpayer should at least be provided a smooth experience in filing/uploading the data required as per the notices received.

4. Issues Facing Taxpayers

The main issues that are being encountered by a taxpayer are discussed hereunder.

1) Notices are being issued to the taxpayer asking for an enormous amount of complex data without providing sufficient time to comply with the same.

2) It is also observed that taxpayers are receiving the same notices again and again in spite of the submission of details called for. It is to be represented that taxpayers should be provided with enough opportunity and time to comply with the submission of details called for. In view of the entire assessment procedure happening virtually, unlike in the past, it is now crucial that a taxpayer communicates in written form in an effective manner.

3) The Income-tax dept has set a limit to the size of taxpayer response to notices under e – proceeding, that is, the response should be provided in less than 4,000 characters in the 'Response/ Remarks' field. The maximum file size of one attachment is 10 MB and the maximum number of attachments which can be uploaded in response to one partial response is ten.

   Essentially, this requires multiple successive submissions of lower size. This is impractical for large submissions. CBDT clarified that the capacity for uploading the information and data called for is likely to be increased to 500 MB but this should be made possible as early as possible.

4) In most of the cases where assessments have been completed, taxpayers were not given enough opportunity to present their case. This resulted in the violation of principles of natural justice on the basis of which the courts have quashed such assessments and set aside such orders passed.

   Recently the Hon'ble Bombay High Court passed strictures on the AO under the Faceless Assessment Scheme for his high-handed approach and set aside the assessment order, show cause notice, and demand notice. In this case, the AO was also fined by the Hon'ble Court -*Parag Kishorchandra Shah [TS-1069-HC-2021] (BOM).*

5) Many glitches are encountered in the portal for uploading submissions by the taxpayers which delay the compliance process. This needs to be addressed as a top priority.

   i. In case a personal hearing is requested by the taxpayer, the concerned Head of the Regional Faceless Assessment Centre (RFAC) can authorize a hearing to be conducted through video conferencing. It is observed that the time granted for video conferencing is a mere 30 minutes.

   ii. Standard Operating Procedure (SOP) issued by CBDT provides that, "the quality of questionnaire must reflect the application of the mind and due diligence of the Assessing Officer". However, in many cases that came up before the Hon'ble High Courts, it was observed that notices were issued in a routine manner without proper application of mind by the AO/AU.

   iii. It is not clear whether rectification under section 154 can be filed under the present assessment system.

5. Recent Litigation

In most of the completed assessments under the faceless assessment scheme, the main point of dispute is the violation of principles of natural justice. In the following cases the Hon'ble Courts have quashed the orders as legally untenable.

- *K L Trading Corporation V. National e-Assessment Centre WP No.4774-HC-2021 (Delhi)*
- *Axis Wind Farms (Anantapur) Private Limited v Union of India and Others WP.No.11812-HC-2021 (Telangana)*
- *M/s Magic Wood Exports Private Limited v National e-Assessment Centre WP No.10693-HC-2021 (Madras)*
- *KBB Nuts (P) Ltd v. National Faceless Assessment Centre [2021] 127.taxmann.com 194 (Delhi)*
- *Parag Kishorchandra Shah v. National Faceless Assessment Centre TS-1069-HC-2021 (BOM)*
- *SAS Fininvest LLP v. National e-Assessment Centre WP.No.5087-HC-2021 (Delhi)*
- *Ekambaram Sukumaran v. National e-Assessment Centre WP.No.10433/2021 (Mad-HC)*

6. Conclusion

The initial experience of the faceless assessment scheme is disappointing as the principles of natural justice are not being followed. All categories of taxpayers, corporate or non-corporate, are provided with a limited window of data submission and time for responding to the notices under the scheme. The present IT Infrastructure does not provide appropriate utilities to taxpayers for compliances on the basis of their status, size, and nature of the activity.

It is essential for the CBDT to come up with a sound Standard Operating Procedure (SOP) in order to avoid unpleasant experiences that are being commonly faced. The IT Infrastructure must be robust and glitch-free so as to facilitate smooth interaction between the taxpayer and the tax administrator in meeting the compliances. It is also imperative to provide in-person hearings (with a team of officers under video recording) in respect of select deserving cases so as to provide enough opportunity to taxpayers to represent their own cases. In this light, it is desirable to have a hybrid system of faceless and In-person assessment with a judicious mix of the two.

CHAPTER 11

REFINING INDIA'S GOODS AND SERVICES TAX—FIVE YEARS ON

Krupa Venkatesh

I. Introduction

Effective 1st July 2017, India ushered in a salutary tax reform, the Goods and Services Tax (GST), after a decade and a half's efforts from economists, policymakers, bureaucrats, and industry. In a multi-party political system, where the Constitution has adopted the spirit of co-operative federalism, getting the States on board to give up some of the autonomy that they previously enjoyed in the matter of taxation of sale of goods, to the GST Council was no mean task. Overnight, India's multi-layer indirect tax system with multiple taxable events was replaced with a single taxable event called 'supply' and a common dual-structured GST across the country came into effect. The transition to the new system was most certainly painful, though not unexpectedly so, for all stakeholders – government, industry, and customers alike.

States were guaranteed compensation of loss of revenue on account of GST introduction via the GST Compensation Act, 2017, for a period of five years from revenues collected from the GST compensation cess collected on sin goods. The year 2022 is significant because it signals the end of the compensation though there is no legal bar on the continuation of the compensation cess, especially in view of exaggerated revenue shortfalls in 2020 due to the disruption to business caused by the Covid pandemic.

The GST Network (GSTN) has settled down over the past couple of years after initial years of glitches, and it is encouraging to see that there are constant improvements that are being brought about to make return filing easier and more transparent and helped the government in detecting fraud and plug tax evasion. GST collections have been progressively increasing – and averaging more than 1.3 lakh crore INR (~ $ 13bn) in the last quarter of 2021-22.[1]

1. See Srinivasan, P V, 'Goods and Services Tax: Analysis, Findings and Suggestions' (2016), for an analysis of the challenges that prevailed in the design of GST prior to its introduction.

It is now time for the government to move to the next level of refining the GST to make it an easier law to comply with and offer stability and certainty to taxpayers so that their costs of compliance can be reduced.

Some areas where reforms are required are identified.

II. Registration – Thresholds and Cancellation

The current registration thresholds are described below, following Diagram 1.

Diagram 1. GST Registration Classifications

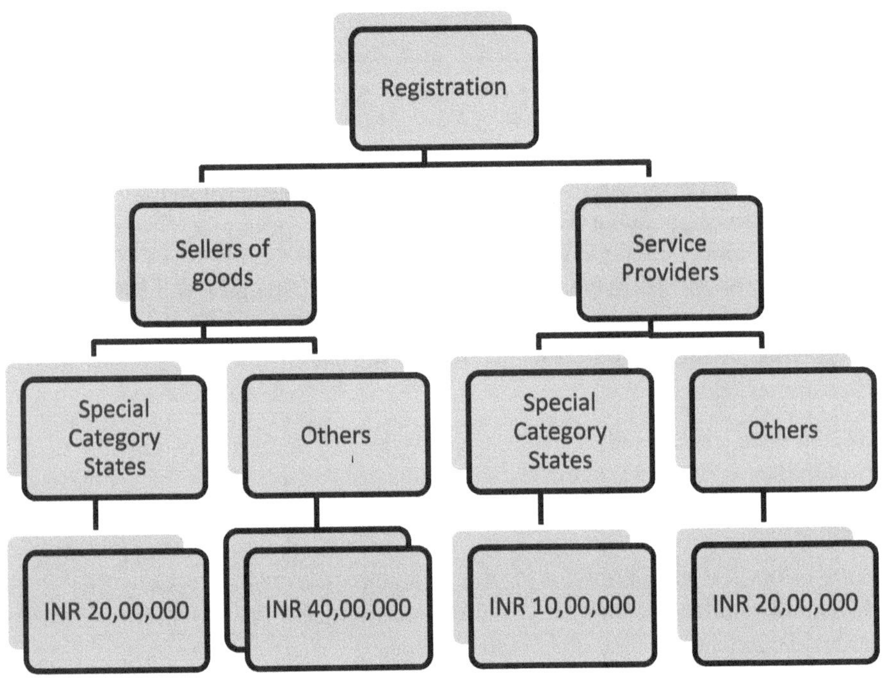

Source: Author

Registration is a very basic requirement under any tax law and must be simple and easy to understand and implement.

Clearly, the current multiple threshold limit structure depicted above is very complex and needs simplification. Some of the threshold limits seem to be influenced by the limits under the erstwhile VAT and Service Tax legislations. As a case in point, there is no reason why the threshold limit for registration for sellers of goods and service providers should be different, except that the registration threshold under the Service Tax law was Indian Rupees (INR) 20 lakhs for service providers.[2] If there are compelling reasons from a revenue perspective to keep a threshold for special category states different from the rest of the country, that should be the only exception and the GST Council must consider keeping a common threshold among all other States, for both goods and services.

As far as the inter-State sale of goods is concerned, taxpayers are liable to register irrespective of turnover[3]. This again is a carry forward of the registration requirements under the legacy of Central Sales Tax Act, 1956.[4] Central Sales Tax or CST was an origin-based tax, and therefore, having no threshold for registration and tax payment served as a protectionist levy to competitors in destination States. It was also necessitated since taxpayers could abuse the system by claiming an exemption threshold in different States. However, those circumstances no longer exist. The GST system monitors taxpayers via the Income Tax Permanent Account Number (PAN) which is common across the country, and it can be ensured that the cumulative turnover for which the exemption threshold is claimed is within the threshold limit. Clearly, there is no case for the continuation of compulsory registration for sellers who make inter-State sales. The distinction between intra and inter-State sales as a threshold for obtaining GST registration needs to be removed, and the cumulative turnover should be the only factor to determine whether a business needs GST registration or not and goes completely against the 'One Nation, One Market' principle.

Currently, the GST law[5] mandates a compulsory registration for sellers who are registered on an e-commerce platform or marketplace, where the latter collects sale proceeds from customers and remits it to them. This is a new requirement that was hitherto not applicable in the pre-GST regime. This provision is more in the nature of an anti-avoidance measure since e-commerce is a relatively new concept in India and perhaps from the government's perspective, there is a fear of loss of revenue. On

---

2. See Venkatesh, Krupa, 'Value Added Tax/Goods and Services Tax in the Digital Era' (2020), for particular challenges of taxing the services component, in particular, cross-border trade. It was legislatively not possible to prescribe a common threshold for Central Excise duty, VAT and Service Tax, since they were governed by different legislations, and administered by different authorities. That difficulty has been removed in the GST regime where the GST Council is the governing body. Works contracts in particular were very complex from an indirect tax standpoint, since they were subject to both service tax and VAT, on a taxable value that was invariably greater than the value of the contract itself. Subsuming both these taxes in GST has removed this problem.
3. Section 24 of Central Goods and Services Tax Act, 2017.
4. North-Eastern and hilly States have traditionally been conferred Special Category Status under tax laws. The lower GST threshold has been adopted in view of lower consumption and per-capita income. Having a higher registration threshold would take most taxpayers out of the GST system itself. This not only means loss of revenue for states, but also breakage in input tax credit chain, which is against the basic principle of any tax system that provides tax relief, in the form of input tax credit.
5. Section 24 of Central Goods and Services Tax Act, 2017.

the contrary, online sales leave an electronic footprint throughout the order and delivery process, and invariably offer a verification trail. Further, e-commerce operators are in any case required to mandatorily register and the government has access to the details of all transactions made on the platform or marketplace at all times, which can be very easily cross-verified. This is a good example of adequate checks and balances, and therefore the compulsory registration of online sellers should be dispensed with. It mainly hurts small sellers who would otherwise have been within the threshold limit for registration but for the mode of sale.

There is now sufficient confidence in the GSTN and the reporting mechanisms, and this is evidenced by the increased fraud detection that has been made possible by elaborate requirements and the government can now focus on making the legislation simpler and easier to comply with.

Cancelling a registration at the request of the taxpayer should also be a simple process. Having a complex or difficult cancellation regime tends to drive away those taxpayers who would have otherwise taken a voluntary registration. It also encourages businesses to artificially split their affairs among various entities so that they can stay within the threshold limit for registration. A registration cancellation request currently entails complete scrutiny by the officers and often queries that have not arisen during assessments or audits are raised, which makes the cancellation process extremely cumbersome. While there must definitely be some checks and balances before cancelling any registration, since the taxpayer then completely exits the system and recovery of any outstanding dues, if any, is impossible, they must be not only reasonable but also effective. The current cancellation procedures require moderation and must facilitate an easy exit for simple businesses and honest taxpayers.

III. Reverse Charge Mechanism

In the entire supply chain, every participant liable to collect indirect taxes (GST, VAT, excise duty, service tax) acts as an agent of the government to collect the tax from his customer and remit it to the government. This is true of every indirect tax regime in the world, and in India, this tenet holds good in the legacy tax and the GST regimes. By its very nature, the incidence of indirect tax is on the person making the supply or sale, but the burden of the tax is always on the end customer.

A reverse charge is a mechanism where the person purchasing the goods or services accounts for the tax that ought to have been charged by the supplier. The reverse charge mechanism for payment of service tax was imposed to bring parity in taxation on domestically procured and imported services. Subsequently, the reverse charge was extended to domestic transactions involving unorganised sectors where compliance was low, and consequently, tax collection was ineffective and inadequate. In all cases, the reverse charge had to be paid for in cash, and input tax credit (ITC) could be availed in the subsequent month.

The practice of discharging the reverse charge liability in cash has been carried forward to the GST regime as well. The logic proffered by the government has always been that the reverse charge represents the output tax of another person; therefore, the recipient's input tax cannot be available for the payment of the same, and the tax claimed as input tax has not actually been paid to the government. This interpretation is very narrow since it is anomalous in those cases where the recipient of services liable to the reverse charge may have a sufficient or large ITC balance. This is particularly true of businesses that accumulate ITC balances during the investment and expansion phase making large capital investments, start-ups or businesses that are yet to make profits, businesses that receive funding from investors for expansion, sometimes considerable, or those with an inverted duty structure, where the rate of tax on outputs is lower than those on the inputs. In all these cases, paying the reverse charge in cash and claiming the same back in the following month, while on the face of it seems neutral, in actuality, adds to the pool of non-utilisable ITC and exacerbates any existing strain on cash flow.

There is very little that the government gains in this whole process which is quite cumbersome even from a compliance perspective. The cash collection on account of reverse charge is counted towards revenue only for a month since the same is given back as ITC in the subsequent month and, looking at the larger picture, there is no revenue loss to the government. The industry has for long been asking for a provision to be inserted in the law where accumulated ITC can be used to pay the reverse charge, but the efforts have so far been futile.

There are two situations now that must make it inevitable for the government to consider this proposal favourably – the uneven post-pandemic economic recovery in various sectors, the continuing rise of new age companies, start-ups, and the ever-growing list of unicorns.[6] This seemingly small measure can go a long way in arresting one source of accumulation of ITC, free up cash flow and ease out at least a bit of strain on working capital, all at once. Just permitting the credit to be availed in the same month instead of the following month, can bring in the desired results.

To elaborate, if reverse charges are shown as output tax in a particular month and are shown as input tax against the same invoice in the same month, it will have a neutral effect on the net tax payable. Those businesses that have accumulated credit will stop further accumulation, and those that have net tax payable will be able to set off the input credit just as they would in the case of any regular purchase.

6. See Shome (2021) on the taxation of robots/Artificial Intelligence (AI) on possible measures to tax this sector (as opposed to the digital economy alone) without damaging its rapid rise or probable contribution to human scientific advancement.

There are sufficient international precedents on this matter. In the European Union (EU) and UK VATs, all business-to-business (B2B) supplies attract a reverse charge, and only when the buyer does not provide a VAT registration number is the VAT charged. Where a person who is VAT registered in the UK or the EU receives services from outside their respective jurisdictions, a reverse charge is attracted, which means that the recipient acts both as the supplier and the recipient. The recipient charges the VAT and reclaims ITC. In most cases, they would be the same, hence the entries would cancel out. In effect, that means that there is no cash outflow on account of the reverse charge. Thus, their VAT in general, and more so the reverse charge, is only 'accounted for' and never really 'paid'; it is always 'charged'.[7] There can be no reason for India not to follow the same principle reflecting that its GST is functioning more smoothly after five years of its existence.

IV. Ad-hoc and Legacy Measures that Need Review

Some of the ad-hoc measures introduced by the GST Council after the GST law took effect, appear to be knee-jerk reactions to specific instances and their continuance needs to be reviewed. A few of them are discussed here.

Utilising ITC: A credit retention of 1% was introduced in December 2020 by which taxpayers could not use ITC to pay 100% of their net tax liability but were restricted to 99%. The avowed purpose of the Rule is to tackle the menace of fake invoices. There is no doubt that the issue of fake invoices that facilitate fraudulent availing of ITC is serious and must be tackled. However, the efficacy of this provision in detecting or preventing input credit against fake invoices needs examination. On the face of it, a 1% retention might not sound like a draconian provision, but this is very cumbersome from a compliance perspective.

The GSTN is well-equipped to match the invoices on which ITC has been availed with the returns filed by the supplier, and already throws up mismatches. Secondly, e-invoicing has been extended to all businesses whose turnover exceeds INR 20 crore, and in the absence of an e-invoice, ITC is denied. Thirdly, where supplies of goods are concerned, there is a system to cross-check invoices with electronic waybills, to curb malpractices where only the invoice is raised to facilitate fraudulent ITC, without matching the supply of goods. With all these checks in place, the 1% retention can well be dispensed with.

Tax Collected at Source (TCS)[8]/Tax Deducted at Source (TDS)[9]: E-commerce marketplaces that collect sale proceeds from customers on behalf of the sellers

7. See: *https://www.gov.uk/guidance/vat-imports-acquisitions-and-purchases-from-abroad.* Accessed on 10th March 2022.
8. Section 52 of CGST Act.
9. Section 51 of CGST Act.

registered on their platforms are required to deduct 1% Tax Collected at Source (TCS). Sellers are required to remit the remaining tax while filing their returns. To illustrate:

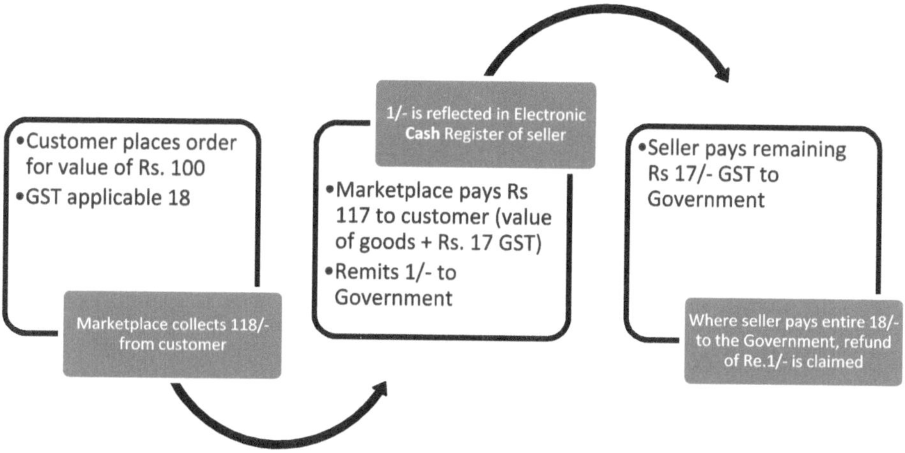

Source: Author

A similar methodology as above is applicable to supplies made to government departments, local authorities, or other persons as the government may specify where vendors are required to remit TDS. Both TCS and TDS are reflected in the electronic **cash** ledger (not the electronic credit ledger). The TDS provision is a legacy of the erstwhile VAT and CST legislations, and the TCS provision is an adaptation of the same, the purpose of which is to bring into the tax fold that class of transactions that the government deems to be susceptible to tax evasion.

There is no data available in the public domain on the additional revenue that has been generated on account of TDS/TCS payments which would otherwise have been lost. On the contrary, many large sellers have filed successful petitions in various courts, in cases of refund of balances in electronic cash ledgers. With the elaborate reporting mechanism prescribed under the GST law, the continuance of these mechanisms needs re-evaluation and, possibly, removal. Especially in the case of e-commerce sellers, where the entire transactions leave an electronic audit trail, there appears to be no reason to impose a measure that is an administrative burden for both the e-commerce platforms as well as sellers. It is probably time for the tax administration to take on this role directly rather than leaving the responsibility for addressing an assumed tax evasion in the hands of the productive sectors themselves. Otherwise, the burden of tax evasion by a few players continues to fall on the entire GST-compliant sector.

<u>**Inverted duty structure:**</u> Inverted duty structure is a legacy issue under the Central Excise law, where the tax on-end products is lower than the tax paid on inputs, resulting in perennial ITC accumulation, for example in highly capital-intensive sectors or priority sectors such as pharmaceuticals. This problem unfortunately has continued in the GST era as well since the rate fitments are guided by the rates prevalent in the pre-GST regime. Since the inverted duty structure was always meant to address a Central Excise issue, the refund of accumulated credit has always been restricted to duty paid on goods only, and not tax on services.

Under the GST regime also, service inputs are not credited out. The accumulated refund scheme is restricted to taxes paid on inputs of goods, and thereby the tax paid on input services lies unutilised in ITC; it thus becomes a 'dead asset' in a taxpayer's books. This has been the subject matter of litigation that has travelled all the way up to the Supreme Court[10], and the Court has observed that in terms of the law as currently drafted, a refund can be permitted of only credit attributed to the purchase of goods inputs and not input services.

With the integration of State level VAT with Central level Service Tax and Central Excise in GST, and all taxes paid on inputs and input services forming part of a common input tax credit pool, there is a need to re-visit the formula prescribed for calculation of refund permissible to those taxpayers where there is an inverted tax structure. While rendering its decision, the Supreme Court also expressed hope that the government would devise a better mechanism for such cases.

<u>**Exemptions and rate rationalisation:**</u> Multiple tax rates and exemptions invariably lead to a multiplicity of litigations and classification disputes. Fewer tax rates and exemptions contribute to ease of compliance, reduce unexpected tax demands from the tax administration, and certainty in projections for tax contributions by taxpayers. Globally, as a general practice, there are three tax rates – a merit rate, a default standard rate, and a demerit rate for sin goods. Currently, there are five tax rates in India – 0, 5, 12, 18, and 28 based on recommendations of the government's rate fitment committee. The government has constituted a rate rationalisation committee to look into a reduction of rate slabs and pruning exemptions. Since this is likely to have revenue consequences, this assumes greater significance with the GST compensation to States coming to an end in 2022.

V. Constitution of Appellate Tribunal

A major issue that needs to be addressed on a priority basis is the constitution of a GST Appellate Tribunal (GSTAT). The constitution and structure of the GSTAT

10. *Union of India v. Mohit Minerals*, 2022 SCC Online SC 657. This case came to the Supreme Court in appeal from a decision of the Gujarat HC.

as proposed in the GST laws were challenged in the Madras High Court (HC)[11] on the following grounds:

(a) The TN GST Act provides for one member (judicial), one member (technical – State), and one member (technical - Centre) which has been challenged on the grounds that the constitution of the GSTAT was not in consonance with those of other tribunals like the Income Tax Appellate Tribunal, or the Sales Tax/VAT tribunals which had one member each – judicial and technical.

(b) Retired Judges of an HC, retired district judges, and officers of the Indian Legal Service who held a position not less than an Additional Secretary for 3 years were eligible to be members of the tribunal. This provision has been challenged on the grounds that only advocates or retired judges could be appointed to tribunals and that officers of the Indian Legal Services could not be appointed to these positions; and

(c) Advocates should not be excluded from being appointed to the tribunal.

The Madras HC, in an Order dated 20th September 2019, struck down the provisions relating to the composition of the tribunal benches where the judicial members were outnumbered by technical members, as well as the eligibility of the officers of the Indian Legal Service to be appointed to the tribunal. As regards the appointment of advocates to the Tribunal, they only recommended that Parliament may consider the same.

Section 109 of the CGST Act and respective State GST Acts will now have to be amended in light of the Madras HC decision, and the tribunals constituted thereafter. There is no easy solution to this problem. However, there is no reason why a single technical member cannot sit upon a dispute involving both State, Central, or Integrated GST, especially when administratively taxpayers have been assigned to a single authority when they pay Central, State, and/or Integrated GST, which presumes that each authority has the capacity to interpret all three laws.

In July 2021, a Public Interest Litigation (PIL) petition has been filed before the Supreme Court requesting a direction to the government to set up the Tribunals in view of the difficulty being caused to taxpayers. The government has issued an order clarifying that the time limit for filing an appeal before the GSTAT would be computed after the jurisdictional GSTAT commences to function. While this will take care of appeals against tax demands, the delay in the constitution of the tribunal is highly detrimental in cases where taxpayers are granted refunds and the government is contemplating an appeal. Refunds for further periods, if applicable, are likely to be put on hold, pending a decision in appeals.

---

11. *Revenue Bar Association v. Union of India*, 2019 4 LW 689.

Interest accumulation poses an additional issue. In the case of demands, there is the unaddressed question of unjustified interest accumulation for no fault of the taxpayer. Interest amounts for five years are almost equivalent to the tax involved and it is certain that a plethora of petitions seeking waiver of the same will begin to appear. This is because there was no legal avenue provided in law to the taxpayer to contest the demand. To sum up, delay in the constitution of the tribunal would lead to a huge accumulation of cases, and therefore, it is important that this issue is addressed at the earliest.

VI. Authority for Advance Rulings

The legacy tax regime also had the route of seeking an Advance Ruling from an authority constituted for the purpose to gain certainty in disputable tax positions. Most States had constituted Advance Ruling Authorities (ARA) under their respective VAT legislations, with two members, both drawn from the VAT department. Under the Central Excise law, however, the authority comprised a member from the revenue authority, and a retired Supreme Court judge. The GST legislation has provided not just an Authority for Advance Rulings, but also an Appellate Authority for Advance Rulings. Members for both fora are drawn from the GST departments, one each from the State and Central GST departments. It is, therefore, not surprising that most of the decisions are against the taxpayer, which reveals an objective of protecting the interest of revenue.

Though the decision rendered by an ARA is binding only on the applicant and the revenue authorities and is not applicable to any other taxpayer, the trend of issuing only pro-revenue orders creates an apprehension that the assessing authorities are most likely to follow the decision of the ARA, where it is decided against the taxpayer, even in cases where no ruling has been sought.

Amending the constitution of the ARA to include judicial members at the State level is impractical since the government has been struggling to fill up vacancies in various Tribunals. So much so, that the Income Tax ARA has been substituted with a Board of Advance Rulings, with representatives only from the Tax Department, to dispose of advance ruling applications in a timely manner.

Since the ARAs are constituted in each State, taxpayers who have a presence in multiple States are required to file applications in each State for the same issue. This is not only cumbersome but could also lead to conflicting decisions from different Authorities on the same question. It is also commonly seen that Authorities render conflicting decisions on the same question. Conflicting decisions on common issues have an unsettling effect and lead to varied practices amongst taxpayers, depending on their appetite for risk and litigation.

It is admittedly a difficult and time-consuming legal proposition to constitute regional or central ARAs, given the experience of the challenge to the constitution of the GSTAT. One alternative that can be considered is to scrap the ARA altogether and instead introduce a process of clarification that can be issued by the GST Council. The clarification process was prevalent in some States, where Commissioners were empowered to issue clarifications or the ARA itself was empowered to do so. While this may not be the perfect solution, and the revenue bias may remain, it could be an acceptable alternative to ensure that conflicting views are not taken on the same issue. It will also help taxpayers having presence in various States to make one single application to the GST Council.

VII. Departmental Adjudication

Chapter 9 of the Economic Survey 2017-18 is titled, 'Ease of Doing Business' Next Frontier: Timely Justice'. This is the latest publicly available data on the performance of courts, various economic tribunals, and data on tax litigation in India. The following paragraph and table pithily sum up the efficacy of departmental adjudication in India:

> 9.23. What is interesting is that the success rate of the Department at all three levels of appeal-- Appellate Tribunals, High Courts, and Supreme Court-- and for both direct and indirect tax litigation is under 30%. In some cases it is as low as 12%....... The Department unambiguously loses 65% of its cases. Over a period of time, the success rate of the Department has only been declining, while that of the assessees has been increasing.

Petition Rate and Success Rate of the Tax Department, as on 31.03.2017

Direct Tax Cases			Indirect Tax Cases	
Court	Success Rate19	Petition Rate20	Success Rate	Petition Rate
Supreme Court	27%	87%	11%	63%
High Courts	13%	83%	46%	39%
ITAT/CESTAT	27%	88%	12%	20%
Source: Survey calculations.			*Source:* Survey calculations	

The success rate of the Department is calculated as the proportion of cases in which the respective court or tribunal rules totally or partially in favour of the Department. Cases that are set aside by the judicial authority are excluded from this calculation.

The Petition Rate of the Department is the percentage of the total number of appeals filed by the Department. The remaining appeals are those filed by the assessees."

Since the tribunal is the ultimate fact-finding authority, and about 80-85% of the cases culminate at this level, the percentage of success for the revenue is almost insignificant. This is reflective of:

- Unsubstantiated litigation
- Poor quality of investigation, evidence, and orders
- Revenue bias

The above is corroborated by the findings of the Tax Administration Reforms Commission (TARC) under the Chairmanship of Dr. Parthasarathi Shome:

> The TARC found that the success rate of the departments in litigation was very low. This is on account of the poor quality of orders and aggressive revenue target-oriented decisions. The TARC recommends that:
>
> - The Boards should ensure avoidance of such decisions by reviewing and improving the quality of orders from the perspective of fairness, legality, and propriety, irrespective of the revenue consequences.
> - They should desist from the filing of appeals against well-reasoned and sound orders passed by their officers simply because they are pro-taxpayers.
> - They should take notice of capricious orders, irrespective of revenue consequence, and discipline the errant officers - even by meting out punishment where required.

The Department of Revenue's website shows this recommendation as 'Implemented'.

The quality of show cause notices issued to assessees in the GST regime, issues raised, and orders passed are not reflective of much, perhaps any, improvement. There is no data to show the outcome at appellate levels since the GSTAT is not yet constituted but, if the experience of the taxpayers is anything to go by, the data is not likely to be very encouraging. In the GST regime, it is to be recalled, that taxpayers also receive notices and orders from State GST authorities, whose performance is not indicated in the above data. Nevertheless, taking the trend of the ARA as an indicator, the revenue bias is likely to be present even where State GST authorities are adjudicators.

The burden of consequences on the taxpayer of frivolous litigations initiated by revenue authorities is not reflected in the above data, but it has led to a poor taxpayer experience, including:

- High litigation costs

- Time cost of resources incurred in defence that could be spread over 4-10 years depending upon the level of appeal
- The implication that this litigation could have on the valuation of a business
- The effect on the financial books of the company

To bring about a tangible change in the experience of the taxpayer in the matter of dispute resolution, the government must consider overhauling the entire departmental adjudication system. The pre-show cause notice consultation process is not effective and has been reduced to a formality for just ticking the box.

VII.1. UK's Alternative Dispute Resolution (ADR) mechanism

UK introduced an ADR in September 2013 as a simpler and less onerous method of helping small and medium enterprises and individuals to resolve tax disputes. It is intended to provide an alternative to a full litigation process, conducted through a VAT tribunal hearing. ADR was introduced by HMRC, the tax department, in September 2013 with this objective. It is conducted through a VAT tribunal hearing. With ADR, an HMRC-appointed mediator trained in mediation skills and techniques works with the taxpayer and the HMRC officer dealing with the case, acting as an independent and neutral observer to aid negotiation between the two parties.

Rather than taking over responsibility for solving the dispute, the aim of the ADR is to re-establish communication, focus on the areas that need to be resolved and help both parties reach a mutual conclusion regarding the best way forward. This could be a concession that one party in the dispute is correct or a compromise agreement; alternatively, it could simply lead to a mutual realisation that a tribunal hearing is definitely required to resolve the matter.

It is possible to apply for ADR at any stage of a VAT dispute, or at any stage of the tribunal proceedings, which means that even existing litigations can be covered under the ADR.

ADR is most commonly opted for:

- When communications between the taxpayer and HMRC have broken down
- When the facts of the case are in dispute, or the conflict may be the result of a misunderstanding
- When HMRC has not agreed with evidence provided to them and the taxpayer wishes to know why
- When the taxpayer is unclear about what information HMRC has used, or if HMRC wishes to explain why more information is needed from the taxpayer

Once a taxpayer agrees to take part in the ADR process, he must commit to providing HMRC with information about the dispute, as well as any correspondence that has been received, sharing required information, and attending meetings promptly.

When ADR was first introduced, many were skeptical about its potential benefits, given that this is an HMRC-staffed, and controlled, offering. However, this scheme is reputed to have met with good success.

India's GST Council should consider adopting a similar ADR as a step before initiating departmental adjudication. This mechanism can potentially be very effective in:

- Reducing the number of frivolous litigations created by revenue officers
- Time of the taxpayer, officers, and appellate authorities will be better utilised to address only those issues where genuine interpretations or questions of law are involved
- Remand of cases by appellate authorities can be eliminated since most of them relate to cases where officers do not consider submissions made by taxpayers
- The issue of constantly filling up vacancies can also be lessened by employing an alternative process such as this.

The government has introduced the Mediation Bill in Parliament which seeks to consolidate the mediation provisions contained in various laws, into one single legislation. The ADR could be included in it so that the processes are streamlined, and appropriate references can be introduced in the GST laws.

The ADR mechanism, if introduced, will also be beneficial to officers who fear taking positions that are pro-taxpayer, in the fear of being brought under vigilance procedures under a charge of accepting gratuity from taxpayers. Instead, ADR forces the officers to consider the evidence provided by the taxpayer and record reasons as to why the same is unacceptable. Such a process would also bring a much-needed improvement in the quality of decision-making by revenue officers.

VIII. Centralised Processing Centre (CPC) and Faceless Assessments

Across the country, taxpayers have been mapped to either the State or Central authority that functions as the nodal authority as far as assessments and administrative control are concerned. In some cases, taxpayers with a multi-State presence may be administered by the State authorities in a few States and the Central authorities in others. There is a dire need to bring uniformity in the manner of communicating with taxpayers and put in a process that should be followed by Central and State authorities alike. To cite an example, where there are discrepancies in GST returns, the same is required to be brought to the notice of the taxpayer in form ASMT-10, and the taxpayer can file a reply in Form ASMT-11, after which the order of scrutiny assessment is to be passed in Form ASMT-12. This is a simple process, but very often taxpayers are directly served with demand notices without following the procedure.

It is also seen that, in many cases, the communication to taxpayers is via a non-official mail address putting at risk the security of the data shared by taxpayers which is sensitive and confidential. These creases need to be ironed out in taxpayer communication since they can become crucial documents in case there is litigation.

The assessment procedures prescribed under the GST law are well-codified and with the wealth of information that is available with the GSTN, most assessments are data-driven and do not require intervention or interaction with the officers. However, with the on-ground implementation challenges persisting, government may consider setting up a CPC either in the GSTN itself or along the lines of the Income Tax CPC where assessment cases are referred to the jurisdictional officers only on an exception basis. This will bring in greater transparency and accountability in the system and contribute to ease of compliance and reduce the cost of compliance as well.

IX. Departmental Audits

India's GST reporting system is one of the most detailed in the world. The GSTN has a wealth of information related to the taxpayer and the administration has transferred a large chunk of work to the taxpayer – whether it is the reconciliation of ITC to purchases, or the mechanism of availing only that input credit that is reflected in returns filed by suppliers, as well as other aspects. While this may appear very onerous on the face of it, the process is actually similar to a self-audit in the matter of payment of taxes, availing of input credit, or reversals.

For successful audits, departmental officers must consider the elaborate reporting system and focus more on risk areas and understanding the business model of the taxpayers. Currently, the guidance on audits and the audit manual focus more on reconciliations and input-output ratios. This would have been a good tool for conducting an audit in a pre-GST era when the GST department did not have so much taxpayer information at its disposal, or when so much automation had not been created. Continuing to follow the traditional method of audit would reduce the exercise to another assessment proceeding and is unlikely to yield any result.

The current audit process must be overhauled in a manner so that intelligence-based methods of analysis are used widely:

- Standard Operating Procedures (SOPs) are published, and the process is transparent and facilitates accountability. The taxpayer's experience must be the same, irrespective of administrative control or jurisdiction.
- Intelligent data analysis should replace the existing audit process. The GSTN already has enough business intelligence tools and audit processes should be developed around utilising the information thrown up by those tools effectively.
- Focus should be on risk review, where taxpayers are profiled based on their business models and control processes, rather than being reduced to a mere reconciliation exercise.
- Dedicated set of officers trained in financial audit techniques and data analytics along with technology specialists should be deployed for onsite audit, especially for large taxpayers using sophisticated technology, as against the current system where officers are simply transferred to the audit wing with no prior training.

The Australian Tax Office follows a process of profiling taxpayers in a risk review, through a detailed understanding of their businesses, and even reaches out to their stakeholders if required, after duly informing the taxpayer. If a need is found to expand the risk review into an audit, based on the findings of the review, a full-blown audit is ordered, which can go up to 18 months, subject to permission from senior officials, against proper documentation to show why the review needs to be converted into an audit. In some cases, the scope of the audit can be enlarged if there is suspicion of tax evasion or fraud.

Such practices in approaching the audit function by tax authorities lend credibility to the audit process if it were to be taken up and is likely to meet with a higher degree of success. In the current Indian scenario, audit officers are given three days to a week to wrap up an audit. Reflecting the limited time, width of focus, and short training period, poor outcomes are not surprising.

X. Training of Officers and Need for Specialization

Emerging business models are very complex, especially in the service sector. Tax departments have mostly been reactive rather than proactive, and tend to create confusion among taxpayers because of knee-jerk, short-term amendments that do not reflect a complete understanding of the industry. Recently, such half measures have been witnessed in the e-commerce and aggregators sectors. More such sectors are bound to emerge given the pace of technological advancements. Businesses will also come up with innovative models, to keep up with trending economic times.

XI. Conclusion

To conclude, implementing a tax regime change as large as the GST is no mean feat wherein all stakeholders have played a constructive part in its rolling success. The suggestions made in this chapter reflect a spirit of constructive criticism and are made in the interest of making India's GST among the best in the world.

Having said that, the GST being a tax on transactions, there is a dire need for industry specialisation among officers or, at the very minimum, an industry-specialised cell whose services are available to officers dealing with taxpayers in that industry. Involving experts from the industry and adopting global best practices can provide valuable insights into trade practices.

State GST authorities have never dealt with taxpayers in the service sector—hence an accentuated need, not just to protect the interest of revenue, but also to ensure uniformity of taxation and actionable guidance, with positions that can withstand legal scrutiny. These cells can also issue position papers that provide insight for taxpayers rather than sudden orders and surprises through tax demands. Bringing greater transparency to the system remains a crucial need that could finally create a regime of trust for taxpayers.

ADDENDUM

GST Returns at a glance[12]

GST Return Form Number	Form Name	Frequency of filing	Remarks
GSTR-1	Details of outward supplies of goods or services	Monthly/Quarterly (for small taxpayers)	
Form GSTR-1A	Details of auto-drafted supplies (From GSTR-2, GSTR-4, or GSTR-6)	—	Not yet implemented
Form GSTR-2	Details of inward supplies of goods or services	—	Not yet implemented
Form GSTR-2A	Details of auto-drafted supplies (From GSTR-1, GSTR-5, GSTR-6, GSTR-7, GSTR-8, import of goods, and inward supplies of goods received from SEZ units/developers)	Auto drafted by the system	It's a read-only dynamic GST return of all inward supplies of goods or services
Form GSTR-2B	Auto-drafted ITC (input tax credit) statement (From GSTR-1, GSTR-5, GSTR-6, and import data received from Icegate)	Auto drafted by the system	It's a read-only static ITC statement made available to the registered person every month
Form GSTR-3	Monthly Return	—	Not yet implemented
Form GSTR-3A	Notice to return defaulter u/s 46 for not filing the return	—	GST Dept issues this notice to the taxpayers whenever they default in filing the return by the due date

12. *Source*: Sravanthi Velagaleti, B.Com, LLB, MA, CA, Deputy Commissioner (State Tax), Telangana Commercial Taxes Department.

GST Return Form Number	Form Name	Frequency of filing	Remarks
Form GSTR-3B	Details of outward supplies and inward supplies liable to reverse charge	Monthly / Quarterly (for small taxpayers)	
Form GSTR-4	Return for the financial year of a registered person who has opted for composition levy or availing benefit of notification no. 02/2019 – Central Tax (Rate)	Annual	
Form GSTR-4A	Auto-drafted details for a registered person opting for composition levy (auto drafted from GSTR-1, GSTR-5 and GSTR-7)	Auto-drafted by the system	
Form GSTR-5	Return for non-resident taxable person	Monthly	
Form GSTR-5A	Details of supplies of online information and database access or re-trieval services (OIDAR) by a person located outside India made to non-taxable persons in India	Monthly	
Form GSTR-6	Return for Input Service Distributor (ISD)	Monthly	
GSTR-6A	Details of supplies auto-drafted form (auto-drafted from GSTR-1)	Auto drafted by the system	
Form GSTR-7	Return for tax deducted at source	Monthly	This is to be filed by TDS deductors
Form GSTR-8	Statement for tax collection at source	Monthly	This is to be filed by the e-commerce operator

GST Return Form Number	Form Name	Frequency of filing	Remarks
Form GSTR-9	Annual Return	Annual	
Form GSTR-9A	Annual Return (for Composition taxpayer)	Annual	This annual return is to be filed by the composition taxpayer
Form GSTR-9C	Reconciliation Statement	Annual	This is a self-certified reconciliation statement to be filed along with the annual return in Form GSTR-9 (applicable only for those taxpayers whose aggregate turnover during a financial year exceeds Rs.5 Crores)
Form GSTR-10	Final Return	Within 3 months of the date of cancellation or date of order of cancellation, whichever is later	
Form GSTR-11	Statement of inward supplies by persons having a Unique Identification Number (UIN)	Monthly (as and when refund is claimed)	This is a statement to claim a refund of taxes paid by UIN holders

Subject Index

D

E

F

H

I

W